Origins and Evolution of the European Union

Edited by

Desmond Dinan

UNIVERSITY PRESS

OXFORD
UNIVERSITY PRESS

Great Clarendon Street, Oxford OX2 6DP

Oxford University Press is a department of the University of Oxford.
It furthers the University's objective of excellence in research, scholarship,
and education by publishing worldwide in

Oxford New York

Auckland Cape Town Dar es Salaam Hong Kong Karachi
Kuala Lumpur Madrid Melbourne Mexico City Nairobi
New Delhi Shanghai Taipei Toronto

With offices in

Argentina Austria Brazil Chile Czech Republic France Greece
Guatemala Hungary Italy Japan Poland Portugal Singapore
South Korea Switzerland Thailand Turkey Ukraine Vietnam

Oxford is a registered trade mark of Oxford University Press
in the UK and in certain other countries

Published in the United States
by Oxford University Press Inc., New York

© Oxford University Press 2006

The moral rights of the author have been asserted
Database right Oxford University Press (maker)

First published 2006

British Library Cataloguing in Publication Data

Data available

Library of Congress Cataloging in Publication Data

Data available

Typeset by Laserwords Private Limited, Chennai, India

Printed in Great Britain
on acid-free paper by
Antony Rowe Ltd, Chippenham, Wiltshire

ISBN 0-19-926792-8   978-0-19-926792-7

1 3 5 7 9 10 8 6 4 2

Outline Contents

Detailed Contents

Preface

This book has had a long gestation period. I approached possible contributors in 2002 and, thanks to the generosity of the American Consortium on European Union Studies in Washington, DC, organized a conference to discuss draft chapters in September 2003, which Jeffrey Anderson, Director of the BMW Center for German and European Studies at Georgetown University, graciously hosted. It took much longer than I had hoped to edit and revise the draft chapters and prepare the manuscript for publication. I am extremely grateful to the contributors, who include scholars at various stages of their careers, based on both sides of the Atlantic, for their cooperation and patience. I am equally grateful to John Peterson and Helen Wallace, editors of the Oxford University Press New European Union series (Helen was the lead editor for this book), and Ruth Anderson, commissioning editor at Oxford University Press, for their forbearance and support. I am honoured to participate in this prestigious and successful series and hope that *Origin and Evolution of the European Union* was worth the wait.

Desmond Dinan

List of Figures

List of Tables

Abbreviations and Acronyms

BBQ	British Budgetary Question or Bloody British Question
BEUC	European Consumers' Organization
BSE	bovine spongiforme encephalopathy
CAP	common agricultural policy
CFSP	common foreign and security policy
CIS	Commonwealth of Independent States (ex-USSR)
CMEA	Council for Mutual Economic Assistance
Comecon	Council for Mutual Economic Assistance
COPA	Comité des Organisations Professionnelles Agricoles
Coreper	Committee of Permanent Representatives
CSCE	Conference on Security and Cooperation in Europe
DBV	Deutsche Bauernverband
DM	Deutsche Mark
EAGGF	European Agricultural Guidance and Guarantee Fund
EC	European Community
ECA	Economic Cooperation Administration
ECB	European Central Bank
ECHR	European Convention on Human Rights
ECJ	European Court of Justice
Ecofin	Council of Economic and Finance Ministers
ECSC	European Coal and Steel Community
ecu	European currency unit
EDC	European Defence Community
EEA	European Economic Area
EEC	European Economic Community
EFSA	European Food Safety Authority
EFTA	European Free Trade Association
EIB	European Investment Bank
EMS	European Monetary System
EMU	economic and monetary union
EPC	European Political Community
EPU	European Payments Union
ERDF	European Regional Development Fund
ERM	exchange-rate mechanism
ERP	European Recovery Programme
EU	European Union
EUI	European University Institute
Euratom	European Atomic Energy Community
FTA	free trade area
G7	Group of seven most industrialized countries (Canada, France, Germany, Italy, Japan, UK, US)
GDP	gross domestic product

GNP	gross national product
GATT	General Agreement on Tariffs and Trade
IAR	International Authority for the Ruhr
IGC	intergovernmental conference
IMF	International Monetary Fund
ISC	International Steel Cartel
ITO	International Trade Organization
JCS	Joint Chiefs-of-Staff
LDCs	less developed countries
MCAs	monetary compensatory amounts
Nato	North Atlantic Treaty Organization
NTBs	non-tariff barriers
OECD	Organization for Economic Cooperation and Development
OEEC	Organization for European Economic Cooperation
PPP	purchasing power parity
PSE	producer support estimate
QRs	quota restrictions
SCA	Special Committee on Agriculture
SEA	Single European Act
SGP	Stability and Growth Pact
UA	unit of account
UDSR	Union démocratique et socialiste de la Résistance
UK	United Kingdom
UN	United Nations
US	United States
USSR	Union of Soviet Socialist Republics
VAT	value-added tax
WEU	Western European Union
WTO	World Trade Organization

List of Contributors

DESMOND DINAN, George Mason University
PETER STIRK, University of Durham
DAVID A. MESSENGER, Carroll College
JOHN R. GILLINGHAM, University of Missouri-St Louis
WENDY ASBEEK BRUSSE, Netherlands Scientific Council for Government Policy
CRAIG PARSONS, University of Oregon
STEPHEN MARTIN, Purdue University
JEFFREY VANKE, Kaplan University
RICHARD T. GRIFFITHS, University of Leiden
ANN-CHRISTINA LAURING KNUDSEN, University of Aarhus
N. PIERS LUDLOW, London School of Economics and Political Science
DOROTHEE HEISENBERG, Johns Hopkins University
JEFFREY J. ANDERSON, Georgetown University
ANNA MICHALSKI, Netherlands Institute of International Relations

Introduction

In a stinging rebuke for the process of European integration, French and Dutch voters rejected the European Union's proposed Constitutional Treaty in spring 2005. Far from being an isolated event, this was a continuation of the expressions of popular concern about the European Union (EU) first voiced when Danish voters rejected the Maastricht Treaty in June 1992 and repeated in other closely-contested referendums on treaty reform. Public opinion seemed increasingly restive about the scope and pace of integration and the unfamiliarity and apparent unaccountability of the EU's institutions. National governments exacerbated the problem by failing to engage national parliaments and publics in the process of European integration and by blaming Brussels for unpopular decisions for which they themselves were often largely responsible.

The trials and tribulations of the EU since the early 1990s attest to the organization's strengths as well as its weaknesses; its successes as well as its failings. The EU pervades everyday life in the member states, ranging from setting farm subsidies and environmental standards to managing monetary policy, although much remains outside its direct control. Apart from what takes place in Brussels itself, politics and policy-making at every level in the member states has an EU dimension. People realize and resent the pervasiveness of the EU while forgetting or dismissing its benefits, such as the single European market, the potential to strengthen internal security, and a powerful voice for Europe in global economic fora. Concerned about the pressures of cultural and economic globalization and the supposed vulnerability of national identities and fragility of costly welfare programmes, many Europeans see the EU as part of the problem, not the solution.

Clearly, the EU has come a long way, for good or ill, from its modest beginnings in the early 1950s as a six member-state organization that sought to establish a common market in coal and steel. This book traces the development of European integration from the immediate post-World War II period, when politicians and the public seemed more than willing to share national sovereignty for the sake of greater security, to the collapse of constitution-building sixty years later, when the EU conspicuously lacked public and political support. The course of European integration was highly changeable during that time, but never dull or uninteresting. Regardless of one's thoughts about the EU today, the process of European integration is one of the most distinctive and important developments in contemporary European history.

Although a uniquely post-World War II occurrence, European integration—meaning the voluntary sharing of national sovereignty in a supranational entity subject to the rule of law—had pre-World War II antecedents. Indeed, as Peter Stirk shows in Chapter 1, national integration (unification) and international disintegration (fragmentation) were endemic in the decades before World War II and strongly shaped developments in the years ahead. So did the outbreak of the cold war which, David Messenger points out in Chapter 2, not only ensured that the United States remained engaged in European affairs but also spurred the process of

European integration while ensuring that it would be confined to the western part of the continent.

Created in the aftermath of World War II and a climate of deepening East–West tension, the European Coal and Steel Community (ECSC) that emerged in the early 1950s was a far cry from what federalists had advocated in the immediately preceding years. Nevertheless, as John Gillingham argues in Chapter 3, it served a vital purpose: to provide a framework for Germany's economic recovery and political rehabilitation that satisfied pressing French security concerns. The European Economic Community (EEC) that followed later in the 1950s was less a successor to the ECSC than a response to the needs of Western European governments to lock themselves into a credible and apparently irreversible commitment to the liberalization of trade in goods and services centred on a resurgent Germany. In Chapter 4, Wendy Asbeek Brusse shows how the European Payments Union, the unsung hero of European integration, resolved the problem of currency convertibility and unlocked the potential of trade liberalization, thereby paving the way for the EEC, which in turn spurred further intra-European trade.

Other, more ambitious schemes for European integration, notably the European Defence Community and the European Political Community, foundered because they lacked a compelling political or economic rationale. In Chapter 5, Craig Parsons examines the competition of ideas in France, the most pivotal country in the early history of European integration, for intra-European cooperation in the 1950s, ranging from traditional intergovernmental arrangements to the sharing of national sovereignty. Parsons sees strong political leadership and the formation of cross-cutting coalitions that commanded a majority of parliamentary support at critical junctures as the main reasons for the triumph of Community Europe, in the form of the ECSC and the EEC. Thus, he argues, the future of European integration, which followed the Community model, hinged on electoral outcomes and parliamentary manoeuvrings in France that had less to do with the forcefulness of the ideas at issue than with unrelated political developments.

In Chapter 6, Stephen Martin contrasts the political suitability of the coal and steel sectors for European integration with their economic unsuitability. He questions the economic impact of the ECSC, showing that it neither prevented price discrimination nor promoted competition, and argues that the member states were reluctant to fulfil their treaty obligations. It was hardly surprising, therefore, that they would continue to suit themselves as much as possible following implementation of the Rome Treaty in 1958 or that the European Commission, constitutionally weaker than the ECSC's High Authority, could not prevail against the perceived vital interests of France.

This brings us to Charles de Gaulle, who dominated the history of the European integration in the 1960s. De Gaulle is notorious for promoting the Fouchet Plan for intergovernmental cooperation on foreign and security policy, blocking Britain's accession to the EEC (in 1963 and 1967), and provoking a constitutional crisis that ended with an agreement (the Luxembourg Compromise) that strengthened the power of national governments in legislative decision-making. In Chapter 7, Jeffrey Vanke examines how policy towards the EEC fit in with de Gaulle's broader European and international objectives, which sought above all to assert French cultural leadership, strengthen French defence, and modernize the French economy. Having denounced the Rome Treaty before coming to power in 1958, de Gaulle ensured the EEC's survival by undertaking financial reforms in France and warding off Britain's effort to negotiate a wider free trade area. His later initiatives sought to strengthen, not weaken, the EEC, but in ways consistent with his vision of Europe and of France's leading role in it.

The other member states and applicant states were relieved to see de Gaulle leave office in 1969. Although a Gaullist, the new president of France accepted the inevitability of British accession, if only as part of a deal to complete unfinished business of particular importance to France—notably securing a permanent financial arrangement for the common agricultural policy (CAP)—and deepen integration in ways acceptable to France—through the launch of intergovernmental cooperation on foreign policy and a plan for economic and monetary union (EMU). In Chapter 8, Richard Griffiths examines the post-de Gaulle revival of European integration, which seemed to come to a halt in the mid-1970s in the wake of enlargement and the first oil crisis. Griffiths takes issue with the usual depiction of the 1970s as a dismal decade in the history of European integration, pointing out that the European Community (EC) continued to develop an impressive body of case law during that time and coped with the challenges of enlargement, the break-up of the international monetary system, and the consequences of slower economic growth. The roots of the EC's undoubted success in the 1980s, he suggests, lie in its responsiveness to the challenges of the 1970s.

One of those challenges was to manage the CAP, the most emblematic, intricate, and expensive area of EC activity. In Chapter 9, Ann-Christina Lauring Knudsen argues that the CAP is a continuation of the agricultural welfare state and can only be understood in political rather than economic terms. Having explained the political imperatives underpinning the CAP, she examines the policy's achievements (income distribution and welfare gains) and unintended consequences (the infamous food surpluses and budget crises, which came to a head in the 1970s and early 1980s). Financial pressure was a powerful incentive for CAP reform in the early 1990s, as was the pernicious international impact of the policy. Concerns about the environment and food safety, and about the possible impact of EU enlargement into Central and Eastern Europe, maintained the momentum for reform. Given the political importance of supporting farm incomes, however, the CAP will probably always be with us in some form or other.

Resolution of the British budgetary question in 1984 was an essential step along the road to CAP reform and unlocked the EC's potential for deeper economic integration. As Piers Ludlow shows in Chapter 10, the success of the European Monetary System and resolution of the British budgetary question paved the way for the launch of the single market programme. In order to ensure the legislative enactment of the programme, national governments negotiated the Single European Act, which also increased the EC's scope by formally embracing environmental policy, cohesion policy, and intergovernmental cooperation on foreign policy. The acceleration of European integration in the late 1980s coincided with the Commission presidency of Jacques Delors, who is often credited with revitalizing the EC. In Ludlow's view, however, national governments deserve most of the credit. Moreover, without the existence of the European Council, the body in which national leaders meet regularly to provide overall direction, the EC might not have revived as spectacularly as it did.

The single market programme seems to have led inevitably to EMU. Yet, as Dorothee Heisenberg shows in Chapter 11, it was French dissatisfaction with *de facto* German dominance of the European Monetary System that set the EC on the road to EMU in the late 1980s. German political leaders sympathized with France and were well disposed towards a new European monetary policy initiative. By contrast, the Bundesbank (German central bank) preferred the *status quo*. The significance of the so-called Delors Committee, established by EC leaders in 1988 to provide a blue-print for EMU, was not Delors's leadership but the participation in it of the Bundes-bank president, who became reconciled to the idea of monetary union. German uni-fication, which triggered fears in neighbouring countries about Germany's role in Europe, tipped the balance in favour of Germany's commitment to EMU but was not the key factor in explaining EMU itself. Heisenberg goes on to trace the conduct and outcome of the Maastricht negotiations on EMU, the rocky road to the launch of the single currency in 1999 (with euro notes and coins following in 2002), and the ex-perience of EMU since then, in particular the difficulty of enforcing the Stability and Growth Pact for fiscal discipline among participating member states.

In Chapter 12, Jeffrey Anderson also touches on the relationship between German unification and EMU, although he is interested primarily in the broader question of the relationship between the acceleration of European integration in the late 1980s and the seismic geopolitical shifts in Central and Eastern Europe, culminating in the collapse of the Soviet Union in 1991. Following a review of relations between the EC and the Soviet Union on the eve of those momentous events, Anderson establishes tenuous links between the rapid integration in Western Europe and disintegration in Central and Eastern Europe. Whereas the acceleration of European integration may not have directly hastened the collapse of the Soviet bloc, the collapse of the Soviet bloc, in turn, had a profound impact on the EU as ten newly-independent Central and Eastern European states clamoured for membership. Having from the outset pro-claimed itself the *European* Community or Union, how could it say no to enlargement?

The pervasiveness and importance of enlargement in the history of European in-tegration is the subject of Anna Michalski's contribution in Chapter 13. Michalski analyzes the process and instruments of enlargement as well as the roles of vari-ous institutional actors and the candidate states and shows how, faced with the likelihood of large-scale Central and Eastern European accession, the EU extended the requirements for membership to include the candidate countries' democratic credentials and economic competitiveness. She shows how the EU has developed a panoply of strategies to deal with growing differences among the member states' socio-economic situations and policy needs without (yet) formally resorting to a division of its membership in concentric circles, core and peripheral groups, or al-ternative frameworks.

The final chapter by Desmond Dinan reviews the historiography of European in-tegration—how scholars have interpreted the process and explained key events and developments. First, Dinan outlines the federalist narrative that predominated in the early decades of the EC, which traced the roots of integration to old ideas about European unity and anticipated the demise of the nation state and the rise of a

federal association of European states. Academic studies of the Communities themselves, including the detailed field work of some of the leading neo-functionalists in
the 1950 and 1960s, contributed to a more realistic appraisal of European integration
and helped pave the way for the onslaught against the federal narrative (and also
against neo-functionalism) by Alan Milward, whose state-centric view of European integration and belief in the mutual interdependence of the nation state and the supranation is now generally accepted. Milward and his devotees have left an indelible
impression on the historiography of European integration that recent federalist neo-
revisionism has failed to erase. Following a review of some of the more current contributions to the history of European integration, Dinan points out that, although EU
historiography has come a long way since the early 1980s, when historical enquiry
into the origins and evolution of the European Communities began in earnest, much
work remains to be done.

The field of EC or EU studies, beginning with the launch of the Communities in
the early 1950s, has been dominated by political scientists trying to understand and
explain the dynamics and significance of European integration from various theoretical perspectives. Historians are equally interested in trying to solve the riddle of
European integration by unearthing detailed information about the causes and consequences of particular events and developments, from a distance of several decades
and with the help of archival documents, the indispensable material of the historian's craft. Political scientists have not always appreciated the contribution of historians, as facts sometimes get in the way of carefully-constructed theories.

Speeches, interviews and diary entries are a useful but often inaccurate guide to
protagonists' motives. Contemporary, confidential records of meetings and conversations generally hold the key to figuring out why the main players acted as they did.
The Schuman Declaration of May 1950, universally cited as the point of departure
for the European Communities, is an obvious example. Taken at face value, French
Foreign Minister Robert Schuman acted out of altruism and an abiding commitment
to Franco–German reconciliation. An examination of French and other state papers,
however, suggests that, notwithstanding his genuine desire for reconciliation with
the former enemy, the timing and substance of Schuman's initiative owed more
to changing international circumstances and the failure of existing French policy
towards Germany. The wellsprings of French President Charles de Gaulle's policy
towards the EC are another example of the value of archival material, although in
this case, as Jeffrey Vanke points out in Chapter 7, not all of the documents are yet
available. According to his oft-quoted public statements, de Gaulle was motivated
largely by geopolitical considerations, especially in relation to Britain's applications
for EC membership. Newly available evidence (not all archival-based and some of it of
questionable value), suggests that economic considerations, such as concerns about
trade and agricultural issues, primarily determined de Gaulle's EC policy.

State archives are an indispensable source for the study of EU history, but are not
the only or the definitive source. Nor will two historians who examine the same documents necessarily reach the same conclusions. Diplomatic historians are trained to
weigh and examine documents in a different way from economic or social historians. Originally thought of solely as diplomatic history, historical enquiry into the
EU increasingly attracts the interest and benefits from the insights of non-diplomatic
historians. As sub-disciplines of history become every more sharply defined,

historical enquiry into the EU stands out as an area that requires a multifaceted approach—cultural, diplomatic, economic and social—from those who conduct it.

Just as the distinction between sub-disciplines of history is becoming blurred in the study of European integration, so too is the dividing line between historians and political scientists less rigid than it once was. Historians and political scientists still approach the subject differently, but no longer entirely separately. Thanks in part to the scholarship of Andrew Moravcsik, a political scientist and trained historian who developed a new theory of big decision-making in the EU using historical case studies, political scientists are increasingly likely to respect and use historical research in their own work. It is no accident, therefore, that a number of contributors to this book are political scientists. Notable among them is Craig Parsons, whose highly-regarded book on France and European integration in the 1950s, on which he based Chapter 5 in this book, demonstrates the benefit of combining history and political science in the study of the EU.

Although it includes contributions from leading scholars of the EU, this book is not an original contribution to historical scholarship on the EU. Rather than interpret the EU in a new way, it aims to familiarize readers with the course and conduct of European integration since the emergence of the European Communities in the singular circumstances of the post-World War II period, when the international situation was highly unsettled and governments struggled to enhance economic welfare and national security. It seeks as well to acquaint readers with contending interpretations of the European Communities' origin and evolution.

The book charts the course of European integration through fifty years of fundamental international change—decolonization, economic crises and monetary instability, the end of the cold war, and the rise of economic globalization. Far from existing in isolation, the EC and later the EU were inextricably bound up with broader regional and international developments throughout that time. It is hardly surprising, therefore, that discontent with the EU is not only an expression of dissatisfaction with the organization's policies and procedures but also a regional manifestation of global angst, as evidenced by the rejection of the Constitutional Treaty in 2005.

Three European communities emerged in the 1950s: the European Coal and Steel Community, the European Economic Community, and the European Atomic Community (Euratom). They were known collectively as the European Communities. The name 'European Community' was sometimes used unofficially to refer to the European Economic Community, until the European Economic Community officially became the European Community under the terms of the Maastricht Treaty in 1993. The Maastricht Treaty also brought the European Union into being. The European Union subsumed, but did not replace, the European Communities, although the European Coal and Steel Community ceased to exist in July 2002 when its treaty expired. The term 'European Community' and abbreviation 'EC' are used in this book to mean the European Economic Community, both before and after the official change of name in 1993.

Part I

Continuity and Change

Chapter 1

Integration and Disintegration before 1945

Peter Stirk

Contents

Summary

Europe experienced both integration (ranging from national unification to international economic interdependence) and disintegration (political and economic fragmentation) in the century before World War II. Examples of integration during that time include the Prussian-dominated *Zollverein* (customs union), established in 1834, and German and Italian political unification later in the nineteenth century. In general, Europe enjoyed a high degree of economic interdependence in the late nineteenth and early twentieth centuries, in contrast to the economic disintegration of the interwar period (in the 1920s and 1930s). The Pan-Europa movement of Count Richard Coudenhove-Kalergi tried to build a groundswell of public support for European federation in the 1920s, but public opinion alone was never enough to determine the actions of European statesmen. French foreign minister Aristide Briand's famous call in 1929 for a 'kind of federal bond' was consistent with French national interests, which inevitably aroused German suspicion.

Other countries expressed concern about its possible impact on the League of Nations and wider economic relations. German plans during World War II for a New Order, however vague, raised the spectre of hegemonic integration while, at the same time, the experience of German occupation and the rise of the resistance movement spurred interest in a possible postwar European federation. Ultimately, however, integration in the form of the European Community and the European Union would be achieved through and by states, not by mass movements guided by far-sighted intellectuals.

Introduction

The era from the middle of the nineteenth century to the end of World War II is often seen as one of nationalism and great power politics, culminating in the disaster of World War I, the subsequent failure of the Versailles settlement and the League of Nations, and the rise of fascism and outbreak of renewed warfare. Only after World War II, even more destructive than World War I and distinguished by the unique horror of the Holocaust, were European statesmen, or at least some of them, sufficiently shaken to embark upon the novel experiment that became the European Union (EU). The period 1914–45, designated by some as another thirty years war, provides a negative contrast, tempered only by the efforts of isolated visionaries and the first hesitant and ineffective steps towards integration, against which the achievements of the postwar era are set. Accounts that cover this period, often referring specifically to the 'idea' of Europe, have tended to focus on the visions that stood in such sharp contrast to the harsh reality of European great power conflict and super-heated nationalism (De Rougement 1966; Heater 1992). They have also invited criticism that the link between the ideas of the visionaries and the interests of the statesmen who launched the European communities is tenuous at best (see Chapter 14).

   Yet the story of a link between the internecine warfare of the period before 1945 and European integration in the postwar era is not without some merit, as can be seen by a brief consideration of three of the key actors involved in the Schuman Plan of May 1950 that started the process of contemporary European integration. The French foreign minister in 1950, Robert Schuman, born in Luxembourg in 1886, had become a German citizen and worked in Alsace, which had been seized from France at the time of the Franco–Prussian war of 1870–1. Consequently, he had served in the German army during World War I but became a French citizen after Alsace returned to France as part of the Versailles settlement. The German Chancellor, Konrad Adenauer, born in 1876, had been a successful mayor of Cologne after World War I and was suspected of sympathizing with plans favoured by France for the separation of the Rhineland from Germany. He died in 1967, four years after the Franco–German Treaty that symbolized postwar Franco–German reconciliation. The third, Jean Monnet, the initiator of the Schuman Plan, was born in 1888 in Cognac. He later recalled that were it not for World War I he might never have left the family business and embarked upon a career as a national and international civil servant. It is notable that his memoirs begin not with his childhood but with the crisis of the French military collapse of 1940, under the heading 'Unity in Peril' (Monnet 1978).

Although the careers of these men clearly bear the imprint of a pre-1945 world marked by nationalism and great power conflict, this chapter suggests that the image of the New Europe of the post-World War II period glosses over more complex processes of integration and disintegration, at both the levels of the state and the international order, that provided powerful motives and models, as well as myths, for later political and economic actors. More specifically, it argues that trajectories of nationalism, tipping over into hyper-nationalism, followed by integration, presuppose an oversimplified contrast between the two processes. National integration, itself very problematic, was a source of myths that formed an obstacle to the consolidation of incipient European integration. The chapter also argues that economic integration did not lead inexorably to political unification and that visions of empire, central to the history of the major European states, challenged the supposed pre-eminence of the nation state and were bound up, in varying degrees, with some visions of integration. Finally, the chapter demonstrates that integration, often assumed to be a peaceful process, in contrast to the violent proclivities of nationalism and the nation state, has not always taken a benign form.

Box 1.1 Key terms

Anschluss: 'union', referring to the union of Germany and Austria, which was prohibited by the treaties of Versailles and St Germain but was brought about by Hitler in March 1938.

Bretton Woods: conference of July 1944 that laid the foundations for the International Bank for Reconstruction and Development (World Bank) and the International Monetary Fund.

Grossraumordnung: a term, difficult to translate, that refers to a large region. It was used by the German jurist Carl Schmitt to refer to continental blocs which he expected to dominate the international scene.

Mitteleuropa: 'central Europe', denoting an area of indeterminate extent but centred on the German-speaking lands and often having connotations of German hegemony.

Risorgimento: 'revival', a term used to refer to the movement for Italian unification in the nineteenth century.

Vichy regime: the French wartime collaborationist regime of Marshall Pétain, based in the spa town of Vichy.

Zollverein: 'customs union', referring to the Prussian-dominated customs union in the nineteenth century.

Zwischeneuropa: 'Europe in between', denoting the European states between Germany and Russia.

Jagiellonian empire: formed by the union of Polish and Lithuanian lands in 1385, it constituted a major European power and remained a symbol of Polish greatness long after the division of Poland at the end of the eighteenth century.

Most-favoured nation principle: enshrined in many international economic treaties, it meant that a state would be treated as favourably as any other. It was intended to promote free trade but did not necessarily do so.

Integration and disintegration before World War I

The *Zollverein*

The Prussian-dominated customs union (*Zollverein*), established in 1834, was one of the most powerful models of integration and continued to exert influence well into the next century. Its presumed legacy was evident in discussions during World War II about the possible political division of Germany. It was taken as axiomatic that a customs union 'would lead to currency co-ordination and so to a monetary union and finally to a political union', as it supposedly had in the case of the *Zollverein* (Goldbach 1991: 144). Many nineteenth-century German nationalists also believed that economic integration had led to political integration. Much later the *Zollverein* would be invoked by advocates of a free trade zone as an example of how sovereign states could pursue a coordinated liberal economic policy without making any significant political sacrifice as well as by advocates of the European Community (Fischer 1961: 105).

Ironically, it was a German, the political economist Gustav Schmoller, who pointed out how odd it was to cite the *Zollverein* as a model for contemporary integration, given that political unification normally preceded economic unification (Schmoller 1916: 529). In fact it was not so much odd as quite misleading. Although disputes about the origins and role of the *Zollverein* continue, most accounts now agree that pragmatic considerations dominated its establishment and subsequent expansion. The high costs of administering separate, often small, customs territories made the idea of a larger, unified customs area attractive to smaller states, especially as the distribution of revenues was deliberately skewed to favour them. Nevertheless too much should not be made of this, given the limited overall contribution of customs revenues to state budgets (Dumke 1991; Voth 2001).

The *Zollverein* did not give the associated states significantly greater leverage with respect to third parties, however. Treaties with Holland in 1839, Britain in 1841 and Belgium in 1844 were widely criticized for what were seen as excessive concessions. In the case of the treaty with Belgium, the *Zollverein* made substantive concessions for little more than the promise that Belgium would not treat it worse than before (Henderson 1939: 135, 161). Doubt has even been cast on the overall impact of the *Zollverein* on economic growth. According to Voth, at the peak of its significance, between 1840 and 1860, the rate of growth in the *Zollverein* was disappointing (2001: 114–16). Nevertheless it can be said that one consequence of the union was to prevent a slide back into protectionist measures between the associated states (Kiesewetter 1987: 99).

The crucial question is whether economic integration led to political integration. Here it is possible to give a very clear answer. When tension between Prussia and the Habsburg Empire to the south finally erupted into war, several of Prussia's fellow members of the *Zollverein* marched against her. The establishment of Prussian hegemony and the associated creation of the North German Confederation were achieved by force of arms against the opposition of Prussia's economic allies. Political and military means decided the issue.

Nationalism and unification

The idea of nationalism readily conjures up two contradictory images: first, an aggressive nation state, where loyalty to the state goes hand in hand with antipathy to other nations; second, the commitment of a group, usually characterized by linguistic, ethnic or religious identity, to break away from an existing state in the name of self-determination. Both images suggest a clear barrier to wider processes of international integration. Yet, as E. J. Hobsbawm's brilliant survey shows, these images were highly misleading for at least the first half of the nineteenth century, and in some respects for even longer. The original 'patriots' were seen, and saw themselves, as radical reformers or revolutionaries (Hobsbawm 1990: 86). The nation they espoused was essentially one constituted by commitment to a particular form of government, in opposition to the existing authorities. It is notable that the French revolutionaries imposed no linguistic, ethnic or religious qualifications for citizenship. Simple residence for a specified period sufficed, though linguistic competence in French was seen as desirable.

The fact that linguistic distinctiveness was insufficient to establish nationality had another side. As Hobsbawm has emphasized, liberals assumed that there was an unspecified minimum size for a viable nation state. It was clearly recognized that not all linguistic groups were big enough and that they would be absorbed, if they had not been already, by larger, more viable units (Hobsbawm 1990: 31–7). Both elements, the idea of patriotism as a revolutionary movement from below and the expansive liberal concept of nationality, could be fused together into what has been called a 'pro-national European nationalism' (D'Appollonia 2002: 180–1). Such sentiments were embodied in the 1834 programme, *Young Europe*, of the Italian nationalist Giuseppe Mazzini. The actual course of Italian unification, however, was to produce a radically different result.

When unification came in 1859–61 it did so predominantly because of the ambitions of the Kingdom of Piedmont–Sardinia and its manipulative prime minister, Camillo Cavour, who was more than willing to exploit those who favoured unification from below but lacked the resources, and indeed sufficient popular support, to achieve their goals without the aid of people who privately despised them. Cavour, for instance, had described the hero of popular unification, Giuseppe Garibaldi, as a 'savage' and a 'disgrace to Italy' (Mack Smith 1996: 183). Yet such remarks had to be extracted from the published historical record in the interests of the creation of a unified myth of the *risorgimento*, a myth that extended to the construction of a series of national monuments, above all in Rome under the new king who ascended to the throne in 1878 (Gernert 1998).

Developments in the German lands were also complicated. One strand of German nationalism exhibited an anti-French tone that was strengthened by fears of a French bid to seize the Rhineland in 1840. According to Heinrich August Winkler, this was a genuine caesura in the development of German nationalism (Winkler 2002a: 87). Yet there is also strong evidence of the continuity of another strand, described by Dieter Langewiesche as 'federative nationalism' (Langewiesche 2000). Here, the singing and shooting festivals that did much to embody the unity of the German nation were also demonstrations of the diversity of the German people, with participants proudly exhibiting the flags and emblems of their respective states and adorning themselves in regional costume. It was indicative of the nature of this 'German' nation that as late as the 1860s Flemings, Dutchmen and Swiss were seen as appropriate participants in such festivities (Langewiesche 2000: 85).

As in Italy, unification in Germany came courtesy of the dynastic ambitions of a particular state. Even at the time of the Franco–Prussian war of 1870–1, a myth of German unity was being constructed and choreographed. In memoirs, speeches and newspapers the war was presented as a justified defence of German honour, supposedly insulted by the French. Highly detailed analogies were drawn between 1870 and 1813, when Prussia rose against Napoleon after a series of defeats and humiliations. The army was presented as the embodiment of the German nation (Becker 2001: 292–376).

Economic integration and international law

The Anglo–French treaty of 1860 inaugurated a period of commercial treaty-making so extensive that it has invited comparison with the ambitions of the EU. According to Marsh, 'Like the twentieth-century [European] Community, the nineteenth-century network embraced virtually all of Western and Central Europe. Both aspired to the creation of a common European market that would transcend the essentially national confines of customs unions such as the German *Zollverein*' (Marsh 1999: 3). But that is an overstatement, for it was not only the bilateral nature of the nineteenth-century treaty network, which Marsh rightly contrasts with the twentieth-century model, that distinguished the two but also the institutions and irrevocable commitment of the European Community that constitute the crucial difference.

Nevertheless, Marsh's point serves to highlight the levels of economic integration that were achieved, in part intentionally, before 1914. By contrast, the years 1914 to 1945—the years of Europe's second 'thirty years war'—would appear as a period of 'disintegration' (Röpke 1942). Intra-European trade had boomed for twenty years or so before the network of treaties was put in place in the 1860s (Ashworth 1974: 304). More striking still is the fact that even after most continental states turned towards protectionist trade policies, levels of integration remained high. Nor was this merely a matter of trade. German and Belgian concerns controlled as much as 35 per cent of the deposits in France's most important iron ore fields. In 1911 French interests established a coking enterprise on the Dutch coast. Shortly before the outbreak of war, two-thirds of the labour force in French Lorraine was made up of Italian migrants. The Ruhr coal mines employed considerable numbers of Poles, despite long-standing, and growing, nationalist antipathy to Polish economic migration (Strikwerda 1993: 1113, 1118, 1120–1).

A strong transnational dimension could also be found in the work of some legal scholars (Koskenniemi 2002). Carl Triepel, a moderate conservative and German nationalist, sought to defend the validity of international law:

> this much seems to be confirmed today, that on the one hand the nation is not the only living form [*Lebenskreis*] that is capable of creating law, that on the other hand, the commonality of important vital interests amongst a plurality of subjects and the consciousness

of this commonality by the members of such a community, must be considered as an essential presupposition of such creation [of law]. (1899: 27)

It was so self-evident that Europe constituted such a community that he simply asserted that this 'requires no discussion' (Triepel 1899: 27).

Visions of empire and integration

Throughout the nineteenth century there were calls for a European federation. From the perspective of 1949, the Frenchman Pierre Renouvin concluded that none of these was of much practical value. Indeed, they had been primarily intended to 'educate public opinion' (1949: 22). That was true, but some placed great faith in the power of public opinion. In the late nineteenth century, the English historian Sir John Robert Seeley considered the prospect of a United States of Europe, explicitly modelled on the United States of America, and noted the enormity of the task. He concluded that the federation was a real possibility though 'it can never be attained by mere diplomatic methods, or be the mere action of governments, but only by a universal popular movement' (Seeley 1871: 446).

Yet it was not European unity but the vision of Empire that prevailed. In a later work Seeley prophesied that in fifty years America and Russia would 'completely dwarf such old European States as France and Germany, and depress them into a second class' (Seeley 1897: 88). Britain's fate would be no better unless it managed to integrate its empire into a true federation. From at least the time of German unification, others counted Germany as one of the potential threats rather than as one of the victims of the supposed trend of global history. Interestingly, James Froude even saw the nature of the threat to Britain as a challenge not to its maritime supremacy by an expansion of the Prussian navy but primarily in the form of an 'extended *Zollverein*' (Neitzel 2000: 215).

Fears that the world was on the verge of consolidating into continental or imperial blocs were fed by the expansion of the United States and Russia, wars of unification on the continent, calculations of surface area and population, and the racism and social Darwinianism of the late nineteenth century. For Britain, following the advice of the prophets of doom would have meant a deliberate break with the free trade policy in favour of imperial integration and protectionism, an option that faded, for the moment at least, with the electoral defeat of the Conservatives in 1906 (Neitzel 2000: 261–3).

The debate in Germany slackened at about the same time. There the idea of an integrated *Mitteleuropa* played a greater role and attracted the interest of prominent politicians as well as the Kaiser. Yet when it came to drawing practical conclusions from these supposed global trends, politicians and business leaders hesitated in the face of the evident risks to the existing levels of European and global economic integration. These visions of empire suggest concern about the successful integration and inherent strength of the European nation states, even when flanked by overseas empires, but, ironically, they ran up against the reality of integration. Imperial integration, whether in the form of the British Empire or a German-led *Mitteleuropa* would have involved considerable international disintegration.

World War I and postwar reconstruction

Mitteleuropa

In the light of the military alliance between Germany and the Habsburg Empire as well as the increasingly effective British blockade, it is not surprising that the idea of an integrated *Mitteleuropa* was soon back on the agenda. It appeared in an internal memorandum prepared for the German chancellor in September 1914. The most renowned publication was undoubtedly Naumann's *Mitteleuropa*, which appeared in the following year (Naumann 1915). The ambivalent response within Germany itself pointed to some of the problems. Naumann had attempted to reassure the non-German peoples of the region that their role would not be merely that of colonial subjects of a German-dominated zone. Not only did he fail to persuade them, but also his very attempt to do so called forth criticism from extreme German nationalists who thought that he was making too many concessions.

Equally significant was the fact that the protracted discussion between the two Central European powers about a customs union achieved so little. Relationships between them were complicated because the Habsburg Empire was a multinational state of whose population only approximately one-quarter was German. The ensuing difficulty became apparent when the German Foreign Office addressed a memorandum to Vienna admonishing it for failing to halt the growing influence of the Slavic elements of the Empire. Vienna replied with understandable bluntness, asserting that this was a natural development and was indeed to be welcomed. Given these intractable tensions, it is tempting to be content with the contrast between the rhetoric and reality of *Mitteleuropa*.

Yet it is possible to indicate what the reality might have looked like by considering Germany's treaties with Russia and Finland in March 1918 and Romania in May 1918, and plans for the fate of Poland and Belgium. In varying degrees they show a set of common factors. First, there was military subordination to Germany with nominally autonomous national armies subject to German command in times of war. Second, there was German control of key raw materials, sometimes through front companies. Third, there was control of transport networks, again sometimes through apparently autonomous holding companies and authorities. Fourth, there was preferential treatment for German goods. Though the successes of German armies, especially in the east, were sufficient to make the outline of *Mitteleuropa* a reality, defeat in the west cut short any further development.

Peace-making and reconstruction

Peace-making at Versailles was a complex affair governed by considerations of security, notably the redrawing of boundaries, especially in Eastern Europe but also beyond Europe, and the idea of a new global organization that took the shape of the League of Nations. The mood of peoples was volatile. In the case of Germany, failure to grasp the reality of defeat and the new international constellation is well summed up in the subtitle of a recent attempt to assess the popular mood: 'The Germans on the way from a misunderstood defeat to an unwanted peace' (Klein 1998).

Of ideas of European integration there was practically no sign. There was, at most, some recognition of the need to coordinate the process of European reconstruction in the creation of a Supreme Economic Council but this body did not last beyond 1920. Subsequently, there were attempts, especially by the relevant German and French ministers, to coordinate reconstruction with the payment of reparations by Germany. Other schemes were touted by the German businessman Hugo Stinnes, and attracted the interest of the British prime minister. They all foundered on a mixture of international economic problems, for which no one took overarching responsibility, and political complications associated with the final implementation of the peace settlement and the attempt to establish relations among the old and new states of Europe. The Treaty of Rapallo between Germany and the new Soviet government was an example of the latter. It also acquired the symbolism of a German rejection of the West that was greatly in excess of its practical significance.

In 1922, the same year as the Rapallo Treaty, Richard Coudenhove-Kalergi proclaimed the cause of Pan-Europe in a Viennese newspaper. He set out from the old idea of the crystallization of the world into a set of continental or imperial blocs. Only the fate of a 'splintered' Europe seemed to be uncertain. The key to Europe's future lay in Franco–German relations: 'So long as France upholds its policy of sanctions and the occupation of the Rhine and Germany its Russian orientation, Pan-Europe will remain a phantom' (Coundenhove-Kalergi 1922). In the following year he developed his ideas at greater length in a book entitled *Pan-Europa*, two minor features of which pointed to wider considerations. One was a map depicting the extent of Pan-Europe. The black shading covered not only the geographic area of Europe, minus Britain, but also large parts of Africa, some areas of the Far East and a tiny portion of South America. This signified the presumption that any bloc needed colonial hinterlands to be viable. It also allowed Coudenhove-Kalergi to generate the statistics of population and surface area that made Pan-Europe look comparable to the other hypothetical blocs. The second was an invitation to subscribe to the Pan-European movement. Here again was the idea that creating a transnational mass movement would push governments towards integration. Whether the small groups that advocated European integration should try to build a mass movement or work through existing elites was a matter of considerable dispute. Despite his own attempt to recruit a mass movement, Coudenhove-Kalergi, an aristocrat, proved particularly adept at working through existing elites.

It was not only publicists who believed that governments could be circumvented or at least shown the way to European integration. After all, it was a former prime minster of France, Edouard Herriot, who wrote that 'The whole problem to be decided is whether public men will have as much initiative and intelligence as private individuals, or whether in politics we are going to be content to walk in the old ways, ignoring the great transformation, which is silently creating a new world' (Herriot 1930: 152). The private individuals he had in mind were the men who had created the International Steel Cartel in 1926. According to one German observer, the cartel could have 'an effect on the political structure of Europe similar to that which the *Zollverein* had on the political structure of Germany' (Pegg 1983: 69).

These hopes, including the revival of the myth of the *Zollverein*, were encouraged by what appeared to be a dramatic improvement in the general climate. In October of the previous year, the Locarno Pact had witnessed German acceptance of its western frontier, but not its eastern borders. The two chief architects of the pact, Foreign Ministers Aristide Briand of France and Gustav Stresemann of Germany, symbolized the hope of many for the reintegration of Germany into the international order and Franco–German reconciliation. But they bargained long and hard for the interests of their respective countries. In September 1926, the same month as the creation of the International Steel Cartel, Germany entered the League of Nations. Advocates of European integration stepped up their activity. In May 1926 a Franco–German Committee for Information and Documentation had been established, with the support of Emile Mayrisch, a key player in the International Steel Cartel. A League for European Cooperation followed in September. The following month Coudenhove-Kalergi organized the first congress of the Pan-European Union. The ideas and debates at this time would later be recalled by Konrad Adenauer (Schwarz 1986: 684), but they were no substitute for acts of state. Nor were the activities of the steel cartel. It worked well enough at managing an agreed distribution of markets but faltered when it came to managing change.

The most dramatic act of state was undoubtedly the offer in September 1929 by Briand to create a 'kind of federal bond'. Briand had referred quite frequently to the idea of a European federation but speculation on such an option usually never advanced beyond an indeterminate assertion. What induced Briand to make a public statement before the General Assembly of the League of Nations was undoubtedly his concern about the long-term security of France. His main lever against Germany, occupation of the Rhineland, was a diminishing asset, scheduled to come to an end in 1935 at the latest. French efforts to secure British and American guarantees against German aggression had not been successful.

But that does not mean that Briand's offer was purely instrumental. He was concerned about the economic divisions of Europe and the continent's comparative weakness in the face of American competition. There may also have been another consideration. A journalist who accompanied Briand on the train to Geneva recalled Briand saying that 'In a democracy one must always feed the mysticism of men. One must stimulate their fantasy' (Siebert 1973: 498). The fact that the crowd psychologist Gustav Le Bon was a friend of Briand and a supporter of European integration may be significant. Belief in the manipulability of the masses was widespread. Yet Briand's hope that his proposal would inspire popular support was no more well-founded than the idea of creating a mass movement in favour of European integration from below.

The reactions of European governments were unenthusiastic. Briand clarified his proposal for them in a memorandum of May 1930. Institutionally, the federation, clearly modelled on the League of Nations, was to consist of a European Conference (an assembly of all participating states); a Permanent Political Committee (consisting of a restricted number of states); and a Secretariat. The 'federal bond' was not supposed to detract from the sovereignty of member states, though how this curious condition was to be attained was not explained. Compared with his speech of the previous September, there was one striking difference. Whereas in September he had clearly emphasized the priority of economic considerations, in the memorandum he asserted the 'General subordination of the Economic Problem to the Political'. In the German cabinet this was taken as self-evident proof that Briand's purpose was the consolidation of French hegemony. What Briand really intended was an 'eastern Locarno', that is the inviolability of the territorial boundaries in eastern Europe and hence the confirmation of German territorial losses at the end of the war. Information suggesting an alternative interpretation, including strong pleas from their own ambassador in Paris, made no impression. In the absence of Stresemann, who had died in October 1929, there was less motivation to look for a compromise with the French.

A host of other reservations was also raised about Briand's proposal, notably its adverse impact on the League of Nations and wider economic relations and its anti-American and anti-Russian implications (Erdmann 1982–90: 158–64, 215–16, 232–5, 264–52, 280–4; Ruge and Schumann 1972). The historical model of the *Zollverein* was inevitably invoked, but this time with unfavourable implications for Germany: 'German *Zollverein*–North German Confederation–German Reich . . . . all based on the predominance of Prussia. By analogy, in Pan-Europe Germany would play the role of Saxony or at best Bavaria' (Auswärtiges Amt 1978: 335). As Bavaria and Saxony had retained their formal sovereignty after 1866 but had become subservient to Prussia, the implication was that this time France would play the role of Prussia, using the idea of Pan-Europe to subordinate Germany.

British officials also considered the possibility that Briand's aim was an eastern Locarno, but rejected it. Nevertheless they expressed concern about its impact on the League, the United States, and other countries. There was also concern about the general impact of 'these regionalising tendencies' which 'might clearly endanger the cohesion of the British Commonwealth of Nations' (Woodward and Butler 1946: 341). In their formal replies Portugal, Spain and the Netherlands also noted their extra-European territories or interests. Several of Europe's states did not consider themselves to be merely European states. The visions of overseas empires were still strong.

Disintegration of Europe

The peace settlement in eastern Europe already entailed a process of disintegration. The successor states carved out of the old empires multiplied Europe's boundaries enormously while mostly failing truly to satisfy the principle of national self-determination. Only Austria and Hungary were substantially ethnically homogeneous. Yet many Austrians were not convinced of the viability of their state while Hungary lamented the loss of territory and the existence of large numbers of fellow Hungarians in neighbouring states. The other states resembled mini-empires in their own right, lacking the economic and security advantages of larger empires while remaining subject to inter-ethnic tension (Pearson 1983). In the case of Czechoslovakia, a nation was invented and the reality of a separate Slovak identity glossed over to maintain the fiction of self-determination, while in Yugoslavia the idea of a common national identity had to struggle against the all-too-evident reality of a multinational state (Krajcovic 1999; Warner 1999). Memories of empire, either feared (as in the case of the idea of a Habsburg restoration) or desired (as in the case of the Polish leader Marshall Pilsudski's nostalgia for the long since disappeared Jagiellonian empire), complicated relationships further (Dziemanowski 1969). Although there were frequent expressions of concern about the disadvantages of economic dislocation caused by the break-up of the previous empires, the underlying problem was well put by Elemer Hantos, a tireless advocate of integration: 'The idea of a customs union in contemporary *Mitteleuropa*, just like the plan for a Danubian federation, is discredited, because in the past it was always related to imperialism, and even today customs union plans (Greater Britain, Pan-America, British Commonwealth) appear as near imperialist movements' (Hantos 1925: 92). The task of national reconstruction or in some cases the construction of an entirely new 'nation' against a background of economic dislocation and fear of past empires was not conducive to integration.

With the exception of the Czech part of Czechoslovakia, one common interest, or rather common plight, was heavy dependence on the agricultural sector. Even before the impact of the Great Depression, a collapse in key global prices for agricultural commodities imposed new strains on these fragile states. One means for dealing with the crisis was a preferential trading system, but this offended against dominant orthodoxy: a commitment to the most-favoured nation principle. In France there were reservations about the principle alongside a strong desire to help east European states that formed part of a system of alliances for containing Germany.

The initial move towards a preferential trading system was prompted by plans for an Austro–German customs union that France rightly perceived as a prelude to *Anschluss*. The Czechoslovak prime minister, Edvard Beneš, saw an analogy with the *Zollverein*. More specifically, he believed that the customs union was based on the treaty of 1828 between Prussia and Hesse–Darmstadt, which was an important stepping stone on the road to the *Zollverein* of 1834 and hence the road to eventual political unification (Auswärtiges Amt 1978: 174). That there was no intention to unify Germany politically in 1828 and that it took over forty years and several wars to do so did little to shake the power of the analogy. Yet Beneš was right in the sense that the Austro–German custom union was intended to lead to *Anschluss*. It was also intended as a lever to exert pressure on his country.

The French proposal of 1931 for a preferential trading system involved a package of measures. Preferential treaties were central but industrial and agricultural cartels would also play a role. It received a discouraging response from Britain and met with outright opposition from the Germans. After the Germans and Austrians had abandoned their planned customs union in September 1931 the French made a second attempt to resolve eastern Europe's problems. The Tardieu plan of 1932 resembled the 1931 proposal but, in its initial form at least, was less attractive for the east Europeans. Whereas in 1931 it was clear that the industrialized western countries were to extend preferential treatment to the agricultural exporters of eastern Europe, in 1932 the suggestion was for a preferential system among the east European states. As the ex-Hungarian prime minister, Count Bethlen, made clear, 'the Danubian agricultural states cannot do without the Italian, German and Swiss markets' (Bethlen 1932: 360).

The French indeed intended that the larger western states should unilaterally concede preferences to eastern Europe, but this ran into opposition from Britain, which had floated, but failed to pursue vigorously, its own plan for a customs union in the east (Boyce 1994; Stambrook 1963–4). Despite recognition by some ministers, officials and business interests of the importance of a positive move to halt the slide into protectionism, Britain opted for imperial preferences at the Ottawa Conference of August 1932 while admonishing others not to enter into regional preferential agreements.

The failure of the western states to develop a coordinated approach to the crisis in eastern Europe based upon multilateral trading patterns gave Germany an opportunity to develop bilateral agreements with the eastern European states. Germany had signed initial agreements with Hungary and Romania in 1931 but these were not implemented because of opposition from the United States. The new Nazi regime decided to pursue a more active commercial policy in the east, partly in response to attempts to create a bloc composed of Austria, Italy, and Hungary. This resulted in the clearing agreement between Germany and Hungary in February 1934, which nonetheless failed to prevent the creation of the Austria–Italy–Hungary bloc. Other agreements followed, including one between Germany and Yugoslavia in May 1934.

Eventually, by the eve of war, Germany had succeeded in building up a Reichsmark bloc and obtaining a high profile in the trade of most of the east European states. Yet this policy, pursued for strategic reasons, was based upon a fundamentally flawed vision of economic integration. Committed as it was to forced rearmament, Germany simply could not export enough to the east Europeans. More significant, however, was the underlying premise of integration between industrially advanced and relatively undeveloped economies. The flaw had been recognized in the 1920s by the economist Eulenburg: 'Exchange between industrial states is, on account of the rising demand, stronger than with pure agrarian states. The latter exhibit a weaker purchasing power and absorptive capacity' (Eulenburg 1926: 116).

The challenge of fascism and National Socialism

It was clear from Benito Mussolini's march on Rome in 1922 that Europe faced a new type of political regime, though British and French leaders had been prepared to cooperate with Fascist Italy, especially while Mussolini remained opposed to any *Anschluss* between Germany and Austria. Despite the presence of small fascist movements in western Europe and the pretension of a coterie of Italian fascist intellectuals that fascism was a 'universal' doctrine, Mussolini declared that fascism was not for export. Mussolini's imperial ambitions focused on North Africa, where his brutal and anachronistic rule led to an attempt to destroy the nomadic lifestyle of the Bedouin in an effort to re-develop Libya as a source of supply of wheat to Italy, which it had been at the time of the Roman Empire (Mack Smith 1996: 41). Italy's invasion of Abyssinia in 1935 and the hesitant and qualified reaction of the League of Nations did much to discredit the latter.

Adolf Hitler's ambitions were of a totally different order. For him, the existing state structure and map of Europe meant next to nothing compared with what he saw as the underlying racial reality. Statesmen who thought in more conventional terms found that difficult to grasp. Hitler's expansionist vision also fit into a broader idea of the mission of a German-dominated Reich, even where its advocates did not think in racial categories. Before Hitler's seizure of power, the authoritarian publicist Giselher Wirsing dismissed Briand's plan for a European federation, which he claimed merely adapted Louis Loucheur's idea of a 'pan-European cartel', as irrelevant to the relationship between the state and the economy in *Zwischeneuropa*, the zone between the west and Russia. Here he claimed that the task of integration, as developed by Rudolf Smend in the context of the state, had to be carried out on a larger scale (Wirsing 1932: 9–10, 210–11). Other prophets of the Reich were much less specific than Wirsing, some even openly stating that their task was a purely educational one. The implementation of the idea was to be left to an unspecified statesman (Breuning 1969: 101–2).

At the end of the 1930s Hitler began to mark out the initial contours of the Reich. The decisive step came with the occupation of the Czech land in March 1939 and the establishment there of the Protectorate of Bohemia and Moravia. In April the German jurist Carl Schmitt concluded that 'The act of the Führer has endowed the idea of our Reich with political reality, historical truth and a great future in international law' (Schmitt 1940: 312). Schmitt was soon joined by others who not only celebrated the German 'mission' evident in the new Reich, but also drew explicit comparisons with the medieval Reich (Winkler 2002a: 65). Schmitt himself soon opted for another term, *Grossraumordnung*, to conjure up a vision of a world divided into continental blocs united by hegemonic powers. The more precise contours of these structures remained elusive for the simple reason that Hitler refused to make any definitive statement about what the New Order in Europe would be and periodically prohibited discussion of the issue (Stirk 1999).

The challenge of the National Socialist new order

German plans

The striking success of German armies in 1939 and 1940 prompted a great deal of speculation on both sides of the Channel. In Germany, a memorandum prepared in the Reich Chancery in July 1940 complained about the 'economic Balkanization of Europe' and predictably identified the settlement at the end of the World War I as an obstacle to the required economic unification. Only a limited number of states was destined to enjoy a close relationship with the dominant German economy, namely the Scandinavian countries, the Netherlands, Belgium and Luxembourg. Among these there was to be a fixed rate of exchange and customs barriers were to be removed, though with quotas to mitigate any economic dislocation (Lipgens 1985: 57–9). Within a matter of days, however, the tone had changed. According to Minister of Economics Walther Funk:

> It was a fantasy to talk at this stage of a unified economy on a European scale, and in the same way it was harmful to use slogans like "currency and customs union" and expect them to solve all difficulties. A currency or customs union could only be envisaged with a country having a similar standard of life to our own. This was not the case in southeastern Europe, for instance, and it was not at all in our interests to confer on that area a similar standard of life to ours. (Lipgens 1985: 63)

Funk's public speech in July glossed over the brutal inequalities of German planning, though there was no doubt about German hegemony. In summary. Funk held out the prospect of stable export markets and exchange rates, payments agreements, a higher standard of living and a 'stronger sense of economic community' within a 'united Europe' (Lipgens 1985: 70-1). Although practical measures to coordinate and exploit the European economy as well as propaganda measures continued and, in some respects, increased in the second half of the war, it is significant that the group set up to prepare for a new economic order was disbanded after Germany invaded the Soviet Union in June 1941 (Freymond 1974: 128).

In reality, the economics of the new order were subject to the contingencies of warfare as well as the racial plans of the Nazis. First, an initial policy of plunder, especially in the east, gave way to more considered efforts to exploit the resources of occupied Europe. Customs unions were formed with the Protectorate of Bohemia and Moravia, the Netherlands and Luxembourg, but discussion about a customs union with Denmark faltered. A more general feature was the distortion of previous patterns of trade, and especially the decline in multilateral trade in favour of bilateral trade between Germany and individual occupied countries. Second, the much promised price stability gave way to inflation, fuelled in part by the competing demands of different branches of the German armed forces for supplies. Third, Germany accumulated enormous debts through the clearing system. Fourth, as the German economy increasingly suffered from a shortage of manpower, it resorted to the forced mobilization of foreign workers in order to maintain its production. Fifth, the Germans imposed occupation costs which amounted to a form of taxation for the benefit of the German war machine.

The impact of these measures on individual economies varied, typically being harsher in the east and south-east of Europe. For the latter, especially, a modern judgement, that 'Chaos, anarchy and partial retardation characterized the economic terrain of Central and South Eastern Europe at the end of the war' (McElligott 1994: 150), coincides with the contemporary view of Leon Baránski that 'between the countries themselves, relations have disintegrated still further, as will become fully apparent when the central controlling authority is broken and collapses. German domination will have hampered and not facilitated the creation of any union of European states' (Lipgens 1986: 394).

Western responses

Even before the fall of France in June 1940 there had been feverish speculation about the future of Europe. The imminence of French surrender spurred on advocates of federation, including Jean Monnet, who persuaded a desperate Winston Churchill to make a dramatic offer of immediate union between Britain and France. There would be joint citizenship, joint policies, and a single war cabinet. It was indicative of the desperation that the offer specified that this single war cabinet would 'govern from wherever best it can' (Monnet 1978: 28).

The offer of Anglo-French union did not succeed in its purpose of keeping France in the war. Faced with the collapse of that strategy British officials and ministers looked to other forms of association, including the idea of a union with the United States. This was even less likely to succeed than the offer of a union with France, though it was a sign of the seriousness of the situation that the British ambassador to Moscow was prepared to contemplate an Anglo-American union in which 'Britain would become merely the European outpost of an Anglo-Saxon group concentrated in the west' (Ryan 1987: 18).

Funk's speech of July 1940 provided a different kind of challenge. The British feared that it would appear all too attractive and would sap the will to resist in occupied Europe. With this in mind the economist John Maynard Keynes was asked to draft a counter-memorandum. In December 1940, Keynes wrote that:

> It would be senseless to suppose that her neighbours can develop an ordered, a prosperous, or a secure life with a crushed and ruined Germany in their midst. Germany must be expected and allowed to assume the measure of economic leadership which flows naturally from her own qualifications and her geographical position. (Keynes 1940: 246)

This was not good propaganda, though Keynes mistakenly thought that it was. Nevertheless Keynes's memorandum revealed a fundamental problem that was to bedevil planning for a postwar world and would not be solved until well after the end of the war: the fact that Germany was indeed essential to a functioning European economy and to European prosperity. The difficulty lay in reconciling that inescapable fact with security against German aggression.

If the importance of the German economy was one problem, German national identity was another one that would not go away. The allies agreed that Prussia should be dismembered after the war. Indeed, it was one of the few things upon which they agreed with respect to Germany. Yet in destroying Prussia they were doing little more than destroying a myth. Ironically, it was the Nazis themselves who had put an end to any autonomous Prussian power base. Churchill, his Foreign Secretary Anthony Eden, and US President Franklin Delano Roosevelt all expressed enthusiasm at some time for a much more thorough dismantling of a unified Germany. In conversations in 1943 Eden and Roosevelt speculated upon the outbreak of separatists tendencies at the end of the war. When pressed about what they would do if such separatism failed to materialize, they had little response beyond falling back on the mantra that Prussia had to be destroyed. Their officials did not generally share their hopes about separatism.

Especially in Britain, there was considerable interest among the foreign policy establishment in the idea of federations of greater or lesser extent. These would strengthen the federated nations, thereby providing a bulwark against Germany, while also resolving some of the interwar problems of economic disintegration. Here, in some respects, there was some basis for hope. After the defeat of Poland in 1939, Polish exiled leaders moved quite quickly in a federal direction. Indeed, even before the war the Polish foreign minister, Jozef Beck, had in mind a 'Third Europe', in some versions of which he presumed the disintegration of Czechoslovakia (Cienciala 1968: 55–7). In a memorandum of November 1940, the Poles proposed a federation of indeterminate extent, but possibly grouping as many as 80 million people, whose cornerstone would be a Polish–Czechoslovak federation. The British were generally favourable, the Foreign Office noting that 'Such a federation is unlikely to become a dangerous expansionist power as, for example, a nationalist Poland might' (Blasius 1984: 229). The Polish and Czechoslovak governments in exile made sufficient progress to sign a declaration of confederation in January 1942.

A little earlier in the same month a Greek–Yugoslav agreement was also reached, though not without Foreign Office pressure on the reluctant Greeks. The more promising Polish–Czechoslovak agreement soon ran into opposition from the Soviets, who, given the memory of the betrayal of Czechoslovakia by the west at Munich in 1938, exercised an effective veto. Careless and futile speculation among elements of the Polish resistance and exile community that the proposed confederation might fulfil the supposed role of the Jagiellonian empire, dating back to 1385, probably did not help and certainly infuriated Poles more attuned to the contemporary reality (Pomian 1972: 116–17). Visions of empire, even if the empire was long gone, were difficult to erase.

In retrospect, the ideas of the exiled governments were to have more lasting significance. Ironically, the experience of exile and the reduced pressure associated with normal political life may have helped the Belgian and Dutch foreign ministers, Paul-Henri Spaak and Belco van Kleffens, to reconsider the commercial strategies of their countries. Businessmen and intellectuals played a significant role in converting both politicians to the idea of a customs union (Laurent 1990: 136). Norwegian, Dutch and Belgian exiles also recognized that their prewar policies of neutrality were bankrupt. Their response was to look to a system of North Atlantic security.

Especially for the Dutch and Norwegians, with their long-standing commitment to neutrality, this constituted a veritable diplomatic revolution. An Atlantic security system, combined with economic integration, was indeed the outcome, but not without tension between Atlantic and continental interests. One Belgian exile did not see the two as compatible. According to Frans van Cauwelaert:

> We are not simply a Belgian frontier province on a continent. We are, like Holland, a door that opens wide upon the ocean. It was the sea that made possible the early and immortal flowering of our Flemish towns. It is the sea that will once again condition the moral and material renaissance that we are expecting after the war. . . . Our international orientation should be maritime and not continental, Atlantic and not European. (Lipgens 1986: 430)

Although exiles—whether Polish, Czech, Belgian or Dutch—could try to lay the foundations of postwar renewal and integration among themselves, the viability of their projects was highly dependent upon the leading Allied powers. Stalin's belated intervention already demonstrated the crucial role that the Soviet Union would play in the east. In the west, Britain's more benign disposition was constrained by a preoccupation with the strategic conduct of the war and dependence upon the United States, a significant factor even before the entry of the United States into the war. After Pearl Harbor, this increasingly meant commitment to the American vision of a new global order that was to result in the Bretton Woods agreements and the United Nations. Britain was also committed to a continuation of the wartime alliance as the foundation stone of the postwar order.

Resistance visions

It was inevitable that the resistance groups within occupied Europe would not be well-informed about the deliberations of the Allied governments and about how far those deliberations diverged from their own. Although Nazi propaganda tainted the idea of European integration in some minds, there was extensive advocacy of often radical, but sometimes vague, ideas of European integration and full-scale federation. It has been argued that the similarity of their views is remarkable, especially given the conditions of occupation which isolated these people from much of their own society let alone from each other. Indeed, many members of the resistance were prepared to consider schemes of integration that involved the extensive sacrifice of national sovereignty. Yet there were significant differences among them due to varying national traditions and the conditions of occupation and liberation. Thus, for the German resistance, moral and religious renewal and a certain distrust of democracy was evident. In France, the existence of the Vichy regime played a retarding role in consideration of European integration. The 'pillarization' of society was reflected in the diverse responses in the Netherlands to the idea of European integration. In Italy, long-standing differences between the north and the south, aggravated by the significant gap between the liberation of the two halves of the country, had an impact.

Altiero Spinelli stood out among the more ambitious figures in the resistance. Spinelli hoped that the resistance movements themselves could provide the political platform for postwar integration. This would not be an easy task, but he expected that:

> In the brief, intense period of general crisis (when the States will lie broken, when the masses will be anxiously waiting for a new message, like molten matter, burning, and easily shaped into new moulds, capable of accommodating the guidance of serious internationalist-minded men), the most privileged classes in the old national systems will attempt, by underhand or violent methods, to dampen the wave of internationalist feelings and passions and will ostentatiously begin to reconstruct the old State institutions. (Spinelli and Rossi 1988: 26)

In short, there would be a small window of opportunity for the unification of Europe from below that would bypass the old nation states.

Yet the idea of making Europe from below was no more realistic at the end of World War II than it had been earlier, despite, and in some senses because of, the unparalleled destructiveness of the war. It was not only that the old 'privileged classes' saw national reconstruction as an urgent task but also that national reconstruction was time-consuming and highly demanding in terms of material and personal resources. The humiliation of defeat and occupation, complicated by the internal divisions that amounted to civil war in Spinelli's Italy and Monnet's France, added another dimension to national reconstruction. In some cases this entailed new myths: that Germany had begun again in 1945 from 'zero hour' or that 'France' had resisted the German invader. In fact, it would take decades before these nations could come to terms with the more complicated and less reassuring reality, much longer than it took for at least some statesmen to grasp the need for reconciliation.

Conclusion

Patterns of integration and disintegration in the century before the end of World War II were highly complicated. There was no linear transition from a condition of disintegration to integration. Not even the idea of increasing national integration leading to hyper-nationalism and a subsequent turn to European integration, as traumatized

Europeans recoiled from the horrors of war, comes close to doing justice to that history. National political integration and international economic integration were not diametrically opposed processes. Moreover, the period was the source of powerful myths about integration: political and economic, national and international.

One of the most powerful of those myths was that of the German Reich. According to Heinrich August Winkler, 'It was not the national state as such that led to catastrophe. The path into the abyss started with the arrogance of those who saw the Reich as more than one national state among others, and wanted it to be so' (Winkler 2002b: 25). The peculiar destructiveness of that national-imperial myth arose from the conjuncture of industrial and military power and a unique set of ideological influences. To that extent, perhaps, one can speak of a linear trajectory. The collapse of the myth was a precondition for postwar integration.

Yet the myth and reality of empire were significant for all the larger European states and even some of the smaller ones. The pretension of being 'lords of all the world' (Pagden 1995) may always have been extravagant but the transition from that ambition to being no more than one national state among others is a measure of the distance that some Europeans had to travel. The experience of empire was significant even for those who had not been able to project their power on an imperial scale, for they had been victims of it.

Empire, of course, did not come to an end in 1945 and disentanglement from empire would be a painful process for many states, especially France and Britain. Integration is often understood as an essentially peaceful process that stands in contrast to the projection of power associated with empire. Yet, as two world wars and numerous processes of national integration show, integration and power are not inevitably opposites. It does of course make an enormous difference whether the projection of power is the mechanism for bringing about integration or whether the basis of integration is acceptance of the status of being one nation among others. That is an essentially political decision which could no more follow from economic integration alone than the German Reich of 1871 followed from the *Zollverein* of 1834.

Economic integration and even a sense of cultural community had been high before World War I, high enough to persuade some that war was no longer conceivable. The subsequent second thirty years war cruelly exposed the shallowness of those hopes. From quite early on in the nineteenth century there had been another hope that was to prove equally unfounded. Empires and wars, it was claimed, could be circumvented and rendered obsolete by the uniting of Europe from below; public opinion and mass movements guided by far-sighted intellectuals could make Europe against the will of governments and states or exploit the temporary weakness of those states at crucial moments. In fact, Europe would be integrated in the post-World War II period through and by states. Only in that way could the institutions be created that would give permanence to European integration.

Further reading

An awareness of wider trends in international history is vital in putting the issue of European integration in context. Hobsbawm (1990) is a brilliant and highly readable account of the changing nature and implications of nationalism. A legal perspective is provided by the detailed studies in Koskenniemi (2002). An orthodox survey of the idea of Europe is provided by Heater (1992). A more eclectic but highly stimulating collection of essays can be found in Pagden (2002). Political and economic developments of the period before 1945 are considered in the first three chapters of Stirk (1996). The early chapters of Arter (1993), which focuses on small and new states, are also useful. Multidisciplinary perspectives on Central and East Europe can be found in Stirk (1994). Pegg (1983) is a very detailed account of the diverse groups advocating European union. A massive collection of original documents relating to the debate about European union during World War II, with valuable introductions to the individual chapters, is provided by Lipgens (1985, 1986).

Arter, D. (1993), *The Politics of European Integration in the Twentieth Century* (Aldershot: Dartmouth).

Heater, D. (1992), *The Idea of European Unity* (Leicester: Leicester University Press).

Hobsbawm, E. (1990), *Nations and Nationalism since 1780* (Cambridge: Cambridge University Press).

Koskenniemi, M. (2002), *The Gentle Civilizer of Nations: The Rise and Fall of International Law 1870–1960* (Cambridge: Cambridge University Press).

Lipgens, W. (ed.) (1985 and 1986), *Documents on the History of European Integration*, Vols. 1 and 2 (Baden-Baden: Nomos Verlag).

Pagden, A. (2002), *The Idea of Europe: From Antiquity to the European Union* (Cambridge: Cambridge University Press).

Pegg, C.H. (1983), *Evolution of the European Idea 1914–1932* (Chapel Hill: University of North Carolina Press).

Stirk, P. (ed.) (1994), *Mitteleuropa: History and Prospects* (Edinburgh: Edinburgh University Press).

Stirk, P. (1996), *A History of European Integration since 1914* (London: Pinter).

Websites

A valuable and extensive collection of historical documents covering west Europe, with sections on Europe as a supranational region as well as specific nations, is available at http://library.byu.edu/~rdh/eurodocs. There is a site devoted to the history of European integration established by R. T. Griffiths at http://www.eu-history.leidenuniv.nl.

Part II

The Postwar Context

Chapter 2

Dividing Europe

The Cold War and European Integration

David A. Messenger

Contents

Summary

The conflict known as the cold war originated in Europe after World War II as the United States and the Soviet Union reached radically different conclusions about the requirements of their own national security. The need to foster the security of the United States and its partners in Europe fostered the Marshall Plan, strengthened the appeal of economic and political integration, and ensured that membership in the ensuing institutions would be limited to the western part of the continent. Countries that opted not to participate in European integration (such as Britain) or were not invited to do so (such as Spain) nevertheless fit into the overarching North Atlantic security framework. The intensification of the cold war in the early 1950s led to American demands for German rearmament, which prompted the French to propose the European Defence Community (EDC). The failure of the EDC was not a serious setback for European integration; nor did it prevent German rearmament (Germany rearmed instead through the Western European Union). The cold war lost much of its salience for European integration later in the 1950s and hardly impinged on the emergence of the European Economic Community.

Introduction

The division of Europe into two spheres, the Western linked to the United States and the Eastern to the Soviet Union, was a gradual process that occurred in the late 1940s. Each of the three major wartime allies—Great Britain, the Soviet Union and the United States—sought to influence postwar arrangements in such a way as to guarantee their own security. The United States and the Soviet Union soon emerged as the dominant powers, whose interactions, debates and disputes over the reconstruction of domestic and international order in Europe led to the emergence by 1947–8 of a new kind of non-military conflict: the cold war. Ideological differences between Communism and liberal democracy played a part in these disputes, as did traditional rivalries and historical enmities. Yet it was the idea of 'national security' that was most significant in breaking up the wartime alliance and generating the cold war conflict, thereby affecting a range of developments in Europe after 1945, including the course of political and economic integration.

Within Western Europe, the integration of political, economic and perhaps even military institutions became one method of organizing the national security of the United States, France, and other states. The cold war itself was not responsible for integration, as a number of proposals involving the sharing of sovereignty had already been made. However, the cold war's emphasis on new policies to foster the national security of the United States and its allies led a number of leaders in Western Europe to embrace integration as a viable means of enhancing protection against the Soviet Union. This chapter traces the relationship between the cold war and the process of integration from the mid-1940s to the mid-1950s. During that time, the cold war encouraged a number of governments to support integrationist schemes in economic and military matters, and ensured that membership in successful integrationist institutions would be limited to Western European countries. Indeed, between 1945 and 1952 the cold war was a decisive factor in promoting the creation of European institutions. However, there were limits to its impact. Integration was not the only manner in which states could affiliate with the Western Alliance, as the cases of Britain and Spain demonstrate. Nor was the cold war the most significant motivation behind the creation of the European Economic Community (EEC) in 1957.

The origins of the cold war in Europe

The Big Three

The Soviet Union under Josef Stalin had one major goal in the immediate aftermath of World War II: territorial security against future attacks, especially from Germany. Stalin was convinced that a number of pro-Soviet buffer states in Eastern Europe and a disabled Germany would provide such security. The most significant buffer state was Poland, through which Hitler had attacked the Soviet Union in 1941 and in which Stalin now insisted on the imposition of Communist rule (Mastny 1996: 20). Stalin wanted a series of pro-Soviet states elsewhere in Eastern Europe, even if their governments included non-Communist as well as Communist parties. Finally, Stalin sought the 'disablement' of occupied Germany through the imposition of severe reparations payments together with economic and military restrictions that would halt German recovery for at least ten to fifteen years.

Like the Soviet Union, the United States pursued a number of goals in Europe as the war came to an end in 1945. In general, the United States wanted to consolidate peace and prosperity in a new European–American relationship. Washington's vision of a Europe that was peaceful, democratic and capitalist was part and parcel of America's efforts to create a 'political economy of freedom' around the world (Leffler 1992: 13).

These differing views of Europe's future were reflected in the agreements reached at the two tripartite (American–British–Soviet) conferences held in 1945, the first at Yalta in February and the second at Potsdam in July–August. At Yalta, Stalin pushed for the establishment of governments in Poland and elsewhere in Eastern Europe that would be friendly towards the Soviet Union. The United States and Britain agreed that the Soviet Union should have a 'sphere of influence' in Eastern Europe, which the existence of the so-called Lublin Poles, a Communist faction loyal to Stalin that had formed a government in liberated Poland, would help to achieve. The two Western allies even agreed that the Soviet Union should gain territory in eastern Poland. US President Franklin D. Roosevelt nonetheless insisted on holding elections in which the non-Communist Polish government-in-exile could run against the Lublin Poles. Roosevelt would accept a Soviet-friendly Poland under some form of Soviet influence as long as the government was not a Soviet puppet and had considerable independence in domestic policy (Trachtenberg 1999: 10–11).

The Yalta conference produced the Declaration on Liberated Europe, which outlined how states freed from German control would return to normal political life and included a statement about the necessity of holding free elections. Despite a general reference to 'Europe', it was understood that the Declaration referred mostly to Eastern Europe, and particularly to Poland. As for occupied Germany, the conference concluded with the creation of the Allied Control Commission as a vehicle for cooperation between the United States, Britain, France and the Soviet Union in the running of the country. The Western allies agreed to key Soviet demands, including the right to reparations.

Despite the existence of seemingly clear-cut agreements, in reality multiple inter-pretations of those agreements existed. Whereas Stalin thought that he had support from the West to treat Poland as a satellite state, many in the US government ex-pected elections almost immediately. The new American administration of Harry S. Truman acquiesced in Roosevelt's acceptance of a Soviet sphere of influence in East-ern Europe. Indeed, it acknowledged in May 1945 that elections were not going to be held in Poland. Yet many in the administration argued that future Soviet actions in Eastern Europe needed to be viewed as a series of 'litmus tests'—opportunities to read Soviet intentions and assess whether cooperation was really compatible with American national security goals (Leffler 1992: 35). Stalin's absolutist interpretation of just what security meant, described by one historian as an 'insatiable craving' for complete control over territory and states, soon undermined his desire for coopera-tion (Mastny 1996: 23). The decision in December 1945 by US Secretary of State James Byrnes to recognize the Bulgarian and Romanian Communist governments, estab-lished by the Soviet Union without elections, led an influential Republican senator to charge Byrnes with following a policy of 'appeasement'. Truman himself concluded that Byrnes had given away too much. The incident illustrated a growing sense within the United States that the Soviet Union was failing the 'litmus tests' implicit in the Declaration on Liberated Europe.

Still, the conflict that became the cold war was not inevitable. Even if the Soviets had failed to live up to their Yalta promises, the nature of the agreements made there, and later at Potsdam, gave considerable leeway to each side to carry out policy in its respective sphere of influence and zone of occupation in Germany. The Pots-dam agreements, despite being based supposedly on the principle of Four-Power co-operation, could just as easily have worked on the basis of division. Certain decisions, like the one giving each of the occupying powers complete independence to act as it saw fit within its own zone, suggested an awareness on their parts that the poten-tial for cooperation was limited, especially in Germany (Trachtenberg 1999: 26). The question was whether intra-Allied differences would lead to a peaceful division of Europe or a sense of distrust and insecurity between the Soviet Union and the West-ern powers. The criticism of Byrnes at the end of 1945 and early 1946 suggested that real distrust of Soviet intentions in Europe was becoming more prominent in the United States. Suitably chastened, Byrnes was very hesitant to seek any accommod-ation with the Soviet Union (Eisenberg 1996: 202). Clearly, the threat perception of both sides was changing.

Changing threat perceptions

Germany was at the heart of the changing threat perception of American policy-makers. What might have been seen as an 'amicable divorce' between the United States and the Soviet Union over German policy now became a fear that the Soviets would seek to expand their influence beyond their existing sphere (Trachtenberg 1999: 35–40). The best expression of the new threat perception came in February 1946 when George F. Kennan sent his famous 'Long Telegram' from Moscow to the State Department in Washington. Kennan, a long-time critic of cooperation with the Soviet Union, focused on the insecurity of Soviet leaders, which, combined with the ideology of communism, he argued, set Soviet policy on an expansionist course. Soon afterwards, Truman seemed to suggest that he too was increasingly distrustful of Soviet intentions in Europe when, in March 1946, he introduced former British Prime Minister Winston Churchill at Westminster College in Fulton, Missouri. Here Churchill delivered perhaps his best-known speech, which Truman had read in advance, denouncing the Soviet Union for imposing an 'Iron Curtain' across the continent, behind which it controlled the Eastern European states. By implication, the West now had to act to prevent the Soviet sphere from growing.

A new American policy gradually emerged in the course of 1946 to try to stop the Soviet Union's supposed expansion (Leffler 1992: 96). The United States would assist Western Europe in order to bolster America's allies against Soviet incursion or subversion. The first significant opportunity to act came in February 1947 when Britain, pleading economic weakness, implored the United States to take over financial and military support of Turkey and Greece, then in the throes of a communist insurgency. The State Department, enthralled by Kennan's analysis, wanted the United States to step into Britain's shoes. In March 1947 Truman asked a reluctant Congress, dominated by fiscal conservatives wary of taking the government into debt so soon after the war, for the financial means to aid Turkey and Greece. Arguing that more than the security of these two states was at stake and that the world faced a choice 'between alternative ways of life', Truman claimed that the United States had an obligation to defend democracy wherever it was threatened by Soviet and Communist expansion. The ensuing Truman Doctrine, and the money spent under its auspices in Greece and Turkey, represented the principle of Kennan's policy of containment in action.

In response to the Truman Doctrine, in September 1947 the Soviet Union convened a conference of primarily Eastern European communist parties and created an organization known as the Cominform. This symbolized the Soviet Union's acceptance of the division of Europe into two irreconcilable 'camps'. A speech by Cominform leader Andrei Zhdanov mirrored Truman's in suggesting that a high level of distrust, suspicion and ideological conflict existed between the superpowers (Nation 1992: 174). In order to prevent the spread of American influence the Soviet Union adopted a policy of 'retrenchment' in Eastern Europe, expelling non-Communist parties from government and purging party leaders who would not follow Stalin's lead (Nation 1992: 177).

Despite the Communist insurgency in Greece, which had triggered the Truman Doctrine, the Soviet Union did not have the military capacity to overwhelm Europe at that time. Instead, the Soviet Union was still in the process of consolidating control and influence throughout Eastern Europe. Few believed that the Soviets wanted to attack Western Europe or take over all of Germany, but many in the West feared that if it co-opted German power, the Soviet Union would acquire the potential to move beyond its existing sphere of influence and perhaps threaten Western Europe in the future (Leffler 1992: 97). The immediate challenge presented by the Soviet Union was a growth in the influence of local Communist parties in Central and Western Europe, eager to exploit internal political crises and economic dislocation. In other words, Western statesmen feared that the policy of retrenchment in Eastern Europe was only the start, not the end, of Soviet efforts to influence and control other states in order to enhance the security of the Soviet Union.

The coup by Czechoslovakia's Communists against their coalition partners in February 1948 reinforced the view that Soviet expansion would not take the form of a military attack, but would happen by other means. Stalin's support for the Czech coup was, in his mind, a continuation of retrenchment, a clearing up of confusion over the composition of each camp, not an attack on the West (Nation 1992: 179). Yet for the United States, the implications of the Czech coup were quite different and led to a recasting of the American policy of containment in more overt military terms. The United States would have to stabilize Western Europe economically and politically in order to prevent the Soviet Union from taking advantage of future political crises, similar to Czechoslovakia's, in states with large Communist parties.

One consequence of this was increased American involvement in the Italian election of April 1948. The State Department, the Central Intelligence Agency and US military intelligence feared the possibility of communist mobilization or even a *coup d'état*. As a result, the newly formed National Security Council, in its first report ever, called for active US intervention before and during the election campaign (Ventresca 2004: 69). Yet the success of the American-backed Italian Christian Democratic Party did little to quell fears about possible Soviet expansion into Central and Western Europe.

Germany and European integration

As seen in Chapter 3, Germany was where policies of reconstruction and revitalization, particularly on the part of the Western allies, ultimately became connected with the conduct of the cold war and the pursuit of European integration. Even without the emergence of the cold war, the four occupying powers had fundamental disagreements about the future status of their former enemy. Once again, threat perception was key. France and the Soviet Union shared the view that Germany posed the greatest threat to the security of both states. Wanting to eliminate the possibility of Germany ever being reconstituted as a single country, as early as September 1945 France opposed the development of central German agencies to assist reconstruction (Eisenberg 1996: 170). The Soviets, by contrast, continued to push for a unified German state, but wanted one that would be friendly towards Moscow and severely weakened economically and militarily. Within their zone of occupation, the Soviets took most of the factories, plants, and equipment while setting up German socialists and communists to administer local government.

Different views in the British and American zones about Germany's future led to very different policies. The Americans soon concluded that economic growth in Western Europe required Germany's resources and industry. The economic recovery of Germany was deemed crucial to establishing the system of free trade and democratic constitutionalism that the United States wanted to see across Europe, or at least in Western Europe (Eisenberg 1996: 234). Thus the national security goals of the United States required the creation of a revitalized and strong state.

By 1946, conflict over the nature of Germany's reconstruction coincided with the emergence of the cold war. Secretary of State Byrnes argued that Germany needed to be restored quickly, that its economic resources were necessary for the reconstruction of Western Europe as a whole, and that a reconstructed Western Europe was necessary to limit the influence of local Communist parties and the Soviet Union.

Byrnes made it clear that the United States was willing to risk the loss of Soviet co-operation in Germany in order to achieve its goals. Indeed, the United States now publicly identified the Soviet Union as the primary threat to the implementation of American policy in Germany and Western Europe (Eisenberg 1996: 248). Plans were soon afoot for the unification of the British and American zones in order to improve economic development in Germany. The French initially remained aloof while the Soviets responded by leaving the Allied Control Commission in March 1948.

In June 1948, the United States, Britain and France cleared the way for a con-stitutional convention that would create the Federal Republic of Germany (West Germany). They also introduced a new currency, the Deutsche Mark, in their now unified zones, and permitted its use in West Berlin, which, although divided among the Western powers, was located within the Soviet zone of eastern Germany. The Soviets quickly retaliated by introducing an East German mark in East Berlin and, more consequentially, by blocking all road and rail access to West Berlin. This led the United States to airlift supplies into West Berlin, thereby triggering an operation that began in July 1948 and continued until March 1949. The so-called Berlin blockade rep-resented the first overt conflict of the cold war. While it took place, West Germany continued moving towards statehood, with the new Federal Republic coming into be-ing in May 1949. This prompted the Soviet Union to create the German Democratic Republic (East Germany) the following October.

While overt and covert intervention (such as occurred in Italy) was one example of how the West responded to new threat perceptions, more notable in the long run was a series of policies that sought to shore up and expand existing democratic and capitalist institutions, with German reconstruction being the first and foremost goal. The integration of Western Europe, economically and politically, became one of the most vital tools in that process, leading to American support for a variety of initiat-ives that emerged over the next several years. Thus, the cold war became one of the most significant factors in the eventual creation of integrated supranationalism in Western Europe that formed the basis for the later European Union.

Marshall planning and beyond

In a speech at Harvard University in June 1947, US Secretary of State George Marshall made a proposal to revitalize Europe — including Germany — economically. The basic premise was that European countries should work together to plan economic recon-struction, with the promise of American financial support if such a plan emerged. Although Marshall's offer covered the entire continent, in effect it was limited by the emerging cold war to Western Europe only. The goals of the Marshall Plan, as it came to be called, were many. First was the fundamental need to rebuild Western Europe's economy. Second was the need to diffuse nationalism, especially a revital-ized German nationalism. Marshall's proposal was partially grounded on the premise that Germany's revival, essential for European economic growth, should not come at the cost of widespread political insecurity. A common, planned approach would work to diffuse German influence. Third was the need to contain possible Soviet expansion into Western Europe. Economic recovery within a multinational framework would serve all these purposes (Hogan 1987: 90).

While the cold war can therefore be seen as one of the factors that led to Marshall's proposal, it did not eliminate all difficulties unrelated to the American–Soviet dispute. Even though the French wanted American assistance, it was not at all clear that they would agree with Washington on Germany's role in Europe. Fearing a possible revival of German nationalism, France opposed the general idea that German recovery was essential in order to lead Western Europe out of economic despair. As it was, the French plan for postwar economic recovery (the so-called Monnet Plan) called for France to supersede Germany in certain industries, notably steel (Eisenberg 1996: 331). By contrast, the Marshall proposal explicitly demanded that West European nations meet and coordinate their recoveries together instead of proposing and pursuing many different national recovery programmes. The American preference for a continental marketplace grounded in a federal system certainly inspired the Marshall Plan and its goal of creating a secure and economically liberal Europe (Hogan 1987: 27).

European officials gathered in Paris in July 1947 and eventually formed the Committee on European Economic Cooperation, which later became the Organization for European Economic Cooperation (OEEC), to determine Western European requirements for assistance. The final report, released in September, disappointed many in the US government who saw it as lacking a real commitment to integrated, transnational planning for recovery. The lack of a customs union and absence of strong, central institutions indicated that the Europeans continued to look at American aid from a national, rather than continental, perspective (Lundestad 1998: 30–1). Moreover, they disagreed over Germany's role in European recovery. In short, European countries continued to think of their individual interests whereas Marshall wanted them to act collectively (Hitchcock 1998: 77). The cold war may have partially instigated Marshall's proposal but it was not enough, on its own, to convince the Europeans to act together.

France, the United States and the institutions of Western Europe

Only in the process of implementing the European Recovery Programme, as the Marshall Plan was officially called, did Europeans themselves come to embrace the idea that economic recovery and national security were more feasible in a western European framework that integrated Germany with its neighbours. Missing from the initial European meetings was a country willing to take the lead in the construction of more comprehensive institutions.

Many American policy-makers had assumed that Britain would play the part. Britain, after all, shared American fears of Soviet expansion and welcomed moves towards a West German state both as an important aspect of containment and as a means of sharing the burden of German reconstruction (Lee 2001: 20–6). Britain had hoped that the Dunkirk Treaty, signed with France in 1947, would, over time, become more than simply an anti-German defensive alliance and act instead as the catalyst for a strong Western European bloc (Bell 1997: 83). Despite rhetoric in favour of integration, however, Britain in the end did not want to lead or even participate in the process of developing supranational ties among Western European states. Indeed, as early as the beginning of talks over Marshall aid, Britain asked the United States for a special status within the scheme, a status suggesting that Britain was aligned more with the United States than with other European nations. Had it had been granted, such a status might have killed the entire programme, not least because of French opposition (Bell 1997: 87).

Another country needed to take the lead in developing common, integrated institutions. France was the obvious contender. Immediately after the war, French policy towards Germany was not that different from the Soviet Union's. Both countries saw Germany as the most significant threat. France therefore wanted Germany to be weakened in a way that would facilitate French recovery (Hitchcock 1998: 43). Disabling Germany's economy and exploiting resources such as Ruhr coal for French reconstruction were important policy goals (Hitchcock 1998: 48). As late as December 1948 and into 1949, French officials continued to believe that institutions such as the International Authority for the Ruhr were intended to limit Germany's freedom of action (Parsons 2003: 45).

Yet signs of change were also apparent. By the time that Four-Power cooperation on Germany formally broke down with the collapse of the foreign ministers meeting in December 1947, France was willing to merge its zone with those of Britain and the United States and facilitate West German statehood. By 1948 and 1949, support for the western, European model proposed by the United States as the solution to France's concerns about security and economic development, as well as a means of containing the Soviet Union, grew within the foreign ministry and other departments (Parsons 2003: 51). Once the Americans realized that there was a willingness within the French government to adopt a European strategy, Secretary of State Dean Acheson pressed the French, in October 1949, to go further (Lundestad 1998: 34). That same month, the head of the Marshall Plan's European office told the OEEC that integration was the only way to achieve real economic recovery (Hogan 1987: 274).

Ultimately, France embraced the American model of a Western European group. This did not represent the 'collapse' of France's position. Rather, the French came to see that integration and cooperative institutions would give them the opportunity to produce 'active and constructive policies' in order to achieve their overriding goal of influencing Germany's recovery. What changed was the means, not the end. Working with the United States, France now sought the integration of Germany's recovery with its own economic plans (Hitchcock 1998: 100). In this way, France would be assured of a non-aggressive Germany, its own recovery, and assistance from the United States. Moreover, taking on the mantle of continental leadership might also extend French influence beyond the country's actual military and economic capacities (Soutou 2001: 44).

The cold war was not the only reason why the French came to accept American proposals for planned cooperation and German recovery, but it did make Franco–American agreement easier to achieve. In what some have called 'double containment'—that is, containment of both Germany and the Soviet Union—the

French and Americans came to see that 'building Europe' through an institutional architecture that tied West Germany into Western Europe was best for their own security. Certainly, double containment was far preferable to dividing Western Europe and possibly aggravating the cold war (Trachtenberg 1999: 74–6).

Yet the process that led France to assume continental leadership was slow and laborious. Well into 1950 there was not a unified French position on how best to proceed. Moreover, it was difficult to move Europe in a new direction, beyond traditional treaties and towards greater transnational and supranational institutionalization. One of the first venues in which the French pressed for integration was the negotiations that led to the Council of Europe in 1949 (Bell 1997: 101). Eventually, in deference to the British, who desired only a cooperative organization that would mirror the Brussels Pact, the Council came into being without any supranational power (Giauque 2002: 31). Nonetheless, French Foreign Minister Robert Schuman and, in particular, economic adviser Jean Monnet strongly advocated the adoption of the integrationist concept as essential for French security and economic development. This provided the catalyst for France to assume a leadership role on the Continent (Gillingham 1991: 137).

The Schuman Plan

Monnet, in charge of economic planning for the French government, was committed to a programme of industrial modernization. He soon saw the benefits of taking up the American offer of aid in the context of continental-wide planning (Gillingham 1991:144). Monnet's efforts led to a series of French initiatives after 1948 for economic cooperation that were inspired in large part by security concerns involving both Germany and the Soviet Union. His primary goal was to reconcile French efforts to contain Germany, economically and politically, with American desires for integration, using supranational management of the Ruhr's coal and steel industries as a model. Sectoral integration had already been the subject of numerous discussions at the OEEC, but no country had so far taken the lead on the issue, or connected it to other concerns (Küsters 1995: 64). That is exactly what France did in May 1950 when, at Monnet's behest, Schuman proposed integrating the French and German coal and steel industries.

Recognizing that the United States was committed to revitalizing Germany, concerned about German resurgence but also steadfast in its belief in the value of a Western Alliance that would confront the Soviet Union, France abandoned its advocacy of separating the Ruhr from Germany and proposed instead the Schuman Plan for supranational oversight of the countries' coal and steel sectors (Trachtenberg 1999: 70). Far from simply falling in line with American and British policies that favoured German revival, France embraced a leadership role that centred on a Franco–German *rapprochement*, using the tools of cooperation and integration (Gillingham 1991: 170). Sectoral integration was a logical starting point for Franco–German reconciliation. The Schuman Plan therefore represented the end of France's 'unyielding' stance against German economic revival and the beginning of an effort to join American and West German leaders in integrating West Germany into Western Europe (Küsters 1995: 65). The result, by 1952, was the European Coal and Steel Community (ECSC).

The Western Alliance and German rearmament

By 1949, Germany and Europe were divided. Efforts to improve the economic security of Western Europe moved forward with the Schuman Plan. However, the question of a new system of military security for Western Europe was still unresolved. Would the United States maintain its troops on the continent? Would West Germany be permitted to develop its own army? What would be the reaction of France and other countries?

Strategic movements and American foreign policy

In March and again in June 1948, Truman offered his European allies a guarantee of continued US military presence in Germany. Yet the Berlin blockade demonstrated the real possibility that war could break out, and thus the need for a more organized and definite security system for Western Europe as a whole. In 1949, the Soviet Union ended the American monopoly of atomic weapons; a gleeful Stalin expressed renewed confidence in his ability to challenge the West (Trachtenberg 1999: 95). Clearly, the security situation in Western Europe was getting worse. Although finally embracing integration, the French insisted that West Germany should not be permitted to rearm, despite the potential for a conflict to break out on its territory. Instead, the United States should make an unequivocal commitment to the defence of Western Europe. In general, Germany's neighbours in the West came to accept the American vision for a revitalized West Germany only because they in turn demanded certain 'terms of their collaboration', including a firm commitment to European defence on the part of the US military (Leffler 1992: 235).

Despite budgetary constraints, American commanders, led by General Dwight D. Eisenhower, agreed. They therefore prepared a defensive strategy that prioritized the American role in Western Europe (Leffler 1992: 274–5). By 1949, the North Atlantic Treaty Organization (Nato) was in place, on paper at least. In the eyes of US military planners, Nato would help deter the Soviets from acting aggressively, as they had in Berlin, and encourage the Western Europeans to participate in their own defence (Leffler 1992: 281). In the event that war broke out, Nato would facilitate the defence of the West.

While the formal commitment to keep US troops in Western Europe should have quelled any concerns about West German rearmament, in fact the opposite occurred. In April 1950, the National Security Council in Washington produced NSC–68, a document that reiterated the importance of containment, given the 'permanent struggle' between the United States and the Soviet Union and raised the question of how to prepare a global military response, involving more than just American forces, to counter Soviet or Soviet-inspired aggression anywhere in the world (Hogan 1998: 296).

As early as 1947 and 1948, military officials in the West, including French military leaders, had raised the possibility of West German rearmament as part of a comprehensive approach to the defence of Western Europe (Large 1996: 35). By 1949, members of the United States Congress, wary of the growing cost of the

American commitment to Europe, advocated West German rearmament as a reasonable demonstration of 'burden sharing' between Europe and the Unites States (Large 1996: 39). Soon after, American military leaders expressed increasing scepticism about their ability to win a war in Europe with current troop levels (Trachtenberg 1999: 98). Given the emerging global commitments implied by NSC–68 and the fact that West Germany was to be integrated into the emerging Western European bloc, the question of West Germany's military contribution to the Alliance became more pressing.

Yet German rearmament was not yet a mainstream idea, even if had been raised in a number of high-level circles. It was extremely unpopular in West Germany, although Chancellor Konrad Adenauer was supportive, seeing rearmament as a way to address a number of concerns, including the threat posed by the growth of East German security forces, the possibility that American troop levels in West Germany would be reduced, and the continued danger of a Soviet attack (Schwarz 1995: 516–18). The outbreak of the Korean war, in June 1950, changed the atmosphere entirely and made German rearmament a respectable topic for politicians, the public and military leaders alike. A consensus soon emerged within the US government that West German rearmament was imperative as the cold war became global. Korea implied a new Communist desire to expand into areas hitherto dominated by the West, or at least to test the West along the East–West divide. The consequences for Germany and Western Europe were immediately appreciated by those who advocated a policy intended to 'stymie prospective counterthrusts' in the region (Leffler 1992: 371). Seeing that West Germany had the potential to be the next South Korea, public opinion there moved much closer to this mindset (Large 1996: 62; Schwarz 1995: 531).

In September 1950, the US government gave a 'virtual ultimatum' to its European allies over the necessity of West German rearmament (Schwarz 1995: 535). Adenauer also pushed his allies on the issue, despite a revival of anti-militarism within West Germany over the course of the summer (Large 1996: 65–78). While fully embracing its role of European leader in the pursuit of Franco–German reconciliation, France was not prepared to permit West German remilitarization, however. Secretary of State Acheson challenged the French to come up with some new ideas, while pointing out that Nato was now committed to defending Western Europe along the Elbe, separating East and West Germany, and not simply along the Rhine, separating France and Germany (Large 1996: 87).

The European Defence Community

France therefore faced the possibility of an open break with the United States as cold-war tensions increased. Two concerns, similar to those expressed by France when the United States had insisted on German economic revival, were uppermost. First was the long-standing French fear of a revitalized and remilitarized Germany. Second, and growing more significant as the cold war intensified, was the fear that a swift German military build-up would lead to Germany, not France, being seen as the leader within Western Europe and America's closest ally on the continent. Such a development would inevitably weaken France's effort to control aspects of Germany's revival, which had been the intention of the Schuman Plan from the start (Hitchcock 1998: 135). Therefore, French foreign ministry officials sought to satisfy American demands within a framework established by France itself and that included French oversight of German rearmament for the foreseeable future (Hitchcock 1998: 137).

The best model available was the integrationist one already used in the Schuman Plan for coal and steel. In this instance, the cold war, intensified by the outbreak of the Korean war, had a very direct role in pushing Western Europe to the next stage of integration. Led once again by Monnet and Schuman, the French hatched a plan to integrate Western European military forces into a single institution, what later became known as the European Defence Community (EDC). Monnet, in fact, called the proposal simply 'an enlarged Schuman Plan' (Hitchcock 1998: 141).

The so-called Pleven Plan, named after French Premier René Pleven, and launched in October 1950, called for the creation of a European army consisting of small battalions under a common military and political authority. The political institutions responsible for oversight—a European parliament and a European defence ministry—were to be created before the army itself was established. Participating states, except West Germany, would be permitted to maintain their existing defence ministries, general staffs, and certain armed forces apart from the European army. The West German army, however, would only exist as part of the continental force. Even more so than the Schuman Plan, the French believed that the Pleven Plan had been forced upon them by the United States. Support within the French government for the Pleven Plan was based upon a determination to prevent the emergence of an independent German force as much as anything else (Parsons 2003: 71). Indeed, many American observers saw the plan, which would take a long time to put in place, as a French attempt to delay German rearmament (Hitchcock 1998: 144; Large 1996: 94). Moreover, the relationship between the EDC and Nato was left unclear. Not surprisingly, the Pleven Plan met with scepticism on all fronts.

China's intervention in the Korean war, in November 1950, pushed consideration of the French proposal forward. It now seemed that Communist states intended to take advantage of perceived Western weakness and would soon extend armed intervention to other parts of the world. The impact in Western Europe was immediate: West German rearmament could no longer be delayed. Adenauer was ready to respond. He and his advisers wanted something more ambitious than the Pleven Plan, including strong German ground, air and naval forces, and a general staff. Adenauer was confident that membership in Nato would suffice to allay fears of German militarism (Large 1996: 97–8).

Global pressures and opportunities

The looming crisis in the Alliance was resolved in part due to Soviet action. In an effort to forestall the creation of a West German force, the Soviet Union offered the Western Allies a Four-Power meeting on Germany. Fearful that France would respond unilaterally, the United States made a counter-proposal to the French, suggesting that if they dropped the political components of the Pleven Plan and accepted the immediate construction of a European army, the United States would concede that German forces should be smaller in size than full infantry divisions and should exist without an independent general staff. Moreover, German units would not be placed directly under the authority of national commanders. The French agreed to this in a revised Pleven Plan.

Talks in Paris among the Nato allies on the American proposal coincided with talks in Bonn between the three Western occupying powers and the West German government on the exact nature of Germany's contribution to the new European army. The United States welcomed this 'two-track' approach for it suggested that a West German contribution to the defence of Western Europe would be achieved in less time than outlined in the original Pleven Plan. Yet France saw in these talks an opportunity to control, limit, or even delay German rearmament, whereas West Germany saw an opportunity to propose its own ideas for rearmament and the achievement of full sovereignty (Large 1996: 107). Either way, the negotiations demonstrated the influence of the cold war on European integration, making explicit the connection between security and integration that also lay behind the Coal and Steel Community. How best to enhance security through integration was nonetheless complicated by competing concerns within the Western Alliance.

Pushed by the global implications of NSC–68, agitated by the Korean War, and wanting to create a genuine 'European group' within Nato, the United States embraced the revised Pleven Plan as a crucial aspect of its national security (Lundestad 1998: 40–3). The revised plan allowed France to balance the need for an American security guarantee, including some degree of burden sharing, with economic and security concerns about a rearmed Germany. Although the French and American positions may have been reconciled, Adenauer was far from mollified. For Adenauer, integration was the means by which West Germany could end the Occupation Statute remaining in place after 1949, rebuild economically, and become bound into the West and the emerging security system represented by Nato. Adenauer did not insist on having a separate German army, but he did see the link between revising the Occupation Statute, restoring West German sovereignty, rearmament, and integration (Küsters 1995: 66). He therefore insisted that German troops would not be used in the defence of Europe until the terms of the country's rearmament were clear and related issues were resolved. There was a risk that the two sets of negotiations could result in completely separate models for defending Europe in the deepening cold war, or, worse, that one or both could break down and collapse.

Germany's hard line led Acheson, for one, temporarily to abandon support for the integrationist solution that the United States had promoted for so long. The EDC, he insisted in July 1951, was too complicated; a permanent American commitment to placing its troops in Europe and managing the Nato system was surely easier to achieve (Trachtenberg 1999: 120) Yet at the same time, the US civilian commissioner for Germany, John McCloy, the Nato Supreme Commander, Dwight Eisenhower, and the US Ambassador to France, David Bruce, all pushed the Truman administration to embrace the EDC as the solution best suited to the concerns of both France and Germany within the Nato system. They argued that a European army was the best and quickest way to achieve the rearmament of West Germany while decreasing the cost for the United States of defending Western Europe; that the French desire to maintain control and influence over German revitalization was worth supporting; that the creation of a separate West German army would jeopardize French support; and finally that Adenauer's demands for a revision of the Occupation Statute and greater sovereignty were also worthwhile (Large 1996: 125–9; Schwarz 1995: 622–3).

Such vocal American support for the Pleven Plan helped foster Franco-German reconciliation while recognizing both France's desire to lead in Europe and West Germany's desire to move closer to full sovereignty and Nato membership as an equal. It was not an easy path; at numerous points both French and German politicians and members of the public raised doubts about the path now eagerly advocated by the Truman administration, and negotiations between France and Germany on many key points did not proceed smoothly (Hitchcock 1998: 155-68; Large 1996: 130-45). Nonetheless, by May 1952, two separate treaties were signed. On 26 May, in Bonn, a new General Agreement between the Federal Republic and France, Britain and the United States replaced the old Occupation Statute; on 27 May, in Paris, the EDC was created.

This explicitly military phase of European integration, one linked directly to the intensification of the cold war, did not last long. As seen in Chapter 5, by the autumn of 1952, French supporters of the EDC, including Schuman, had lost their pre-eminence in government. For many in France, the EDC meant that 'France lost its army [and] Germany gained one' (Hitchcock 1998: 168). Even a revival of the idea of a political assembly to oversee the European army did nothing to counter such criticism, especially by Gaullists and other French nationalists in the parliament and press. Skittish French governments refused to bring the EDC Treaty before parliament for a vote of approval, fearing certain defeat. Meanwhile the United States under President Eisenhower became increasingly hesitant to accept other models for West German rearmament besides the EDC. Adenauer, having achieved considerable success through his policy of linking rearmament with greater sovereignty, was equally determined to support the EDC. Ultimately, a new French government brought the treaty to a parliamentary vote in August 1954, but it was roundly defeated. The relationship between security policy and integration remained unresolved.

The Soviet Union and European integration

Perhaps the most visible way in which the cold war became connected to European integration was the Soviet Union's reaction to various stages of the process. As with the United States, the Soviet Union eventually saw integration as a policy grounded in the different approaches taken by the two sides to the reorganization of the continent and especially to the question of German reconstruction. As the cold war gradually emerged, the Soviets saw American support for integration as a threat to their security, which inevitably coloured their views of the integration process itself. Soviet perceptions and actions therefore help explain how integration became part and parcel of the cold-war conflict.

Stalin's focus on reconstructing Europe in the name of Soviet national security gave Soviet policy in Eastern and Central Europe two significant aspects. First, security was defined territorially. Stalin's chief goal was to create pro-Soviet states between Germany and the Soviet Union. This was apparent in Poland in 1944-5, with the formation of a Communist government, and in other Central and Eastern European states in 1946–8, including the Soviet zone of Germany. Second, as the construction of the Soviet sphere of influence progressed, it became increasingly apparent that the Soviets would determine policy there unilaterally rather than in cooperation with the national governments.

In the midst of this came the Marshall Plan, which 'put European integration on the agenda of international diplomacy' (Schwabe 2001: 19). As already seen, European recovery organized with American aid represented a form of political and economic containment of the Soviet Union. Yet the offer to participate in the initial European conference called in response to the American initiative went to all European states, including the Soviet Union and its allies. Although the State Department anticipated a Soviet rejection, the Soviet foreign minister attended the meeting in Paris in July 1947 to coordinate the European response.

American policy-makers and British and French officials alike saw the Soviet Union's ostensible inclusion in the invitation for Marshall aid as a necessary 'tactic', for in reality the plan was meant for Western Europe alone (Schwabe 1988a: 40). Indeed, the foreign ministers of Britain and France were even more committed to limiting American assistance to Western Europe than Marshall was. Ernest Bevin, the British foreign minister, was deeply suspicious of the Soviet Union. Georges Bidault, his French counterpart, felt obliged to support the offer to the Soviet Union because of the strength of the Communist party in France. Nevertheless he was primarily concerned with securing much-needed American assistance, regardless of any previous agreement with the Soviet Union over the future of Germany (Hitchcock 1998: 74–5). In any event, the proposal seemed unlikely to appeal to the Soviet Union. First, as the United States surely knew, ideological conflict and the growing atmosphere of tension that marked the onset of the cold war meant that any American proposal was bound to raise Soviet suspicions. Second, American insistence on European cooperation for a continent-wide recovery, instead of having countries submit a laundry list of individual projects, seemed to go against the emerging Soviet preference for a unilateral approach consistent with its security concerns (Mastny 1996: 27).

Nonetheless, there were equally good reasons for the Soviet Union to accept the invitation and show up in Paris. The cold war had not yet gelled. On the German question, there were signs that a resolution was possible, for the Soviets accepted the idea that the German economy could be run as a single unit if in return the Western allies would permit the Soviets to take reparations from current West German production (Trachtenberg 1999: 57). Moreover, the Marshall proposal gave the Soviets some hope that American monies might still be available for their own reconstruction. The Soviet foreign minister was well aware that a number of Western European states were concerned about the American desire to promote integrationist or cooperative planning for recovery. Indeed, American policy-makers were quite angry with the Europeans for promoting individual national interests instead of collective European ones (Hitchcock 1998: 77). If there was any possibility of obtaining American aid without having strings of cooperation attached, then the Soviets would certainly want to participate (Mastny 1996: 27). American–Soviet talks on bilateral assistance to replace wartime Lend-Lease aid had been broken off only in 1946; the Marshall proposal offered an opportunity to get money that the Soviet Union needed in order to recover from the devastation of war.

Almost immediately after arriving in Paris, the Soviet foreign minister received information from Soviet intelligence indicating that the American plan to aid Europe was motivated by the desire to create an anti-Soviet front in Western Europe and to encourage the economic revitalization of Germany at its centre (Zubok and Pleshakov 1996: 105). This prompted the withdrawal of the Soviet and Eastern European delegations from the conference. Although it was not the only factor in the Soviet decision to leave—after all the very idea of integration and cooperative planning for economic recovery seemed to go against Soviet conceptions of postwar reconstruction—clearly the cold war had played a crucial part.

Indeed, the reasons behind the Soviet Union's rejection of the European Recovery Programme were self-reinforcing. The Marshall Plan came to represent, for the Soviets, a 'closing of ranks' among the United States and its Western European allies. In response, Stalin secured his own sphere in the East (Zubok and Pleshakov 1996: 131–2). Soviet policy was reactive, one of retrenchment. As noted earlier, Stalin drew the lines tighter around his own sphere of influence, purged non-Communists in Eastern European governments, and initiated the Cominform and a 'two camps' view of Europe.

The Soviet Union's response to the American effort to create a separate West German state was similarly reactive. Thus the Soviets walked out of the Allied Control Commission in March 1948 in response to talks among the Western allies aimed at forming a West German government; blockaded Berlin in June 1948 when the United States introduced a new currency in the western zones of the city; and established a separate East German state, the German Democratic Republic, in October 1949 following the declaration of the Federal Republic earlier that year.

Only when the Korean war broke out and the Soviet sphere was successfully consolidated did Stalin take a more proactive approach towards German policy. Content to accept the division of the continent, Stalin was still not prepared to accept full West German revival as part of the postwar settlement. Since 1945, the Soviet Union had wanted to create a unified, weak, and neutral German state. The emergence of the cold war did not change this. Developments since 1947 seemed to have favoured the West, which hoped to tie its part of Germany to Western Europe for reasons of economic recovery and military security. Integration was emerging as a useful means of doing so. Beginning in 1950, however, Stalin took the diplomatic offensive in hopes of ending Germany's division and thwarting the further integration of West Germany with Western Europe and the United States. Hence his call for a German peace treaty to replace the existing Occupation Statute as well as various other initiatives.

A growing perception that European integration was simply a means to perpetuate the cold-war division of the Continent and make permanent the division of Germany was the primary factor in Stalin's decision to act. Documents prepared by the Soviet foreign ministry highlighted the connection, in Soviet eyes, between integration and the strengthening of the Western Alliance. With reference to the European Coal and Steel Community, Soviet officials argued that supranational control of Germany's coal and steel industries was one way to deprive the Soviet Union of any say in the management of these resources and was contrary to the goal of a neutral, unified and demilitarized Germany (Mastny 1996: 136). The connection between integration and efforts to tie West Germany into the Western Alliance was made even more explicit in the eyes of Stalin and his advisers when the Western powers announced that they would consider new 'contractual agreements' with West Germany, excluding the Soviet Union, and that negotiations based on the Pleven Plan to create a European army were close to reaching a successful conclusion.

Hence the famous Soviet note of March 1952, which proposed immediate talks aimed at creating a neutral and unified Germany (Large 1996: 132–45). Stalin suggested a formal peace treaty with Germany, an end to occupation within one year, and a ban on German participation in an alliance aimed against any of the four wartime allies. The note, described as a 'bombshell', received a great deal of publicity in the West (Schwarz 1995: 652). Historians have long debated whether it was a serious proposal or simply a last ditch effort to disrupt the Paris talks then in progress to establish the EDC. There is evidence to support both interpretations (Mastny 1996: 132–7; Large 1996: 146). In any event, the Western Powers rejected the Soviet overture within two weeks. When the Soviets issued a second note in April 1952, proposing talks on all-German elections, the US Secretary of State responded by urging immediate resolution of the EDC and West German treaty negotiations (Schwarz 1995: 658). Acheson's almost simultaneous suggestion that all-German elections might work in some circumstances was really designed to give the Soviets a counter-offer that 'they could not accept' (Large 1996: 147). Similarly, Adenauer, fearful that public opinion would embrace the Soviet idea, was determined to reject the initiative in order to achieve West German rearmament (Schwarz 1995: 653). In the minds of both Western and Soviet policy-makers, integration, especially as it related to Germany, had become a key method or tool in the construction of the cold-war settlement in Europe.

Alternatives to integration

The failure of the EDC in August 1954 left open the question of German rearmament. Yet soon thereafter, West Germany was rearmed outside a supranational framework. Thus the case of German rearmament after the EDC's failure, as well as the unique position of states like Great Britain and Spain, demonstrate that while the cold war might have fostered some aspects of integration, integration was not the only approach available in the West to construct its cold-war alliance. It might be said that the preferred method of building the Western Alliance was integration if possible; otherwise, the primacy of the cold war required policies in Europe that were not necessarily supranational ones.

The WEU and Nato

The immediate problem for Britain, France, and the United States after the defeat of the EDC was that the General Agreement of 1952 between them and the German Federal Republic had to be renegotiated, while the question of rearming West Germany remained unresolved. The Eisenhower administration still wanted some sort of supranational framework for rearmament but no one could come up with a plan likely to win a parliamentary majority in France. Yet the failure of the EDC did not come as a surprise to most governments on the Continent and alternatives were proposed almost immediately. Months before the French vote, Adenauer had floated the idea that West Germany simply be admitted to Nato as an equal, an idea that squared with his interest in renegotiating the General Agreement in order to give West Germany full sovereignty (Küsters 1995: 67). A Nato solution would give Germany equality and the right to have its own national army and was, for Adenauer, preferable to the perceived anti-German or 'control' aspects of the proposed EDC. Nonetheless, the popularity of the EDC among the fairly pacifist German public, French opposition to a separate German army, and strong support for supranationalism by the United States were all significant obstacles facing Adenauer.

Britain, which had declined to participate in the EDC negotiations, suggested after the initiative collapsed that West Germany could accede to the Brussels Treaty, originally signed in 1948 by Britain, France, and other Western European states as a defensive alliance against Germany. This would end the anti-German aspects of the treaty, making it instead a mutual defensive alliance of Western European states. Moreover, the proposed new Western European Union (WEU) would be integral to Nato. Although an intergovernmental rather than a supranational organization, the WEU would satisfy Adenauer's desire for greater equality within the Western Alliance and provide the French with a measure of security as well. By October 1954 the London Agreements on WEU and West German accession into Nato were signed. Simultaneously, talks took place in Paris on revising West Germany's contractual agreements with France, Britain and the United States. The Paris Accords, signed in October 1954, granted West Germany full sovereignty by May 1955 with only the status of the city of Berlin remaining part of the peace settlement overseen by the four wartime allies. American and European troops would share the burdens of defence against possible Soviet attack, thereby enhancing Western European security. Integration certainly had contributed to the reconciliation between West Germany and its neighbours, but integration was not the only solution to security dilemmas on the continent.

Britain

It was perhaps fitting that Britain proposed the solution to German rearmament after the failure of the EDC, for the British, in contrast to the French, excelled as leaders and participants in the Western Alliance without embracing integration as the means of doing so. There were certainly individuals within the British government, such as Foreign Secretary Ernest Bevin, who saw Marshall Plan as a means of building a Western European bloc within the broader Western Alliance (Bell 1997: 83). However, Britain was consistently unwilling to take the lead in basing the Western European arm of the Alliance on integration and supranationalism. Instead, Britain wanted a special status within the proposed cooperative structure (Bell 1997: 87). As time went on, and the United States came to embrace integration more explicitly, Britain consistently backed away, leaving the door open for France to establish itself as the Western European leader.

British hesitancy flowed from a belief that Britain's commercial and military interests existed outside the continent as much as within it (Reynolds 1997: 179). Britain's priority on the continent was to secure an American commitment to the defence of Europe. The Brussels Treaty of 1948 laid the foundation for this, and the

North Atlantic Treaty of 1949 provided the superstructure. Clearly, Britain preferred intergovernmental options rather than supranational ones. Thus, when the French proposed supranationalism as a way to tie Germany into Western Europe, Britain was supportive but not interested in participating. The Schuman Plan proposed a European union based on Franco–German reconciliation; Britain was absent, and content to remain so. For the French, integration was a solution to the dilemmas raised by the cold war and German recovery. Sensitive to French concerns, the United States supported integration for similar reasons. The British did not have a German dilemma, in that they were committed to German reconstruction with or without integration. Moreover, they had strong ties to the Commonwealth and colonies outside Europe. Thus for Britain it was possible to be an active player in the cold war and a committed partner in the Atlantic Alliance without embracing integration.

Spain

The cold war division of Europe reinforced the fact that integration and other developments associated with French, British, and American policy on the continent became Western European, not continent-wide, initiatives. However, the cold war did not mean that all of Western Europe was to be integrated. As in the British case, there were alternative paths to westernization for many states. This fact alone demonstrates the primacy of the cold war in the period. If the cold war was the reason for the Western Alliance, it was not necessarily the case that all members of the Alliance were to be part of the integration project. In the British case, absence was voluntary. But the case of Spain demonstrates that the cold-war division of Europe did not necessarily mean that all non-Communist states were welcomed in the process of integration.

Spain under General Francisco Franco was a dictatorship with many fascist tendencies. Although officially neutral during the war, Franco's regime had come to power in the Spanish Civil War with the help of Nazi Germany and Fascist Italy. Moreover, during World War II, Spain had sent 'volunteers' to fight alongside Nazi troops in the Soviet Union, as well as supplying Hitler with significant economic resources. Despite an interest in removing Franco from power as a vestige of fascism, the Truman administration concluded that the potential chaos that might ensue in Spain would only benefit the Soviet Union and the spread of Communism (Byrnes 2000: 152). By 1947, with the enunciation of the Truman Doctrine, the United States increasingly saw Spain primarily in the context of the emerging East–West conflict (Guirao 1996: 80). Thus the maintenance of the *status quo*, which would prevent any chance of the Spanish Communists coming to power, became the overriding US goal in Madrid. British policy paralleled American policy in the aftermath of the war. If anything, Britain's desire to see Franco continue in power preceded that of the United States (Dunthorn 2000: 69).

If Franco provided Spain with anti-Communist stability in Western Europe, however, the potential for economic dislocation that might lead to a Communist revolution was just as great there, or even greater, than elsewhere on the continent. Thus some in the US Congress argued that Spain was a legitimate candidate for Marshall aid (Guirao 1996: 81). Moreover, as the threat of a European war grew in the minds of US military planners after the Czech coup and Berlin blockade of 1948, Spain's strategic value also grew (Guirao 1996: 83). Because the State Department and President Truman himself opposed including the Franco dictatorship in major American aid programmes, Spain ultimately did not receive Marshall assistance (Guirao 1996: 84). More significantly, American allies such as France, itself forced by domestic opposition to Franco to impose sanctions unilaterally against Spain, encouraged the United States to exclude Spain from the Marshall Plan.

As early as 1948, once France ended its sanctions, Britain raised the possibility of allowing Spain to enter into the various arrangements being made by the Western European nations (Marquina Barrio 1986: 151). In particular, the British proposed that Spain be admitted to the Brussels Treaty. France refused even to consider such a request. Although the United States accepted this situation, the National Security Council in Washington concluded by mid-1948 that ideally Spain should to be a part of Western Europe's military arrangements if not its economic ones (Marquina Barrio 1986: 180).

As the rearmament crisis developed in the aftermath of the Korean war—the crisis not only of German rearmament but also of the slow pace of rearmament in other European countries—the possibility of involving Spain as part of the Western European system was again raised. By January 1951 the Truman administration decided that it could no longer ignore the potential that Spanish territory held for the military defence of Europe. Aware that inclusion of the Franco regime in the Nato alliance was still unpalatable to its European partners, the United States decided to pursue a bilateral military agreement with Spain outside both Nato and the integrationist EDC (Guirao 1996: 86). The primacy of the cold war was again demonstrated: integration if possible, security at any cost.

The Western Europeans, particularly the British and French, welcomed a bilateral US–Spanish deal as the best way for the United States to achieve its goals while allowing its European allies to avoid another contentious issue. Negotiations between the United States and Spain, opened in March 1951, culminated in the Bases Agreement of September 1953. The United States received land for military bases on Spanish soil in return for a financial commitment to assist Spain's military through a \$465 million programme of aid and cooperation, from 1954 to 1957 (Guirao 1996: 90). Soon after, Spain was admitted to the OEEC, the United Nations and eventually Nato. Nevertheless, Spain remained outside the purview of European integration led by the Europeans themselves until after Franco's death in 1975, despite its desire to be included. In the Spanish case, paths to the Western Alliance were opened up even as the doors of integration remained closed.

Conclusion

Without a doubt, the conflict known as the cold war fostered important moments in the history of integration and directly contributed to certain stages in the development of European institutions. The connection made by American and French officials—notably Jean Monnet—between economic development, national security and the double containment of Germany and the Soviet Union was of great significance.

The model of the Marshall Plan, intended to further security through economic growth, encouraged intra-European cooperation and led to a number of initiatives culminating in the Schuman Plan for coal and steel integration and the birth of supranationalism. The cold war also shaped integration by making it a preserve of Western European states, for the politics of the cold war created and cemented the division of Europe in the immediate postwar era.

The EDC, a proposed supranational solution to a military challenge on the border between East and West, suggested that rising cold-war tensions might lead to another round of integration. Yet the failure of the EDC did not mean the failure of the United States and its allies to solve the problem of German remilitarization. The accession of Germany to Nato in 1955, in response to which the Soviet Union established a rival military organization, the Warsaw Pact, deepened the cold-war division of the continent. The failure of the EDC raised the possibility that the West might abandon integration as a viable tool in the creation of its cold-war institutions and structures.

For a variety of reasons, however, Western European countries continued to embrace integration and supranationalism. The economic imperative had always been present. The desire of the Adenauer government to pursue integration as part of a general policy of achieving German equality within the West, despite the EDC experience, was another factor (Giauque 2002: 12–13). In the case of France, the defeat of the EDC coincided with the bloody loss of its colony in Indochina (Vietnam). In 1956, France experienced another humiliating failure following its military intervention in the Suez Canal zone. For France, leadership in Europe, first linked to the German question, now became bound up in a more general search for prominence, and thus became the most important aspect of the country's foreign policy (Giauque 2002: 17–18). Continued integration represented France's best chance to lead the European wing of the Western Alliance.

Nevertheless, the cold war became less significant as a driver of European integration in the second half of the 1950s. President Eisenhower and his influential Secretary of State, John Foster Dulles, recognized this. The two continued to support the idea of integration, but increasingly believed that the Europeans themselves had to take the lead (Giauque 2002: 14–15). Eventually, the Western European desire to press forward for economic reasons led to the Messina conference of June 1955 that resulted in a series of negotiations on a customs union and atomic energy cooperation. The ensuing Rome Treaties of March 1957 established the EEC and the European Atomic Energy Community.

Although the cold war had less to do with the emerging EEC than it did with the Marshall Plan and the EDC, it was not irrelevant to integration in the latter part of the 1950s. American support for the negotiations that culminated in the Rome Treaties, particularly the negotiations on atomic cooperation, was grounded in a perception that any strengthening of Western Europe generally would strengthen the Atlantic Alliance in particular. The EEC required the United States to adjust the structure of its economic relationship with its allies, and led to the Dillon Round of the General Agreement on Tariffs and Trade (GATT) in 1958, but it did not require a new conception of European integration as something separate from the Atlantic Alliance and thus the cold war. Indeed, the EEC was seen as a new and important pillar in the Atlantic Alliance, an economic arm that complemented Nato's military one (Giauque 2002: 32; Lundestad 1998: 53–4). As seen in Chapter 12, only the end of the cold war, a seemingly remote possibility as the EEC got off the ground, would make possible the conception of integration as something that went beyond Western Europe and the real and artificial borders created by the protracted East–West conflict.

Further reading

Understanding the various dimensions of the German question, its relationship to the origins of the cold war, and the later significance of the German rearmament debate is a good place to start further investigation of the question of the impact of the cold war on European integration. Eisenberg (1996) and Hogan (1987) provide detailed analysis of the political and economic underpinnings of American policy towards Germany, while Large (1996) offers a highly readable account of how German and American officials came to focus on rearmament in the 1950s. Hitchcock (1998) provides an important argument concerning France's commitment to the Western Alliance that centres on the German question. Lundestad (1998) specifically addresses the question of European integration in an analysis of how economic reconstruction led to greater political and military ties with the United States and ultimately within Western Europe itself. Trachtenberg (1999) makes an argument about the emergence of American support for integration and subsequent Western European leadership on the same issue not only for the late 1940s, but through the rearmament debates of the 1950s. He, like Giauque (2002), develops important ideas about the 'Nato system' that emerged at that time. Although not focused on integration at any specific point, Mastny (1996) provides one of the best accounts of Stalin's policy towards Europe and the emerging cold war after 1945.

Eisenberg, C. (1996), *Drawing the Line: The American Decision to Divide Germany, 1944–1949* (Cambridge: Cambridge University Press).

Giauque, J. G. (2002), *Grand Designs and Visions of Unity: The Atlantic Powers and the Reorganization of Western Europe, 1955–1963* (Chapel Hill: University of North Carolina Press).

Hitchcock, W. I. (1998), *France Restored: Cold War Diplomacy and the Quest for Leadership in Europe, 1944–1954* (Chapel Hill: University of North Carolina Press).

Hogan, M. (1987), *The Marshall Plan: America, Britain and the Reconstruction of Western Europe, 1947–1952* (Cambridge: Cambridge University Press).

Large, D. C. (1996), *Germans to the Front: West German Rearmament in the Adenauer Era* (Chapel Hill: University of North Carolina Press).

Lundestad, G. (1998) *'Empire' by Invitation: The United States and European Integration, 1945–1997* (Oxford: Oxford University Press).

Mastny, V. (1996), *The Cold War and Soviet Insecurity: The Stalin Years* (Oxford: Oxford University Press).

Trachtenberg, M. (1999), *A Constructed Peace: The Making of the European Settlement 1945–1963* (Princeton, NJ: Princeton University Press).

Websites

A comprehensive website on the history of European integration and the European Union is maintained by Richard T. Griffiths at the University of Leiden, Netherlands, and includes archival documents, bibliographies and links to other sites, including cold-war sites: www.eu-history.leidenuniv.nl. Europa, the Gateway to the European Union also has a history section with summaries and documents at http://www.europa.eu.int. There are numerous cold war-related sites.

Chapter 3

The German Problem and European Integration

John R. Gillingham

Contents

Summary

One of the greatest accomplishments of the process of European integration is the contribution that it made to the so-called German Problem—the problem of managing Germany's political rehabilitation and economic resurgence in the post-World War II period. The achievement rested not only on the Schuman Plan and the ensuing European Coal and Steel Community (ECSC) but also on cooperation among French and German coal and steel producers in the interwar period. The adoption by the new Federal Republic of homegrown economically liberal policies, which complemented and implemented the wartime vision of American postwar policy, was another decisive factor. Over time, domestic reform in Germany and elsewhere unlocked the integration process and helped establish what Friedrich Hayek called the economic conditions of interstate federalism. Thus, the solution of the German Problem not only lay to rest the unhappy legacy of the past but also set the stage for the unfolding of a better future.

Introduction

The greatest single accomplishment ascribed to European integration is that by merging Germany into Europe and fusing Europe with Germany the process cured the ailment thought responsible for causing the two world wars of the early twentieth century. Such is, at any rate, the usual legitimization provided for the familiar yet elusive process still under way and leading, it is presumed, to some form of European economic and political union. Little doubt remains that the malady known as the German Problem has now received proper treatment and that the famous Schuman Plan of May 1950 was part of the remedy. The cure cannot, however, be explained satisfactorily simply by reference to the standard integration narrative that identifies the reconciliation of Germany and Europe with the events that led to the formation of the ECSC in 1951 and the European Economic Community (EEC) in 1957.

Instead, the solution of the German Problem emerged from a broad restoration and reform process that comprises part of a larger, more complicated and interesting story than usually told. It involves a contest at the level of ideas, institutions, and individuals between the market and the state, but also interaction at the international, national, and regional levels. Postwar European integration began with a diplomatic breakthrough—a mutual accommodation of the larger civilization and the nation that had been the greatest threat to it—but has since advanced chiefly through the operation of the market mechanism. It can be said to have resulted from an asymmetrical, interactive interdependence game, one always in flux, whose origins and outcomes are unpredictable and which includes such inescapable variables as human agency and random events.

This mutable, polymorphous, and refractory process can move history forward but also resist change (Gillingham 2003). It has often made fools of those who have tried to chart its future course. Yet it can be said that 'negative integration'—limited to the imposition of rules to make markets function properly—generally succeeds, while 'positive integration'—aimed at the use of state power to shape events—normally leads to complications, delays, and failure (Gillingham 2003: 85–97). As befits the complexity of the integration process, the EEC has been the agent of both approaches. In pursuing 'negative integration', and creating what Friedrich Hayek termed the economic conditions of interstate federalism, the EEC has nevertheless made a contribution of historic dimensions to the reconciliation of Europe's peoples, as well as of Germany and Europe.

The postwar framework

The most formidable of the many great challenges facing Western statesmen after the war was to tie Germany into Europe and Europe into Germany. Many of them realized from the outset that this linkage would have to take place as part of a larger recovery process that would restore an economically liberal Europe more closely resembling that of the nineteenth century than anything of recent memory. Yet there was no single prescription to heal the ailing body. Economists like John Maynard Keynes, a wartime adviser to the British Treasury, thought state intervention necessary to restore markets to proper operation; others, like Hayek, an internationally influential public intellectual, looked to markets to do the job on their own. These divergent positions merged in what political scientist John Ruggie termed 'embedded liberalism', the philosophy that shaped the institutions designed by the allies during the war to regulate world markets after it. Embedded liberalism posited interpenetration and interweaving of state and market power in order to buffer regulated national economies from exogenous shock, set the stage for recovery from depression and war, and led to the eventual restoration of an open economy and polity. The embedded liberal system lasted until the collapse of the Bretton Woods agreements in the early 1970s. Thereafter, it was gradually replaced by a more open version of liberalism in which, by exercising market power, private agents would seize and recover the 'commanding heights' of the economy from the state (Gillingham 2003: 3–6).

Reflecting embedded liberalism, postwar international economic and political institutions would, in varying degrees, influence both behaviour and expectations. The Bretton Woods agreements of 1944, which resulted in the International Monetary Fund (IMF) (to regulate international payments) and the less important World Bank (to finance development projects), had little immediate impact, because European currencies, nearly all debauched by funny-money policies of the 1930s and wartime inflation, were not convertible. The trade counterpart of IMF also had a rocky beginning. Ambitious plans for the International Trade Organization (ITO), designed to bring down tariffs worldwide, failed to pass in the US Congress. Substituted for it, by executive decree, was the General Agreement on Tariffs and Trade (GATT), today the World Trade Organization (WTO), which first became active in reducing tariffs during the 1950s. The Marshall Plan—formally the European Recovery Programme (ERP)—brought the GATT to life and spawned two other organizations instrumental in European recovery. One was the Organization for European Economic Cooperation (OEEC), which played an important early role in eliminating tariff quotas. The other, the European Payments Union (EPU), restored currency convertibility in Europe and then, like an egg-laying salmon, died after completing its arduous upriver trek (Gillingham 2003: 37–41).

The Marshall Plan

Abstract institutional delineations such as the OEEC and the EPU mean little in the absence of any attempt to describe the force animating them, in this case the Marshall Plan. Likened at the time to a flying saucer whose origins, destination, workings, purposes, and consequences remain a mystery, the Marshall Plan had many different dimensions. It was first of all a loan programme to provide the scarce US dollars needed to import goods for public subsistence and economic recovery. In the 1950s it developed into an agency for technical assistance—the transfer of industrial technology and management expertise. Of greatest significance over the long term, the Marshall Plan became an engine of economic and political liberalization. To this end, it sponsored 'European integration'. Paul Hoffman, the administrator of the ERP, appears to have coined the term, which he equated with a single large customs area freed of internal barriers to trade and regulated by the competition principle (Gillingham 1997: 25–30).

Yet no still-intact and well-paved highway in war-wrecked Europe could be found leading to such an outcome. Hoffman called upon Europeans themselves to find the route. The search took place under the auspices of an agency that would become the OEEC but which, as seen in Chapter 2, was originally set up to encourage recipient nations to devise an overall aid programme and implicitly also to establish a governance framework of some kind for economic policy-making at the European level. Nothing similar had ever been seriously attempted before. In the event, European recalcitrance meant that the ERP determined aid allocation nation by nation, based on the hurly-burly of contending aspirants, priorities and ideologies, each backed by a corresponding faction within the national Marshall Plan missions. The recipients usually got what they sought, but national programmes varied substantially from country to country, according to economic need and domestic politics. The OEEC gradually morphed, for its part, into a forum for quota removal and, later, into a think tank, the Organization for Economic Cooperation and Development (Esposito 1994; Gillingham 2002; Hogan 1987; Price 1955; Wexler 1983).

The economic importance of the EPU, an offspring of the OEEC, was, during its short-lived existence, in fact far greater than that of the European Coal and Steel Community would ever be. As seen in Chapter 4, the EPU provided automatic mechanisms for the multilateral settlement of clearing balances between the OEEC countries. Each member nation received a quota based upon its total foreign trade, which if exceeded on the deficit side would owe amounts debited in dollars and soft currencies, according to a sliding scale. Creditor countries would receive dollars and soft monies on a fifty–fifty basis, providing a strong incentive to generate surpluses. Credit surpluses would accrue to the EPU, increasing its capital. Transactions did not have to be settled, as the dollar balance more than doubled during the years of its operation. The system required an initial US loan of $350 million, the existence of effective national capital controls, and over-valuation of the dollar. It worked well. The world trade of the EPU members increased by 1.7 times between 1949 and 1966; the intra-European trade by 2.3 times. The success of the EPU was due partly to the requirement that countries participating in it accept the OEEC's trade liberalization code (Eichengreen 1995: 171–82).

The German boom

The success of the EPU also owed much to the German boom. German GDP (1950 = 100) grew to 162 by 1958. Industrial output nearly doubled between 1950 and 1955. Total foreign trade more than tripled between 1950 and 1959, with exports rising from about a quarter to 40 per cent of total output. The Federal Republic's intra-European trade grew even more rapidly in these years, and within it the import share rose steadily in the 1950s. The German export success provided growing markets for neighbouring countries as well (Giersch et al. 1994; Kramer 1990: 81–3).

Minister of Economics Ludwig Erhard was the architect of this so-called economic miracle. The June 1948 currency reform brought the market economy to life and opened the first great phase of his reforms. The second, even more significant, measure was the introduction of unilateral tariff cuts ahead of other OEEC nations. Erhard acted in this respect as a disciple of Wilhelm Röpke, a leading light of the so-called Freiburg School or Ordo-liberal economists. In 1946, Röpke indeed supplied *The Solution to the German Problem*, as he titled his book of that year. Röpke found an answer to the dilemma facing the pariah nation in 'absolute and, if necessary, even one-sided free trade' that would compel 'Germans to bring into play exceptional re-sourcefulness, adaptability, and abstinence'. Free trade conducted on such a basis would, even if unreciprocated, break down the excessive (and protected) concentra-tion of industry, he argued, and force Germany to become dependent upon interna-tional trade as well as turn the former Reich into an 'enlarged Belgium' incapable of building up an 'autarchic war industry' (Röpke 1946: 259–61). Harsh controls over the German economy would become unnecessary, it follows, because a prosperity that would rest upon interweaving the German economy with those of its neighbours would both obviate the need for a prolonged occupation and provide a necessary means of national reconciliation.

Röpke was an associate as well as a disciple of Hayek. Also convinced that the future of Europe depended on solving the German Problem, Hayek developed the political as well as economic logic to make the two interdependent. In 'The Eco-nomic Conditions of Interstate Federalism', published fatefully on 1 September 1939 (the day that Germany invaded Poland and triggered the outbreak of World War II), Hayek presents a compelling explanation of why open markets and political union go hand in hand and are, in other words, both co-dependent and co-evolutionary (Hayek 1948). The logic behind this thinking has figured into the classical liberal approach to European economic integration up to the present.

Hayek opens his case with a verifiable hypothesis: no instances can be found of suc-cessful political federations without counterpart arrangements for the unimpeded movements of labour, goods, and capital. He then posits that the absence of trade bar-riers stands in the way of an identification of economic and political interests and so limits the pursuit of independent policies by member states of the federation. Con-sequently, it is difficult for them to manipulate prices, adopt independent monetary policies, discriminate against one producer in favour of another, levy harmful taxes, or impose social or regional policies having differential impacts. It would, further-more, be harder for a federation than individual member states to make invidious distinctions between producer groups. Economic planning at a higher level would also become more difficult. Rather than legislate poorly, he suggests, a federation should limit itself to the proscription of anti-market policies. The weakening of fed-eral and state power in a market-based union, he concludes, would result in the de-volution of functions to the regional or local level, where they could be carried out more efficiently. Competition between these small units would, in turn, provide a salutary check on excessive growth and encourage innovation.

Conditions in postwar Europe were anything but propitious to classical liberal solutions. Apart from the fact that Germany was occupied—its fate unknown and at the mercy of the cold war—and that the Soviets were believed to be at the gates, the moral and material conditions prevailing on the devastated continent dictated that priority be assigned to the prevention of famine, unrest, and revolution. The legit-imacy of governments and the rule of law had to be restored and Europe, at least temporarily, be fed by the United States. There was little pressure from Wall St for a 'private Marshall Plan', analogous to the post-World War I Dawes Plan for financial stability, to restore the European economy. Demand at home appeared to be insatiable. Nor could anyone in a position of authority seriously contemplate introducing the 'gale of creative destruction' needed to optimize the allocation of investment; it would have hit postwar Europe with hurricane force, taking everything before it and leaving only destruction in its wake. Institutions had to be built so that markets could work properly. As indicated by the development of the new US-inspired international regulatory agencies, this, too, would take time. In the short run, sound policy-making would require improvisation and have to be forged from the elements at hand (Gillingham 2003).

Jean Monnet

One of these elements—an historical force in his own right—was Jean Monnet. No individual played a larger role in shaping postwar Europe (Gillingham 2003). Monnet was the indispensable intermediary between the United States and Europe. He disposed of a wealth of international experience unequalled by any man of his generation. The highlights of his extraordinary career included (as a young man) serving on the inter-allied commission for regulating the international commodity trade in World War I and advising the French delegation at Versailles. In the 1920s Monnet led the economic directorate of the League of Nations and set up the 'little Dawes Plans' to bail out bankrupt European nations. In the depression decade he tried (in vain) to take over the Bank of America, launched an (unsuccessful) national economic development plan for Kuomintang China and, in the late 1930s, created and directed a critical aircraft purchasing programme in the United States for a beleaguered and soon to be defeated France. Though by no means a technocrat—indeed lacking even a baccalaureate—Monnet was most effective when operating internationally along the interface of government, finance, and industry. He was an expert in using the power of the state to 'make things happen' in the economy. Never comfortable operating within the confines of a bureaucracy, he drew on a huge inventory of powerful friends and associates to tackle problems larger than could be dealt with through the machinery of any single European state (Duchêne 1994; Gillingham 2000; Monnet 1976).

Monnet had little personal wealth, but greater access to un-earmarked public money than nearly anyone in the postwar world. The Frenchman's influence rested on his special role as flow regulator along the American aid pipeline. He served as the human conduit through which passed the subsidies that supported the Free French government in Algiers and the armed forces of Free France, and he channelled the funds towards General Henri Giraud, whom President Roosevelt much preferred to the imperious and temperamental General Charles de Gaulle as future head of the French provisional government. This was the source of much later bad blood between de Gaulle and Monnet. In early 1946, Monnet returned to Washington as behind-the-scenes negotiator of the so-called Blum Loan for France, more than half the proceeds from which he pre-empted for the *Plan de Modernisation et de l'Equipement* (the so-called Monnet Plan for industrial development), which he inspired, designed, headed, and staffed (Brinkley 1991; Gillingham 1998).

Monnet immediately grasped the importance of the Marshall Plan. Facing economic management problems of unprecedented size and scope, the Economic Cooperation Administration—as the ERP's headquarters in Paris was called—relied heavily on him for advice and endorsed his proposal that each recipient nation set up an equivalent to the French *Plan* to serve as foundation stones in a veritable pyramid of economic control. The failure of this visionary scheme (due to British-led opposition) did not discredit Monnet in American eyes. On the contrary, his influence over American—and therefore also French—policy-making grew over the five years between the end of the war and the announcement of the Schuman Plan, which he devised (Gillingham 1997).

The centrality of the Ruhr

The Schuman Plan was both an outgrowth from French policy towards the Ruhr (*Ruhrpolitik*) and a break with it. Each of the western Big Three (Britain, France, and the United States) had different aims with regard to Germany, but in the end French policy was the most influential, thanks largely to US support. Winning over the Americans was neither easy nor painless. France was no longer a great power but a recently defeated nation of mid-sized proportions that had to return to respectability on its knees. It confronted a backlog of outstanding social and economic problems, aggravated by the hardships and injustices of the occupation, and faced critical shortages of foodstuffs and raw materials, especially coal. France was not invited to the Yalta conference in February 1945 and only included at the Potsdam discussions of July–August 1945 concerning German occupation thanks to British intervention. The French had little standing as one of the Big Four (Britain, France, the United States, and the Soviet Union). To make its voice heard on occupation policy France had to shout, to be noticed it had to annoy, and to have any influence it had to obstruct. Yet the extremism that characterized its behaviour was tactical. Like post-1918 *Ruhrpolitik*, the ultimate French goal was to strengthen the country's bargaining position in preparation for a definitive settlement with Germany, this time, however, one underwritten by the Americans (Gillingham 1991: 137–47).

Anglo–American policy

French success in this respect can be partly ascribed to the policies of the United States and the United Kingdom. British occupation policy usually gets more credit from commentators than it deserves. Britain sought, and received, the largest and economically strongest zone, but punitively limited output on the one hand, while half-heartedly attempting to nationalize industry on the other. The British zone, moreover, faced a foodstuffs deficit that Britain had no intention of closing. The war-weary victors had different priorities. The British government confronted severe economic problems, had difficulty feeding its own population adequately, and committed the meager strategic resources at its disposal to maintaining overseas influence. The formation of the Anglo–American condominium known as Bizonia in early 1947 relieved the United Kingdom of the obligation to sustain its German charges, but at the cost of a voice in policy-making. British *Ruhrpolitik* remained largely passive until, belatedly, in 1948 the military government in Germany began an outrageous and counterproductive campaign of factory dismantlement to stave off future competition (Gillingham 1991: 121–37).

American *Ruhrpolitik* travelled the road from the malign Morgenthau Plan to benign Schuman Plan in only five years, rejecting sponsorship of a proposal to destroy German heavy industry in favour of a scheme to make it a nucleus of a new political and economic Europe. The shift was part of a broader movement from planned disengagement to constructive engagement with Europe. President Roosevelt's wartime Grand Design called for the Big Four to police the world jointly until international law had been established and borders opened—then go home. Its failure left a policy vacuum. On-the-job learning was necessary and initially slow. The despicable Morgenthau Plan, intended to keep Germany forever weak, soon gave way to a directive (known as JCS 1067) authorizing the American commander in occupied Germany to take actions necessary to avert 'famine and unrest'. Although an improvement over the Morgenthau Plan, JCS 1067 was inadequate for policy-making as it provided no guidelines for restoring or reforming the German economy (Gillingham 1991: 148–87).

At the Potsdam conference, Britain, the United States, the Soviet Union, and France divided Germany into four zones of occupation and agreed to govern them jointly. It makes no sense to speak of the 'breakdown' of these arrangements because they never operated. The refusal in May 1946 of the American military governor, General Lucius D. Clay, to deliver reparations from the American to the Soviet zone in violation of agreements reached at the wartime Yalta conference—an act from which the subsequent division of Germany is often said to have stemmed—merely provided Stalin with a pretext to proceed with a decision made earlier to 'Sovietize' his country's zone of occupation. The only serious economic understanding reached by the Allied military governments was the March 1946 Level of Industry Agreement, which authorized seizures and removal of 'excess' plants. It had no influence on either output, which lagged far below authorized maxima, or seizures, which would have continued at their own pace even in the absence of an agreement (Cairncross 1986; Mee 1975).

With the formation of Bizonia, the American military governor in Frankfurt held the upper hand in economic policy in Germany (excluding the Soviet Zone). Yet division and indecision beset his office. Only after the adoption of the Marshall Plan did recovery take priority over reform. The latter turned on 'deconcentration and decartelization', something that could be viewed in two possible ways, as punishment or opportunity. Trust busting could be used on the one hand to dispossess shareholders and weaken the economic power of the state, but on the other as a chance to break up inefficient, inflexible, and unprofitable organizational dinosaurs. With administrative confusion and mistrust general, it was often difficult to determine which of the two ends the policy was actually meant to serve. Within the US Office of Military Government, a radical reform faction close to Henry Wallace viewed trust busting as a second-best to the earlier but no longer acceptable Morgenthau Plan, but it got purged in early 1947 (Martin 1950). A suspicious senior German management was also disposed to consider 'decartelization and deconcentration' little more than a watered-down version of the earlier industrial wrecking scheme, but under the circumstances—mass arrests took place—its voice was muted (Sohl 1983).

A small, market-oriented coterie within German senior management thus rose to short-lived prominence. The temporary eclipse of the dominant group enabled Heinrich Dinkelbach, whom the British named steel trustee in late 1946, to break up and reorganize Vereinigte Stahlwerke—a trust amalgamated in the late 1920s that controlled nearly half of the total Ruhr steel output. The shopfloor was initially the only base of support for such a policy and the fledgling union soon got on board. Dinkelbach's quid pro quo was to offer organized labour half the seats on the supervisory boards (*Aufsichtsraete*) of the new firms, thereby introducing the subsequently famous principle of co-determination (*Mitbestimmung*) into German industry. Belatedly sanctioning Dinkelbach's reforms, a British–American military law of November 1948 also left the eventual disposition of steel industry assets up to 'the German people', to whom sovereignty would soon be restored. The ownership issue was left completely unsettled. The companies themselves were bankrupt in all but name (Gillingham 1991: 197–204).

At the same time, management power remained intact. Industry continued to operate with familiar methods. The British, and later Bizonal, administrators depended no less than Hitler and his economic henchmen on coal and steel cartels to allocate raw materials, place orders, and deliver to markets. The cartels were of course renamed, launching a process of pouring old wine into new bottles that would resume with successive political re-shuffling and end only years after the European Coal and Steel Community was up and running. On the level of industry organization, continuity with prewar Germany was the rule in the Ruhr (Gillingham 1991: 191–3).

The Marshall Plan was the turning point for German heavy industry. This was not evident at the time. In the months between late 1947 and early 1950, some 700 million DM worth of steel plant would be unbolted, disassembled, cut apart with blowtorches and carted away—by weight and value a third of the initial dismantlement plan target of what was intended to be a mini-Morgenthau Plan. The British occupation authorities ran the programme, whose ostensible purpose was to eliminate future German export competition. The French supported it, if only because it increased the availability of coking coal for their own rapidly modernizing steel industry, into which the first *Plan de Modernisation et de l'Equipement* ploughed vast amounts of public investment. Tens of thousands of Germans were thrown out of work as, month after month, factories fell to the wrecker's ball. The common threat faced by employers and employees rekindled a sense of national solidarity, blunted the sharpness of socialist attacks on private ownership, and restored a measure of public respectability to the old combines. The curtailment of the *Demontagen* gave the young and shaky government of Konrad Adenauer its first great victory, greatly increasing the likelihood of the eventual restoration of private ownership in the Ruhr.

The economic consequences of the campaign were less severe than feared; the elimination of inefficient production units merely accelerated a process that the market might otherwise have performed. The execution of the campaign was nevertheless brutal. It raised the hackles at the Economic Cooperation Administration (ECA), triggered opposition in Congress, angered union leaders in Britain and the United States, met with popular disapproval in both countries, directed public opinion to the critical role of the Ruhr in European recovery, and helped re-focus French policy of *controle organique* or 'effective management' of sales and supply. It was thus a step towards the eventual Schuman Plan (Först 1979; Gillingham 1991: 205–15).

The evolution of French *Ruhrpolitik*

French *Ruhrpolitik* grew out of a profound conviction that '[i]f France should have to submit to a third assault during the next generation, it (may) succumb forever' (Monnet 1943). To prevent such a catastrophe Monnet had insisted, at a crucial discussion of the provisional government in Algiers in 1943, that France must break with past practice and, by right of an 'historical mandate' take the lead in achieving a new industrial settlement by creating a 'European entity' to open large markets and prevent competitive rearmament. Such views, though not always visible on the surface of French Ruhr policy, had wide and deep support from within the veteran policy-making community. France opposed the Morgenthau Plan, ruled out another Ruhr occupation like the disaster of 1923, and emphatically rejected the westward spread of Soviet influence in Germany. To build up German economic strength without increasing the nation's political power, a searching policy analysis undertaken by the Foreign Ministry recommended eliminating armaments factories, but opposed long-term restrictions on production and further rejected expropriation, the displacement of industry, and suppressing new lines of production. The proposed solution would require *controle organique*, a partial break-up of the trusts, supervision (by 'extra-European' as well as European states) of cartel relationships between producers in French and German industry, the maintenance of a long occupation, and adaptation to changing circumstances. The ultimate goal would be 'to integrate the productive forces of Germany into a new international order' (Gillingham 1991: 137–48).

Years would pass before France was in a position to disclose this objective officially. Not until March 1946 could the French participate in the meetings of the Allied Council of Ministers, which drafted treaties with the minor defeated powers. That goal attained, the next one was to block every step towards Four-Power agreement on German policy, since 'no imaginable solution could offer France stronger guarantees than those [of] participating in the present occupation' (Gillingham 1991: 154). A third goal was to gain Allied consideration for French proposals for the political and economic reorganization of the 'Ruhr-Rhenanie', the name proposed for the future German state. Envisaged were radical political decentralization, international management of mine and mill, economic controls, and territorial parcellization into tiny customs areas. Such hare-brained schemes were concocted partly for the consumption of a *Boche*-hating public. They also gave Foreign Minister Georges Bidault precious bargaining chips. In any case, long-range planning had to cede priority to the pressing French need for coal, especially during the severe winter of 1947, but also in light of the projected future requirements of the French steel industry (Gillingham 1987).

At the Moscow conference of foreign ministers in early 1947, Bidault secured British–American assent to a 'sliding scale' guaranteeing both France's basic requirements for Ruhr coal and a greater German share as output increased. In August 1947, several weeks after the Marshall Plan announcement, Bidault struck an important deal with William Clayton, the chief of economic affairs in the State Department: France would drop its wild and woolly proposals for sole control of the Ruhr if guaranteed that German recovery would not outpace French and if a suitable agreement for international management of the Ruhr could be reached. Bidault proposed:

> the creation of a ... board [to] allocate the Ruhr production of coal, iron, and steel and possibly chemicals between Germany and other countries. After the peace treaty such a board would be composed of representatives of US, UK, France, Benelux, and Germany. Prior thereto it would be composed of the same countries minus Germany. (Gillingham 1991: 157; see also Bidault 1965)

French plans underwent one important additional change. Knowing that the British–American decision to restore heavy industry assets to the German people would eliminate any possibility of French control at the factory level, in January 1948 Bidault instructed the military governor of the French zone that 'German recovery in the cadre of Europe should take place as rapidly as possible'. The foreign minister emphasized that 'the first phase of the occupation is now over and our main concern is no longer to right past wrongs but to prepare for the future'. Ruled out were 'direct occupation of the Zone and exploitation for our own profit'. 'Everything', Bidault concluded, 'must be done to develop useful contacts with Germans'. Indeed, Frenchmen should miss no opportunity to explain to them that 'we [did] not attempt to dominate but merely [desired to] play an honorable role in a united and cooperative Europe' (Gillingham 1991: 159, 162–3).

Over several months in 1948 a tripartite conference of the three Western allies met in Paris to set the guidelines for organizing what would become the Federal Republic. The conference also dealt with German heavy industry. In February, the French proposed creating an International Authority for the Ruhr (IAR), whose key power would be to divide the Ruhr coal supply between exports and domestic consumption in a manner calculated to assure that 'the resources of the [area] should not in the future be used for aggression but in the interests of peace'; guarantee 'European powers operating in the common good ... non-discriminatory access' to Ruhr coal and steel; and promote both tariff reduction and German democratization (Gillingham 1991: 161). The final IAR agreement also specified that a control period would remain in force until the Allied governments chose to end it and, further, that the approval of a new a Military Security Board, representing the three Western occupation governments' powers, would be required for all future factory construction in order to prevent the reconstitution of an armaments industry. Except for British participation and the fact that it operated under the auspices of the military government occupation authorities, the IAR, in short, provided the gist of the Schuman Plan: international supervision, coal supply guarantees to France, relinquishment of economic controls upon evidence of appropriate behaviour, the enforcement of fair trading practices, and eventual Franco–German partnership. In 1949 the British would effectively opt out of supervisory responsibility for Ruhr coal and steel and the military governments, at State Department behest, would be replaced by civilian Allied High Commissioners. Although the Schuman Plan—a *coup de théâtre* of historic dimensions—would appear like a bolt out of the blue, the stage had already been set for it.

The Schuman Plan negotiations

A month after the historic May 1950 announcement of French Foreign Minister Robert Schuman, who spoke on behalf of Monnet, the actual drafter of the text, negotiations began in Paris for the new European Coal and Steel Community (ECSC), whose design was supposed to make war economically impossible as well as politically unthinkable (Gerbet 1962; Monnet 1976). Joined by the Benelux countries and Italy as well as France and Germany (though with Britain remaining a bystander), the conference would conclude with the initialling of the Treaty of Paris eleven months later. The text reflects the complicated and often difficult compromises arrived at during the intense and sometimes disjointed multidimensional negotiations over this period (Gillingham 1991: 228–98).

The Franco–German relationship was always the chief concern of the Paris conference, but right behind it, as well as closely related to it, was the issue of the future 'economic constitution' of Europe. Monnet's *dirigiste* views had counterparts in an official Washington still deeply stamped by the New Deal. Contesting this position were the voices of organized business from the Ruhr but also eventually from France and the other participating countries. In Germany, free marketers like economics minister Erhard were largely conspicuous by their silence in the heated debates that went on for months, both openly and behind the scenes. Chancellor Adenauer held the German foreign-policy reins firmly in hand throughout negotiations. Profoundly committed to reconciliation with France, Adenauer supported Monnet as chairman of the coal–steel conference proceedings, backing him even in the teeth of dogged opposition from Ruhr producers and the indifference of Erhard. Behind Monnet was a strong but officially silent American partner—his not-so-secret weapon.

By making German rearmament inevitable, the outbreak of the Korean War in June 1950 shifted the power balance in Western Europe decisively, thereby also jeopardizing the coal–steel conference. The transformation of Nato from a US-directed headquarters based in Europe into a standing army composed of American and European units, in which a German military identity could be subsumed, ultimately re-created the necessary conditions for Western European security. The terms of the eventual settlement, which involved the relinquishment of residual occupation controls, would nevertheless take years to work out. As seen in Chapter 2, as a stopgap to save the Schuman Plan, Monnet devised the so-called Pleven Plan in October 1950, calling for a European defence force composed of nationally integrated contingents. This ultimately-rejected proposal would lead the integration process off in the wrong direction. It was, however, sufficiently reassuring to the French public, at least for a time, to keep the negotiations for the coal–steel pool from derailing (Gillingham 1991: 263–5).

The compromises needed to conclude the Treaty of Paris left many issues unresolved, were satisfactory to no one, and created a heavy work load for the so-called Interim Committee, which met in continuous session from May 1951 until the High Authority of the ECSC opened its doors in Luxembourg in June 1952 (Gillingham 1991: 293–6). This informal, embryonic body deserves to be remembered as the progenitor of the Eurocracy. The considerable operational shortcomings of the ECSC, which eventually caused Monnet to resign the presidency of the High Authority in disgust, were due as much to circumstance as to faulty design. By the mid-1950s, economic and strategic change had relegated historic Western European coal–steel problems to the back burner (Gillingham 1991: 299–364). Notwithstanding its increasing irrelevance, the ECSC substituted for a treaty settlement that ended the war against Germany. It was the necessary diplomatic forerunner of the economic and political integration that would unfold later and under different auspices.

French and German positions

Monnet's concept for the ECSC was similar to the New Deal's Tennessee Valley Authority in calling for a programme of economic expansion anchored in a key industrial sector governed centrally through a code of business conduct restricting the powers of private enterprise. The centrepiece in his plans was the creation of the High Authority: a directorate with extensive regulatory powers. A so-called *Document de Travail* (1950) spelled out Monnet's ideas. Acting as chairman (as well as head of the French delegation), Monnet would set the agenda for the Paris conference. Monnet operated independently of governmental or parliamentary control and refused to consult the French steel industry or the employers' association, neither of which had any direct influence on the negotiations. He lacked organized support, except from the Americans (Schwabe 1988*a*).

Adenauer replied to Schuman's proposal with unbridled enthusiasm, claiming to have waited twenty-five years for such a welcome offer. Determined that nothing should be allowed to let the talks fail, Adenauer allowed Monnet to veto appointments to the German delegation and accepted both his conference leadership and the *Document de Travail* as blueprint. Although he could be tough with the occupying powers when necessary, during the Schuman Plan negotiations Adenauer's chief concern was to bring his own troops in line. The smokestack barons of course wanted to slip the noose placed around their collective neck in 1945 and to return as soon to possible to a simulacrum of business as usual. Adenauer, too, sought to end the occupation but, fully confident that over the long run Germany's underlying strength would tell, he feared that his impatient constituents might undermine the restoration process (Schwarz 1979).

The German chancellor also appreciated the seriousness of the American reform commitment, as notably manifest in US Secretary of State Dean Acheson's knee-jerk reaction that the Schuman Plant amounted to little more than a ploy to revive the International Steel Cartel. Adenauer was also aware that John J. McCloy, the American High Commissioner, was Monnet's close friend and fellow-spirit and could not be counted upon to support the German position in the coal–steel negotiations. The American embassy in Paris, the ECA-office headquartered there, and the French Marshall Plan mission were also outposts of American Monnetism. Key members of the US Parisian policy-making complex, such as like David Bruce (head of the Marshall Plan mission to France) and Tommy Tomlinson (representative of the Treasury in Paris), served as unofficial members of the Monnet 'team' (Gillingham 1991: 235; Schwartz 1985).

Adenauer could be proud of his first months in power, when he had to skate on thin ice. Elected to office by the narrowest of majorities and by a public whose support for his distinctive policy—the *Westintegration* of a truncated German state into a politically phantom 'Europe'—had not been secured, Adenauer needed to convince a sceptical electorate that his approach served the interests of the new state. Adenauer's first, purely symbolic victory—a token of his paltry standing—was to insist that he and McCloy be photographed together on the same carpet (an incident that became known as *Teppichpolitik*). The promise of equal treatment in the Schuman Plan negotiations, which took place before the organization of a German foreign service, represented a giant step towards winning respect for the Federal Republic as a sovereign power. Above all, West Germany still remained under occupation: any change in its status would have to occur as an outcome rather than at the onset of the Paris conference. Two circumstances nonetheless favoured Adenauer: the 'economic miracle' and the need—recognized, however grudgingly, even by the French—for German rearmament in the face of the Soviet threat (Schwarz 1980).

Arduous negotiations

Beginning in late June 1950 at the summit of European diplomatic triumph, the Paris negotiations followed a tedious, meandering downhill route, which by autumn had led to swamps of bureaucratic manoeuvring in the national interest. Little remained of the *Document de Travail* and of Monnet's conception of the ECSC's institutional architecture. Monnet had envisioned the High Authority as a powerful directorate acting collectively on the basis of majority vote but dominated by its president, who would be *primus inter pares* among the commissioners. There would be a court to which governments might appeal, and a parliament limited to powers of interpellation providing the sole restraints on the exercise of executive power. Three separate committees composed of producers, consumers and labour would advise the High Authority upon request, but otherwise lack statutory authority. Monnet also envisioned regional producer organizations, whose size, composition, and functions were not specified, serving as transmission belts to convey High Authority directives to industry as well as provide it with necessary data.

According to Monnet's *Document*, the High Authority was supposed to act on the basis of powers assigned to it by the member states. Included in this transference of sovereignty was the authority to create a 'social market (*marché unique*)', to 'pool production' and specifically to eliminate 'all privileges of entry or exit, tax equivalents and quantitative restrictions of the circulation of coal and steel products'. The High Authority could likewise abolish 'all aids or subventions to industry', 'all means of differentiation between foreign and domestic markets in transportation rates' as well as in coal and steel prices, and all other 'restrictive practices' (Griffiths 1988; Küsters 1988).

Other draft provisions rendered these liberal ones mostly nugatory. If, on the one hand, the High Authority was supposed to eliminate 'falsification' of competitive conditions, it was, on the other, obliged to equalize wages and working conditions and enforce 'identical delivery conditions for coal and steel at the point of departure from mine or mill'. Pricing policy served various inconsistent ends: to protect consumers against discrimination; prevent producers from engaging in 'disloyal' practices; 'assure' the steady expansion of markets and output; and 'guarantee the spontaneous allocation of output at the highest level or productivity'. Wage and price policy was similarly fanciful. Thus the document committed the High Authority to preventing wage cuts during slumps, eliminating 'exploitative competition', guaranteeing 'coal and steel workers the highest standard of living compatible with economic equilibrium', and introducing 'wage equality' by imposing assessments on production. Other articles empowered the High Authority to impose manufacturing programmes upon firms; steer investment; recommend changes in tariffs, banking regulation, and transport rates; and fine miscreant producers (Gillingham 1991: 240).

While (with one important exception) accepting the general framework of Monnet's *Document*, the basic German working paper for the conference contained the gist of an alternative scheme that rested chiefly on industrial self-government. In effect, the Federal Republic sought to create a High Authority too weak to interfere with a Ruhr restoration. The Germans therefore took up a key Dutch proposal to establish a Council of Ministers with veto authority and further recommended both giving the proposed European court broad review powers and creating supervisory committees to enable the assembly to oversee the High Authority. The German draft also precluded the High Authority from the exercise of social policy, emphasizing that the principle of economic efficiency should instead guide policy-making. Moreover, the German draft specifically denied the proposed executive the authority to set prices, establish manufacturing programmes or engage in long-term production planning, except for situations in which 'recent new projects [had] been built in the wrong place' (in other words, outside Germany) (Gillingham 1991: 240–1).

The German paper assigned powers stripped from the High Authority to producer associations. Monnet envisaged a role for such bodies, but his language, which alluded to the importance of the 'transnational' principle, strongly hinted at a dilution of Ruhr power. To head off the threat of being either out-muscled by a single association of French and Benelux producers or split up into different producing districts, the German text stipulated that future producer groups should be 'created on a geographical basis without respect to international frontiers'. The most memorable passages in the German document unsurprisingly describe the legal character, organization, and powers of the regional groups: these should not be purely private associations but semi-public ones which, while self-governing, could be deputized to discharge responsibilities on behalf of the coal–steel pool (Gillingham 1991: 240–1).

Solidarity, born of defeat and persecution suffered under occupation, underpinned the German position. Industry enjoyed the support (albeit sometimes only tacit) of the economics ministry, the labour unions, and a portion of the Social Democratic Party for a hard-nosed policy to defend the German industrial tradition of organized capitalism. Overt resistance to Monnet being politically difficult in the still-occupied country, the most feasible strategy was quietly to subvert his work while operating with the support of the other participating countries as well as of powerful interests unrepresented by their official negotiators (Gillingham 1991: 242).

Monnet expected the Schuman Plan conference to last three months, with technical discussions conducted at the level of specialized working groups being quickly concluded in a plenary session. By the time these working groups were abolished in October 1950 they had, however, reduced the structure of the *Document de Travail* to unvariegated rubble. Upscale wage equalization went by the board, the only support for it being from the Belgians, who, after threats to walk out, were kissed-off with a cheap gratuity—a levy on coal output from the Ruhr, whose labour force was underpaid, raised to cross the palms of overpaid but under-productive Belgian miners. The High Authority also lost the power to forbid wage reduction nationally at the hands of the relevant working group. All the non-French negotiating delegations objected to the proposed High Authority's exercise of investment controls. As for production controls, the High Authority should be allowed to enact them, the specialists agreed, only in times of manifest surplus or scarcity, and even then only at the request of national producer groups (Gillingham 1991: 244; Griffiths 1988).

Guidelines for price policy emerged from the committee discussions but were too vague and confusing to be of value. In attempting to arrive at some form of common, ECSC-wide pricing that would simultaneously provide producers an adequate return, keep costs to consumers low, support wages at socially accepted levels, and eliminate market distortion, Monnet had tried to square the circle. In the end, the working group dealing with the issue compromised by agreeing to adopt some variation of the American basing point system—perhaps the most distorting non-tariff barrier in American economic history. Discussion of the powers and composition of the regional groups never really got off the ground. Indeed, the specialized technical discussions resolved none of the fundamental operational questions facing the conference (Gillingham 1991: 245–7).

What eventually curtailed the activity of the working groups and shifted responsibility to the heads of delegation was not lack of progress but a bombshell that Acheson dropped in New York in September 1950, when he announced unexpectedly that the United States had decided to rearm Germany (that is, create an army and lift restrictions on war production). Acheson's explanation that this decision was a component of a larger policy that included stationing American troops in Europe, organizing an integrated command structure for the Atlantic Alliance, and subordinating future troops from the Federal Republic, did little to reassure the panicky French. The uncharacteristic gaffe of the polished Secretary of State threatened, in short, to knock down the Schuman Plan negotiations at a single blow. Monnet saved the day in October 1950 by hatching the Pleven Plan for a European Defence Community and placing it front and centre on the European policy agenda (Gillingham 1991: 250–6; Kaplan 1988: 39–40).

Ruhr-bashing

The Schuman Plan discussions now entered their most critical phase, which lasted until March 1951. The fate of the ECSC would hinge not only on discussions carried on in Paris but also on the outcome of a US–German struggle in Bonn over 'deconcentration and decartelization'. Previously a forceful advocate of ending economic controls in Germany, American High Commissioner McCloy abruptly turned about face in order to promote the greater good of European integration after Monnet persuaded him of the potentially devastating consequences of the Acheson bombshell. A memorandum by Monnet in late September 1950, virtually repudiating the recommendations of the working groups, set the stage for the new no-holds-barred negotiating phase in Paris.

At the same time, an uncharacteristic threat by Adenauer to walk out of the negotiations unless the trust-busting regulations of a new Allied-imposed law were modified increased the tension (Gillingham 1991: 256). The regulations in question ordered the break-up of the six leading trusts, a cut in the ties between the coal and steel industries, and the organization of no less than fifty separate mining companies. The angry Germans countered with a compromise plan in November 1950 while Monnet further raised the ante by insisting in a succession of notes that the High Authority be empowered to authorize or forbid all past, present, and future formal or informal arrangements between producers, as well as producers and their customers, and to approve or disapprove all future mergers and fusions (Gillingham 1991: 257).

The bashing of the Ruhr was about to begin (Gillingham 1991: 266–83). For three-and-a-half months Americans would pummel the body with one gut-punishing flurry after another, while Monnet, feinting and occasionally jabbing, prepared the knock-out punch. Knowing that the German government had ultimate authority to dispose of coal and steel assets and could, by nationalizing industry, escape detrustification altogether, Monnet tried to force the Germans to enact a law consistent with international agreements for deconcentration and decartelization as required by the United States. He also sought a transfer of power from the occupation authorities to the ECSC. Once this was accomplished, and the planned reorganizations completed, the French government would relinquish its occupation powers—that is, allow the International Authority for the Ruhr to die and eliminate the military security boards, whose powers would then revert to the High Authority (Gillingham 1991: 270).

The scheme presupposed that the High Authority would have the power to act under draft Articles 60 and 61 of the proposed treaty. Because the existing law governed the mills but not the mines, Monnet, in a show of force, included provisions in the two articles that would result in the break-up of coal cartels, which in fact applied only to the Ruhr—in glaring violation of the 'equal treatment' principle (Gillingham 1991: 269). In early December 1950, Erhard recommended walking out and letting the negotiations die, a step that Adenauer was no longer quite ready to take. Leading industry figures, aware of the Korean War-induced boom on steel markets, thought the time had come to 'call the bluff on the Schuman people' (Gillingham 1991: 270). Later in December, Adenauer intimated to Monnet that in order to head off co-determination he was ready to nationalize heavy industry, a move that would have pulled the carpet out from under the dapper Frenchman and sent him sprawling. The Germans also benefited from the spontaneous support of other national steel industries, which reasonably feared that they, too, could fall victim to trust busting. In January 1951, the head of the German delegation, acting upon orders from Adenauer, informed Monnet that Germany would only sign the treaty under protest if differences concerning Articles 60 and 61 were not ironed out (Gillingham 1991: 270).

To prevent the collapse of the Schuman Plan, McCloy simply dictated the terms of the settlement, using his authority under the existing law. Failure of the noble experiment, he declared in February 1951, would set the clock back two years, make it impossible to revise the still extant agreements limiting steel production, hopelessly compromise the Pleven Plan, in general undermine *Westintegration*, and even open the way to an undesirable 'Austrian' solution: Four-Power rule and the neutralization of Germany. Thereupon McCloy summoned Adenauer for a dressing down, blamed German stubbornness for delaying the negotiations for two months, and warned that the United States and France would impose their own decartelization scheme if necessary (Gillingham 1991: 279).

McCloy's terms were the same as offered earlier: the German coal cartel (*Deutsche Kohlenverkauf*) would be dismantled by October 1952 and remain subject to Allied authority during the transition period; twenty-seven steel companies were to be carved out of the existing seven; and only eleven of these would be allowed to own coal mines. Over vehement Ruhr protest, Adenauer accepted, paving the way for the treaty to be initialled on 18 April 1951.

The Treaty of Paris

The Treaty of Paris establishing the ECSC left the outlines of Monnet's original scheme mainly intact, but key questions continued to be unanswered. The High Authority remained the exclusive source of executive power and would exercise responsibility for its own internal organization, although the treaty called for the creation of an Advisory Committee of thirty to fifty-one members representing by thirds the interests of producers, organized labour and consuming industries (appointment was to be made by the relevant private national associations). The economic sections of the document, which reveal strong antitrust influence, establish modernization as the guiding principle of the ECSC and set as priorities opening common markets, reducing prices, increasing efficiency, and eliminating all forms of discrimination. To this end, the High Authority disposed of numerous disciplinary and regulatory powers—it could set and require the publication of prices; impose punishments for falsification of data, rebating, as well as price gouging; and subsidize mine operations. The lengthy decartelization provisions (the eventual Articles 65 and 66) enumerate various circumstances calling for High Authority intervention. The treaty's omissions were also significant. Regional groups were unmentioned and the relationship between producer groups and the High Authority left undefined and therefore open to dispute. The regulatory problems that had vexed the working groups remained unresolved. Intended to serve as a constitution, the treaty did not even amount to a cease-fire agreement. It was merely an interlude in the ongoing struggle over the control of West European heavy industry (Gillingham 1991: 280).

That struggle would resume with increased ferocity within the new Luxembourg *apparat* and set in motion a process of institutional reformation which, contrary to the High Authority's intentions, would restore the old *Konzerne* as well as the sometimes derided 'dictatorship of business associations' (*Verbaendediktatur*), now complemented by the co-optation of the labour unions into junior partnership. The state also moved closer to industry, thanks to the 1952 investment aid law. Designed to offset the thinness of German capital markets, this huge tax credit won the endorsement of both management and labour and had the complete support of McCloy, who, in still another shift, now supported partial mobilization of the economy to meet the demands of rearmament. Thus the Schuman Plan negotiations contributed inadvertently to the creation of that tripartite corporatist relationship known as 'Germany Inc.' (Adamsen 1981; Gillingham 1991: 283).

The Schuman Plan likewise revived the tradition of coal and steel cartelization in Western Europe. In January 1951, the International Association of Schuman Plan Nations came into existence. The prologue of the charter of this federation for national industry *Verbaende* opened with a blast against the 'super-dirigism' of the proposed High Authority, something 'unknown in democracies and drawn from the most totalitarian regimes'. The document called for suppressing the future High Authority's powers to borrow, tax, lend, and underwrite investment programmes and insisted upon the devolution of remaining ones from the purportedly omnipotent planned directorate on the grounds that only producers could manage the transition to a common market. The resolution further urged that national producer associations be empowered to establish joint production programmes, set up common supply systems, define prices, conditions and terms of sale, and set up investment programmes (Gillingham 1991: 292).

Of more immediate concern, the Interim Committee, comprising senior civil servants from the member states, made two decisions, each in the teeth of opposition from Monnet, of fundamental importance in the future. It designated Luxembourg as the seat of the ECSC, instead of a future extra-territorial Saar, and also assigned the staffing and structuring of the organization's administration to the member states. These decisions all but guaranteed the continuation of the struggle between *dirigisme* and corporatism within the ECSC, as well as between Monnet and industry. The coal–steel poll's future as integration model and motor would not be decided, however, in a struggle between old contestants. In the end, the ECSC would simply be eclipsed by change (Gillingham 1991: 94–296).

The agreement to create a heavy industry pool in Western Europe changed no borders, created no new military alliances, and reduced only a few commercial barriers. It did not even end the occupation of the Federal Republic, a process that began with the agreement of May 1952 on German sovereignty between the Western Powers and Germany. Instead, the Schuman Plan negotiations shifted the diplomatic context, cleared (sometimes by indirection) a logjam of unresolved practical problems, and persuaded sceptical publics that Franco–German cooperation could be more than a pipe-dream. In doing so it eliminated political obstacles to future economic partnership. A supranational authority had for the first time been created in Western Europe, but it would have to deliver as promised in order to become the nucleus of a future European government.

The eclipse of Monnetism and the founding of the EEC

As seen in Chapter 5, the ECSC would in fact be a disappointment. The continuous infighting and bickering that characterized the policy-making process made a mockery of official Euro-idealism, but such unpleasantness would have counted for little if, in the end, the ECSC produced significant results. The record was not barren of achievement. Common markets for coal and steel opened, albeit with little economic impact. Knowledge gains were more important. Growing out of the problems of administering transnational markets, a number of new technical insights and innovations short-cut customary managerial approaches and often proved valuable in future economic and legal applications.

Yet, these were secondary gains. 'Spill-over', as predicted by Monnet and his academic admirers, such as Ernst Haas and Leon Lindberg, did not occur; an integration servo-mechanism did not generate change spontaneously. Rather, a premature

hardening of the arteries set in at Luxembourg. The ideal of European integration failed to capture the imagination, tended to be overlooked in public discourse
and was often forgotten altogether. The Monnet model of centralized bureaucratic
transnational governance failed as a harbinger of future development. Nothing was
gained in the attempt to rejuvenate it by creating complementary institutions in the
fields of security (the European Defence Community) and politics (the European Political Community). Both (fortunately) went nowhere. The representatives of the Six
ECSC member states who met at Messina in June 1955 to kick-start the stalled integration process may not have had a single purpose, or even necessarily a clear sense of
where they were headed. They were of one mind, however, about what they wanted
to avoid—Monnet and a Monnetist approach to supranational institution-building,
which had become a drag on the healthy interdependence produced by liberalization
and economic growth (Marjolin 1989: 276).

Back to the future

The spirit of contentiousness prevailing in Luxembourg stemmed in part from the
industrialists' new feeling of power, which derived from the re-founding of the old
partnership of the prewar International Steel Cartel. In November 1951 the direct-
ors of the French and German employers' associations met in Düsseldorf to form an
entente. Steel names were prominent on both sides of the table. The wide-ranging
talks touched on labour, public relations, patent and brand-name exchanges, and
productivity. Their main theme was 'the European idea'. Representatives of the national steel associations of the ECSC member states would meet twelve times with
the Interim Committee in order 'to clear up problems with the [High Authority] in
advance' and to place as many industry representatives as possible in the bureaucracy. The effort was repaid. A German mining engineer and a senior manager of
ARBED, the big Luxembourg steel company, ran the Main Branch for Production. The
business manager of the Ruhr steel producers' association directed the section responsible for investments. The chief economist of the German coal cartel was number two in the statistical section. A French civil servant managed financial matters;
senior French and German railway men shared responsibility for the transportation
sector; an Italian official headed the (largely inactive) labour office; and an Italian
nobleman directed the office staff. Two of the three important legal counsels were
German. None of the aforementioned was a 'Monnet man', and to locate supporters
the High Authority President often had to search beyond the confines of the Luxembourg Eurocracy (Gillingham 1991: 313–18).

The so-called Advisory Committee was the locus of industrialist power within the
High Authority. Monnet wanted little to do with this essentially non-statutory body,
which was in fact 'the last of the five important community organs to begin operating', and convened it from fear that otherwise producers might have sabotaged the
openings of the common markets for coal and steel scheduled for early 1953. His fears
were exaggerated: instead of resisting planned changes, the producers stitched up
markets in a succession of meetings beginning in November 1952. In fact, Monnet
had little scope for policy-making. In coal, subsidization was in effect throughout the
ECSC. Competition would have created a bloodbath; imposing a high tariff would
have been inflationary. In Germany, the *Deutsche Kohlenverkauf* (coal cartel) continued

to set domestic prices, which the government then sanctioned—a relationship in effect since the 1920s. The International Authority for the Ruhr continued to allocate coal exports—a power Monnet curiously chose not to take over—upon which the French levied a tonnage fee, which was then paid into an equalization fund to compensate consumers of domestic coal. French prices were fixed. Compared to the many non-tariff barriers that regulated the coal trade, tariffs were unimportant; lifting them had a cosmetic function (Gillingham 1991: 218–21).

The opening of the common market in steel was also less significant than it seemed (Gillingham 1991: 321–30). To be sure, external tariffs were harmonized and slightly lowered. A 'liberation of prices' did take place, but from government controls; cartels immediately filled the gap. The basing point system was retained. French and German producers worked out a new agreement for splitting up the south German market. The most extensive pre-opening discussions concerned a technical matter, the standardization of pricing for custom manufacturers, but producers eventually agreed to adopt the German nomenclature community-wide. Other producing districts, after initial objections, accepted the German system of rebating on direct sales and of cross-subsidizing at the wholesale level.

Monnet blamed the steady price increases of early 1953 on such collusion and convened the Advisory Committee in April to convey his 'extreme displeasure'. Instead he received a fifteen-hour savaging from the angry producers and left the meeting 'troubled, very troubled' (Gillingham 1991: 330). This is hardly surprising. In the first quarter of 1953, twelve new European steel syndicates formed for cooperation on third markets, two for the community, four for France and one for Germany. Capping the edifice was the International Steel Export Cartel, set up in March 1953, which set price minimums for a quarter of ECSC output; a higher percentage, in fact, than the old International Steel Cartel of the 1930s had done.

In the Ruhr of the early 1950s, the preface 're-' gradually supplanted the 'de-' of the 1940s. There was *re*investment, *re*assemblage (*Remontage*), *re*concentration and, finally, *re*storation (*Restauration*). The reorganization process was immensely complicated, but by 1975 there were 'as before World War II ... eight *Konzerne* dominating the west German steel industry that together control 79 percent of Ruhr pig iron production, 75 percent of ... steel production, 60 percent of rolled steel production, and 33 percent of coal production'. Although the bloated steel trust Vereinigte Stahlwerke had been split up, Thyssen and Krupp still produced a quarter and a seventh of total steel output. The four traditional middle-sized firms divided the rest. Thanks to the boom, the German share in overall European production continued to mount (Gillingham 1991: 352).

Nevertheless the High Authority's accomplishments must not be overlooked. It set up a European scrap cartel to end monopoly pricing by national ones, reduced transport rates and ended 'rupture charges' for hypothetical trans-shipment at borders, and harmonized tax law (though not taxes themselves) (Gillingham 1991: 343–8). Yet Monnet could only play King Canute for so long. The most serious obstacle to his plans was not stubborn, backward-looking coal and steel men, but the process of economic change, which eroded their influence too. By mid-decade auguries boded ill for the traditional 'tied-in' German economy, as well as its imitators elsewhere. Petroleum and cheap coal from overseas broke the Ruhr monopoly. The mines entered the final phase of secular decline. New steel plant was built on littorals with easy access to overseas sources of supply. Consumption sector growth outpaced that of heavy industry. Market responsiveness and innovativeness began to edge out planning and product reliability as gages of competitiveness. The economic importance of the ECSC faded with that of old industry.

From Monnet to Messina and Rome

Such realities contributed to general frustration in Luxembourg but were not the sole cause of Monnet's abrupt resignation as President of the High Authority in June 1954. He feared that the impending failure of the European Defence Community (EDC) would break down the postwar settlement in Western Europe (Gillingham 1991: 349–50). German rearmament had been made conditional upon acceptance of this scheme, which called for the merger of national units at the lowest feasible operational level and whose fine print, in effect, would have placed German foot soldiers under French command indefinitely. The EDC was, it should be added, a purely political project. It had no military value and was firmly embedded in the Nato command structure. Nato itself had no operational independence. Decisions governing its use were to be made in Washington.

Except in the United States and, for obvious reasons, in West Germany, the EDC was wildly unpopular, even in France, which had proposed the idea in the first place. Monnet's attempt to sugar the pill by proposing to merge the EDC and ECSC into a grandiose European Political Community, in addition to being reckless, impressed almost no one. French ratification of the defence community treaty thus dragged on for years; it would continue to do so until France no longer depended on American aid to wage the war in Indochina. With that condition satisfied, the French National Assembly rejected the treaty in August 1954. The US State Department panicked (Gillingham 2003: 30–3). Yet the end of the EDC meant little. A compromise brokered by British Prime Minister Anthony Eden, which called for treating Germany's Nato contingent units like any other, within the framework of the Western European Union, won the prompt approval of the United States, Britain, and France alike. The German Problem had disappeared almost unseen.

The prosperity of the 1950s was the hidden hand directing this mysterious yet welcome development. The statesmen who met at the famous Messina conference of June 1955 in order to 're-launch' the integration process thus shared the overarching goal of institutionalizing West Germany's new role as model and motor of economic growth. The delegates grappled with two main issues. The first was to sidetrack Monnet. He was barred from the ensuing negotiations and his 'baby', the European Atomic Energy Community (Euratom), did not, as planned, become a nuclear counterpart to the ECSC; it turned into a talking shop. Second, a jittery France had to be bought off. The ill-starred common agricultural policy was subsequently endorsed to give the French economy a leg up on those of its neighbours, while subsidies would be provided in Europe's name as a special reward to uncompetitive industrial exporters in order to prop up the ramshackle French overseas union or empire (Gillingham 2003: 34–7, 43–55).

As seen in Chapter 4, the greatest threat to the formation of the future EEC stemmed from a potential competitor, the proposed European free trade area (FTA), which could well have absorbed the EEC under slightly different circumstances.

Launched by the British and officially sponsored by the OEEC, the FTA proposal foresaw the creation of a common customs area but eschewed federation as an aim as well as the creation of a special regulatory (protectionist) regime for agriculture. If fully successful, the FTA would have become a larger, looser union than the EEC, and included British membership (Curzon 1979). All OEEC member states participated in the FTA discussions, which ran simultaneously with those for the EEC. The FTA had broad support: from the small, export-oriented nations of western and northern Europe, from the neutrals, and even from Germany, where Erhard was a vigorous champion. The British provided weak leadership, however, and the Monnetist US State Department firmly backed the more 'political' EEC. Adenauer, in a conscious choice between preserving the special relationship with France and encouraging liberalization, repudiated his economics minister and committed German resources to strengthening the position of the French government in power—in the critical months of transition between the French Fourth and the Fifth Republics. In December 1958, President Charles de Gaulle would proclaim his first Euro-historic '*Non!*' and, Germans in tow, pull out of the FTA talks. A truncated FTA, in the form of the European Free Trade Area Association, would survive in the shadow of a stronger EEC.

The promise of a German wealth transfer to French coffers via the common agricultural policy was one element essential to the viability of the EEC, but the so-called Rueff reforms were more important (Rueff 1959). Against the rapidly deteriorating economic background of early 1958, Finance Minister Jacques Rueff put France on a course parallel to the one charted a decade earlier by Erhard: he devalued the currency and introduced convertibility; balanced the budget; eliminated quotas; drastically reduced tariffs; and ended indexation of wages and prices. Within a year inflation had been checked, real wages rose, production boomed, the trade balance stabilized, and reserves, which had dwindled to nothing, recovered. In six amazing months a seriously debilitated France had become fit for competition in a European common market and a precedent had been set for future economic convergence. New economic muscle did not at once quell French fear of its powerful eastern neighbour, but enabled France to negotiate with West Germany on its own, without an American big brother lurking in the shadows, during a crucial early phase in a still fluid integration process.

The Treaty of Rome, which created the EEC, was, in Andrew Moravcsik's terms, a liberal framework document. The treaty provided for a common external tariff and a single customs area, which, though non-tariff barriers remained in place, was to be regulated by the competition principle—that is, optimally, by the invisible hand of the market. The creation of the common agricultural policy amply demonstrated that no direct route would lead to this result. The European integration process has indeed been a history of zigs and zags, of false starts, delays, and even backsliding as well as of solid long-term accomplishment. It could nevertheless not have started in the early 1950s and would not have continued had the Federal Republic not convinced fearful and sceptical neighbours that peaceful economic competition within and between borders trumps political and military rivalry among states, regions, and civilizations. This recognition has been the keystone of European peace ever since.

Conclusion

The greatest political accomplishment of the integration process remains its contribution to solving the German Problem. It is hard to imagine such a solution in the absence of Jean Monnet. He had vision, no doubt (but so did many others), as well as extraordinary determination (a quality that particularly impressed devoted associates).
But he also had at his disposal an international circle of exceptionally well-placed
friends with access to levers of power and spigots for cash and credit flows. Monnet
was a man with a special knack for keeping one step ahead of the game. He dared undertake those things that supposedly wiser heads thought impossible; experienced
many setbacks, but never admitted defeat. Monnet was indispensable to the breakthrough that led to a new German relationship with Europe. So was Adenauer. There
was no serious modern precedent for *Westintegration* and no other German statesman
capable of holding the Federal Republic to such a course. Without Adenauer, West
Germany might, by force of circumstance, have been rearmed and incorporated into
an American-led European security system, but without the benefit of *détente* and reconciliation with France except, perhaps, by means of the traditional, partly suspect
manner of international cartelization.

Apart from the impact of Monnet and Adenauer, a number of essential ingredi-
ents were required to advance integration at the early stages, when Europe was
still recovering from the war. Institutional transnational commercial cooperation
in Western Europe, upon which the ECSC rested, was the first of them. As seen
in Chapter 1, it has an antecedent in the interwar history of cross-border cooperation-
tion which, if economically undesirable, nevertheless brought about *détente* from a
post-1918 Franco–German relationship that resembled the post-1945 cold war. This
tradition proved sufficiently durable to weather the collapse of the world economic
system in the 1930s and provided the essential administrative structures of what became Hitler's European New Order. Interwar *cooperation*, in short, led to wartime *collaboration*. The interrelationship between both national producer communities and
traditional suppliers and customers, in heavy industry as well as in other sectors, survived the war at the national level and was revived internationally in the course of
the Schuman Plan negotiations. It was that interrelationship, rather than the formal
quasi-constitutional framework of the ECSC, that provided the real sinews of 'community' in the new Europe (Gillingham 1985: 112–62, 1991: 1–28, 29–77).

A new postwar context also figured in the events that led to the formation of the
ECSC. The existence of potentially hegemonic American world power set it apart
from the Europe-directed system of the 1920s and 1930s. The Truman administration, as heir to the free trade tradition of the Democratic Party, did not, however,
try to divide and conquer or colonize the defeated and abject peoples of the wrecked
civilization, or attempt to subordinate them to leadership from Washington, but
hoped instead to instigate, at least within Europe, the creation of an empire-by-
consent in a world governed through international law and open markets by sovereign democratic states. The administration envisaged a pluralistic global order
which, as recovery and growth took hold, would eventually enable the United States

to share responsibility for the good conduct of the world's affairs with other great powers of comparable strength (Gillingham 2003: 37–41).

Policy-makers as well as historians have sometimes lost sight of this decent and liberal vision. Consensus on how best to realize it has also often been missing. Yet having been gradually approached over the past fifty years, power-sharing with some like-minded European entity—the red thread in long-term American policy—has had consequences far different from anything that might have been predicted in Washington. Even with its many shortcomings, American policy has given European civilization a new lease on life (Gillingham 2003: 3–5).

The boldest claim made on behalf of the Schuman Plan—that it would prevent a recurrence of war in Europe—must also be examined in light of larger security considerations. Official wartime Washington counted on neither the break-up of the alliance with the Soviet Union, the onset of cold war, the creation of the national security state, or the establishment of Nato; nor did the US administration thereafter expect the alliance to become the anchor of a *pax Americana*. In the 1950s and 1960s, furthermore, not even the purported experts could adequately understand the hegemonic implications of fast-breaking changes in military technology, atomic weaponry and nuclear strategy. Indisputably, US military power and the American presence have pre-empted the possibility of large-scale warfare in Europe since World War II and, in the bargain, provided the nations of the formerly warring continent with low-cost security. The role of the European Communities and later the European Union (EU) as peacekeeping institutions has been, in an immediate sense, slight, albeit over the long run highly significant. Surely the reconciliation of Europe's peoples would survive Nato's and the EU's disappearance (Gillingham 2003: 16, 23, 32–3, 307–8, 407, 499).

In addition to the horrific memories of the last great war and the strong likelihood that the next one would be a nuclear holocaust, Europe's blessed new love of peace has had many sources, including the legacies of successful economic problem-solving and continuous prosperity; the recovery of the world market; the spread of multinational corporations and international finance; increases in personal mobility and population interchange; the development and acceptance of common tastes, values and ways of life; and the rise of secularization. Nevertheless a tradition of European self-government is not one of them. No *demos* yet exists. The lack of this vital but still wanting spirit is due in part to the early history of European integration. Imposed from the top down and legitimized by technocratic efficiency rather than democratic procedure, the European Communities excluded public participation.

The unfolding integration process did not result in the creation of unambiguously successful institutions as measured by the efficiency criterion—at least not all at once. In spite of its diplomatic importance, the ECSC scores low in terms of practical accomplishment (Gillingham 1991: 313–47). The architects of the EEC therefore understandably broke with *dirigisme*, the failed operating principle of the ECSC. With recourse to a different strategy, they endeavoured to create a customs union with a common tariff which, governed by the competition principle, would at some future date ideally be freed of non-tariff barriers to trade as well (Marjolin 1989).

Like the ECSC, the EEC was initially also only a partial success. Customs barriers fell, stimulating economic growth, which reinforced Germany's new role as economic hub of Europe, promoter of free trade, and agent of constructive change through the market. But the common agricultural policy, an egregious and stultifying endeavour, wasted resources on a vast scale and blew the integration process off course. In 1965, furthermore, a zealous bid by Walter Hallstein, the intellectually overheated president of the European Commission, to run Europe from Brussels triggered a major political crisis. The ensuing institutional gridlock, along with a succession of futile attempts to impose central economic direction upon recalcitrant national bureaucracies, brought the integration progress to a halt (Gillingham 2003: 53–72). The EEC was immobilized for another twenty years, until the Single European Act of 1986 got it going again.

Both before and since its revival in the late 1980s, the EU has struggled with Monnet's *dirigiste* approach, which was undemocratic, rigid and (contrary to expectations) proved to be inefficient. At its worst, when unchecked, it could be reckless and irresponsible. Yet the long-term alternative to a top-down approach to European integration—a market-based customs union governed by the competition principle—was not a viable alternative in postwar Western Europe. A difficult process of institution-building—itself preceded by the reinstatement of government under law—had to come first. The ECSC was hardly the only new international regulatory body to suffer teething problems after 1945. The International Trade Organization never got off the drawing board. GATT, a substitute for it, directed successive rounds of tariffs cuts in the early 1950s and then went into a long hibernation. The OEEC did not provide the desired framework of supranational governance, although, as seen in Chapter 4, it was useful in eliminating import quotas. The other Marshall Plan offshoot, the European Payments Union, was an undoubted success but, as intended, soon wound up operations. The International Monetary Fund could not begin operating until the end of the 1950s, and the dollar–gold exchange standard that it upheld worked satisfactorily for less than a decade.

Such liberal framework organizations may have set their sights properly but could not operate in a vacuum. They required reinforcement—compatible economic regimes—at the national level. None existed in Europe immediately after World War II. Erhard's Germany set the liberalization pace, as recommended by Wilhelm Röpke. Most of its European trading partners followed suit in the 1950s and France, thanks to Jacques Rueff, picked up the slack as the decade drew to a close. These developments hardly ended organized capitalism or French-type *dirigisme*— they were only first steps—but did make deep and permanent inroads into such systems. Over time, liberalization restored the power of the market domestically and unlocked the potential of the integration process to bind peoples in peaceful union. It helped establish what Friedrich Hayek termed the economic conditions of interstate federalism. The solution of the German Problem not only lay to rest the unhappy legacy of the past but also set the stage for the unfolding of a better future.

Further reading

Röpke (1946) provided an early and compelling answer—economic liberalization—to the problem that his country posed for European stability and prosperity in the immediate aftermath of World War II. Gillingham (1991) deals specifically with the German Problem at that time, culminating in the launch of the European Coal and Steel Community. Hogan (1987) and Wexler (1983) examine the German Problem more generally in the context of the Marshall Plan. Duchêne (1994) and Gillingham (2000) assess the pivotal part that Jean Monnet played in tackling the German Problem in the early 1950s. Gillingham (2003) provides a thorough assessment of the significance of the German Problem throughout the history of European integration.

Duchêne, F. (1994), *Jean Monnet: First Statesman of Interdependence* (New York: W.W. Norton).

Gillingham, J. (1991), *Coal, Steel, and the Rebirth of Europe, 1945 – 1955* (Cambridge: Cambridge University Press).

Gillingham, J. (2000), 'Jean Monnet and the New Europe', in Schuker (ed.), *Deutschland und Frankreich vom Konflikt zur Aussöhnung* (Munich: Oldenbourg Verlag).

Gillingham, J. (2003), *European Integration, 1950 – 2003: Superstate or New Market Economy?* (Cambridge: Cambridge University Press).

Hogan, M. (1987), *The Marshall Plan: America, Britain, and the Reconstruction of Europe, 1947 – 1952* (Cambridge: Cambridge University Press).

Röpke, W. (1946), *The Solution of the German Problem* (New York: G. P. Putnam's Sons).

Wexler, I. (1983), *The Marshall Plan Revisited: The European Recovery Programme in Economic Perspective* (Westport, CT: Greenwood Press).

Part III

Shaping the European Community

Chapter 4

Liberalization, Convertibility, and the Common Market

Wendy Asbeek Brusse

Contents

Summary

The launch of the European Economic Community (EEC) in 1958 can be understood as the outcome of an ongoing search since the end of World War II for ways to manage national policies for economic growth and prosperity in a context of reconstruction, intra-European trade expansion, and growing international interdependence. The Bretton Woods system for worldwide currency convertibility and non-discriminatory trade liberalization proved ill-suited for the immediate postwar requirements of economic reconstruction. Following the launch of the Marshall Plan, the Trade Liberalization Programme of the Organization for European Economic Cooperation (OEEC) and the European Payments Union (EPU) became intermediate routes towards solving Europe's reconstruction problems and obtaining a one-world system for trade and payments. The flaws and temporary nature of the OEEC eventually prompted several European countries to propose permanent preferential schemes for trade liberalization, some of them supranational in nature. For economic and political reasons, France and Germany were indispensable to such schemes. Yet wooing France required extensive economic and political concessions, which only a more flexible 'customs union plus' could accommodate. The EEC's package deal provided this. Crucially, it also firmly anchored Germany's vast export market into the larger Western European whole, thereby solidifying mutual trading gains. The United Kingdom initially remained aloof from these initiatives, hoping to maintain leadership of Europe and the Commonwealth by pursuing a one-world system of full currency convertibility and non-discrimination in trade. When this proved unfeasible, Britain pushed for the creation of a wider industrial free trade area in hopes of scuttling the proposed EEC.

Introduction

The days are long gone when European integration was described as a self-propelling, functional process or the sole outcome of visionary politics. Yet it is not uncommon to see the history of European integration still explained almost entirely in terms of the (supranational) European ventures of the six countries that formed the European Coal and Steel Community (ECSC). Such accounts usually start with the advent of Marshall aid, the creation of the ECSC in 1951 and the subsequent failure of the European Defence Community and European Political Community in 1954, only to end with the successful conclusion of the Rome Treaty in 1957. This chapter argues that in order to understand the timing, shape and competencies of the EEC, it is necessary to look beyond the efforts undertaken by the six ECSC member states to share and pool sovereignty, and to examine the nature of the trade and payments problems facing European countries both in the worldwide and European contexts. Regional trading institutions emerged partly as a result of the immediate postwar reconstruction problems and partly in reaction to the flaws of the worldwide trade and payments system of the Bretton Woods regime. This system was itself heavily influenced by economic experiences of the interwar period. Although by no means the only considerations, concerns about national economic reconstruction and commercial stability played a vital role in the search for cooperative arrangements throughout the 1940s and 1950s. The successful outcome of the negotiations leading to the signing of the Rome Treaty can largely be attributed to the lessons of earlier successes and failures to secure a stable environment for economic growth and trade expansion, as well as to the fast rate of intra-European trade growth after 1953.

The chapter begins with a short overview of the main international economic events during the pre- and immediate postwar periods that form the backdrop to the institutional setting under examination. It then analyzes the role of the Bretton Woods system, including the General Agreement on Tariffs and Trade (GATT), which aimed at creating worldwide currency convertibility and trade liberalization. The failure of these worldwide multilateral arrangements to secure European reconstruction spurred a preferential approach to trade and payments liberalization, once it became clear that Europe's recovery itself was a prerequisite for the proper functioning of

Table 4.1 Concepts of trade liberalization	
Concept	Features
Multilateral reductions of trade barriers	Trade liberalization within GATT
Preferential reductions of trade barriers	Trade liberalization among a group of countries
Examples:	
1. OEEC's Code of Liberalization	1. Reducing quantitative barriers
2. Free trade area	2. No visible trade barriers among members
3. Customs union	3. Free trade area plus common external trade regime
4. Common market	4. Customs union plus free movement of labour and capital

Source: Asbeek Brusse (1997*b*); Pelkmans (1997); Adapted from Young and Wallace (2000)

multilateral arrangements on a world scale. This is examined in the third section, which focuses in particular on the strengths and weaknesses of trade and payments liberalization within the OEEC and the EPU, and on several national and collective attempts to modify these arrangements to new requirements. The final section of the chapter shows how the common market of the Six emerged from this search for alternatives, as the deficiencies of trade and payments liberalization in existing institutions prompted several countries to find alternative policy arrangements that better suited their interests.

The chapter pays systematic attention to the trade and payments problems facing national governments; the timing and motivation of the cooperative solutions chosen; and the nature (institutional framework, membership, main policy clauses and policy competences) of these solutions. Table 4.1 outlines the major features of relevant concepts of trade liberalization used in the chapter.

Trade and payments before and immediately after World War II

The behaviour of European states in the 1950s trade and payments system was at least in part conditioned by their specific national experiences during the interwar period and the immediate postwar years. Trade imbalances caused by the economic depression of 1929 led most European states to adopt domestic deflation policies. However, once a financial crisis swept across Europe in the summer of 1931, a series of new responses and priorities manifested themselves. Based on their policy reactions, three different groups of counties can be identified. The first, known as the Reichsmark bloc, consisted of Germany and the successor states of the Austria–Hungarian Empire. Facing speculation against their currencies, these states began imposing exchange controls. Intended initially as crisis measures, these were soon integrated into programmes to determine both the size and the direction of foreign trade. The second group centred on the United Kingdom, which, as speculative pressure mounted, resorted to a policy of currency devaluation to save reserves. Because this had the additional effect on trade of making British exports cheaper and imports dearer, it was followed by the Scandinavian and Baltic States, Ireland, and Portugal, whose trade depended on Britain and much of the Commonwealth. As a result, a third group of states (notably the Benelux countries—Belgium, the Netherlands, Luxembourg—France, and Switzerland), which had decided to ride out the speculative wave, found themselves high and dry with overvalued currencies. They responded by raising tariffs and, more importantly, by imposing quantitative trade restrictions, until they too were forced to devalue (in 1935 for Belgium and 1936 for the others). Each group of countries left these policy instruments intact for most of the 1930s, even after the upturn in economic activity. This explains why intra-European trade recovery during the interwar period lagged far behind the recovery in manufacturing output.

The economic depression not only witnessed a panoply of trade and payments barriers but also was accompanied by deliberate attempts to alter the direction flows in goods and money. One noticeable effect was the rediscovery of colonial links. In this respect, the United Kingdom was the most successful. Many of its colonies already formed a currency area with Britain, meaning that they accepted sterling in commercial transactions and also kept their reserves in sterling. Britain deflected trade towards these countries by the use of preferential tariffs, quotas and other incentives, thus reducing uncertainties and the leakage of foreign currency. France, Belgium and the Netherlands followed the same policy, and for much the same reasons. However, the smaller size of their colonial empires meant that the impact was less in terms of the share of total trade.

After World War II, the trade and payments situation was even worse than during the 1930s. The war had destroyed large parts of Europe's production apparatus and infrastructure. It had also reduced capital income from foreign property, destroyed Eastern European grain supplies to Western Europe, and undermined Europe's dollar earnings from trade with Latin America. Immediate needs of reconstruction, the need to repress consumption to allow room for investment, and desperate balance of payments positions (especially in dollars) forced governments to keep in pace the full array of import controls and regional preferences. This situation was aggravated by Allied policies in Germany. Apart from restricting the rate of German output recovery, the Allies had also limited the use of reserves of German currency (or credits) to buy German goods. As European traders would thus lose hard dollars from buying German imports and obtain soft currency from their export sales to Germany, trade with Germany dwindled still further, causing intra-European trade recovery to lag behind the recovery of industrial output. The absence of Germany as the linchpin in Europe's trading network and the major supplier of manufactures meant that Europe rapidly developed a trade deficit with the United States that dwarfed any normal, prewar deficits. In the short run, this gap also widened as most European countries developed ambitious industrialization plans that required high and sustained levels of capital imports and investments.

Postwar approaches to convertibility and liberalization

The postwar institutional architecture for trade and payments known as the Bretton Woods system focused more on lessons from the interwar years than on the emerging problems of the immediate postwar era (Reisman 1997: 82). It was designed to avoid the recurrence of excessive restrictions on trade and payments that were expected to lead to worldwide economic depression and economic nationalism. The monetary system was seen as the key component of the new political and economic order, as governments would not reduce trade barriers if exchange rate policies were still allowed to distort competitive conditions (Gardner 1997: 187). Bretton Woods also reflected American postwar dominance in designing institutional blueprints. Its core was formed by a gold-backed dollar as the world's leading currency, with the International Monetary Fund (IMF) and the International Bank for Reconstruction and Development (better known as the World Bank) functioning as supporting institutions. The IMF was supposed to administer the rules governing currency values and convertibility and to provide supplementary monetary reserves to protect countries with temporary balance of payments deficits against speculative attacks on their currencies. Contrary to British hopes, its reserve funds were modest.

To ensure that currency convertibility would come about, states would in principle have to remove all their existing exchange controls and abstain from any discriminatory currency practices. The Americans had agreed to two main exceptions to this rule. First, the obligation not to impose restrictions was limited to buying and selling currencies to pay for goods and services (current-account transactions); countries remained free to regulate transactions on their capital account. Second, countries were allowed to defer convertibility obligations during a transitional period, which was the case in most European countries after the war.

Immediately after 1945, the United States contributed about $15 billion in *ad hoc* aid to Europe for relief and reconstruction under the auspices of the United Nations Relief and Rehabilitation Administration. In 1947 the IMF and the World Bank finally began to release funds to Europe. This prompted the US Treasury to use its veto powers to insist that money be given only to countries ready to tighten their monetary policy and correct their balance of payments deficits. The IMF thus prescribed a harsh and, to most countries, unacceptable recipe of anti-inflationary policies and currency devaluation to reduce reliance on US aid and to bring countries closer to the post-transitional obligations of Bretton Woods (Kaplan and Schleiminger 1989: 145). Pushed by the US Treasury and the terms of an American loan of $5 billion, Britain made sterling convertible into dollars in May 1947, allowing about 75 per cent of world trade to be conducted in convertible currency. In less than six weeks, sterling convertibility had to be suspended again because the loan was exhausted by European countries' cashing of sterling for dollars. It was not until 1958 that these countries formally introduced currency convertibility on current account.

The postwar discussions on the Havana Charter for the International Trade Organization (ITO), the third key Bretton Woods institution, also illustrated the difficulties of reconciling general aspirations for freer trade and global prosperity with the day-to-day politics of fostering national reconstruction, employment and growth. Nothing demonstrated this better than the negotiations on quotas and employment. While all parties claimed to support the general principle of applying quotas in a non-discriminatory way, most European countries insisted on separate clauses permitting trade discrimination to protect the balance of payments and domestic employment policies. American negotiators had to concede that a multilateral trading system could not be maintained in the face of widespread and protracted unemployment. If domestic stability and worldwide trade liberalization came into conflict, the former would receive priority (Diebold 1997: 155). When the Charter was finally put to a vote, however, it could not satisfy anyone, least of all the US Congress, which eventually rejected it in 1950, leaving the provisional GATT to deal with worldwide tariff negotiations (Diebold 1997: 156).

The vicissitudes of the Bretton Woods system, including the failure of the ITO to come into being, demonstrated the growing discrepancy between wartime planning for a smoothly working international economic order and the messy realities of postwar European recovery. The failed convertibility experiment showed that the sterling crisis and European dollar hunger were intertwined. Within Europe itself, creditor countries such as Belgium and Switzerland had initially been prepared to support the recovery effort by adopting liberal import policies and by granting large export credits. However, as imbalances persisted and as convertibility was delayed, they began refusing credits, insisting on debt repayment and a strict balancing of bilateral trade flows. This pushed trade into even more inefficient channels and threatened to hinder the reconstruction effort (Asbeek Brusse 1997b: 45–6). US State Department officials appreciated the need to change course. As deflationary policies risked undermining the social and political stability of Europe, making it more vulnerable to communist influences, they urged a more realistic foreign policy that accepted European trade and payments discrimination as a stepping stone towards greater economic and political unity in Europe (Vernon 1997: 62). Intra-European trade and payments recovery was seen in Washington as the means of achieving the long-term strategic goal of worldwide trade liberalization and convertibility.

Regional routes

With the announcement of the Marshall Plan in June 1947, US foreign policy shifted decisively from worldwide ambitions to Europe's immediate economic reconstruction problems, as the United States gave priority to a structural programme for military and economic assistance. In the course of 1947 and 1948, Washington agreed that Marshall aid would be allocated to individual countries on the basis of the size of their dollar deficit on foreign trade. By April 1948, the sixteen European nations that had accepted the offer signed the Convention setting up the OEEC, which was responsible for strengthening cooperation among its members and helping them fulfil their international and national programmes. After bitter internal debates and heavy pressure from Congress, the Americans decided that a new agency, the Economic Cooperation Administration (ECA), independent of the State Department and the Treasury, would be in charge of implementing the programme. The United States also insisted that the Europeans had to do much more than draw up (competing) national programmes for spending dollar aid and would have to engage in real efforts to advance closer cooperation among themselves, preferably by creating a customs union based on joint political institutions. Such a development, the Americans hoped, would reconcile the multiple objectives of US policy-making by ensuring a more effective allocation of aid to Europe, transforming Europe into a strong and united economic and military ally and attractive market for US exports and investment, and offering a framework to control Germany's recovery for the benefit of the entire free world. Last but not least, it could be a regional step towards establishing a fully functioning system of worldwide multilateral trade and payments. With that in mind, the Americans pressed Britain and France to take the lead in coordinating efforts for regional cooperation.

The French government had already explored the conditions under which regional projects for integration would satisfy its economic interests. France wanted a controlled environment in which it could safely promote reconstruction and industrialization by expanding production and exports without experiencing cut-throat market competition from its nearest competitors. This almost inevitably meant a customs union with relatively high tariff barriers—directed mainly against Germany. The option of supplanting Germany as Europe's traditional supplier of heavy industry had been the driving force behind French efforts since 1944 to join Benelux, the preferential regional association of Belgium, Luxembourg and the Netherlands. But these efforts had floundered on Benelux's unwillingness to exclude Germany, its main trading partner, from any commercial arrangement. In 1949, when pressed by the Americans to take the lead in Europe (and to allow West Germany's entry at a later stage), the French repeated their advances. This time, the offer was diverted by the Benelux countries and Britain into a study examining the feasibility of a pan-European customs union.

Although the Americans pressed Britain even harder to show leadership in liberalizing European trade and payments, the British kept a low profile. In 1947, the British government concluded that the long-term losses from joining a Europe-wide customs union would be too large, certainly compared to the preferred strategy of maintaining independent leadership within the Commonwealth and upholding a special relationship with the United States. As it was unlikely that the Americans would allow the Commonwealth into a customs union, Britain's trade relations with this area would be destroyed. Even if British trade did not decline, Britain would probably find itself in an emerging economic and political union in which important areas of economic policy would be harmonized. For Britain, such a loss of freedom in policy-making was intolerable. At the same time, however, Britain could not be seen to oppose a customs union, as this would leave the door wide open to French leadership of a continental zone that could be even more damaging to British commercial interests. These considerations prompted the Foreign Office to consider the Western Union, established in 1948 when Britain, France, and the Benelux countries signed the Brussels Treaty, as more than simply a military alliance. For a while, the Western Union, which became the Western European Union in 1955, served as a fallback position for closer economic cooperation with continental Europe as well as a vehicle for joint French–British initiatives within the OEEC (Milward 2002: 33).

When the OEEC was set up, France and Britain had insisted that the organization's ministerial Council take decisions by unanimity and that the implementation of such decisions be left to individual member states. While this struck a blow to Americans hopes for OEEC-led initiatives for political unity, a further disappointed came with the OEEC's failure to make even the slightest progress on the road towards a customs union. With the Marshall Plan already nearing its third year, the US administration used the presentation of its mid-term report to Congress and the voting for Marshall aid as leverage to secure closer cooperation from European governments. By mid-1949, the US administration and the ECA insisted that unless something bold was done in the field of trade liberalization, the continuation of dollar aid would be in jeopardy. If, on the other hand, the Europeans came up with a significant liberalization venture, they could expect extra dollar aid. US pressure eventually bore fruit when Britain proposed a staged removal of quota restrictions (QRs) within the regional framework of the OEEC. Britain sought to expose France's lack of commitment to genuine trade liberalization, to rival France's bid for a customs union with Italy and the Benelux countries and to diffuse any far-reaching American plans for a monetary union (Milward 2002: 39). Having given its qualified approval to the British initiative, the ECA insisted that such a scheme could not run effectively without a working payments system. Thus, solving Europe's payments problems and multilaterally reducing quota restrictions to intra-European trade emerged at the top of the OEEC's agenda and eventually resulted in the EPU and the Code for Liberalization.

The European Payments Union

The Intra-European Payments Agreements in place since 1947 suffered from several defects. They compensated small balances only, provided perverse incentives by their dependence on Marshall aid and remained essentially bilateral in nature because they were tied to bilateral trade agreements. Such trade agreements were not only highly distorting but also inhibited the expansion of European trade. By the end of 1949, therefore, the ECA and the State Department proposed establishing the European Payments Union, under a strong managing board, which they hoped would have enough authority to develop into a laboratory for a future European political entity (Dickhaus 1997: 188). The EPU would pool surpluses and deficits and make OEEC members' currencies automatically transferable up to specific credit limits. Each member country's automatic credit limit was expressed as an initial currency quota, determined on the basis of the estimated value of its foreign trade. All quotas together, plus $350 million funding from Marshall aid, would make up the working capital of the EPU.

Domestically, the ECA had to sell the idea to sceptical officials in the US Treasury, the Federal Reserve and the IMF. It argued that the regional payments scheme would not evolve into a permanent discriminatory arrangement ready to damage American interests by blocking progress towards worldwide convertibility or multilateral trade (Dickhaus 1997: 187; Milward 1992: 349). Internationally, the ECA had to get the British and Belgians on board. An EPU without Britain, Europe's most important trading partner, and sterling, its largest currency, made no sense. Yet Britain had pushed the Trade Liberalization Scheme as a way of forestalling the advent of the clearing union, which it feared would impose unfavourable common payments rules on sterling and would inhibit Britain's worldwide role (Milward and Brennan 1996: 53–5). The failed convertibility experiment of 1947 had shown that such fears were not unfounded. If European creditor countries such as Belgium once again rushed to exchange their accumulated sterling balances for dollars or gold, Britain had to keep its hands free to reimpose QRs and obtain safeguards for sterling. Belgium, in turn, refused to join an arrangement by which it would be forced to provide automatic credit to European debtors.

As a result of these and other issues, the EPU agreement of July 1950 gave Britain guarantees that sterling could be kept to a limited degree as a reserve currency. Existing sterling balances could be used by EPU members to exchange debts among themselves. Sterling balance holders within the EPU could negotiate with Britain the terms for repayments over the two-year duration of the EPU agreement. If the negotiations failed, Britain had another two years before having to repay in dollars or gold. The agreement gave Belgium lower credit obligations than initially proposed, as well as some compensatory direct Marshall aid. More important, Britain and the other European governments obtained concessions from the Americans which limited the authority of the proposed Managing Board, whose seven members could only make recommendations by majority vote, subject to automatic credit settlement rules and to the ultimate responsibility of the OEEC's Council. Any major disagreements would therefore always end up in the Council, where decisions were made on the basis of unanimity (Barbezat 1997: 37).

Quota restrictions

With the EPU agreement in place, the remaining obstacles to formalizing the Trade Liberalization Programme also disappeared. The ensuing Code for Liberalization urged member states to remove QRs to their mutual trade 'as fully as their economic position would permit'. This had to be done in a non-discriminatory way, as the multilateral settlements mechanism of the EPU meant that there were no longer any balance of payments reasons to apply trade discrimination. By October 1950 at the latest, OEEC members would have to remove quotas covering at least 60 per cent of all their intra-European trade. Moreover, a new target was set for an overall liberalization of 75 per cent, to be reached in February 1951, including targets of at least 60 per cent within three separate product groups: food and feeding stuffs; raw materials; and manufactured products. Balance of payments problems and serious economic disturbances were still legitimate reasons for suspending quota liberalization, although countries in such a situation would have to resume liberalization within eighteen months. Moreover, the OEEC could examine whether maintaining these restrictions had been justified and, by using 'peer group pressure', insist on their removal. However, it lacked sanction mechanisms to enforce its decisions.

At the start of the Liberalization Programme in 1949, the ECA had hoped that QRs on intra-European trade would be completely abolished by 1951. This grossly overestimated both the willingness of most member states to relinquish their restrictions and the programme's effectiveness in imposing policy changes. Most countries began by lifting QRs on essential imports such as raw materials and capital goods needed for economic reconstruction. Usually, countries already allowed such products to be imported without any real limitations, other than requiring a licence. By formally declaring these products liberalized and allowing their import without official government licence, countries could easily 'liberalize' in the OEEC's official meaning. Reaching the OEEC's first targets of 50 and 60 per cent was therefore little more than an administrative exercise that had little impact on real levels of quota protection. Only when targets were raised beyond 60 per cent, made non-discriminatory and set *within* product groups did the liberalization exercise bite. That was precisely when progress stagnated. After all, at stake was the entire panoply of QRs aimed at fostering vested producer interests, government-sponsored infant industries, and strategic trade bargaining efforts. Such restrictions had been imposed at various times during the depression in the 1930s, the war years, and the immediate postwar reconstruction effort. Countries needed much more than the threat of losing Marshall aid to dismantle them.

The liberalization method itself had several built-in deficiencies that accentuated governments' dissatisfaction with parts of the programme. At various times during the 1950s these slowed down the pace of intra-European trade liberalization, distorted countries' effective liberalization efforts, and created severe imbalances in their trade gains. One major problem concerned the method for calculating liberalization percentages. A country's official liberalization performance at a given date was expressed as a percentage of the total value of its private imports, thus excluding goods imported on government account. This meant that the formal liberalization percentages of countries whose imports included a large share of state trade (normally subject to fixed quotas to match a government's precise import requirements), usually overstated the real value of imports freed from quota restrictions. Britain, for instance, which was by far the largest potential European market for agricultural exporters, purchased in 1951 more than 35 per cent of the total value of food imports on state accounts (Milward and Brennan 1996: 62). As the OEEC's calculations covered private trade only, Britain's official liberalization percentage for food amounted to 87 per cent. France's overall OEEC percentage of formally liberalized imports trade amounted to over 78 per cent in 1956, yet almost one quarter of the country's total imports were government imports still subject to quota restrictions. Countries with exports unevenly affected by state trade therefore pressed for a different calculation method and insisted on a common list of commodities to be liberalized.

A second major problem concerned the reversibility of national liberalization measures and the limited amounts of credit available under the EPU. In February 1951, the Allied authorities forced West Germany to reimpose quotas after a strong surge in domestic demand coincided with an exceptional delay in the financing of its export income and put Germany into an extreme debtor position within the EPU. Fortunately, Germany soon moved into the role of a structural creditor, but not before the crisis brought the EPU and the OEEC's trade liberalization scheme to the brink of collapse (Dickhaus 1997: 189). In the course of 1951, Britain and France also faced balance of payments problems that forced them to reverse their trade liberalization efforts. Both responded slowly to pressure from their trading partners within the OEEC to remove quotas, France much more so than Britain. The OEEC also failed to put French quota restrictions under formal scrutiny and expose the country's use of quotas for 'hard core protectionism', as the French government simply refused to appear before a panel of experts to justify its position (Asbeek Brusse 1997a: 130). Such high-handedness exposed the vulnerability of countries whose exports and balance of payments situation relied so heavily on unrestricted access to Europe's large economies. It also showed that the OEEC was virtually powerless in the face of stubborn non-compliance to the rules of its liberalization programme.

Yet another deficiency was the Trade Liberalization Programme's virtual silence on tariff protection. It was the OEEC's formal objective to create a single and united European market free from tariffs as well as quotas. However, the British government in particular had insisted early on that tariff matters be left to the GATT. Britain's standard reply to OEEC partners was that meaningful reductions in tariff protection could only be obtained in a worldwide framework, where large trading nations such as itself, the United States, and Canada negotiated comprehensive bilateral tariff bargains, which could then be multilateralized through GATT's most-favoured-nation clause. In fact, Britain considered tariffs not only as useful bargaining chips in negotiations on multilateral free trade and convertibility, but also as indispensable instruments for preserving commercial and political links with the Commonwealth and protecting specific industries from damaging import competition (Asbeek Brusse 1997b: 193–203). The fact that countries such as France, Germany and Italy also reactivated previously suspended tariffs in the wake of the Trade Liberalization Programme showed that Britain was hardly the only country to resort to such measures. Given its eagerness to avoid discussions of a customs union, expose French protectionism, and bring Europe into the one-world system via the OEEC and EPU, Britain frequently faced a difficult dilemma, a point underscored by its persistent conflicts over tariffs within the informal 'Low Tariff Club'. Britain's position ended up holding the entire Liberalization Programme to ransom.

Modifying the OEEC and the EPU

A loose, informal coalition of small, low-tariff European countries such the Benelux countries, Sweden and Denmark had formed on and off since 1949 to press the point that a more balanced distribution of the gains and losses from the Trade Liberalization Programme also required cuts in high tariff barriers. Two main considerations motivated the group. First, being too dependent on cheap imports to use (high) tariffs, those countries had, as a rule, traditionally relied on quotas for protection and trade bargaining. For instance, several sectors in their postwar industrialization programmes depended on so-called infant-industry quotas to provide (temporary) shelter in the face of growing European trade competition. Secondly, by 1951 the small, low-tariff countries had consolidated more than 80 per cent of their tariffs under the GATT. With quotas eventually disappearing, quotas under state trade being exempted under the rules of the Liberalization Programme, and tariffs making a comeback in Europe as a fully accepted commercial policy instrument, they faced a weakening negotiating position while coming under increasing pressure from sheltered domestic producers and export-oriented industries to table tariffs more forcefully and to halt the process of quota liberalization.

Attempts in the early 1950s to change the rules of the programme had all ended in vetoes, usually invoked by either Britain or France. The Netherlands and Denmark had pushed for an enquiry into the use of high tariff barriers that distorted the impact of removing quotas, which Britain, France and Italy blocked. The Netherlands had continued its battle by producing the so-called 'Stikker Plan of Action' only days after French Foreign Minister Robert Schuman made his famous declaration on coal and steel, in May 1950. The Stikker Plan entailed removing quotas, tariffs and state trade in Europe on a sector-by-sector basis. Shortly after having raised their own, formal tariff levels, the Italians produced their own plan (the Pella Plan) to form a European free trade area within the space of ten years by progressively eliminating quotas, reducing tariffs automatically (albeit at a slower pace than suggested by Stikker), liberalizing invisible transactions, and freeing the movement of labour across Europe to solve Italy's problem of excess manpower. The Italians also raised the possibility of establishing a joint European Integration Fund for promoting investments to provide assistance to regions suffering from transitional or structural economic problems (Fauri 1997: 142–3). A third, French proposal—the so-called Petsche Plan—emerged to counter these ideas. This suggested establishing a European Investment Bank to help carry out capital-intensive investments needed to improve Europe's competitiveness towards third countries, in particular the United States. The fact that tariffs were not mentioned suggests that France's priorities were to prepare its domestic firms for increased competitiveness, not to dismantle the protective devices that would assist such a transformation into modern, internationally competitive units (Asbeek Brusse 1997b: 102–3). Britain was hostile to all of these proposals, having publicly committed itself to the Trade Liberalization Programme and to securing adequate tariff protection to maintain what it called 'a reasonable level of protectionism for the general run of . . . industries'.

The possibility of liberalizing intra-European trade in agriculture had first been addressed by France. Its plan for a so-called Green Pool was directed at the members of the Council of Europe, where talks lasted in effect from 1952 to 1955, ending in the creation of a Committee of Agricultural Ministers within the OEEC. From beginning to end, the Netherlands pushed for a supranational common agricultural policy, only finding sympathy for this in France, which was nonetheless unwilling to sacrifice the option of striking bilateral agricultural deals with any of the other OEEC members. Whereas Britain completely opposed any discussion of agricultural trade liberalization, Italy wanted better market access for its agricultural exports by obtaining stricter rules on the application of tariffs and state trade. The other European countries were completely opposed to supranationality or to any other automatic measures that would impinge on their domestic agricultural support.

What kept the talks on agricultural going for so long was the prospect of one or more countries striking preferential agricultural deals with France. As with the OEEC's other trade problems, however, the issue of trade in agriculture was at a stalemate. Moreover, member countries' efforts to boost agricultural production by any domestic policy means could be at the expense of other countries' export positions within OEEC markets. The classic example was Britain, where subsidies to domestic egg producers transformed the country within a decade from a major egg importing country to self-sufficiency, at the expense of other egg exporters. That is why Dutch policy-makers were so insistent on bringing not just frontier measures but all domestic agricultural policies under supranational control. The form and fate of these proposals to solve Europe's trade and agricultural problems prefigured the negotiations for the EEC later in the decade. In the meantime, however, most other policy-makers shifted attention to the issue of balance of payments problems and the future of the EPU.

Like the OEEC, the EPU was considered to be purely transitional. It was supposed to be a two-year arrangement to facilitate Europe's move towards full convertibility. In the end, it would take until December 1958 for most European currencies to become formally convertible into dollars. Why the delay? The EPU's Managing Board concluded by mid-1952 that Europe's economic situation did not warrant a return to convertibility in the very near future. Somewhat later it was forced to revise this conclusion, for two reasons. First, by 1952 there were unmistakable signs of an improvement in Europe's economic situation. Although the trade and payments shocks of 1951–52 still left most governments cautious about the extent and durability of the upswing in production, productivity and trade, it was clear that Europe's overall payments situation was beginning to ease and its dollar gap starting to shrink. Second, these positive economic developments prompted the new Conservative government in Britain to consider introducing sterling–dollar convertibility at a floating exchange rate, and leaving the EPU. By the end of 1952 a secret plan emerged—the so-called Collective Approach to Freer Trade and Convertibility. This aimed at replacing the fixed exchange rates of the Bretton Woods agreement by more flexible ones, setting a wider margin on both sides of the IMF registered par rate and simultaneously introducing dollar and sterling convertibility among a small group of European currencies (Milward and Brennan 1996: 84). The word 'collective' did not refer to a joint plan designed in consultation with its EPU partners; rather, it meant relying on support from Britain's partners in the sterling area, as well as from the United States and the Europeans. Britain asked the Americans to provide a support fund for convertibility through the IMF and adopt a 'good creditor policy', which also involved opening up US domestic markets by cutting the most restrictive import tariffs. The Europeans would have to adopt convertibility according to a British timetable to minimize the risks for sterling (Asbeek Brusse 1997*b*: 108–9; Schenk 1994).

The Americans received the plan early in 1953. American caution reflected an ongoing debate in Washington between the two different conceptions of US foreign economic policy that had emerged at the start of the Marshall Plan, pitting the State Department and the ECA against the Treasury. The former gave priority to developing European economic integration, whereas the latter stressed the urgency of implementing the Bretton Woods system of multilateral trade and payments. In bilateral talks with the British in March 1953, the views of the State Department and ECA seemed to prevail, with the Americans complaining that the early introduction of sterling might disrupt the Trade Liberalization Programme, destroy the EPU, and endanger the highly-sensitive discussions then taking place on the European Defence Community (Asbeek Brusse 1997*b*: 122). Britain retorted that the EPU was 'a nice little working mechanism' that nonetheless failed to offer a worldwide approach to problems (Schenk 1994: 122). Less than a year later, however, after a special bipartisan Commission under the ardent free-trade supporter Clarence Randall had called for expanding world trade under a revised GATT and for reintroducing world wide convertibility, the Treasury view was in the ascendant, thereby reviving British hopes for a more supportive American position.

The Europeans received a softer version of the plan at the OEEC's Council in late March 1953, qualified with British promises of cooperation on the convertibility issue, safeguards to intra-European trade liberalization, the EPU's continuation for yet another year, and even a rise in British official liberalization from 44 to 58 per cent. Still, European reactions were mixed. The loss of the sterling area would significantly reduce the EPU's attractiveness to most members. France's trade and payments transactions in Europe relied very heavily on sterling; the EPU allowed France to run large deficits with the sterling area and with other European countries. Liquidating these arrangements would mean a loss of the EPU's easy credit arrangements and would force France to write off the gold it had already paid to the Union. Italy, whose EPU trade amounted to more than 65 per cent of its total trade, also preferred to continue the clearing arrangement, its balance of payments having been severely hit by the reimposition of British and French import restrictions. Italy therefore called on Britain and France to step up their quota removal and proposed renewing and possibly hardening the EPU provisions for persistent debtors.

Belgium and Germany, both creditors within the EPU, were torn between the financial and trade implications of a move towards convertibility. A year earlier, Belgium had again raised the issue of its extreme creditor position, threatening to leave the EPU unless all surpluses beyond the allocated EPU quotas be settled for 100 per cent in gold and dollars. This was totally unacceptable to debtors such as Britain, the Scandinavian countries, and the Netherlands. It was only after long negotiations that Belgium agreed to a compromise that solved the crisis and opened the way for another one-year renewal of the EPU agreement. Under the circumstances, the British proposal to restore convertibility had the advantage of allowing EPU credits to pay for dollar imports. However, by 1953 Belgium decided that for the moment its main interest still lay in preserving the existing system, as more than 60 per cent of its exports went to EPU partners. Convertibility would therefore have to be obtained using an institutional approach aimed at hardening the rules by gradually increasing the gold/credit ratio and repaying debts (Dickhaus 1997: 192).

The German government made a similar assessment, although not unanimously. The foreign ministry considered that Germany's reliance on EPU export markets was too large to risk breaking up the EPU and causing trade stagnation. By contrast, Economics Minister Ludwig Erhard believed that Germany's economic future lay in reducing its narrow dependence on European markets and in expanding towards overseas markets in South America, Africa, and the Commonwealth. Therefore he strongly advocated a speedy move towards convertibility and worldwide tariff reductions within the GATT.

Despite speculations about its imminent demise and almost permanent German threats to leave the EPU, the agreement was renewed annually until 1958, with its credit terms modified to increase the gold/credit ratio. These year-on-year renewals resulted partly from the change in economic circumstances during 1955, when the system began to suffer from heavy disequilibria. France and Britain experienced large balance of payments problems and saw their debtor position increase at an alarming rate. After the ill-fated French and British intervention in Suez in October 1956, both sterling and the franc came under heavy pressure. Ironically, this led to a dependence on German credits that allowed Germany successfully to push for an increase in the gold/credit ratio in exchange for gold loans to the EPU, which in turn enabled it to provide extra individual grants. European countries were thus caught in their own convertibility trap; as the system hardened, disciplining creditors became imperative, whereas softening the credit terms implied a step back on the road towards full convertibility. Eventually, the European countries 'escaped' this trap after the British balance of payments situation improved at the end of 1957 and Britain took the lead in the move towards convertibility (Dickhaus 1995: 90–1).

Creating the common market

Throughout the 1950s, the Netherlands was in the vanguard of countries trying to amend the OEEC's trading rules and decision-making procedures. The Dutch had failed to obtain majority voting in the OEEC's Council as well as an opt-out clause for countries unable or unwilling to join tariff and quota removal within a particular sector. They had also realized that approaches through sectoral integration or product lists were likely to fragment rather than integrate European markets by creating overlapping preferential zones in Europe with differential membership. Neither integration by sector nor trade liberalization within the OEEC would therefore provide secure and long-term access to Europe's—and especially Germany's—burgeoning export markets. What the Dutch began to envisage was a solid commitment in advance by a more limited group of European countries to form a customs union. They used the discussions in 1953 for a European Political Community to push the so-called Beyen Plan for a supranational customs union among the Six with an automatic timetable for removing internal trade barriers, supranational institutions being necessary for the enforcement of collective decisions and for arbitration. Thus, they felt, participating countries would avoid the kind of stalemate that the Trade Liberalization Programme (and the Benelux customs union) so frequently faced. Moreover, having suffered the earlier failure to create an OEEC-wide supranational customs union, the Americans were likely to lend a renewed effort their full support, even though the ensuing arrangements could solidify trade discrimination against American exports and give the Europeans strong bargaining chips in future GATT negotiations.

Formally, the collapse of the European Defence Community (EDC) in August 1954 brought down the European Political Community and with it the Beyen Plan. Informally, the other prospective participants had rejected the plan as too rigid and ill-timed to accommodate their interests. Several factors explain this. First, the French cabinet that came to power in early 1953 was cool towards the idea of supranationality and also faced severe economic difficulties. Earlier, France had suspended its quota liberalization commitments within the OEEC because of a rapidly deteriorating external position that reflected the weak competitive position of French industry and triggered a search among industrialists and politicians for a new national economic strategy. Under the circumstances, the French government saw very little point in joining a rigid, predetermined scheme for creating a customs union that lacked any escape clauses or provisions for economic and social policy coordination.

Second, a mere customs union also failed to satisfy the other potential participants. Italy insisted on obtaining full labour mobility among the Six in order to 'export' excess labour, whereas Belgium and West Germany wanted full capital mobility. They also argued that the only way to guarantee internal trade liberalization from coming about and to prevent France from constantly invoking escape clauses would be to introduce far-reaching economic policy coordination. The discussions during 1953 and 1954 on the customs union nevertheless provided valuable insights into the feasibility of future attempts at economic integration. Automatic, time-fixed and complete liberalization of trade in goods alone clearly could not satisfy all six ECSC members. Provisions for the free movement of labour and capital as well as other flanking policies might be necessary as well. This raised the possibility of a common market that went beyond trade liberalization to include also the removal of barriers to labour, capital and services. However, as seen in Chapter 5, virtually everything hinged on France's ability and willingness to join.

What motivated the Benelux countries to take the lead so quickly after the EDC's failure? It is often argued that the federalists' disappointment with the demise of the EDC prompted committed pro-Europeans like Belgian Foreign Minister Paul Henri Spaak to table new proposals for integration. This is a very small part of the story. Indeed, Spaak discussed the feasibility of sectoral communities and a customs union with Jean Monnet. Both believed that France would reject a customs union but could perhaps be tempted to play a leading role in a supranational nuclear energy community. However, without the Dutch there could not be a joint memorandum. Having made their modified customs union proposal a precondition of their support for any new initiative, the Dutch insisted that Spaak present a joint memorandum calling for a customs union as well as Monnet's preferred atomic energy community. The Belgians in any case were eager to table a commercial initiative, in response to warming bilateral relations between France and Germany.

Having resolved the contentious questions of German rearmament (through membership in the Western European Union) and jurisdiction over the Saar (through a resumption of German control), France and Germany launched a number of ambitious initiatives. These ranged from talks on joint investment projects in French North Africa, to an agreement to canalize the Mosel river, to improvements in cross-border trade. Benelux producers, who had never really managed to penetrate French colonial markets, which were heavily protected by preferential quotas, subsidies and exchange controls, now looked aghast as France and Germany discussed possible trade and investment cooperation in French overseas territories. At the same time, mutual trading deals boosted French exports into Germany, possibly to the detriment of exports from the Benelux countries. Agriculture was a further source of worry. After the failure to solve the agricultural issue within the Green Pool talks and the OEEC, France and Germany in January 1955 concluded a preferential agreement allowing France to sell parts of its wheat surplus to Germany (Asbeek Brusse 1997b; Lynch 1997). The Benelux countries would be quite content if improved Franco–German relations benefited all of Western Europe. If France increasingly ignored 'Europe' by using bilateral channels, however, the Benelux countries could easily lose out

(Griffiths 1995*b*: 29). Such considerations strengthened Benelux determination to play the European commercial card.

Negotiating the Treaty of Rome

A number of issues in the ensuing negotiations for the new European communities stand out. One is the link between the proposed common market and the atomic energy community. France strongly supported the atomic energy community from the start of the talks, but was equivocal about the common market throughout the negotiations. It was clear that the French government was extremely reluctant to abandon its arsenal of protective regulatory policy measures such as export subsidies, import taxes, quota restrictions, and multiple exchange rates for fear of exposing industry too quickly to external competition. In an effort to overcome French reluctance, the German government actively used the leverage of the nuclear community (known in Germany as the so-called 'Junktim') once it was clear that the new French government of Guy Mollet was seriously interested in the customs union. Having conceded the establishment of the atomic energy community as part of the deal for the economic community, the former became somewhat of a sideshow and the Cinderella of European integration.

There is little evidence that the Suez crisis of October 1956 played a decisive role in the French decision to acquiesce in a customs union. Backed by French industrial and agricultural pressure groups, the Mollet government stipulated fairly detailed conditions for joining the customs union well before the crisis. These included the requirement of a unanimous decision by the Council of Ministers in order to move from the first to the second transitional phase of the customs union; harmonization of social charges; inclusion of the French overseas territories within the customs union; and permission to maintain tariffs and export subsidies for balance of payments reasons. Moreover, France demanded a temporary exceptional status in case of balance of payments problems, allowing it to enjoy all the benefits from internal trade liberalization by the union's member states without itself having to impose such measures. Mollet and German Chancellor Konrad Adenauer announced a compromise on these issues at a meeting in October 1956, the outlines of which had already been agreed. The aftermath of the Suez crisis did contribute to a sense of urgency among the negotiators, however, due to fears that the pro-European French government might not be around much longer, thereby hastening efforts to conclude and ratify the treaty. This rush to reach an agreement explains the odd combination of detail and vague formulations in the treaty. The agricultural clauses provide a good illustration: as seen in Chapter 9, time pressure and fundamental disagreement on the form and the level of agricultural protection resulted in largely procedural provisions, which merely stated that the 'common market for agriculture must be accompanied by the establishment of a common agricultural policy'. The treaty assigned responsibility for designing such a policy to the European Commission.

The customs union lies at the heart of the common market. Its highly detailed provisions on tariffs and quotas (certainly compared to the minimalist references to the provisions on the free movement of labour, services and capital) reflected the preoccupations of policy-makers at the time and the need to pay lip-service to GATT requirements on customs unions (Pelkmans 1997: 62). The customs union would be created in three successive steps of four years each, covering the removal of tariffs on intra-EEC trade and the establishment of a common external tariff. The treaty option of a three-year overrun of the scheduled transitional period of twelve years suggests that its designers planned for the eventuality of a temporary economic setback. They certainly did not foresee the economic boom of the 1960s that would actually allow the customs union to be created ahead of schedule, in July 1968. The new common tariff schedule was calculated in advance, but time pressure meant that some particularly problematic items were put on a separate list (the so-called list G), whose precise common tariff would be calculated after the treaty was signed. Interestingly, over 80 per cent of the items on this list covered chemical products, which earlier in the 1950s had been the cause of OEEC skirmishes between low- and high-tariff countries.

Provisions for the internal removal of quota restrictions reflected recent OEEC and GATT experiences. First, the treaty called for the simultaneous removal of quotas and tariffs among the member states. Second, quota removal also covered state trade and agriculture. Third, by the end of the transitional period all discrimination with regard to imports, domestic procurement and marketing or distribution had to be abolished. Fourth, just as in the case of tariffs, the irreversibility of quota removal was guaranteed by a combination of automaticity (based on specified liberalization percentage targets and timetables), across-the-board coverage instead of discretion, and a ban on the unilateral reimposition of quotas. Fifth, again just as in the case of tariffs, 'measures with an equivalent effect' to quotas were also banned.

Steps for the creation of the common external quota regime were also laid out in detail. After the first year, any remaining bilateral quotas had to be opened up to all other member states. Quotas then had to be enlarged in overall value by 20 per cent annually and at least 10 per cent per product. After ten years all quotas had to equal a minimum of 20 per cent of national production of the relevant product, and after the end of the transitional period all quota restrictions had to be eliminated (Pelkmans 1997). Supranational oversight of the common market was embodied in the European Commission's monitoring role over market integration and sole right of initiative across a range of policy areas, as well as in the European Court of Justice's rulings.

Crucially, the treaty's voting procedures for the decision to progress to the next stage of the customs union were closely linked to the special provisions for France and to the agricultural issue. At French insistence, the decision to proceed from the first to the second stage of the customs union would be taken by a unanimous vote in the Council of Ministers. Failing that, the first stage could twice be extended for a year, implying that in the worst case only after six years would the Council shift to voting by qualified majority. The same treaty article contained a key provision on agriculture, which stipulated that progress through the stages of the customs union was conditional upon equivalent progress in agriculture (Griffiths 1995b: 52). This encapsulated the principle that equivalent access to industrial and agricultural markets was a crucial part of the EEC's package deal, which would later strengthen the Commission's position against Germany's opposition to a common agricultural policy. At the same time, it implied that the Commission's proposals for such a policy needed member states' unanimous approval in the Council and that France could always fall back on bilateral agricultural deals with Germany if the Commission's proposals were not to its liking.

Apart from the articles on the customs union, the treaty contained a large set of separate clauses that provided extra flexibility and/or extra compensations compared to the original customs union proposed in the Beyen Plan. Together these formed crucial elements of the package deal that secured the final agreement for the treaty establishing the EEC, signed in Rome on 25 March 1957. Many critics of the treaty within Germany and the Netherlands nevertheless refused to see a common market of the Six as their final aim. They became ardent supporters of Britain's efforts to join a wider free trade area with the remaining OEEC countries.

Britain and the wider free trade area

Although the Six accounted for more than half of Western Europe's foreign trade and production, a formidable and sophisticated European market remained outside the EEC's orbit, including those OEEC countries with which the Six shared a common experience of trade and payments liberalization and growing economic interdependence. Both inside and outside the Six, awareness of that fact motivated the search for trade arrangements to encompass a larger membership. Among the Six, Germany had strong export interests in the Scandinavian countries, Austria, and Switzerland. It also had Erhard, a vocal minister of economic affairs, who stressed German exporters' ambitions and opportunities on the world market and who criticized the Six as too inward-looking, protectionist, and *dirigiste*. In the Netherlands, too, there were widespread misgivings about membership in a customs union that excluded Britain, its largest trading partner outside the Six, and that would adopt a common external tariff that on average exceeded the existing Benelux tariff. Outside the framework of the Six, Denmark, Sweden, and Switzerland had been part of the *ad hoc* coalition of OEEC countries pushing for tariff reduction. More importantly, by 1956 Britain had begun to explore ways to neutralize the impact of the seemingly discriminatory bloc, preferably by steering it towards the OEEC.

At the insistence of the Benelux countries, Britain had been invited to attend the landmark Messina meeting of June 1955, which had kick-started the process of European integration. Britain's initial response was lethargic (Milward 2002: 200). The government saw no reason to change its earlier position towards a customs union. With 13 per cent of British exports in 1956, the Six were Britain's single largest export market. British exporters could presumably increase their market share if such exports faced no trade barriers, although it was doubtful if they were competitive enough to make further inroads into Germany's fast-growing domestic market. The share of British exports going to the four largest, admittedly slower-growing Commonwealth markets was more than double that towards the Six, and another 7 per cent of total exports went to the United States. The British government therefore responded cautiously. While it did not want to be excluded from a large, fast-growing continental market, Britain saw major disadvantages in the Benelux proposal, which would limit the country's right to set its own tariffs and disrupt relations with its traditional trading partners. Britain would also be unable to continue giving preferential treatment to Commonwealth import commodities. As a result, some 20 per cent of British exports would probably experience a loss or elimination of reciprocal preferential treatment in Commonwealth markets (Milward 2002: 199). Moreover, Britain would experience increases in agricultural prices as it would no longer be able to maintain low food prices through duty free imports of Commonwealth produce. Beyond these economic calculations, the Commonwealth was also seen as an integral part of Britain's heritage, an exemplar of worldwide responsibilities and of Britain's claim to world power status. Any government, whether Conservative or Labour, would find it difficult publicly to distance itself from the Commonwealth in favour of the Six (Griffiths and Ward 1996: 10).

British officials initially presumed that the Messina process would collapse of its own accord without any interference from London, thereby allowing Britain to pick up the pieces, take over the initiative and lead the Six back on to the safe track of the OEEC. When that did not happen, British officials begin to look for an alternative policy. After a considerable period of soul-searching, they came up with the initiative for a wider industrial free trade area (FTA) among OEEC members. It involved eliminating all quotas and tariffs on intra-OEEC trade but left open the option of preferential access for Commonwealth exports. It also left existing protection for agriculture intact. The timing of this initiative was hardly fortunate: the Six having just entered the final, decisive phase of their common market negotiations. The fact that Britain launched its initiative in the OEEC, just before the OEEC was due finally to examine the issue of tariff disparities, did not help either. Understandably, the Six saw Britain's move as a cheap and transparent attempt to sidetrack the Messina process and the low-tariff club initiative (Asbeek Brusse 1997b: 172–3; Griffiths and Ward 1996: 11). Nevertheless, when presented with the plan in February 1957, the OEEC's Council created three working parties under British chairmanship to study the matter.

Among the Six, the Dutch and Germans were the most ardent supporters of linking the EEC and the wider industrial FTA, fearful as they were of being locked up in a high-cost, protectionist club. Yet even they saw the FTA only as a complement, not an alternative, to the common market of the Six. Moreover, their support was not enough to secure an agreement. France proved to be outright hostile towards the proposal, which failed to provide the carefully designed common policies that made the EEC such an attractive, controlled environment for French industrialists and farmers. Eventually, France successfully united the Six around its negative position, and the British proposal was rejected in November 1958.

Conclusion

The struggle in the late 1940s and 1950s to create preferential European trade and payments arrangements reflected the failure of the existing worldwide multilateral system to secure European reconstruction. Indeed, Europe's rehabilitation itself became a prerequisite for the proper functioning of multilateral arrangements on a world scale. The OEEC and the EPU had been helpful at first in assisting Europe's trade growth and in preventing debtor crises, such as that in Germany in 1951, from spreading. As Europe's production and trade began to expand faster after 1953, the degree, speed and commitment with which countries opened up their domestic markets to each other's exports remained very uneven under the Trade Liberalization Programme, which allowed most states to keep sizeable parts of their domestic industries sheltered from foreign competition. Moreover, there were no hard mechanisms in place to prevent countries from reintroducing trade and payments barriers in times of economic recession.

The shape, timing, and origins of the various proposed alternatives to, and modifications of, the existing arrangements suggest that such proposals were motivated by a wide range of national considerations. France's early proposal for a small European customs union, for instance, was mainly designed to strengthen its political and economic weight *vis-à-vis* Germany. When this strategy failed and Germany's full economic recovery seemed imminent, France put forward the Schuman Plan. The Dutch integration initiative, inspired by the Schuman Plan, sought to preserve the position of strong Dutch export industries in the German market while leaving other industries temporarily protected. The problems with trade liberalization within the OEEC and the GATT gradually drove the Benelux countries towards proposing a supranational customs union for market integration. By combining internal free trade with outward protection, such a union would offer a compromise between the economic interests of relatively open and relatively closed European countries. What mattered most politically, however, were the sequencing and tempo of internal trade liberalization and the availability of common policies (including the common external tariff) to mitigate potentially disruptive effects. Most countries were not prepared to join schemes for automatic internal trade liberalization without sufficient escape clauses and compensatory policy arrangements. Discussions of the Beyen Plan in the early 1950s were a learning process that greatly contributed to the successful outcome of the EEC negotiations later in the decade. By negotiating a package deal that went beyond a traditional customs union, the Six eventually satisfied French needs and anchored Germany's economy into the common market.

Further reading

There are relatively few histories of the trade and payments dimensions of early European integration. A good starting point is Griffiths (ed.) (1997), which covers the period 1945–60 from an OEEC-wide perspective. The two volumes by Milward (1984 and 1992) provide thought-provoking criticism of orthodox views on European integration. Asbeek Brusse (1997) links the multiple locations of European trade governance (in the OEEC, EPU, Council of Europe, EEC, etc.) to the global level (of transatlantic relations, GATT etc). Kaplan and Schleiminger (1989) examine the EPU context, whereas Kirshner (ed.) (1997) offers the GATT perspective. Two other useful collections of archive-based research are the volumes edited by Trausch (1993) and Serra (1989), which contain thematic and single-country approaches. Trausch deals with integration efforts during 1951–5, and Serra covers the Treaty of Rome negotiations.

Asbeek Brusse, W. (1997), *Tariffs, Trade and European Integration, 1947–1957: From Study Group to Common Market* (New York: St. Martin's Press).

Griffiths, R. T. (ed.) (1997), *Explorations in OEEC History* (Paris: OECD).

Kaplan, J. and Schleiminger, G. (1989), *The European Payments Union: Financial Diplomacy in the 1950s* (Oxford: Clarendon Press).

Kirshner, O. (ed.) (1997), *The Bretton Woods – GATT System: Retrospect and Prospect after Fifty Years* (New York: M.E. Sharpe).

Milward, A. S. (1984), *The Reconstruction of Western Europe, 1945–51* (London: Methuen).

Milward, A. S. (1992), *The European Rescue of the Nation State* (London: Routledge).

Trausch, G. (ed.) (1993), *Die Europäische Integration vom Schuman-Plan bis zu den Verträgen von Rom: Pläne und Initiativen, Enttäuschungen und Misserfolge (European Integration from the Schuman Plan to the Treaties of Rome: Projects and Initiatives, Disappointments and Failures)* (Baden-Baden: Nomos Verlag).

Serra, E. (ed.) (1989), *Il Rilancio dell'Europa e i Trattati di Roma: La Relance Européenne et les traités de Rome (The Relaunching of Europe and the Treaties of Rome)* (Brussels: Bruylant).

Websites

An annotated collection of historical documents and other resources, including photographs and sound clips, are available at the University of Leiden's site on EU History–History of European Integration: http://www.eu-history. leidenuniv.nl/index.php3?m=10&c=11&garb=0.40408187313677024&session=.

The so-called European Navigator at http://www.ena.lu/mce.cfm offers a multi-media website with an extensive range of articles, treaties, maps, photographs and soundclips.

Chapter 5

The Triumph of Community Europe

Craig Parsons

Contents

Summary

'Community Europe'—the organization of economic cooperation along supranational lines—triumphed in the 1950s over two alternatives that might have been equally viable: 'confederal' and 'traditional' models of international cooperation. The triumph of community Europe in France, the key political battleground in postwar Europe, was due to strong leadership and the formation of powerful coalitions on other issues that resulted in majority support in the National Assembly for the European Coal and Steel Community (ECSC) in the early 1950s and the European Economic Community (EEC) in the late 1950s. By contrast, the outcome of domestic elections and coalition-building in the mid-1950s was inimicable to ratification of the treaty establishing the European Defence Community (EDC). Regardless of objective structural imperatives or alleged spill-over from one area of sectoral integration to another, it was the consistent ideological crusade of an elite minority, filtered through an unrelated process of domestic coalition-building, that set France and Europe on the path of supranationality.

Introduction

In the 1950s and early 1960s, Western Europe adopted a regional format that has since made it increasingly unique in international relations. Beginning with the ECSC proposed in 1950, the 'community' projects of that decisive decade created unprecedented supranational institutions at the regional level. With the implementation of the much broader EEC in the early 1960s, the supranational community format was consolidated as the core architecture of postwar Europe. From that point of departure—already the most substantial instance of voluntary international institution-building in history—Western European countries delegated more and more power to the regional level, effectively creating a new category of polity, culminating in today's European Union (EU).

Why did Western Europe give rise to such unique regional institutions in the 1950s? As seen in Chapter 14, two answers dominate EU scholarship. For 'structuralists' like Andrew Moravcsik and Alan Milward, the community project responded to objective structural imperatives (Moravcsik 1998; Milward 1992). Various patterns of international interdependence were particularly acute in postwar Europe, encouraging societal groups, their political representatives, and government bureaucrats to seek particular internationalized solutions to a variety of policy challenges. For 'institutionalists' in the tradition of Ernst Haas, structural imperatives may have driven initial postwar institution-building, but subsequent steps were heavily path-dependent. Once some power was delegated to supranational agents in the ECSC in 1952, those agents crafted new projects and mobilized coalitions to extend supranational institutions. Such 'spill-over' carried Europe on to the EEC Treaty in 1957, and later to the EU (Haas 1958; Sandholtz and Stone Sweet 1998).

This chapter argues that both approaches overlook the range and historical strength of alternatives to a community-model Europe, and so mischaracterize why it emerged victorious. Postwar structural conditions may have generated widely-perceived incentives to European cooperation, but similarly-placed actors consistently disagreed over the appropriate format for that cooperation. Institutional path-dependence helped consolidate the contested EEC institutions after 1958, but there is practically no evidence of spill-over from the ECSC to the EEC. Instead, the triumph of the community model is a much more contingent story. Only a scattered minority of European elites advocated supranational institutions as the solution to many European problems. They confronted equally well-supported elites who advanced less revolutionary alternatives—'confederal' and 'traditional' plans for European cooperation. Only because advocates of the community model episodically achieved national power through support *on other issues* did they gain the authority to strike deals and the leverage to rally reluctant majorities behind them. Europe took a supranational path only because aggressively integrationist leaders used a series of *faits accomplis* to resolve a wide battle over alternative Europes.

The key battleground was France. All accounts agree that the institutionally strong, geographically limited EEC came about above all because the French government demanded it. Though internal arguments over community, confederal, and traditional alternatives took place in Germany and the Benelux countries,

their governments ultimately preferred broader and weaker institutional options—mainly to include the British, who flatly rejected any supranational format.
It was French insistence on a community Europe that forced Germany, the Benelux
countries and Italy to choose supranationality over cooperation with sovereignty-
conscious Britain. The central goal of this chapter is to show that this French
demand resulted from aggressive, unrepresentative leadership, not clear structural
imperatives or institutional constraints. Due to domestic elections and coalition-
building that operated on unrelated (mainly right–left) issues, community-minded
individuals gained power in the early 1950s and struck the ECSC deal; lost power
in 1952–4 and so lost the battle for the EDC and unexpectedly regained control in
1956–7, resulting in the EEC Treaty. Thus the consistent ideological crusade of an
elite minority, filtered through an unrelated process of domestic coalition-building,
set France and Europe on their unique regional path.

The battle begins: competing models of Europe

The massive environmental changes of World War II made 'Europeanist' ideas
broadly salient by 1945–6, but the real political battle over the format of European
cooperation only emerged with the outbreak of the cold war. The rise of the
superpowers, the destruction of national economies, and delegitimation of the nationalist far right turned old utopian musings about European federalism into active discussions as the postwar era opened. Older ideas survived as well, however,
and the meaning of 'federalism' was initially so vague as to be meaningless. Thus
when the development of the cold war put the first serious pressure on several
countries—above all France—to develop a new policy of European cooperation,
political elites did not simply shift *en masse* to advocacy of a supranational Europe. Instead they began to diverge around a wholly new political cleavage about European
institution-building.

   This new cleavage emerged most sharply in France because of the utter failure
of early French postwar plans. French elites initially shared a wide consensus on
their basic postwar goal: to perpetuate German weakness while rebuilding French
strength. Their means were direct controls on occupied Germany, bolstered by alliances and economic cooperation with other European powers. As tensions with the
Soviet Union increased, however, the Americans demanded the rapid revival of a
West German state as a bulwark and ally against the Soviets. Pressure on France increased with the Marshall Plan in June 1947, which offered badly-needed economic
aid on condition that France coordinate its recovery with Germany and other countries (Lundestad 1998; Milward 1984). The London Accords of June 1948 confirmed the
creation of the new West Germany, and the failure of French policies. As Milward
writes, for France, 'The inevitable moment of choice had arrived' (1984: 157). But that
choice would not be an obvious one.

Streams of thought

Despite their failures, some French elites continued to defend traditional strategies. They retained a familiar *realist* analysis of the European scene, with legitimacy and security located in the independent nation state. Although the attempt to block Germany's recovery had been frustrated, traditional options remained. Some direct controls on Germany could be salvaged; military and economic alliances with other powers could still be sought; if necessary, bilateral deals could even be struck with the Germans themselves. All would uphold the balance of European power, protecting French interests better than uncontrollable international organizations. Such a strategy was also more worthy of 'Great Power' France, whose independence was sacrosanct, and whose peers were Britain, the Soviet Union and the United States—not other European countries.

But other French elites soon began to advocate 'confederal' strategies. They based their analysis on *liberal* thinking: the nation state remained the source of legitimacy and security, but like-minded states should cooperate closely given their interdependence. France's natural partner was her liberal sister, Britain; together they would preside over pragmatic cooperation in broad European fora, while supervising the illiberal, atavistic Germans. Only combined Franco–British leadership would prevent the Germans from dominating Europe—ruling out narrower Franco–German projects. Broad but weak organizations could provide a platform for a European 'third way' between the superpowers, and for economic cooperation, without requiring direct losses of French sovereignty.

Still other elites soon began to call for a more radical departure from standard diplomacy, advocating 'community' strategies. Their analysis drew on *functionalist* thinking: legitimate policies were those that best provided welfare. Two world wars and the rise of the superpowers showed that European welfare required more than the nation state. Only new 'supranational' institutions, partly independent from governments, could lead fractious Europe to peace and prosperity. In particular, weak intergovernmental accords could not hold the Germans down. In order to make such control acceptable to the Germans, however, France would have to submit to it as well. This might entail a break with the British, who abhorred supranationality. Thus a supranational solution meant forsaking the security of Franco–British balancing against Germany. But the result could be real 'integration', leading to a 'United States of Europe' as powerful and rich as the United States of America.

If these models divided most clearly around the 'German Problem', as outlined in Chapter 3, their key difference was not pro- or anti-Germanism. Some traditionalists soon proved quite willing to deal bilaterally with Germany. Some non-traditionalists arrived at confederal or community strategies out of visceral fear of Germany unfettered. Instead, the fundamental distinctions among French elites concerned the 'master frame' linking France itself and its European environment. Protagonists in the debate suggested different 'constitutive rules' about France as a player in a European game (Ruggie 1998: 855–85; Searle 1995). Each side packaged a set of normative and causal claims that defined France's position *vis-à-vis* her neighbours.

Crucially, these different views of Europe had no direct connection to the right–left cleavage that dominated French politics. Each model's constitutive rules

were general enough to link to various lower-level 'regulative rules'. Political actors (except for the Communists) could picture the competing models—traditionalist,
confederal, and community—as either advancing or impeding goals across both left
and right. For the left, a supranational community could undo conservative legacies
at the national level—or mean capitulation to the German *Konzerns*. For the right,
supranational integration could open France to broader markets—or emasculate
national strength and identity. Since right, left, and centre had their realists, prag-
matists, idealists, Anglophiles, and even Germanophiles, domestic political allies
gravitated to different European strategies. Some sought to mobilize coalitions in
favour of community projects; others in the same parties and bureaucracies called
for confederal or traditional alternatives.

The parting of the ways: the ECSC

The early debate about these contending models, from 1948 to 1950, was quite inco-
herent. Only with the first serious proposal for a community project—the Schuman
Plan of May 1950—did positions crystallize. The battle lines were soon drawn around
the French foreign minister's call for France, Germany, and other countries to pool
their coal and steel industries under independent 'supranational' institutions.

Structural accounts present the Schuman Plan as a direct response to clear imperatives. Geopolitically, it would initiate Franco–German reconciliation while giving France oversight of Germany's nascent foreign policy, while responding to US
pressure for European collaboration. Economically, it would secure long-term access
to German coal and supervision of German heavy industry. These obvious advantages cast the ECSC as the 'rational' French strategy (Hitchcock 1998: 10; Milward
1984: 380).

This orthodoxy overlooks actual French reactions to the proposal, however. Rather
than reflecting clear preferences within parties, interest groups or bureaucracies,
Schuman's self-described 'leap in the dark' provoked a deeply divided response.
Early support was weakly scattered across Schuman's diverse 'Third Force' coalition,
which allied the full range of pro-parliamentary parties—from the conservative Independents, to Schuman's Christian Democrats, to the centrist Radicals and Union
Démocratique et Socialiste de la Résistance (UDSR), to the Socialists—against the
Communists and Gaullists who, for different reasons, wanted to alter the Fourth Republic's parliamentary institutions. Only about a third of the majority saluted the
plan, including major figures in each party: a third of the sixty-seven Independents, around Paul Reynaud and Antoine Pinay; perhaps fifty of the 166 Christian
Democrats, behind François de Menthon and Pierre Pflimlin; a score of the fifty-
two centrists, such as René Mayer and René Pleven; and another twenty of the
128 Socialists, around André Philip and Gérard Jacquet. Schuman also drew support from some prominent bureaucrats, like Hervé Alphand, a senior diplomat,
and Jean Monnet, head of the plan for economic modernization and author of the
Schuman Plan.

Concerns and criticisms

The other two-thirds of the majority, the opposition, most high officials, and all interest groups, criticized Schuman's proposal. About one-third of the coalition voiced confederal concerns, supporting coal and steel cooperation but fearing supranationality and partnership with Germany. They favoured plans within two weak organizations under Franco–British direction, the Organization for European Economic Cooperation (OEEC) or the Council of Europe. They counted close to half of Schuman's own Christian Democratic Party, including Prime Minister Georges Bidault, party head Maurice Schuman, and Secretary of State for Economic Affairs Robert Buron; at least a third of the Independents, most notably Finance Minister Maurice Petsche; a similar portion of centrists like Pierre Mendès France (Radical) and Édouard Bonnefous (UDSR); and perhaps 70 Socialists (Callot 1986; Criddle 1969; Delwit 1995: 61–4; O'Neill 1981; Poidevin 1984: 73–97; Soutou 1991: 267–306). Ministers Petsche and Buron even initiated secret talks with the British about replacing the ECSC with OEEC plans. Similar critiques arose across the bureaucracy. Alphand's deputy in the Foreign Ministry's economic division, Olivier Wormser, joined Finance Ministry officials to try to shunt coal and steel discussions into the OEEC (Bossuat 1992: 752). These officials saw 'Britain as France's irreplaceable partner against Germany ... [and] tended to regard community with Germany as suicidal or a betrayal of France's great-power prerogatives' (Duchêne 1994: 206). Ambassador René Massigli later wrote:

> From the moment when Jean Monnet rallied Robert Schuman to the idea of European federalism, to which the supranational system he invented was meant to lead, I fought tirelessly for the victory of a confederal conception to which it would be possible, with time, to rally Great Britain; I could not conceive Europe without Great Britain. (Massigli 1978: 212–21)

Approximately another third of the majority, some bureaucrats, the opposition and interest groups attacked Schuman with traditional arguments. They wanted to defend the Occupation coal and steel arrangement, the International Authority for the Ruhr (IAR). Renegotiation was to be avoided, as it would necessarily upgrade German status. A dozen Christian Democrats, such as Léo Hamon and André Denis, like their close associates among the Gaullists, denounced any retreat from occupation controls. They were joined by the remaining twenty Independents behind Louis Marin and Pierre André, a similar number of Radicals behind the influential Édouard Daladier, and about twenty Socialists like Defence Minister Jules Moch and French President Vincent Auriol. Officials under Alphand in the Foreign Ministry were similarly preparing a new push to expand the IAR's powers in May 1950 (Milward 1984: 388). The least divided section of the government were the officials responsible for coal and steel in the Ministry of Industry, who closely echoed the traditional views of coal and steel firms and the broader employers' association, the Conseil National du Patronat Français. The interest groups flatly opposed being subjected to supranational authorities, feared competition with the Germans, and wanted to retain the IAR (Ehrmann 1954; Poidevin 1988: 105–15).

Critics of the Schuman Plan had good reason to think that confederal or traditional strategies were viable domestically and internationally. Domestically, in single-issue terms, traditionalists and confederalists would support each other's plans over supranationality. The confederal middle ground was the path of least resistance for new initiatives; without new initiatives, policy would default to its traditional track. Internationally, the British were fixated on the OEEC/Council of Europe (Bullen 1988: 199–210). Benelux leaders and industrialists too were wary of supranationality (Kersten 1988: 285–304; Milward 1988: 434–52). The Germans, seemingly the beneficiaries of Schuman's overture, had many sceptics as well. Industrialists and Economics Minister Ludwig Erhard echoed the hostility of business groups elsewhere. Even the Americans signalled opposition to the ECSC-like plans circulating in 'Europeanist' circles before May 1950, fearing they would recreate interwar cartels. Only when Monnet and Schuman sold US leaders on its political appeal did they come to favour the ECSC (Acheson 1969: 278). Overall, French confederal or traditional strategies faced no more international obstacles—and probably less.

The pursuit of consensus

It was the institutional authority of Schuman's position as foreign minister that allowed him to select among these viable options. The divisions in his coalition and party showed that he did not owe that position to his pro-community views; as another Christian Democratic leader later remarked: 'One cannot say it was the [party] which pushed [Schuman] to take his European initiative' (Callot 1986: 144). But his position let him set the French agenda. In late May 1950, Schuman insisted on immediate and rapid negotiations of the ECSC. He collaborated purposefully with Monnet to limit input from other actors in Paris. The Germans, Benelux, and Italians agreed, though they consistently pleaded for British involvement and fought to limit the ECSC's supranational provisions (Gillingham 1991). After difficult negotiations, which almost failed due to German intransigence, the treaty was signed in March 1951.

The final, daunting step was ratification. By late 1951, Schuman had used issue linkages and coalitional pressures to assemble a hesitant majority. This was not because the ECSC had become more popular during its negotiation. Public opinion remained ill-informed and neutral. Among politicians, not even his Christian Democrats displayed increased enthusiasm. Haas notes: 'Clearly, there was no "majority" for integration among the French parties in 1951–1952…' (Haas 1958: 123). Yet with leverage unrelated to the ECSC—leverage that followed simply from being in government, which could have been used to build support for *any* of the options—Schuman rallied a majority. Most broadly, he presented the treaty as a *fait accompli*: he had used his ministerial prerogatives to negotiate away IAR controls. Having alienated the British, Schuman argued that the choice was now between the ECSC and no supervision of Germany at all. In coalitional terms, the Third Force was faltering over other issues (religious schools and social policies), and the risk of dividing further over the ECSC pressed confederal and traditional critics reluctantly together. Most blatantly, Schuman made side payments on colonial policies to secure centrist and Independent votes. By December, he had assembled one of several possible majorities behind his own ideological preference.

Schuman later wrote: 'The road towards Europe reached a parting of the ways in 1950' (Schuman 1963: 132). But the ECSC's creation did not lock France and Europe on to the path to the EEC. It introduced a new 'community' framework for French interests, but also crystallized support for the alternatives. Now the battle of ideas was truly engaged.

The battle widens: the EDC

From 1951 to 1954, the ECSC debates echoed across several issue areas. Confederalists and traditionalists tried to reorient French policies to their strategies. Community champions tried to imitate the ECSC with proposals for a 'European Agricultural Community', a 'European Health Community', a 'European Transports Community' and, most important by far, a 'European Defence Community' (EDC).[1] France's pursuit and then rejection of the EDC animated 'the greatest ideological and political debate France has known since the Dreyfus affair' (a notoriously divisive issue in late nineteenth-century France) (Aron and Lerner 1957: 8).

Nonetheless, recent studies of the EDC downplay ideas, tracing French choices to structural pressures in geopolitics or economics. All accounts (including this one) begin with the outbreak of the Korean war in June 1950, which brought intense US pressure to rearm Germany. In the geopolitical view, this led the French straight to the EDC, since a supranational 'European Army' offered the tightest controls on Germany. After the treaty's signature in 1952, however, geopolitical shifts undermined French support. Fears of German dominance inside the EDC grew when the British refused to join, and as French forces became bogged down in Indochina. Stalin's death in 1953 lessened cold-war pressures. By 1954, the French had changed their minds, and the Assembly rejected the treaty (Hitchcock 1998: 133–202). The economic account argues that Third Force leaders conceived the EDC to preserve social spending despite US pressure for rising defence outlays, by sharing the latter among Europeans. French support for the EDC declined after early 1952, when the Third Force was replaced by a conservative coalition with no such social agenda (Pitman 1998).

Yet as older French accounts suggest, a huge problem for both geopolitical and domestic economic accounts is that neither French elites in general nor Third Force leaders in particular *ever* agreed on the EDC (Aron and Lerner 1957; De la Gorce 1979; Elgey 1993). Nor did any changes in constraints lead individuals to change their views of French interests from 1951 to 1954. Straightforward geopolitical pressures did put German rearmament on the table, but French elites consistently responded to these pressures with the three views they had formulated on the ECSC. As of late 1950 and through to 1954, community advocates among the Independents, Christian Democrats, Radicals, UDSR, Socialists, and the bureaucracy called for integrating German units into a supranational European Army. Confederalists in the same parties and ministries preferred to incorporate German forces into looser organizations under

Franco–British direction. Their traditionalist peers either rejected German rearmament outright or favoured a standard alliance framework.

Assessment of viability

As with the ECSC, it is clear that none of these actors was irrationally misreading the environment. All three strategies were viable internationally. The community option led to the EDC treaty in May 1952. It was ratified by the other ECSC members and supported by the United States, leaving it to France to ratify or reject. A traditional solution, rearming Germany without new institutions, was also clearly possible, since the French alone opposed this path against American and European pressure in 1950–1. The confederal option was equally viable as a compromise; indeed, it quickly emerged after the French rejected the EDC. *Ceteris paribus*, French choices were selecting between outcomes as different as a European Army and simple German entry into Nato.

The French pursued the EDC through 1952 not because the Third Force coalition coherently supported it, but because pro-community leaders controlled the foreign policy agenda. Encouraged by Alphand and Monnet, Schuman shifted French policies from stonewalling to pushing for an ECSC-style framework in summer 1951. No one else in Paris was consulted on this change (Elgey 1993: 295). Monnet, still a national official in 1951, played a key role in convincing US leaders to focus on the EDC rather than the Nato track (Winand 1993: 28). At home, the shift to a community strategy soon led Third Force traditionalists and confederalists to abandon Schuman. As they feared, the British ruled out joining any supranational solution in late 1951. Schuman and Alphand also steadily conceded more generous terms to Germany within the EDC. By early 1952, traditionalists were denouncing the EDC, and large confederalist groups among the Independents, Christian Democrats, Radicals, and Socialists moved into quiet opposition. An open rebellion erupted inside the Foreign Ministry (Alphand 1977: 228). Even before Schuman signed the treaty in May, he knew that only a scattered minority supported it.

Still, many observers believed a ratification vote could have passed in early 1952 (Fauvet, in Aron and Lerner 1957: 128–64). Had the negotiations proceeded slightly faster, Schuman could have used the same coalitional pressures and issue linkages that secured the ECSC in late 1951. As it was, an unrelated coalitional realignment in March 1952 erased these pressures and eventually removed Schuman from office. The Third Force collapsed over religious schools and social policy (not over Europe, which had never united it to begin with) and was replaced by a centre-right coalition and left opposition. The key consequences were that in opposition, more than fifty confederalist or traditionalist Socialists were no longer pressed to support the government; within the majority, the addition of anti-EDC Gaullists encouraged others to voice their own criticisms. Pro-community sections of each party were left isolated. At Gaullist insistence, Schuman was replaced as foreign minister by his Christian Democratic ally—but EDC opponent—Georges Bidault in early 1953. After attempting to renegotiate the EDC, Radical premier Pierre Mendès France called a vote in August 1954 (while himself abstaining). The Socialists split 50 for, 53 against; the Radicals and UDSR voted 41 for, 44 against; and the Independents divided 66 for, 28 against. The hierarchical Christian Democrats maintained cohesion for the

EDC only by expelling several members, and despite known hostility from much of the party (Aron and Lerner 1957: 9; Elgey 1993: 329–79; Irving 1973: 170). Gaullist and Communist opposition decided the outcome.

The fate of the EDC

In sum, the EDC did not emerge from majority support and die when policy-makers changed their positions. The 1952 realignment reflected no broad shift on European issues. The public was ill-informed about the EDC and its alternatives (Stoetzel, in Aron and Lerner 1957: 72–101; Rioux 1984). Neither before nor after 1952 did any substantive agreement on European policies help unite the governing coalition; the Independents and Radicals who led governments from 1952 to 1955 were the groups *most* divided over Europe. Instead, the EDC drew its support consistently from minority groups in each of the governing parties. It rose and fell as they obtained and lost agenda control on the *other* issues that dominated coalition-building.

The degree to which the new cleavage around the EDC cross-cut pre-existing lines in French politics was remarkable. Daniel Lerner has shown that it lacked a regional pattern (Aron and Lerner 1957: 198–225). Erling Bjøl has demonstrated the same within the parties and their currents (Bjøl 1966: 169). Sectorally, while the French aeronautical and electronic industries would receive guaranteed contracts from a European army, many of their political representatives (like Gaullist deputy and aircraft magnate Marcel Dassault) opposed the EDC for traditional reasons. Sectors like textiles and steel stood to lose from the EDC, and their business associations campaigned aggressively for rejection. But many of their normal political mouthpieces (Independents like Pinay or André Mutter) were EDC supporters (Aron and Lerner 1957; Balassa 1978: 69–79; Ehrmann 1957: 413; Elgey 1993: 360). Lerner summarized: 'The traditional universe of internal French politics, and the new universe of political sentiment evoked by EDC, simply do not coincide' (Aron and Lerner 1957: 207).

The EDC's defeat highlighted the fact that pro-community elites were scattered across most parties. Their strategy could only be successful if they obtained power on other cleavages. For the moment, they had little to show for their efforts. The ECSC was a narrow sectoral organization that had stimulated as much hostility as support for supranationality. In August 1954, almost everyone thought the community adventure was over. Not even the strongest community advocates would have believed that they stood on the verge of the decisive triumph of the supranational format.

Choosing the community model: the EEC

In the same way that the ECSC's success sparked a rash of community projects, the EDC's fall re-energized confederal and traditional plans. Premier Mendès France—a confederalist who declared in August 1954 that '[t]he axiom of French policy must be to stick to Great Britain!'—moved quickly to frame German rearmament in a Franco–British-led intergovernmental organization, the Western European Union (WEU). The EDC signatories and Britain drafted the much looser WEU deal in four weeks. French confederalists were ecstatic. One Socialist rejoiced: 'The accords deliver us from the Europe of Six and the risks of German hegemony which it contained; today it is the Europe of Seven!' (Cophornic 1994, in Bossuat and Girault 1994: 262; Lapie 1971: 262). In 1955, they hoped to expand the WEU to cooperation in arms production and foreign policy, refounding Europe on a 'Franco–Anglo–German triangle' (Bossuat 1993: 147–206). Parallel plans emerged for OEEC cooperation in atomic and other forms of energy, and transport.

Traditionalists in every party, meanwhile, rejected the WEU or accepted it reluctantly, seeing it (like the EDC) as an 'Anglo-Saxon' plot relegating France to a non-global role in minor European organizations (De Gaulle 1970: 621). France needed to assert itself as a global power, while technical European problems could be handled in standard bilateral deals. French business, bureaucrats in the technical ministries, and traditional politicians pushed in 1954–5 to develop new bilateral accords in trade, atomic energy, armaments production, and transport. They focused especially on new ties with the rising German economy, showing that traditionalists too acknowledged environmental change. All French elites saw incentives to cooperate with Germany, but they still differed over *how* to do so.

Community advocates also rejoined the fray in early 1955. Like their peers, they saw incentives to cooperation in atomic and classic energy, armaments, and transport. But their solutions were to extend or imitate the ECSC. Foreign Minister Antoine Pinay (Independent), an EDC champion, considered several such options, though he feared supranational initiatives were impossible after the EDC (Massigli 1978: 506). Then bureaucrat-turned-activist Monnet focused pro-community attention on plans for an atomic energy community (the so-called Euratom). French anti-supranationalism could be overcome, argued Monnet, by capitalizing on widespread faith in an impending atomic energy revolution, fear of a separate German atomic programme, and the appeal of sharing expensive atomic investments. As these reasons appealed less to other Europeans, who preferred atomic cooperation with the more advanced British or Americans, Monnet reluctantly agreed to package Euratom with a Benelux plan for a European Economic Community (EEC) of trade liberalization within managed safeguards (Duchêne 1994: 262–79).

Bilateral ties and supranationality

All three kinds of proposal were active when the ECSC foreign ministers met at Messina, Italy in June 1955. Internationally, confederal and traditional options were strong possibilities. The WEU was pushed by the British and accepted by the Germans as the appropriate forum for political and armaments cooperation. British, German, and most Benelux leaders strongly supported the OEEC forum for economic issues (though Belgian Foreign Minister Spaak and Dutch Foreign Minister Beyen were personally pro-supranationality). Economics Minister Erhard and German business were particularly intent on liberalization in the OEEC (Küsters 1986). In atomic energy, all of France's partners wanted to include the advanced British (Lee 1995: 38–54). Traditional bilateral ties were also active alternatives. Bilateral export contracts remained the norm in intra-European industrial trade, which doubled from 1953 to 1957. In agriculture, all governments except the Dutch defended the *status quo* of bilateral contracts. Bilateral cooperation in armaments production was moving forward slowly on several fronts. The Germans were receptive to (if not eager for) cooperation with the French in atomic energy (Soutou 1996: 42–9).

Inside France, confederal or traditional options were universally seen as *more* viable than supranational ones. The anti-EDC majority stood ready to quash community proposals. Even Euratom—constructed by Monnet as the supranational plan most likely to appeal in France—drew little support from the best-informed French elites. With few exceptions (like the prominent Louis Armand), civil and military atomic experts strongly favoured either OEEC or bilateral alternatives over Euratom. They saw collaboration with the backward German, Benelux, or Italian programmes as far less appealing than with Britain or Switzerland. Euratom might also impede French military research. François Perrin, head of the Atomic Energy Commissariat, championed a British-sponsored OEEC project. Pierre Guillaumat, director of the secret military programme, favoured bilateral deals and dismissed Euratom as 'dangerous nonsense' (Elgey 1993: 581; Goldschmidt 1980: 147–53; Scheinman 1965: 148–57).

The EEC's prospects in France were worse. If Beyen and Spaak judged correctly that practically all French elites thought liberalization acceptable only within managed safeguards, other aspects of their plan made it *less* appealing to French business than its alternatives. Liberalization in bilateral deals or the OEEC allowed governments to impose safeguards as they saw fit; liberalization in the EEC would be automatic, with safeguards authorized by supranational administrators. Consequently, and contrary to common wisdom, French business and economic officials did *not* see the EEC as the safer route. A major Finance Ministry study in 1955 concluded: 'The problems of forming a common market of the Six were no less than liberalizing trade within the OEEC since imports from the Federal Republic, Benelux and Italy represented 70 percent of all imports from the OEEC' (Lynch 1997: 176). Businessmen added that unilateral German tariff cuts already gave them favourable terms of trade. In July 1956, business representatives in the French Economic and Social Council voted *unanimously* to relocate the EEC talks to the OEEC. The prospect of automatic, supranationally-administered liberalization in 'little Europe' frightened them more than did the wider (but weaker) OEEC. At least in the OEEC, they hoped, broad liberalization could be 'indefinitely delayed', and channelled into sectoral, bilateral accords between business associations (Balassa 1978: 79–95; Mahant 1969: 79–95; Szokolóczy-Syllaba 1965: 287).

Even French farmers—similarly miscast in common wisdom as the EEC's champions—opposed community-style accords in 1955. Though the largest French farmers were among the most competitive in Europe and French surpluses were mounting, agricultural organizations unambiguously favoured the continued pursuit of bilateral contracts. They saw the ECSC Six as too small a framework for French exports. Germany was its only major importer, and the Dutch and Italians were more competitors than potential markets. Institutionally, farmers had come to oppose supranationality during the fight over a European agricultural community in 1951–3, denouncing the ECSC model as 'too heavy, too rigid, too authoritarian and *dirigiste*, and weighted towards consumer interests' (Délorme and Tavernier 1969: 20; Neville-Rolfe 1984: 116). Even Milward calls the notion that French farmers dictated the EEC format a myth that 'ought to be laid to rest' (Milward 1984: 283).

Political cleavages

Under these conditions, France did not return to community policies because object-ive economic interests or institutional spill-over from the ECSC formed a majority to demand it. Instead, pro-community leaders unexpectedly gained opportunities to reassert their views. This occurred in two steps. First, conservative Foreign Minister Pinay went beyond his instructions at Messina, which ruled out even discussing the EEC, to accept studies of all the proposals. Pinay had been a prominent supporter of the EDC, and consciously sought to relaunch the community institutions (Lynch 1997: 172). He proposed that Spaak, the most pro-community participant, chair the studies, and sent an ultra-Europeanist young deputy, Félix Gaillard (Radical), to rep-resent France. These selections were highly consequential. When talks in the 'Spaak Committee' became bogged down at the technical level, Gaillard and the other deleg-ation heads dismissed their bureaucrats and allowed Spaak's aides to draft the entire final report themselves. The result was a coherent plan that, wrote one French diplo-mat, showed 'considerable distance from all aspects of French positions'.[2] It linked the EEC and Euratom, but focused on the former. Institutionally, both were expli-citly modelled on the ECSC. In the 'Common Market', liberalization would proceed in automatic stages. All quotas and subsidies would be quickly eliminated. An unspe-cified 'agriculture policy' was left to the future. Safeguards operated at the discretion of a supranational 'Commission'.[3]

With few exceptions, French bureaucrats' reaction to the Spaak Report was 'gla-cial' (Bossuat 1995: 87–109; Marjolin 1986: 282). Diplomats wrote that the EEC's 'fundamental risks' included 'economic and social disruption which cannot be underestimated'.[4] The Ministries of Finance, Industry and Commerce, Agriculture, Transports, Social Affairs, Public Works, and Overseas France echoed them. Inter-ministerial meetings rejected negotiations based on the Report, accepting to discuss only an initial four-year phase of liberalization.[5] Some officials wanted to shift the talks to the OEEC, arguing (like business) that its weak commitments were safer despite its wider scope.[6] They also insisted that French interest groups would never support the EEC. A Foreign Ministry note accurately characterized interest-group positions in early 1956:

> It is obvious that a consultation with the directly interested economic and syndical groups would lead very rapidly to a negative assessment that could only limit the gov-ernment's possibilities for manoeuvre and crystallize the heretofore latent opposition to the Common Market. In particular, this would be the case if such a consultation sought to determine the advantages and the disadvantages that our country could draw from the establishment of a Common Market.[7]

Agricultural lobbies remained unconvinced of the Common Market's promise (Küsters 1986: 142). French business was overwhelmingly hostile to the Spaak Report, though the employers' association—careful after its failure against ECSC—complained about the details rather than rejecting it outright (Balassa 1978; Ehrmann 1954: 414; Mahant 1969: 177).

While the Spaak Committee met, however, a coalitional shift allowed the second step to a French community strategy. In January 1956 a centre-left coalition won a razor-thin legislative victory. The new majority was neither pro-community nor pro-liberalization; it won on a social policy platform led by EDC-killer Mendès France, who was expected to become premier. But President René Coty (a conservative Independent with little love for anyone in the coalition) instead nominated Mendès France's less popular electoral partner, doctrinaire Socialist head Guy Mollet. He did so partly because Mollet opposed Algerian independence, and partly because he and Mollet shared pro-community sympathies (Duchêne 1994: 267; Elgey 1993: 477; Fauvet 1959: 308; Lefebvre 1992: 156; Lynch 1997: 173). Though his Socialists remained deeply split over Europe and broadly hostile to liberalization, Mollet soon set a treaty based on the Spaak Report as his main goal. He assigned European policies to a strongly pro-community Radical, Maurice Faure, along with a team of similarly-minded officials (Delwit 1995: 71; Criddle 1969: 82; Küsters 1986: 142).

Rather than being lobbied *by* interest groups, Mollet's team began lobbying *them* to support the EEC. They began with the farmers. In what one participant called 'the most prolonged, and at least for a while, the most difficult discussions' of the process, they argued to farmers that the EEC promised stable export contracts, not menacing liberalization (Marjolin 1986: 292). Though the agricultural organizations 'remained until almost the last moment suspiciously antagonistic of anything more complicated [than bilateral contracts], especially anything that would provide a market for other peoples' surpluses in France', they endorsed EEC talks in summer 1956 (Milward 1984: 293). French positions were set in favour of a network of long-term intergovernmental contracts within the EEC, without any demand for a 'common policy', which farmers still feared meant liberalization.

The farmers' endorsement made a deal imaginable, but hostility to the EEC still dominated the majority and opposition. Mollet's approval of the negotiations, based on the Spaak Report in May 1956, was 'manifestly contrary to the general sentiment of the ministers present' (Serra 1989: 282). Finance Minister Paul Ramadier led opposition to the EEC in Mollet's Socialist Party (Criddle 1969: 82; Delwit 1995: 71; Mahant 1969: 154; Prate 1995: 17). All but the most die-hard 'ultras of Europe' in the Christian Democratic Party were also sceptical. Party statements paid the EEC no attention until late 1956 (Bjøl 1966: 145; Brunet 1993: 233–50). The Radicals and Independents still divided into three camps. Traditionalists like Édouard Daladier (Radical) or François Valentin (Independent) opposed anything beyond existing frameworks. Confederalists like Mendès France (Radical) or André Boutemy (Independent) argued for intergovernmental, non-automatic accords that allowed France to control the pace of liberalization and cooperation. Community champions like Faure and Gaillard (Radical) or Paul Reynaud (Independent) marshalled every conceivable economic or geopolitical argument for the EEC and Euratom (Bjøl 1966: 168–205). But even with their Socialist and Christian Democratic allies, the latter still counted no more than a third of parliamentarians by late 1956.

Hoping to conclude a ratifiable treaty, Mollet's team attempted in the early EEC talks to block automatic trade liberalization. Germany refused categorically, even as Erhard pushed aggressively to replace the EEC with a new British proposal for an OEEC-based 'free trade area'. Mollet faced a choice between failure and fundamental concessions. Most of his bureaucrats, his finance minister, and his party preferred failure, but the pro-community prime minister thought that a major supranational project justified substantive compromise. In early November, Mollet met German

Chancellor Konrad Adenauer and dropped the key conditions on automatic liberalization. Recent accounts agree that the two leaders reached this understanding regardless of the geopolitical crises in Suez and Hungary (Bossuat 1995: 324; Küsters 1986: 285–304; Milward 1984: 215; Moravcsik 1998: 119). Thereafter, despite continued internal complaints from Finance Ministry officials and Socialist ministers, the negotiations sped to their conclusion. The delegations agreed on phased liberalization and preferential long-term agricultural contracts (with undefined future discussions of a 'common agricultural policy'). To Mollet's chagrin, opposition to a strong Euratom from the Germans, Benelux, and France's own atomic officials diluted the second community into a minor research pool.

The one remaining battle inside the French government concerned the overseas territories. Mollet pushed hard for German side-payments in investments and aid for the French Union. Although in hindsight such payoffs look clearly beneficial to France, many traditionalists and confederalists actually saw the EEC's intrusion into colonial relationships as another reason to oppose the Rome Treaty. Bureaucrats and deputies among the Independents, Christian Democrats, Radicals and Socialists wanted to 'safeguard the French Union' against 'Europeanization'.[8] Not only did liberalization threaten the territories; even *aid* from other countries would undercut French control. Finance Ministry officials insisted well into the EEC negotiations that France's 'natural ally' was Britain, and that France should:

1) Push for European integration in the OEEC framework, trying to establish a Franco–British common front ... 2) Not discuss, even in principle, the integration of the Overseas Territories of the franc zone before the principles of European integration are established and have begun to be executed. 3) Activate as much as possible the economic, financial, and tariff integration of the franc zone (notably Morocco) with France, and not envisage the adhesion of this zone to Eurafrica until its own internal ties are sufficiently consolidated to avoid all risks of dislocations.[9]

But this 'was an argument that Mollet rejected completely' (Lynch 1997: 204). Unlike many more liberal actors, he thought the nationalist trading system anachronistic. He succeeded in obtaining a five-year fund, of which 88 per cent would go to French territories. Ironically, this was not a side-payment that many French elites had even wanted him to demand.

Movement towards ratification

Once the treaties on the EEC and Euratom were signed in Rome in March 1957, Mollet turned to ratification. Three factors explain why, four months later, an EEC majority coalesced despite widespread scepticism. All resulted either from the direct leadership of Mollet's team, or from its use of unrelated coalitional pressures and issue linkages that, as in the case of the ECSC, could have created support for *any* of the three active European options. First was the mobilization of farmers. Despite persistent divides in agricultural opinion on the EEC—with the strongest opposition coming from the heavily rural-based Gaullists and Poujadists (followers of Pierre Poujade, a leader of discontented farmers and merchants), and prominent members of farmers' organizations—many rural politicians were persuaded that the

EEC offered attractive long-term opportunities (Mahant 1969: 221). The farmers' support convinced sceptics among the Radicals, Independents, and even some dissident Gaullists. Second were coalitional pressures. The fifty Socialists who had swung the balance against the EDC felt unable to reject a treaty identified so closely with their party boss (Delwit 1995: 72). Third was issue linkage to Algeria. In the opposition, at least twenty EEC sceptics voted 'yes' only in order to uphold Mollet's stance against Algerian independence.[10] Public inattention also aided ratification. France was gripped by the Algerian débâcle. A growing economic crisis—caused by Algeria and Mollet's profligate domestic budgets—suggested that the EEC might go unimplemented in any case. Amid such disinterest that only thirty deputies voted in person, the 'Treaties of Rome' were ratified in July 1957 by 342 votes to 239.

Thus Mollet used his agenda-setting power and issue linkages to build coalitional support for his own European ideas. The availability of equally strong (or stronger) domestic support for confederal or traditional choices was obvious in 1955–7. Nor did Mollet owe his agenda-setting power to any electoral or coalitional upswell for a community Europe. He became premier against all contemporary predictions, campaigning for social policies that fit poorly with liberalization. By far the most popular French politicians during the EEC negotiations were its two strongest leaders before and after that process, Mendès France and Charles de Gaulle, who incarnated confederal and traditional thinking, respectively. France chose EEC over these alternatives because certain leaders asserted their views amid a deeply cross-cutting battle of ideas. These diverse politicians—the conservative industrialist Pinay, the Socialist boss Mollet, the rural centrist Maurice Faure—shared little besides a vision of Europe's future. They achieved power on other issues, used their authority to direct European policies, and built French strategies around their unrepresentative ideas.

Conclusion

This chapter makes two basic points. First, in all the negotiations on European co-operation in the 1950s, the major players besides France (Germany, Britain, and the Benelux countries) tended to prefer some combination of geographically broad, institutionally weak cooperation—a confederal model—flanked by traditional bilateral deals in certain areas (like agriculture or atomic energy). This claim attracts no objection from the historical literature, and so has received little elaboration here.

Second is the much more novel argument that the erratic French insistence on an institutionally strong, geographically limited 'community' framework—successful in the early and late 1950s, but unsuccessful in the middle of the decade—did not reflect any sort of straightforward response to geopolitical imperatives or the demands of French economic interest groups or bureaucrats. Interest groups and bureaucrats were themselves divided over the appropriate institutional shape for European co-operation in a variety of issue areas, but mostly favoured relatively conservative, familiar projects along traditional or confederal lines. Politicians, by contrast, were split in relatively even thirds by a new battle of ideas that cross-cut the main organizing lines of French domestic politics. In the bitter debates about the ECSC and the

EDC shortly thereafter, individual politicians became deeply wedded to particular views of appropriate European institutions in a pattern that separated almost entirely from their party or other ideological affiliations. This divided polity then chose to advance the ECSC and EEC projects (and to defeat the EDC) not because clear majorities dictated these strategies, but because leaders with support on other issues used their institutional authority to craft one of several potential coalitions behind their own European ideas.

That electoral coalition-building was unrelated to leaders' European views does not mean it was irrelevant. The EDC made clear that community strategies depended on a centrist majority. Under the Third Force, Schuman and pro-community figures in all the centrist parties could invoke party and coalitional pressures to press confederalist and traditionalist peers into line. When the centre divided into right and left in 1952, it lost coalitional leverage over the centre-left. Socialist confederalists and traditionalists in the opposition had no reason to support government policies, and were themselves sufficient to swing the vote against the EDC. Only when the Socialists returned to a centrist coalition in 1956 (for non-European reasons) did it become possible to assemble another reluctant majority behind community plans. Still, if only centrist majorities allowed for community choices, they certainly never demanded that strategy.

The conventional wisdom that European policies were the 'glue' for centrist majorities reverses the real dynamic. Far from being united over Europe, the centre was the part of French politics *most divided* over Europe. Only the Communist and Gaullist extremes had common European preferences: both were staunchly traditionalist. All parties in between included community advocates, confederalists and traditionalists. Consequently, not only did community plans not help centrist leaders form a majority, but committing to *any* European track provoked opposition from at least half their electoral allies. Schuman could only pass the ECSC by expending political capital from other issues. The same was true of Mendès France with the confederal WEU plan and Mollet with the EEC. Centrist majorities created permissive conditions for community policies, but did not cause them.

A third argument is necessary to explain fully the triumph of community Europe. The emphasis here on French and European support for alternatives to the EEC begs a huge question: if so many actors wanted something else, why did the EEC endure when the fall of the Fourth Republic brought the deeply traditionalist de Gaulle to power in May 1958? The answer overlaps somewhat with institutionalist scholarship and draws on the basic notion that new institutional deals constrain subsequent interaction. Such an approach is crucial to understanding the implementation and consolidation of the Communities under de Gaulle, which is discussed in Chapter 7.

The ECSC was a narrow sectoral arrangement that did not decide the overall architecture of European cooperation, and so debate over various formats continued after 1952. The EEC, by contrast, was a broad accord that both its supporters and its opponents conceived as laying down fundamental organizing principles for the European arena. In 1958, even the powerful de Gaulle found his strategies deeply altered by the EEC inheritance. In terms of constraint, the Germans and other Europeans quickly made clear to de Gaulle that they expected him to maintain France's EEC commitments; if he wanted to pursue his personal priority of European foreign policy cooperation, he needed to begin by respecting the EEC treaty. Even though they had not themselves demanded the EEC format, at least it gave them *an* acceptable framework for liberalization to which they could hold the unpredictable new French regime. In terms of incentives, the EEC offered de Gaulle a golden opportunity to exclude the pro-American British from a European framework. This had not been intended by most of the EEC's French negotiators—the British had excluded themselves from the community discussions—and de Gaulle himself would never have advocated supranational institutions in order to distance the British. As his predecessors had conveniently done this for him, however, de Gaulle opted not to scuttle the EEC. Instead, he would maintain and attempt to alter it into a platform for his distinct foreign policy ambitions. The ironic outcome was that de Gaulle greatly consolidated the EEC as he tried and failed to advance his agenda of a French-led European 'third way' between the superpowers. Despite his own preferences, and despite the availability of a wide range of other options before the negotiation of the EEC, de Gaulle left behind a Europe organized on community lines.

The existing literature is thus wrong to see Europe's adoption of a unique supranational path in the 1950s as dictated by structural configurations or by the incremental momentum of institutional spill-over. Most Europeans simply did not see a community Europe as necessary or even desirable at the time. European problems were only connected to the community-model solution by the aggressive leadership of ideological champions of supranationality, whose episodic control of national policy-making allowed them to bind all their compatriots into their European vision.

Notes

1 *All* these proposals were serious enough to provoke formal international talks. On agriculture, see Noël, (1988); Délorme and Tavernier (1969). On the proposed health community, see Parsons (2003).

2 French Foreign Ministry (FFM) archives, DE-CE 613, 24 February 1956. Sécrétariat d'État aux Affaires économiques, 'Note: marché commun européen'. Comment on early Report draft.

3 FFM, DE-CE 613, 21 April 1956. 'Rapport des chefs de délégation aux ministres des Affaires étrangères'.

4 FFM, DE-CE 613, 21 April 1956. Service de coopération économique, 'Note: marché commun'.

5 FFM, DE-CE 613, 23 May 1956, 'Résumé du projet de document de travail sur l'établissement d'un marché commun, préparé par la Commission interministerielle réunie à la Présidence du Conseil'.

6 'Note: Marché commun', Direction Générale des affaires économiques, 2 February 1956, in *Documents diplomatiques français*, 1956, 1 (67): 127–40.

7 FFM, DE-CE 613, 23 February 1956. No author, 'Note'.

8 FFM, DE-CE 613, 21 April 1956. Service de coopération économique, 'Note: marché commun'; Mahant, *French*, 94, 105, 148.

9 FFM, DE-CE 613, 19 October 1956. DREE. 'Note pour Monsieur Clappier. Objet: l'intégration européenne de la zone franc'.

10 *Le Monde*, 24 January 1957.

Further reading

For a masterful overview of the economic and political context prior to the European Coal and Steel Community (though this chapter contests some of its overall conclusions), see Milward (1984). In a similar vein, the best English-language overview of French economic issues in the early postwar period is Lynch (1997). Duchêne (1994) is probably the most informative, readable and insightful account of the early manoeuvrings on postwar European projects. An excellent account of the background and process of the ECSC negotiations is Gillingham (1991). On the crucial but often misunderstood episode of the European Defence Community, by far the best English-language account remains Aron and Lerner (1957). For the EEC negotiations, de Gaulle's European policies and French strategies *vis-à-vis* European integration through the 1990s, see the expanded version of this argument in Parsons (2003).

Aron, R. and D. Lerner (eds.) (1957), *France Defeats EDC* (New York: Praeger).

Duchêne, F. (1994), *Jean Monnet: First Statesman of Interdependence* (New York: W.W. Norton).

Gillingham, J. (1991), *Coal, Steel, and the Rebirth of Europe, 1945 – 1955* (Cambridge: Cambridge University Press).

Lynch, F. M. B. (1997), *France and the International Economy: From Vichy to the Treaties of Rome* (New York: Routledge).

Milward, A. (1984), *The Reconstruction of Western Europe, 1945 – 1951* (London: Methuen).

Parsons, C. (2003), *A Certain Idea of Europe* (Ithaca, NY: Cornell University Press).

Websites

Probably the most useful website on the early history of European integration is maintained by historian Richard Griffiths at Leiden University, at http://www.eu-history.leidenuniv.nl/. Also very useful is the searchable European Integration History Index offered by the European University Institute at http://vlib.iue.it/hist-eur-integration/Index.html.

Chapter 6
Building on Coal and Steel
European Integration in the 1950s and the 1960s

Stephen Martin

Contents

Summary

The choice of coal and steel for the first European Community had great symbolic value for Franco–German *rapprochement* and great utility for France, but the two sectors were singularly unsuited for economic integration. Although no studies of the coal and steel sectors were undertaken before the Schuman Declaration, their characteristics suggested that the establishment of a common market would likely entail an extended period of disequilibria with substantial political and economic costs. Inevitably, the adjustment was a difficult one. Nor did the European Coal and Steel Community (ECSC) meet its stated goals. The High Authority was buffeted by the strong interests of the member states, which often prevailed. The experience of the ECSC was that community institutions can negotiate and cajole but not compel member-state adherence to treaty commitments. This was a leading indicator of the experience of European integration in the 1960s, when the Commission advocated deeper integration in the face of strong French resistance and France successfully challenged one of the basic instruments of supranationalism (the use of qualified-majority voting).

Introduction

From the point of view of the long process of European integration, arguably the 1960s began with the election of Charles de Gaulle as the first President of France's Fifth Republic, in December 1958, and ended with his resignation in April 1969. This slightly off-sync decade was preceded by the ECSC and (barely) by the Treaties of Rome establishing the European Economic Community (EEC) and the European Atomic Energy Community (Euratom). Beginning with the Hague summit of December 1969, it was followed by a series of steps that laid the foundations for financial reform, foreign policy coordination, monetary policy cooperation, and the accession of Britain, Denmark, and Ireland to the EEC in January 1973.

But the decade itself is notable more for the stumbling blocks encountered than for the advances made. The ways in which those stumbling blocks were dealt with ensured that when the process of European integration began again to go forward, in the early 1970s, it did so on terms different from those which might have been expected going into the 1960s. By the same token, the experience of the ECSC in the 1950s suggested that national governments would not willingly fulfil all their treaty obligations under the Rome Treaties and that the European Commission would not survive a clash with a headstrong member state.

The experience of the ECSC

Based on the Treaty of Paris of April 1951, the ECSC came into effect in July 1952 for a period of fifty years. The treaty created an institutional framework, including a High Authority based in Luxembourg, to manage the integration of the coal and steel markets of the six member states (the Benelux countries, France, Germany, and Italy). The ECSC also touched upon the markets for iron ore and scrap, as well as sectoral transportation and labour markets.

The Schuman Plan that led to the ECSC embraced the strategy of pursuing Franco–German *rapprochement* and European unity by way of market integration. If the means of the Schuman Plan were microeconomic, however, the goals were political. As Jean Monnet put it in his memoirs:

> ... une autre guerre est proche devant nous si nous ne faisons rien. L'Allemagne n'en sera pas la cause, mais elle en sera l'enjeu. Il faut qu'elle cesse d'être un enjeu, qu'elle devienne au contraire un lien. Seule la France peut actuellement prendre une initiative. Qu'est-ce qui pourrait lier, avant qu'il ne soit trop tard, la France et l'Allemagne, comment enraciner dès aujourd'hui un intérêt commun entre les deux pays... (Monnet 1976: 342)

The coal and steel sectors, upon which Monnet settled as a means of forging ties between France and Germany, had historical, symbolic, and practical advantages as choices for economic integration. There was a history of vertical relationships between French coal and German steel, not to mention the cooperation embodied in the International Steel Cartel (ISC) of 1926. The ISC had not been particularly successful and (evidently) the economic ties that it forged had not prevented the run-up to World War II.

But one must take one's history as one finds it. According to Gerbet:

> In the eyes of the masses, and particularly of the French, coal and steel possessed a certain psychological value. French–German difficulties had often assumed the form of a struggle for coal. ... As for steel, it simultaneously evokes 'the arms makers' and German military power. To internationalize steel thus had to appear as a commitment to peace among nations. On the other hand, to unify coal and steel, to begin organizing basic industries ... had for Monnet the immense advantage of giving the pool considerable possibilities for expansion. ... Coal and steel were thus the point of attack of the effort to build Europe, a point of attack chosen more for political than economic reasons. (Gerbet 1956: 542)

There were practical advantages of several kinds as well. France, under its first postwar plan for economic modernization (supervised by Jean Monnet) had substantially expanded its steel capacity. A common market in coal and steel would at once ensure French access to coal for its forges and an outlet for its steel products (Abelshauser 1994; Haas 1958: 242).

The French interest in introducing vertical disintegration between German coal and German steel fit nicely with the American deconcentration and decartelization drive of the early years of the occupation (Berghahn 1986). Given the *dirigiste* bent of French microeconomic policy, American hostility towards cartels had the unfortunate aspect of being general rather than specific. William Diebold, a contemporary observer, noted more than three decades later that:

> So far as Americans were concerned, the cartel issue went beyond Germany. It is not always remembered nowadays that the American interpretation of the interwar experience put considerable stress on the iniquities of international cartels. Partly that was economic analysis and partly it was a reaction to the Nazi use of German firms, notably I.G. Farben ... to penetrate other countries. (Diebold 1988: 26)

Against this background, it is not surprising that the initial reaction of many American observers (including then-Secretary of State Dean Acheson) to the Schuman Plan was that the ECSC would simply be a cover for the revival of prewar cartels (Gillingham 1991: 234; Monnet 1976: 356). The lasting legacy of this American reaction sprang from the steps taken by Monnet to assuage American concerns. He contacted John J. McCloy, the American High Commissioner for Germany, and arranged to use the services of the American diplomat Robert Bowie, who drafted the first versions of what became Articles 65 and 66 of the Treaty of Paris (Ball 1973: 88; Bowie 1989; Monnet 1976: 413; Spierenburg and Poidevin 1994: 28). There were changes in language and in nuance, but Articles 65 and 66, the direct ancestors of Articles 85 and 86 of the Treaty of Rome, are themselves direct descendents of Sections 1 and 2 of the Sherman Act.

The unsuitability of coal and steel for economic integration

Despite these historical, symbolic and political advantages, the settling on coal and steel as the lead sectors for European integration carried with it one negative point: economically, they were singularly unsuited for integration. Although no particular economic studies of the coal and steel sectors were undertaken in advance of the Schuman Plan proposals (Gerbet 1956: 542), their economic characteristics suggest that integration of the member states' markets should have been expected to entail an extended period of disequilibrium, with substantial political and economic costs. Indeed, '[t]he coal and steel industries were not the most tractable ones with which to start the experiment of freeing trade and prices because freight costs in both industries tend to create separate markets, because of the structure of ownership and the long history of concerted practices, because individual governments exercise strong influence over the two industries, and because the coal industry is so labor intensive' (Lister 1960: 403).

The adjustment was a difficult one. The decline of the coal market, and particularly of Belgian coal, began very soon after the formation of the ECSC (see Figure 6.1). The political response to it may be seen as perhaps the first example of the enduring tradition of the granting of massive amounts of state aid, often in violation of competition policy rules, for the purpose of delaying as long as possible structural adjustments that are a consequence of market integration (and, in fact, a prerequisite for the full benefits of integration to be realized).

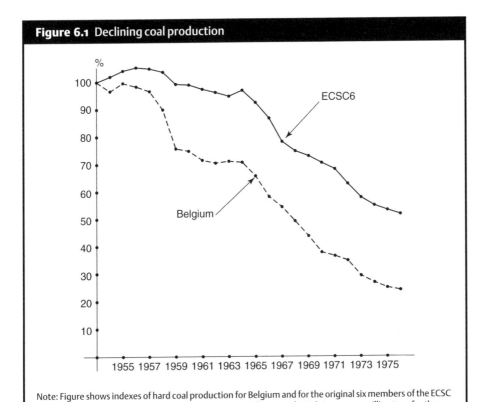

Figure 6.1 Declining coal production

Note: Figure shows indexes of hard coal production for Belgium and for the original six members of the ECSC with 1953 as 100. The levels of output in 1953 were 30.1 million tons for Belgium, 242.3 million tons for the ECSC6.

Source: European Commission (1977: Table 30)

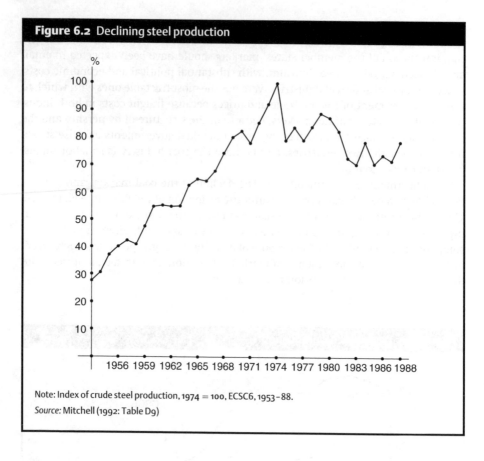

Figure 6.2 Declining steel production

Note: Index of crude steel production, 1974 = 100, ECSC6, 1953–88.

Source: Mitchell (1992: Table D9)

The decline of steel came later, after the 1973 oil shock (see Figure 6.2). The use of crisis cartels to deal with it was an indication of a fundamental unwillingness to rely on the marketplace as a resource allocation mechanism (Heusdens and de Horn 1980).

Substantive ECSC price policy is laid out in:

- Article 4(b), which prohibits 'measures or practices which discriminate between producers, between purchasers or between consumers, especially in prices and delivery terms or transport rates and conditions, and measures or practices which interfere with the purchaser's free choice of supplier';

- Article 60(1), which bans unfair competitive practices and prohibits 'discriminatory practices involving, within the common market, the application by a seller of dissimilar conditions to comparable transactions, especially on grounds of the nationality of the buyer' (thus repeating the content of Article 4(b));

- Article 60(2)(a), which provides that for the purposes of accomplishing the prohibitions of Article 60(1) 'the price lists and conditions of sale applied by undertakings within the common market must be made public to the extent and in the manner prescribed by the High Authority…'.

There is no clearly stated rationale for the banning of price discrimination. It is understandable that a European common market would not permit discrimination based on national identity. But the prohibition of price discrimination contained in the treaty is a general one. As price discrimination is a normal form of rivalry (that is, of competition, in the lay sense in which the word is used in the treaty) in imperfectly competitive markets, it follows that by seeking to prohibit price discrimination in general, the treaty sought to prohibit a normal form of oligopolistic competition.

For Haas, the prohibition of price discrimination had a protectionist purpose:

> Monnet's specific proposals on market rules, prices, access to raw materials, non-discrimination, subsidies, re-adaptation, and exemptions during the transitional period were accepted in essence in the final version of the Treaty, including the rigorous inter-pretation of Article 60 which made 'nondiscrimination' almost the equivalent of 'no price competition,' a deliberate device to limit the flow of German steel to the French market. (Haas 1958: 245)

The rationale for the publication of prices was to provide consumers with information that would allow them to make the best choice of supplier. Writing of the rules for steel, Spierenburg and Poidevin point out that:

> Under Article 60, producers were obliged to publish their prices. Accordingly, the High Authority drafted rather elaborate rules to cover not only basis prices but also conditions of sale, delivery dates, standard surcharges for special qualities and discounts for quant-ity and loyalty. It explained clearly that steel producers 'must ensure that users are able to ascertain the quality and calculate precisely the cost of the products they are consider-ing buying, and also to compare offers from various suppliers'. (Spierenburg and Poidevin 1994: 101)

Ensuring that users have the ability to make such comparisons ensures as well that any producer cutting prices would know that rivals would be aware of that price cut in advance and be able to match it. This brings out a point that seems to underlie much of US and later European Community competition policy: very often, policy-makers seem to have no coherent vision of markets in mind when they formulate policy. When there is an implicit market model behind policy formation, it often seems to be the model of a perfectly competitive market that is in long-run equilib-rium; when such policies are applied to imperfectly competitive markets, the con-sequences can be quite different from those intended.

So it proved to be for steel in the ECSC. The anti-collusion provisions of Article 65 applied to agreements restricting competition 'within the common market'. In an imperfectly competitive market, one might expect that participation in an ex-port cartel would, of necessity, affect the home markets of participating firms, but the High Authority did not take this view. ECSC steel firms formed an export car-tel. When the ECSC came into effect and freed producers from national price con-trols, firms raised prices for the ECSC member states up to the higher level set by the export cartel. Further, under Article 60(2) of the Treaty, steel firms set up a basing point system (Phlips 1983: 27–30).

In coal, neither the High Authority nor the national governments seemed to take the idea of market competition seriously. As Lister observed at the time: 'That there is need of centralized regulation of production, prices and sales in order to mitigate the effects of the business cycle is a proposition that goes nearly unchallenged in Europe' (Lister 1960: 260).

Diebold, another contemporary observer, noted that the underlying policy goal was to keep all ships afloat:

> ... most of the Community's coal is covered by price equalization arrangements and compensation schemes. Though costs differ, all the mines in the scheme sell at the same price. Part of the return to the more efficient mines is distributed to less efficient ones. This makes it possible to keep prices lower than they would be if they had to be remunerative to the high cost mines, but prevents any coal being sold at the lowest price the most efficient mines could offer. (Diebold 1959: 274)

Yet such a policy prevents an efficient allocation of resources, as Meade et al. (1962) observed:

> Keeping the prices charged by each basin closely geared to costs prevents the lower-cost producers from realizing the extra profit without which they are unlikely to expand at the appropriate rate, if at all. It follows that if progress towards the attainment of the common market's basic aim—an improved distribution of resources—is the criterion, then the price-fixing policy of the High Authority and of the member governments is open to question. (Meade et al. 1962:218)

By the time initial negotiations and legal skirmishes over the introduction of some form of managed competition for coal had played themselves out, the fact of secular decline in coal had become undeniable (see Figure 6.1). From that point, the task of the High Authority was to organize a retreat.

Article 58 of the treaty empowered the High Authority, with the approval of the Council of Ministers, to declare a state of manifest crisis and impose production quotas:

> In the event of a decline in demand, if the Commission considers that the Community is confronted with a period of manifest crisis and that the means of action provided for in Article 57 are not sufficient to deal with this, it shall, after consulting the Consultative Committee and with the assent of the Council, establish a system of production quotas...

The High Authority sought to use this provision and declare a state of manifest crisis in the coal sector in 1958, but the Council declined to agree with its request.

Based on output levels alone (see Figure 6.1), one might take the view that there was no manifest crisis in the ECSC as a whole in 1958. There was a crisis in the Belgian coal industry, and the Belgian government asked the High Authority to take appropriate measures (based on a request from a member state and with the advice, but not requiring the consent, of the Council) if an action of the High Authority or a failure to act by the High Authority had caused 'fundamental and persistent disturbances' in the member state's economy. Acting in the belief that the failure to declare a state of manifest emergency under Article 58 validated Belgium's request, the High Authority limited imports from other ECSC countries and granted aid to unemployed mineworkers in return for Belgium's closure of uncompetitive mines (European Commission 1977: 83; Spierenburg and Poidevin 1994: 493–8). The Belgian government later implemented a market-sharing agreement with the Ruhr and in 1961 established a public directory to control coal prices, output, and sales.

Table 6.1 Changes in intra-community steel trade, 1952–5 (thousands of tons)

	Increases in exports	Increases in imports
Germany	530	1,777
France and Saar	1,462	754
Netherlands	276	570
Belgium and Luxembourg	1,230	295
Italy	59	160

Source: Diebold (1959: 580).

Table 6.2 ECSC trade in steel (as percentage of ECSC production)

	Intra-ECSC exports	Exports to third countries	Imports from third countries
1952	5.2	14.3	1.1
1953	6.8	15.4	1.8
1954	8.2	13.9	1.5
1955	9.2	13.7	1.7
1956	7.8	15.3	1.7
1957	8.5	15.1	1.8

Source: Diebold (1959: 584).

Spierenburg and Poidevin regard the directory as 'clearly incompatible with the ECSC Treaty' (Spierenburg and Poidevin 1994: 498).

Limited sectoral integration

Yet in terms of the flows of goods and changes in business conduct, there is evidence of some sectoral integration under the ECSC. Table 6.1 shows increases in the levels of incoming and outgoing intra-ECSC trade flows in steel, by member state, in the first three years of the Community. Germany, in the throes of reconstruction, was a substantial net importer, whereas Belgium and Luxembourg, and to a slightly lesser extent France, were net exporters.

Table 6.2 shows a generally upward trend in intra-ECSC trade in steel, along with respectable levels of exports outside the ECSC, as well as modest levels of imports from outside the ECSC.

Figure 6.3 shows a generally flat level of intra-ECSC trade in the coal sector, after which the trend is upward.

But correlation is not causality. The level of tariffs applying to trade among ECSC member states had been low before the ECSC came into force (Haas 1958: 60; Meade

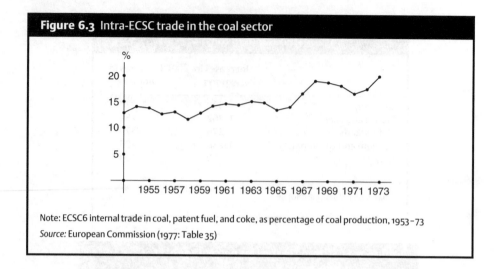

Figure 6.3 Intra-ECSC trade in the coal sector

Note: ECSC6 internal trade in coal, patent fuel, and coke, as percentage of coal production, 1953–73

Source: European Commission (1977: Table 35)

et al. 1962: 200), and the first twenty years of the ECSC were a golden age of growth. Overall growth would have come with or without the ECSC. Similarly, trade flows, intra- and extra-ECSC, would have increased with or without the ECSC. That said, the impact of the ECSC on trade flows was no doubt positive:

> one should consider the substantial increase in interpenetration of Community markets in steel and certain parts of the coal trade. There can be little doubt that ... the opening of the common market contributed to this expansion. The contraction of 1956 is, however, a warning about the limits within which measures directed primarily at trade barriers can have an effect, owing in part to the somewhat marginal character of much intra-Community trade. (Diebold, 1959: 589)

One of the sources of gains from market integration is the concentration of supply in the hands of most efficient producers. Some such specialization occurred in coal, although this must be seen in the perspective of the overall decline in coal shown in Figure 6.1. The Commission stressed in a report published in 1977 that 'as regards types of coal intra-Community trade has increasingly concentrated on German coking coal and coke. These products accounted for some 40% of trade in 1954, rising to two-thirds in 1973' (European Commission 1977: 54).

Adler (1969–70) examined intra-ECSC trade flows in steel and concluded that what developed was the sort of intra-industry trade that would be predicted by so-called 'new' theories of international trade, those based on the realization of economics of scale in markets for differentiated product varieties rather than on the classical theory of trade flows based on comparative advantage. He found a clear movement towards intra-industry trade during the early years of the ECSC.

Market integration may manifest itself without the physical movement of goods, through its impact on business conduct. The behaviour of Italian steel prices is instructive. Exceptionally, Italy had negotiated the gradual reduction of steel tariffs over the first five years of the Community (Diebold 1959: 148–51; Ranieri 1988: 353). Tariffs were finally abolished in February 1958. From January 1957, Italian prices began to fall, as Italian producers anticipated the lower prices that firms based else-where in the Community would be able to offer on the Italian market (Lister 1960: 244–6).

Steel firms located outside Italy were able to offer low prices in Italy without lower-ing their entire price schedule by aligning on French prices, which were low follow-ing currency devaluations in 1957 and 1958 (Meade et al. 1962: 66; Spierenburg and Poidevin 1994: 433). That Italian firms would expect firms outside Italy to seek to supply the Italian market, and act pre-emptively on the basis of that expectation, is evidence of market integration. Thus steel market integration not only affected the conduct of firms but also confronted national governments with the fact of the microeconomic consequences of their macroeconomic policy decisions.

The reaction to a January 1959 average price increase of 9 per cent for French steel provided further evidence of steel market integration, with German steel producers expressing 'grave concern at the new French price lists, which, if they were not re-vised, would force German producers to "reduce their own prices to the same level"' (Spierenburg and Poidevin 1994: 434).

Lessons from the ECSC

The ECSC was a stalking horse of European integration, leading the way for the EEC and Euratom, which followed the ECSC by just five and half years. In leading the way, the ECSC showed not only the heights that could be attained by successful market integration, but also the obstacles to be overcome, and the obstacles it encountered anticipated those that met its successor Communities.

The ECSC treaty was to establish a supranational infrastructure to manage the in-tegration of European coal, steel and related sectors. It was widely held to have pre-vented price discrimination and to have promoted competition. In fact, it did neither. The High Authority expended great effort on the supervision of joint-buying and joint-selling agencies, which were often referred to as cartels. Yet the price transpar-ency mandated by the treaty was more effective in reining in competition than overt or tacit private collusion could possibly have been.

The High Authority's task, prescribed by the treaty, was to negotiate a path between 'not enough' competition and 'too much' competition. As the Commission pointed out much later:

> the provisions of the ECSC Treaty designed to combat practices which would restrict com-petition are not intended to permit unlimited competition between the various undertak-ings. The main aim is to ensure that minimum margin of competitiveness necessary for the achievement of the aims of the Treaty, which include in particular ensuring that the most rational distribution of production at the highest possible level of productivity is not jeopardized by agreements which form obstacles to production. ... (European Commission 1977: 62)

In both coal and steel, the treaty proved to be a straitjacket that prevented the realization of a rational distribution of production. Judging by their actions, member states were willing to accept some increase in price competition as a consequence of market integration. They were not willing to accept the efficient re-allocation of production that increased price competition would bring. The result of this rejection of the market mechanism was repeated failure by the member states to adhere to the terms of the treaty, failures that lasted either until a judgment by the Court of Justice compelled compliance or until an accommodation had been worked out with the High Authority.

'Supranational', by dictionary definition, means 'transcending national boundaries, authority, or interests'. Jacques Delors, Commission president during the halcyon days of European integration in the late 1980s, has given a favourable assessment of this aspect of the ECSC's performance in his foreword to Spierenburg and Poidevin's history of the High Authority:

> Readers of this book will discover what strengths the High Authority drew from its collegiate system and from the independence of its members in discharging its supranational responsibility. The collegiate system was the touchstone of equality between the Member States, but it could have ended in deadlock if the members of the High Authority had remained under their influence. (Spierenburg and Poidevin 1994: xviii)

Against his rosy assessment must be set the more somber conclusion of Milward, who opined that:

> The High Authority, as the decisions at the end of April 1955 made clear, was not the triumph of functionalism, but a powerful international committee within which separate national representatives argued for separate national policies. Common decisions and policies were only possible where there were wide areas of agreement between nations. (Milward 1992: 117)

The experience of the ECSC suggests that Community institutions can negotiate and cajole but not compel member-state adherence to treaty commitments. This was a leading indicator of the experience of the EEC during the 1960s.

The development of European integration

The Korean war began in June 1950. The resulting demands on US military resources led the American government to see the wisdom of having Western Europe, including Germany, assume a greater share of the burden of its own defence. German rearmament was a development many in Europe would have preferred to avoid, but if it could not be avoided, they would try to control it. Thus in October 1950, not quite six months after the Schuman Declaration, French Premier René Pleven proposed the establishment of the European Defence Community (EDC). The Pleven Plan would have made German rearmament palatable by carrying it out under European political control. German troops would serve under the authority of a European defence minister, who in turn would be responsible to the ECSC Assembly.

Negotiations over the EDC were complicated by the questions of its relationship with Nato and its implications for the rearmament of Germany (Willis 1968). The EDC treaty was not signed until May 1952, some thirteen months after the ECSC treaty. It provided that the functions assigned by the Pleven Plan to a European defence minister should instead be carried out by a Council of Defence Ministers of the member states (thus anticipating a feature of the later European Communities). To provide political legitimacy to the proposed European army, Article 38 of the EDC treaty also provided for an *ad hoc* assembly to examine the organization of a democratically-elected permanent assembly, 'so conceived as to be able to constitute one of the elements in a subsequent federal or confederal structure, based on the principle of separation of powers and having, in particular, a two-chamber system of representation'. The permanent assembly was also to deal with the question of coordinating the activities of the 'different agencies for European cooperation already established'.

With the Luxembourg Resolution of September 1952, the foreign ministers of the ECSC member states gave the ECSC Assembly the task of implementing Article 38. In March 1953, that group adopted a draft treaty establishing the European Political Community, having a structure with a family resemblance to what later took form under the Rome Treaties (Griffiths 1994: 21–2). Thus a scant eight years after the end of World War II in Europe, the stage seemed set for political and military unification among the Six, to accompany the sectoral economic integration already in place. The inclusion of other European states was explicitly envisaged.

But it was not to be; at least not then. Whereas Germany ratified the EDC treaty almost immediately after it was adopted by the ECSC Assembly, the debate in France dragged on through a change of government. As seen in Chapter 5, some French resistance reflected an unalterable opposition to German rearmament; some was motivated by the views that political integration should come before military integration and that political integration should cast its net beyond the Six (Willis 1968: 158). The French Assembly rejected the EDC treaty in August 1954. When the EDC died, the project for a European Political Community died with it.

The European impulse was not to be denied, however. On the initiative of the ECSC Assembly, the foreign ministers of the Six looked down the path of economic integration that had been opened up by the ECSC. At their meeting in Messina in June 1955, the foreign ministers adopted as a goal the establishment of a common market, without internal barriers to trade and with a common set of tariffs applying to non-members. They established an intergovernmental committee under the direction of Belgian Foreign Minister Paul-Henri Spaak to work out proposals for the common market. The Spaak Report (*Comité Intergouvernemental* 1956) became the foundation for the Rome Treaties, signed in March 1957 and with effect from January 1958, establishing the EEC and Euratom.

The economies of the Six were strong in the years immediately after the EEC came into being and the EEC took advantage of this strength. According to Stirk and Weigall:

> Trade in industrial product between the Community member states doubled in four years and the average growth among the economies of the Six in the 1960s reached between 5 and 6 per cent. Predictions that the weaker economies—France and Italy—would lose from increased competition within the common market proved groundless, since France and Italy in fact increased their trade far more than the other member states. . . . Germany . . . also made gains of her own, particularly in catching up with French manufacturers in the private car market. (Stirk and Weigall 1999: 155)

Barriers to trade among the Six were removed more rapidly than had been provided for in the treaty, but three interrelated issues clouded the horizon. These were the place of agriculture in the common market; the on-again, off-again possibility of UK membership; and the nature of the political infrastructure that was to accompany economic integration.

Agricultural tensions were rooted in the need to define a treatment for former colonial possessions and the conflict between the wish of the Benelux countries for low tariffs on food imports while France, Germany, and Italy were willing to use high tariffs to protect their agricultural sectors (Stirk and Weigall 1999: 156). Member states eventually agreed on the common agricultural policy (CAP) in mid-January 1962, back-dated to the end of 1961, the deadline set in the Treaty of Rome (Stirk 1996: 196).

The first British application to join the EEC came in July 1961 and negotiations lasted well past the adoption of the CAP. The possibility that UK entry might trigger revisions in the CAP was one complicating factor. Indeed, Moravcsik (1998) emphasizes the protection of agriculture as a driving force in European Community developments throughout this period. But the real sticking point lay elsewhere, in competing British and French strategic visions of Europe's future. In the event, de Gaulle vetoed Britain's application in January 1963.

At a summit in February 1961, the heads of state or government of the Six established an intergovernmental committee under the chairmanship of French Ambassador Christian Fouchet. The ensuing Fouchet Plan of November 1961

> envisaged that major political decisions on foreign and defence policy matters ... were to be taken unanimously by the heads of government at state summit meetings. ... There would be a separate European Political Commission comprising officials of the foreign ministries of the Six, who would reside in Paris and coordinate agendas for meetings of foreign ministers and of the heads of state. (Stirk and Weigall 1999: 157)

As seen in Chapter 7, the vision of the Fouchet Plan—de Gaulle's vision—was of an intergovernmental Europe. Thus, 'In [de Gaulle's] view, the task of the Community executives was to prepare studies, and that of the Parliament to hold debates. But final policy was to be made by the representatives of the national states in the Council of Ministers' (Willis 1968: 322).

France consulted bilaterally with Germany and Italy before presenting the Fouchet Plan at a meeting of foreign ministers in Paris in April 1962. At the meeting, the Netherlands rejected the Plan, an explicitly stated reason being that the Benelux countries had not been consulted in advance of the meeting (Willis 1968: 298). But the contrast between the French vision of the Community's political infrastructure and that implicit in the Rome Treaty was another reason for the rejection.

Nor was the vision embodied in the Rome Treaty entirely implicit. The transition timetable contained in the treaty specified that the Council of Ministers should at first reach decisions unanimously but shift to a system of qualified majority voting by January 1966. The combination of the prospect of this change and proposals submitted by the Commission in March 1965 for administration of the European Agricultural Guidance and Guarantee Fund (EAGGF), which paid for the CAP, triggered a French revolt—the so-called Empty Chair Crisis—with enduring consequences for the EEC.

Those proposals were that the Commission, subject to the oversight of the European Parliament, would collect tariff receipts on agricultural imports and eventually industrial imports as well and use them to finance the agreed-upon EAGGF subsidies. Accordingly, the Commission would have become the executive branch and Parliament the legislative branch of a genuine supranational European government. This prospect was simply unacceptable to France, and from July 1965 French officials of any importance withdrew from the Council of Ministers and its working groups.

In December 1965, de Gaulle was re-elected President, but not as handsomely as he had hoped. Chastened by his electoral experience, de Gaulle sought an end to the stand-off. The Luxembourg Compromise of January 1966 induced France to take its place again at the Council table. Under the terms of the agreement, despite the terms of the treaty, unanimous approval was to be required for decisions that, in the view of a member state, affected its vital interests.

The Luxembourg Compromise was a temporizing device. The EEC could not do without France and the compromise gave France what it most wanted: the ability to block decision-making in the Council of Ministers. But it did so by stepping outside the formal structure of the EEC, which therefore remained to be taken up when it was once more possible to do so two decades later.

The Empty Chair Crisis was but one front in the campaign for European integration. It was followed by a second French veto, in 1967, of Britain's application to join the Community. But an amendment to the Rome Treaties, which provided for the merger of the three communities (and, not incidentally, the rescue of the ECSC), had been signed three months before the Empty Chair Crisis erupted. The merger went forward as planned in July 1967. In a separate policy development, the Commission represented the member states in the Kennedy Round negotiations of the General Agreement on Tariffs and Trade (GATT).

De Gaulle's resignation in April 1969 paved the way for the Hague Summit the following December, at which EEC leaders commissioned two reports. One, the Werner Report, laid the groundwork for monetary union (although the target, 1980, was not reached). The other, the Davignon Report, set up a framework for European Political Cooperation, a mechanism for foreign policy cooperation based on regular meetings of the foreign ministers of the member states. The Hague Summit provided for the Commission's own budget resources, on a smaller scale than had been sought in 1965. It also prepared the way, finally, for the accession of Britain (as well as Denmark and Ireland) to the EEC in January 1973.

Conclusion

A common aspect of the ECSC in the mid-1950s and the sideways progression of European integration in the 1960s was the non-cooperative—in the game-theoretic sense—position of the member states vis-à-vis their formal treaty obligations. The ECSC treaty gave the High Authority far more power, on paper, than it was ever able to exercise in fact. The Rome Treaty paved the way for the development of a supranational authority (the European Commission) that could not stand against the perceived vital interests, primarily but by no means uniquely, of France.

De Gaulle once famously said that 'Treaties are like maidens and roses—they last while they last'. European integration in the 1960s was on one level an exercise in *realpolitik*: sovereignty remained with the member states and it passed to the supranational level only when and to the extent that they were willing to cede it. The events of the 1960s were the basis for later (than might otherwise have been expected) progress in European integration and ensured that that progress took place no more rapidly than the member states were willing to permit.

Further reading

De Giustino (1996) and Stirk and Weigall (1999) are good collections of documents on European integration. Gillingham (1991) is a comprehensive treatment of the European Coal and Steel Community; Berghahn (1986) deals specifically with the postwar experience of the German economy. Moravcsik (2000a, 2000b) presents a provocative interpretation of France's role in European integration in the 1960s.

Berghahn, V. R. (1986), *The Americanisation of West German Industry 1945–1973* (New York: Berg).

Gillingham, J. (1991), *Coal, Steel, and the Rebirth of Europe 1945–1955* (Cambridge: Cambridge University Press).

De Giustino, D. (1996), *A Reader in European Integration* (Harlow: Addison-Wesley Longman).

Moravcsik, A. (2000a), 'De Gaulle between Grain and Grandeur: The Political Economy of French EC Policy, 1958–1970 (Part 1)', *Journal of Cold War Studies*, 2/2: 3–43.

Moravcsik, A. (2000b), 'De Gaulle between Grain and Grandeur: The Political Economy of French EC Policy, 1958–1970 (Part 2)', *Journal of Cold War Studies*, 2/3: 4–68.

Stirk, P. M. R., and David Weigall, D. (eds.) (1999), *The Origins and Development of European Integration* (London: Pinter).

Websites

The History of European Integration website at Leiden University (http://www.eu-history.leidenuniv.nl/) is an invaluable gateway to information on its chosen topic, as is the European Navigator (http://www.ena.lu/mce.cfm).

Chapter 7

Charles de Gaulle's Uncertain Idea of Europe

Jeffrey Vanke

Contents

Summary

Having returned to power in 1958 in the waning days of the French Fourth Republic, General Charles de Gaulle sought to use the newly-established European Economic Community (EEC) to help achieve a number of long-standing objectives: to place France at the head of cultural developments in European civilization; to maintain allies for French defence; to develop the French economy in a European setting; and to leverage French power globally by carving out a European organization of nation states that would turn to France as its natural leader. Accordingly, he undertook domestic financial reform and facilitated implementation of the customs union, which he linked to implementation of the common agricultural policy (CAP). At the same time he attempted to build an intergovernmental organization for foreign and security cooperation (the Fouchet Plan) on the political foundation of the EEC. Not wanting to risk French leadership of the Community, de Gaulle twice vetoed Britain's application for membership. De Gaulle is probably best known in the history of European integration for withdrawing French representation in the Council of Ministers and thereby triggering the so-called Empty Chair Crisis of 1965–6. Although bound up in negotiations about CAP financing and proposals for institutional reform, de Gaulle's drastic action aimed primarily to prevent provisions of the Rome Treaty for greater use of qualified-majority voting, an instrument of supranationalism, from coming into effect. De Gaulle prevailed when the other member states agreed to his demand that any national government be allowed to block decision-making in the Council on points opposed to its 'very important interests' (the so-called Luxembourg Compromise). De Gaulle's policy towards the EEC was part of a larger European strategy that often seemed unsteady as the constellation of European and world powers realigned even within a seemingly rigid bi-polar order.

Introduction

From the shores of England and Algeria during World War II, as leader of the Free French Movement, General Charles de Gaulle inspired resistance to German occupation and planned for a new organization of Europe to restore the continent's vitality. From the halls of power in Paris, Prime Minister de Gaulle acted from 1944 to 1946 to restore order and strength to his country and to its European and global positions. From the wings of opposition, Citizen de Gaulle, ever General de Gaulle, frustrated by years of premature quasi-retirement, campaigned for his vision of French independence in the cold-war world. In the chaos of the Algerian war, General de Gaulle returned to office first as prime minister of the decrepit Fourth Republic in 1958, then as president of the new Fifth Republic in 1959. He imprinted his most enduring legacy for Europe in the decade that followed: a largely intergovernmental European Community that integrated agricultural markets as well as industry and capital. What were his grandest ambitions for Europe unity? Why did he fall short? How did de Gaulle develop his policies and how much did his projects change over three decades of statesmanship?

Charles de Gaulle had a mind for the long term, *la longue durée*. For France itself, the General made a consistent push for ever-increased strength and unity in politics, economics, and defence. In foreign relations, on the other hand, President de Gaulle's approach was mixed. He wanted French independence, but he knew that France was too small to secure this on its own and that his country would paradoxically have to develop interdependent partnerships in security and trade. If de Gaulle had 'a certain idea of Europe' from 1940 to 1969, ancillary to his 'certain idea of France', it was fourfold: (1) to place or keep France at the head of cultural developments in European civilization, which he valued highly; (2) to maintain allies for French defence; (3) to develop the French economy in a European setting; and (4) to leverage French power globally by carving out a European organization of nation states that would turn to France as its natural leader (De Gaulle 1954: 1). His certain ideas of Europe were to preserve French sovereignty, to suppress the sovereignty of Germany (a nation he never fully trusted), and to use Europe to boost French power abroad.

However, the uncertainty of de Gaulle's European policies lay in his evolving judgement of which national partners and which international projects would best fulfil those goals. Fickle he was not, but even after 1945 several foundations of the European interstate system shifted or settled dramatically. By the end of the 1940s, the cold war's intractability made the Soviet Union, not Germany, the greatest immediate threat to French security. Within another ten years, even as empires crumbled, Britain's devotion to the Commonwealth and partnership with America clearly still took precedence over relations with Europe. The mid-1960s saw a less aggressive Soviet leadership; a peaceful, solidly democratic, but increasingly assertive West Germany; and diminishing British power and prestige. Each of these developments gave pause to de Gaulle. Besides Britain, Germany, Russia, and France, de Gaulle's calculations always included the European power of the United States, which seemed constant even where it was unsteady. When de Gaulle changed policies towards Britain or Germany or Soviet Russia, and therefore towards Europe, it was usually because one or more of those three countries were changing.

Constantly promoting French international power, de Gaulle was usually predictable in his European policies—but not always. Whenever Europe experienced one of its tectonic shifts, or whenever its faultlines rumbled, de Gaulle was prepared to adapt, adjust, or change his policies according to the new landscape. For example, in June 1940, General de Gaulle endorsed an ultimately unavailing proposal for an Anglo-French union to bolster the French government's resolve to carry on the fight. Yet within two years, with the Americans and the Soviets now in the war, de Gaulle already looked forward to France's liberation and a very different international position than he had contemplated in 1940. France's closest partnerships, he imagined, would be with neighbouring continental countries, certainly to the exclusion of Britain.

If de Gaulle's initial embrace of Britain was due to the extreme circumstances of 1940, other changes in de Gaulle's European policies reflected less dire, more predictable developments. Even the much less momentous example of European political union offers a remarkable turnabout on de Gaulle's part within the span of a mere five years. From 1959 to 1962, the French president pushed hard to get six continental countries to sign on to his decades-old vision for a European political organization, under the so-called Fouchet Plan. After two rare multilateral summits, his public failure at the hands of the Dutch was a humiliation he did not soon forget. Yet a few years later he consoled himself for his good fortune in not having the European union that he originally espoused, possibly restricting France's *force de frappe* (independent nuclear deterrent), which he had been developing since his first days back in power.

Across three decades of national leadership, de Gaulle consistently adhered to a French national idealism in his domestic and international goals. And within the confines of the cold war and modern democracy, he was a *Realpolitiker* in European affairs, certain about the value of French independence, less certain and more flexible about the best means to enhance it. To some degree, de Gaulle believed in the cohesion of European civilization as well as Europe's historical role of world leadership. To a greater degree, he recognized that different European nations would live and prosper together or whither and die together. But he faced a fundamental paradox that he seems never to have fully acknowledged. His vision of full French strength depended upon independence from the United States and Britain and also upon their security guarantees against Germany and sometimes against the Soviet Union. For de Gaulle, that meant a continuous balancing act between two imperatives: strategic security and independence from stronger allies. He frequently switched emphasis between the two according to the ebbs and flows of international developments far beyond his control. The international constraints on de Gaulle's certain idea of France thereby yielded his evolving, uncertain idea of Europe.

World war and cold war

General Charles de Gaulle emerged as an eminent French leader during the Battle of France in 1940. With Hitler's generals close to defeating France, de Gaulle travelled to England to endorse a vague, emergency call for Anglo–French Union that Prime Minister Winston Churchill offered in a failed attempt to steel the French government's nerves for a drawn-out fight against the Germans. For the next year, while Britain stood alone against Hitler's Europe, de Gaulle professed his deepest commitment ever to Anglo–French friendship, not only for the sake of France but also as a basis for organizing Europe. He insisted that 'the spirit' of the Anglo–French Union remained in place and that only a 'loyalty of sentiment with regard to allies ... will permit ... the reconstruction of Europe in law and freedom'. Together, France and England (as he usually called it) were history's 'champions of liberty'. Nor had 'so many artificial factors of division ... in any way altered the confidence and inclination of the French people ... to the British people' (Jouve 1967a: 5; Jouve 1967b: 95, 96).[1] In these early years of war and crisis, de Gaulle saw in England France's greatest partner and best friend in the world.

Looking to the future

At the same time, the entire German race merited perpetual suspicion and Germany itself deserved disarmament and dismemberment. Germany was 'drunk with pride', the bellicose 'German people' bore responsibility for war after war and never 'cease[d] to secrete Bismarcks and Wilhelm II's and Hitlers'. If alliance with Soviet Russia was necessary, it was because the Franco–Russian pair offered a 'guarantee of balance' of power to the abuses of German might (Jouve 1967b: 97, 107, 102, 101, 116–17).

By late 1942, with the Russians and Americans in the war, de Gaulle could look forward to a new postwar order. Although he never gave up the principle of full national sovereignty, his ideas for European and world organization were revolutionary in comparison to the past, if not in comparison to contemporary idealists. For the next several years, until he recognized the dangers of Soviet Russia in the cold war, de Gaulle promoted what amounted to a four-layered vision of international organization. First, national reconstruction was paramount, if symbiotic with international arrangements. At the next level, France would lead a west European international organization to coordinate trade, promote freedom and control the vast coal resources of western Germany. The corollary was de Gaulle's insistence that

Germany be permanently dismembered, harkening not to the future but to the pre-Bismarckian past. Third, and most loosely, de Gaulle suggested a Europe-wide organization with Paris and Moscow and perhaps London as its poles. While courting an alliance with the Soviet Union against Germany, de Gaulle insisted that his envisioned West European organization would not constitute any kind of bloc, 'because Europe is one'. Finally, de Gaulle agreed on the desirability of an effective postwar world organization (Jouve 1967b: 112, 113, 114, 115, 125, 127).

This vision for postwar Europe began to emerge in de Gaulle's Armistice Day speech in 1942. After elaborating on France's natural geographic position of leadership as Europe's 'bridgehead', he continued:

> [France] wishes henceforth to do everything so that those in Europe whose interests are joined with hers — the problem of their defence and the needs of their development — join with her, as she with them, in a practical and durable fashion. At the same time, she intends to play the role that matches her effort and her gifts. (Jouve 1967b: 102)

In early 1944, de Gaulle speculated on which countries those might be. The Benelux countries — Belgium, the Netherlands, and Luxembourg — always figured in, as did some version of a detached German Rhineland under international control. To this 'federation', Great Britain 'could attach itself'. 'Between England and us', he later added, 'there is a notable community of European and world interests' (Jouve 1967b: 111, 113).[2]

Yet as postwar planning took on more tangible forms, with France excluded from the conferences of the 'Big Three' (Britain, the Soviet Union and the United States) at Yalta and Potsdam in 1945, de Gaulle warned that Britain risked burning its extensive political goodwill in France. When he complained that 'Europe' was being excluded from planning its own future, de Gaulle implied that Britain did not represent Europe as France could, or perhaps that Britain was not fully European. Yet he continued to name France and England as the anchors of Western Europe's natural historical tendency 'to economic and cultural cooperation', and to plead for improved relations between the two (Jouve 1967b: 125, 122, 123, 134).

In other directions, eastward and southward, de Gaulle drew some lines in the sand and extended others. Eastern Europe could not belong to his West European organization because of its different river basins, different 'economies' and different borders. But in the Mediterranean, Italy — France's 'cousin' and latter ally — belonged to the West, as did Iberia, as soon as Spain (and presumably Portugal) returned to democracy (Jouve 1967b: 127–8). While refining his geographical concepts of European organization, de Gaulle added 'cultural' cooperation to defence and economics.

By mid-1946, shortly after he resigned as provisional prime minister and began a protracted period in the political wilderness, de Gaulle launched a short-lived attempt to use his conception of Europe to dampen the incipient cold war. An effective Europe could provide a 'balance' between America and Russia. But now he repudiated Soviet Russia for its domination of Eastern Europe and its ambitions to subjugate France (Jouve 1967b: 133, 134, 137, 139). Otherwise, though, the legacy of World War II still dominated his vision of Europe. Independent German states, as 'sons' of Europe, could join if they wanted (here his familial characterization of Germans was slightly more generous than during the war). But the 'indispensable foundation of all truly valuable and effective European construction' remained 'the real and sincere accord of England and France' (Jouve 1967b: 138).

Ambivalence about Germany

Given that, in his view, the 're-establishment of Europe' depended upon American aid, de Gaulle welcomed the Marshall Plan. He was especially pleased to accept an invitation for Europeans 'to constitute themselves ... into a whole and to establish a plan common to all states that wish to unite themselves to lift themselves back up. There is here a perspicacious initiative, and which one can hope will be fertile, precisely because it compels Europe to solidarity' (Jouve 1967b: 138). Yet the next two years saw a fundamental revision of de Gaulle's idea of Europe. He was furious when the English and Americans, thanks partly to the impact of the Marshall Plan, created a comprehensive West German state. At the same time, along with all of Western Europe, he shuddered at the threatening Red Army across the Iron Curtain.

In what way did de Gaulle change his vision for European organization? Not in its geography, which had always centred on the northwest of the Continent, and not in its content, which had ranged from defence to economics and then culture. Now, though, he abandoned Britain as his principal European partner and began to focus on France's relations first with a confederation of German states, then with the *fait accompli* of the West German state, as the core of the 'European union', which would bring a permanent solution to the German question. By early 1949, he insisted that European defence could not focus on England and that 'Europe must be done, with an accord between the French and Germans as its basis'. France, he still assumed, would be the 'head' of the 'organization of western Europe'. This organization would be held out to the Germans to give them 'hope' and to 'call them to the West' (Jouve 1967b: 151, 153, 157, 141, 148).

Excluded from power and able to comment upon developments but not to steer them, de Gaulle endorsed the 1947 plan for a Franco–Italian customs union, which never got off the ground, while pointing out its incompleteness. He derided the Council of Europe, founded in 1949, as ineffectual. Nevertheless the Council of Europe moved de Gaulle to develop his notion of a European organization grounded in the legitimacy of popular referenda across all member states, because a truly effective European organization required 'popular act[s] of faith'. The Schuman Plan for a coal and steel community he dismissed as a hodge-podge inadequate to the task of uniting Europe (Jouve 1967b: 143, 151, 159, 161, 166).

The symbiosis between a restored France (presumably under his leadership) and Europe, de Gaulle claimed, could send such reverberations across the Iron Curtain that the 'atmosphere' would change from the Atlantic to the Ural Mountains. In a speech evidently delivered before hearing about North Korea's attack on the South, de Gaulle praised his own activity for European unity: 'We have ... done everything so that, despite the suffering, the rancour, [and] the furore, the policy of the unity of Europe may be accepted by hearts and minds (*par esprits*)' (Jouve 1967b: 166, 166–7, 167).

Two weeks into the Korean War, de Gaulle stated that he was 'certain' that the war's purpose was 'to prepare the action in Europe', that is, to weaken Western

Europe in preparation for a possible attack from the East. In this context, he explored the possibility of German rearmament (a mere five years after the end of World War II), as long as it rested on a Franco–German accord and a 'European federation incorporating the new Germany' (Jouve 1967b: 168). Almost certainly de Gaulle intended to use the proposed accord to extract security guarantees from the Germans and enforcement mechanisms for the French. Moreover, he clearly saw European union as France's best guarantee for the perpetual containment of Germany.

The Korean war thereby led the General explicitly to accept the unity of West Germany and also to relax his positions towards Britain and Spain, both of which he would encourage to join the Franco–German pair in defending Western Europe. De Gaulle exhorted the Americans to 'Defend Europe!' and reminded the English of their interest in defending the continent. Although by the summer of 1951 de Gaulle no longer predicted an attack on Western Europe, he stood by his endorsement of a German defence contribution, albeit with treaty restrictions. He essentially repudiated the Franco–Soviet pact (against Germany) of 1944 and professed confidence in Germany under the leadership of Chancellor Konrad Adenauer (Jouve 1967b: 169, 173–4, 176–7).

Nonetheless, de Gaulle rejected the proposed European Defence Community (EDC), which he believed would result in the demise of the French army and the 'resurrection' of the German one. He complained that such 'detrimental (*facheux*) projects', or 'Frankenstein[s]', as the EDC threatened to destroy the European project by leading it down false paths. De Gaulle insisted on real checks on German rearmament, while proclaiming his European *bona fides* by trying to 'introduce Germany into a confederated Europe'. De Gaulle (and many others) wanted to contain Germany in a new Europe in which 'each nation ... [would] bring its [own] patriotism' for the common defence, but not by abandoning national forces or by giving Germany equal rights. During the most hysterical years of the cold war, in the late 1940s and early 1950s, de Gaulle believed the Soviet threat so urgent that he had dared renounce his pact with Stalin. Not any longer: with German rearmament seemingly headed out of French control, de Gaulle asserted that France 'is always Russia's ally in the event of a German threat' (Jouve 1967b: 179, 178, 181–3, 200). During the heated political debate about the EDC, Germany once again moved to the top of the General's hierarchy of French security concerns. After Stalin's death in 1953, when many westerners held out hope for a quick end to East–West tensions, de Gaulle looked to the Soviet Union for protection against a remilitarized Germany.

Even while he regretted that successive French governments had signed away the ability to control Germany, de Gaulle continued to espouse positive notions of European union, which he saw as the organization of European defences, economies, and culture, 'an association of nations in a confederation of states' (Jouve 1967b: 193, 195–6). Beyond that, de Gaulle observed, Europe did not command the 'congenital loyalty of its subjects', the mark of a nation, with 'millions of men will[ing] to die for it'. Yet as the EDC debate reached a feverish pitch in 1954, the normally implacable de Gaulle found himself increasingly drawn in, momentarily contradicting many of his own decade-old notions of European integration. He repudiated 'a Franco–German group that would be made to live under German hegemony within the frontiers of Charlemagne'. Suddenly, de Gaulle insisted on a geographically Greater Europe, 'from Gibraltar to the Urals, from Spitzberg to Sicily'. As always, his Europe was 'composed of indestructible nations, forged at the fires of History', not subject to the 'derisory puerility of wanting to smelt' any of them together. After the EDC failed to pass the French National Assembly in August 1954, de Gaulle pronounced himself cautiously optimistic about the intergovernmental arrangement that took its place to facilitate German rearmament and about the possibilities for East–West *détente* in the post-Stalin period (Jouve 1967b: 204, 210).

Around this time, frustrated by his continued exclusion from power, de Gaulle turned away from most public activity and devoted himself to composing his memoirs. Nevertheless he denounced the Rome Treaty of 1957 for the European Economic Community (EEC) as an unacceptable surrender of French sovereignty. Whereas Gaullist opposition had helped to scuttle the EDC in 1954, the Gaullists were weaker three years later and opposition to the EEC was much less intense. A sullen and seemingly isolated de Gaulle looked askance at the launch of the EEC in January 1958.

Accepting the EEC

Soon afterwards, de Gaulle returned to power as the saviour of French democracy, following an attempted coup by French army officers who feared that the government in Paris was on the verge of 'selling out' to nationalists in Algeria. With France on the brink of civil war and the Fourth Republic on its deathbed, de Gaulle agreed to head a temporary government and reconstitute the regime. The Socialists and Christian Democrats who entered de Gaulle's government in June 1958 insisted that the General accept French membership in the EEC. He did so, and by the end of 1958 went a long way towards defining French participation in it.

Having rejected the EEC in 1957, why did de Gaulle accept it a year later? Was it only because of political expediency—a sop to the pro-EEC Socialists and Christian Democrats? Some of de Gaulle's defenders insisted that it was because the General intended to honour France's international obligations. A more compelling explanation is that de Gaulle considered that membership in the EEC might help realize his visions for France and Europe. That was certainly what Maurice Couve de Murville, an influential colleague from resistance days and soon-to-be French foreign minister, tried to convince the General.

Mixed motives

First and foremost, Couve argued, the common market would force French industry to modernize and compete more than it otherwise would, or at least than was the inclination of about half of French industry. Couve understood that the more dynamic half, such as auto-makers, looked forward to expanded European markets, under the right conditions.[3] Couve's point strengthened de Gaulle's fundamental determination to force the French not just to adapt to the modern world but to be ambitious enough to lead it. The common market, Couve convinced de Gaulle, would bring French industry closer to world competitiveness levels. De Gaulle made this idea his own: the common market would 'awaken French industry'.[4] The General's first reason for accepting the EEC therefore lay in the interest of aggregate French economic strength, a key determinant of France's strategic strength.

Second, de Gaulle appreciated the EEC because it provided a small organization of continental European states, which France could lead, just as the General had envisioned since the early 1940s. Here was a new organization in place that could provide the momentum that had been missing during the chaotic period of the mid-1940s, his last time in office. And unlike what he envisioned at that time, the existing EEC well represented the General's more recent emphasis on a European union based on France and Germany, but not England. 'The essential point', he argued at an early meeting of his top officials on foreign affairs, 'is the Common Market which, in itself, is not a bad thing, and especially the political and cultural organization of Europe'.[5] In fact, the General would use precisely this grouping of the 'Six'—France, the Benelux, West Germany, and Italy—for his most substantial proposals for European union in the years to come.

His third motive for embracing the EEC was something that de Gaulle discussed less often by that time: the containment of Germany. In fact, if de Gaulle discussed it at all with Adenauer, who was also suspicious of Germany's long-term tendencies, such candour is not to be found in available records. Instead, de Gaulle told Adenauer at their summit in September 1958 that he understood the 'new Germany' to be a stable and peaceful country, committed to friendship with France, which wanted Germany as its 'one possible partner'. De Gaulle sincerely believed what he said, yet he always maintained a fundamental ambivalence about Germany's future, especially as it had lost so much territory and had been forcefully divided after the war. As he told British Prime Minister Harold Macmillan during their summit in December 1959, de Gaulle still feared an eventual German revisionist '*Drang nach Osten*', a push to the East. He therefore continued the work of his French predecessors to anchor Germany in the West. 'It is because it ties the Germans to us', de Gaulle had earlier told Adenauer, 'that I finally accepted the Common Market, of which I was not originally a partisan, as you know' (France, Foreign Ministry 1993: 344, 78). Neither of de Gaulle's counterparts in London and Bonn heard the full story of why he had accepted the common market or what he thought about Germany.

The British could easily see that de Gaulle enjoyed the privileged European role provided for France by the EEC—as long as Britain remained on the outside. In 1958, Britain's strategy for keeping a foot in European trade was to swallow up the common market into a looser free trade area (FTA), a proposal that predated de Gaulle's return to power. After several months back in office, Prime Minister de Gaulle rejected the FTA in a move that demonstrated his clear preference for a small European organization centred on the Franco–German pair. To be sure, there were economic reasons for de Gaulle's move. French industry would have no safeguards in the FTA and the British refused to purchase expensive French agricultural products in order to offset what de Gaulle perceived as France's competitive disadvantage in industry. This emphasis on Germany over Britain would arise several times during de Gaulle's next decade in power. Yet the General wanted to maintain friendly relations with the English. Hence, when the first reductions of tariff barriers took place within the Common Market in January 1959, de Gaulle agreed with his EEC partners to extend those trade benefits not only to Britain but also to all other GATT and most-favoured nations.

De Gaulle's ability to nudge France towards trade liberalization depended on his political will as well as on his ability to reform the French economy and finances. The Algerian war had so drained the French Treasury that previous governments had resorted to preserving French currency reserves by curtailing imports. The Rome Treaty stipulated that the first tariff reductions would take place only at the end of 1958. In the interim, France actually raised import restrictions instead of preparing to lower them. De Gaulle used his political strength to re-write the French budget and devalue the franc so that French exports would become more competitive on international markets. Although he did not announce it until December 1958, de Gaulle promised Adenauer during their September summit that France intended to honour the timetable for the customs union.[6]

What were the international consequences of de Gaulle's dramatic embrace of the EEC? Exasperation by the British, but relief among the other member states. Just months earlier, France had wavered between democracy and dictatorship. Now de Gaulle preserved the former while leading a stronger France as an active partner in the EEC. Especially in business circles and among political champions of liberal economic policies, early scepticisms about de Gaulle's intentions gave way to muted appreciation of his leadership. Perhaps most impressively, German Economics Minister Ludwig Erhard, an early opponent of the Common Market on liberal economic grounds, expressed relief to Douglas Dillon, US Assistant Secretary of State for European Affairs, that under de Gaulle, 'France was stronger politically and economically, as a result of which the Common Market had developed faster and more effectively than expected' (FRUS 1993: 58).

The common agricultural policy

De Gaulle's support for economic aspects of the EEC accelerated after 1959. Even as he laboured through France's Algerian war and pushed a specific proposal for the European organization that he had contemplated for almost twenty years, de Gaulle—now President of the Fifth Republic—pursued a myriad of detailed negotiations on implementing the economic clauses of the Rome Treaty.

De Gaulle himself was not usually involved in the negotiations. Nevertheless he approved further concessions by the EEC to outside trading partners and endorsed an acceleration of the twelve-year schedule for implementing the customs union of the Six. De Gaulle continued to welcome the EEC's challenge to French industry to modernize and compete.[7] But because he saw French industry as disadvantaged in both coal resources and innate vigour in the face of German competition, de Gaulle insisted that the Germans absorb excess French food production. De Gaulle's economic thinking was largely mercantilist, with an emphasis on exports over imports, to enhance state power. 'Our industry can face the competition', de Gaulle argued, 'but if our agriculture had to remain outside the Common Market, the weight that would result for our industrialists would not be bearable' (Peyrefitte 1994: 302).

In 1960, Germany produced only about one-third of its own food requirements; naturally it preferred to purchase the difference at the lowest prices available, largely from American and British Commonwealth producers. French prices were not competitive on world markets and French farmers were producing greater surpluses annually following stimulus packages designed during the lean years after the war. De Gaulle lamented that more than a century of French demographic trends had left the country with only 50 million souls, rather than the 100 or 150 million he opined were optimal. Absent all those mouths to feed, France would have to look to the EEC for guaranteed agricultural exports (Jouve 1967b: 242; Willis 1968: 287–92, 336–53).

Although it took de Gaulle two or three years back in office before he emphasized the clauses of the Rome Treaty for the common agricultural policy (CAP), he had long highlighted agricultural trade as a key component of his vision for a Franco–German accord. In 1951, at the beginning of Europe-wide brainstorming on agricultural integration alongside that of coal and steel, de Gaulle outlined his own thoughts in a press conference: 'One of the reasons [why] I foresee [a] broad and complete economic accord with Germany, is that on the German side there are markets that would voluntarily be buyers of our agricultural exports' (Jouve 1967b: 175). De Gaulle took up the idea again in July 1960, but his steady insistence began in earnest in May 1961, less than a year before the EEC was due to advance to the second stage of implementing the customs union.

That transition could not happen, de Gaulle insisted, until and unless France secured permanent agricultural guarantees from its EEC partners, principally Germany. In addition to his mercantilist concerns, de Gaulle worried about domestic pressure from the highly vocal French farmers' lobby. Little wonder that he described agriculture as France's second greatest problem, after the Algerian war. At his summit with Adenauer in May 1961, de Gaulle therefore laid down the line: 'Now, our cooperation that exists on an economic basis, *will not continue* if we do not take political decisions, and this is true particularly for agriculture.' The General continued: 'We cannot therefore do a Common Market for industry that does not extend to agriculture, and that depends very much on you' (Peyrefitte 1994: 302).[8]

In December 1961, shortly before the deadline for moving to the next stage of the customs union, Adenauer wrote to de Gaulle asking him to accept vague principles for an agricultural common market, but de Gaulle flatly refused.[9] The entire EEC stood in jeopardy. In fact, implementation of the treaty's terms for the second stage of the customs union was suspended when member states agreed to 'stop the clock' and engage in marathon negotiations on agriculture. The French finally got several important concessions on 14 January 1962, including the promise that member states would give preferences to Community agricultural products and would jointly subsidize excess production and even exports to third countries. That allowed the EEC officially to proceed with completing the customs union. Although some aspects of the agricultural agreement were delayed until 1965, de Gaulle had secured not only a commitment by Germany to purchase French surpluses, but also a stream of nearly direct German subsidies for French agriculture. His economic idea of Europe—controlled competition for French industry and extended markets for French agriculture—was finally coming together, centred on the Rhine and Franco–German partnership.

European Union

De Gaulle's notions of European union for political and defence purposes met with less success. Along with economics, culture, and another category that he had recently developed called 'political' Europe, defence figured strongly in de Gaulle's project for what he sometimes called 'European Union'. As seen above, the General had pursued something of the sort since the early 1940s. In his first months back in power, as he told Adenauer in September 1958, de Gaulle imagined that 'all Europe', not just the Six, should engage in European cooperation (France, Foreign Ministry 1993: 344). But by mid-1959, the French president returned to his earlier vision of a smaller European organization, now focused on the Six, to the exclusion of Britain. He repeatedly insisted that his organization would be more meaningful than existing ones because it would be bolstered by popular referenda, notwithstanding the fact that he refused to allow direct elections for the EEC's Parliamentary Assembly.

De Gaulle reiterated that this Europe could change global politics by introducing a third power between the superpowers, even as he reassured the Americans of his commitment to alliance with them. In his most candid moments, de Gaulle also acknowledged that he envisioned his European organization as a means for leveraging French power globally. If the EEC participated in it, and if France dominated the organization, then France could act on the world stage with the strength of six countries. 'Europe', he once privately explained, 'is the means for France to recover what she ceased to be after Waterloo: first in the world' (Peyrefitte 1994: 159). For all his lifelong harping on Germany's recent history of warmongering, however, de Gaulle did not dwell on the European aggressions of Louis XIV and Napoleon Bonaparte.

The global context

De Gaulle's proposal should be understood in its global context. Within months of his return to power, the cold war took a turn for the worse. In November 1958, Soviet leader Nikita Khrushchev issued an alarming ultimatum to the Western allies: leave West Berlin, an island of freedom behind the Iron Curtain, within six months. In response, for the second time since World War II, de Gaulle momentarily placed the imminent Soviet threat above his longer-term concerns about Germany, without, however, forgetting those concerns entirely. While he could envision the Western allies using force if the Soviets blocked access to West Berlin, he thought that the Soviets 'seem to want to obtain' the same sort of 'advantages' in Germany as France did. His country would work to 'prevent the return' of woes wrought by Germany in the past. Still, 'today's Germany does not threaten us', he insisted. 'She constitutes an essential element in the life and progress of Europe and the entire world.' Furthermore, German reunification 'seems to us to be the normal destiny of the German people', as long as current borders are not questioned, and as long as the Germans 'integrate themselves one day in a contractual organization of all Europe for cooperation, freedom, and peace' (Jouve 1967b: 221–2).

For the next several years, de Gaulle continued to hedge between German and Soviet threats. In November 1959, six months after the Soviet ultimatum had passed without incident, he sounded a more optimistic note about the possibilities for *détente* with Khrushchev. Nevertheless, de Gaulle's nascent atomic defence policy in the next decade was aimed first and foremost against the Soviet threat to Western Europe. Yet if the Germans ever acquired atomic weapons, even if only in joint control with the Americans, de Gaulle threatened privately but sternly to re-engage the alliance with Russia, France's natural ally against German military might. De Gaulle fretted that the American proposal for a multilateral force threatened such a possibility. 'We don't want the Germans to have any bombs, and we would join the Russians to prevent them from it.' So while de Gaulle pointed his own bombs at the Soviets in the event of an attack, however unlikely in the mid-1960s, he was prepared to join with the Soviets to counter Germany's acquisition of nuclear arms. What that meant, he does not seem to have fleshed out in detail, beyond an immediate 'end' to the Atlantic alliance (Jouve 1967b: 225; Peyrefitte 1997: 60, 72; Vanke 2001a: 119–26).

To be sure, France was in an unenviable position: next to a strong and peaceful Germany, but a Germany that would not recognize its postwar territorial losses; across the continent from a Soviet Russia that wavered between peaceful overtures and menacing behaviour; and allied to a United States that demanded military subservience as a condition for protection. With France's middling resources, de Gaulle found it difficult to be anything but 'uncertain' about his country's European options in defence matters. Therefore, de Gaulle started small, with a proposed European organization of France, West Germany, Italy, and the Benelux. An earlier effort having failed, following the abandonment of foreign ministers' meetings in 1959, de Gaulle began anew in 1960 with much more personal involvement and a much more ambitious plan (France, Foreign Ministry 1995: 35, 46, 208; Gerbet 1994: 235–36).

The Fouchet Plan

The French leader launched his initiative with a 'Note on the subject of the organization of Europe', at a summit with Adenauer (De Gaulle 1985: 382–3). A more specific title could have been, 'Proposal for an Independent and Intergovernmental European Union': independent in that it would be 'organized by itself and for itself, in the political, economic, [and] cultural domains, and in that of defence'; intergovernmental in that it would oppose the tendency towards 'supranational bodies' and proceed instead from regular summit meetings. De Gaulle would ground the legitimacy of the proposed European union in popular referenda and in a parliament of secondary importance (composed of national parliamentarians, not directly elected). Based upon bilateral Franco–German cooperation, his European union might include Italy and the Benelux as charter members—the same grouping as the existing EEC.

When Adenauer proved receptive, de Gaulle seized the moment. 'We must forge the iron of the Organization of Europe', he wrote Couve de Murville, 'for this iron is hot'. He instructed Couve to study the idea extensively, including the possibility of 'profound reform' of the EEC as well as the Atlantic Alliance. If the other four governments hesitated, de Gaulle instructed, then France and West Germany could sign an accord as early as October 1960 (De Gaulle 1985: 383–4). Here de Gaulle's European idea was as focused on Germany as ever it would be.

In fact, three of the other four governments responded favourably as well. The fourth, the Netherlands, nonetheless accepted the invitation to discuss de Gaulle's proposal. The enthusiastic French president had to wait until all six could assemble for a summit in February 1961, by which time a number of them had raised concerns about the integrity of Nato and the EEC—precisely those institutions that de Gaulle hoped to erode and supersede. Adenauer took some offence that de Gaulle was courting the other four EEC member states just as closely as he was courting Germany and wanted to determine the new Kennedy administration's position.[10] Finally, the EEC Commission, under Walter Hallstein, scorned de Gaulle's efforts as an assault on European integration as embodied in the Rome Treaty.[11] De Gaulle therefore ran up against a roadblock at the February summit when several delegations expressed reservations, the strongest coming from The Hague. As a result, the summit merely produced an intergovernmental committee to examine the idea, named the Fouchet Commission after its French chair, Christian Fouchet.

In May 1961, the impatient French president renewed his suggestion that France and West Germany reach a bilateral agreement, open to others to sign or reject as they liked. De Gaulle spoke to Adenauer of Dutch objections:

> Our partners fear that in this domain, the fact of *Franco-German domination is establishing itself*. This is not entirely false, but what can we do about that? For the first time in their history, France and Germany can collaborate closely. They should not allow themselves to be stopped by their partners' objections.[12]

De Gaulle seemed to be forgetting wartime collaboration, but he was expressly acknowledging that his European union would take in smaller countries without according them much of a role. Yet de Gaulle remained frustrated by Adenauer's ambivalence and by the failure of another summit of the Six in Bonn, in July 1961. At the same time Britain seemed to be moving towards a closer relationship with the EEC and soon applied for membership. De Gaulle's partners wanted to encourage Britain's participation in Europe before constructing a new organization that would exclude London.

Suddenly, in October 1961, with de Gaulle's initiative losing momentum, the French government unilaterally produced the so-called Fouchet Plan: a draft treaty for a European 'union of states' (Bloes 1970: 487–92). This spanned the wide ambitions that de Gaulle had held since the beginning, including defence, although it made no reference to Nato. When West Germany, Italy, and Luxembourg responded relatively favourably, Belgium and the Netherlands were left to lead the opposition. Dutch tactics switched from resisting formal treaty negotiations to insisting on British participation. Against French opposition, the other delegations got the Fouchet Plan amended to include explicit reference to the Atlantic Alliance. Nevertheless in January 1962, de Gaulle shocked the others by producing a new draft treaty, a revised Fouchet Plan, which dropped concessions that his diplomats had made during the previous two months of negotiations. Fouchet himself expressed 'regret' that his government had adopted the latest draft (Bloes 1970: 493–7).[13]

The French leader had so affronted even Rome and Bonn that he agreed in bilateral summits to compromise marginally in order to salvage his cherished European union. De Gaulle would once again agree to mention the Atlantic Alliance in the union treaty. Nevertheless, he told Adenauer, a Franco-German 'agreement ... should be imposed' on the others.[14] Adenauer was not so sure. Nor would Belgium and the Netherlands succumb to French pressure to accept the Fouchet Plan, which they firmly and definitively rejected at a foreign ministers' meeting in April 1962. De Gaulle found himself standing alone.

The Elysée Treaty

Yet the story does not end there. Within hours of the final meeting of the Six, de Gaulle revived the alternative of a smaller Franco–German union. From the French perspective, this represented a coda to the Fouchet negotiations, their fulfilment on a reduced scale. Yet even that achievement was painstaking for de Gaulle, who worked for months to secure Adenauer's agreement, through two summits and a massive publicity campaign in which he personally courted large crowds during a tour across West Germany. Still the chancellor hesitated. Only in November 1962, after seven months of intense wooing by de Gaulle, did he agree.[15] De Gaulle and Adenauer signed the ensuing Treaty of Franco–German Friendship at the Elysée Palace in Paris, in January 1963, to great fanfare.

Nonetheless, when Adenauer faced a revolt in the German parliament because the Franco–German treaty seemed to threaten the EEC and Nato, he agreed to a German preamble that endorsed those institutions. German parliamentarians were particularly upset at the treaty's timing, just one week after de Gaulle vetoed Britain's membership in the EEC. De Gaulle's disappointment with the preamble was palpable: all he had to show for three or four years of pursuing a European union was a truncated bilateral version of his original idea. De Gaulle's efforts to use Europe to bolster French international strength had failed. Although he would politely entertain intermittent German and Italian suggestions to renew talks on political union in the coming years, de Gaulle decided that this avenue of European policy was futile for his purposes.

The British Question

In 1958, when he rejected Britain's effort to establish a broader and looser free trade area, de Gaulle had preserved the EEC as a smaller organization of deeper economic integration. Britain's response in 1960 was to construct a parallel European Free Trade Association (EFTA) with six other European countries outside the EEC. But Macmillan's government increasingly desired to participate in the EEC's early successes. Hence its decision to pursue membership.

This did not come as a surprise to other European governments. Macmillan had laid the groundwork for months. De Gaulle, in turn, was more than ready. Even before the British applied to join, de Gaulle and Couve de Murville explained their ambivalence about British membership to the German government. Fearful that Britain and the United States would 'absorb' the Common Market, de Gaulle declared that his government was 'not very ardent' about British membership. Couve then predicted the outcome with stunning precision: talks would last for two or three years, 'and ... [then] will end perhaps by a rupture on France's initiative', as had been the fate of the free trade area.[16] And so they did, but in half as much time. Couve's prescience reflected de Gaulle's fundamental hostility to British membership. France played the prominent political role in the EEC and de Gaulle did not want to share this pond with the English.

By December 1962, fourteen months of negotiations on British membership had made some progress but an accession agreement was still out of reach. First, de Gaulle wanted a complete British commitment to privilege EEC agriculture over Commonwealth food imports. France sought markets for its expanding grains surpluses and Britain produced only a fraction of its food needs, which it generally filled with products from anglophone countries at costs well below what the French could deliver. Second, the geopolitical irritant of special Anglo–American relations continued to exacerbate Britain's courtship of the EEC. When, during a meeting with Kennedy at Nassau in the Bahamas in late December 1962, Macmillan secured an exclusive nuclear defence agreement with the Americans, de Gaulle's rage perhaps accelerated the timing of the rupture that Couve had predicted from the start.

Nevertheless the French president's sudden and firm rejection of British membership surprised most observers. Britain, after all, had stood for an entire year (1940–1) alone against Nazi Germany, a feat that conferred an aura of respect upon it and made Britain a natural leader of postwar Europe. Such respect was not yet diminished by the economic weakness that would accelerate Britain's decline towards mediocre power status by the end of the 1960s. But the Rome Treaty constitutionally enabled de Gaulle to limit the Community's membership and in his famous press conference of 14 January 1963, he listed the litany of Britain's disqualifications. First, Britain refused to embrace France's version of the CAP. Second, the EEC served a cold war security purpose. In de Gaulle's view, the Nassau accord symbolized how disruptive Britain could be to that purpose. Third, Britain's 'insular' attitudes were incompatible with Continental 'civilization'. Fourth, too much geographic expansion would destroy the EEC's 'cohesion'. Fifth and most generally, the United Kingdom was a 'Trojan Horse' for the United States; if the EEC admitted Britain, the United States 'would make the rules' (De Gaulle 1970–1: vol. 4, 66–71; Peyrefitte 1994: 282).

Why did de Gaulle wait eighteen months to veto Britain's application? After all, it seems unlikely that he wanted to give Britain the opportunity to accept his terms of entry. Personal pique may have played a part: de Gaulle forever resented the second-rate treatment that he had received in exile in London during World War II. More fundamentally, de Gaulle was unwilling to share European leadership with Britain, which would have required either a radical change in British thinking or French dependence on British security guarantees. Ironically, it was precisely the extent of American involvement in postwar European security, which de Gaulle cited against the British application, that allowed him to dismiss the British so easily in 1963—for the American presence eroded Britain's importance as well as that of France.

The timing of de Gaulle's veto was significant, coming as it did after the conclusion of the Algerian war and just before the signing of the Elysée Treaty. Given that the veto was sure to anguish France's EEC partners, the stronger France was, the more it would be able absorb any resulting international difficulties. By January 1963, France was almost a year removed from its colonial war and the young EEC had had more time to entrench itself in the minds and practices of its member states. Indeed, barely anyone reacted to de Gaulle's veto by suggesting that the other member states should spurn French partnership in favour of Britain.

By scheduling the veto so close to the celebratory deal with Adenauer, de Gaulle posed a Franco–German alternative to Anglo–American leadership of the Atlantic Alliance. The veto seemed not to surprise the German chancellor, who attended the already arranged Paris summit despite a flood of pleas to postpone it. Adenauer was known to harbour misgivings about Britain's application to join the EEC, and the timing of the veto successfully associated the long-time German leader with de Gaulle's action. With his veto and its timing, de Gaulle adroitly asserted foreign policy leadership of the Six both by restricting the other member states' options for relations with Britain and excluding competing leadership claims from across the Channel.

The Empty Chair Crisis

Notwithstanding de Gaulle's aspirations to lead the EEC for the glory and economic benefit of France, the General more than once threatened the Community with an ultimatum: do it his way or France would destroy the entire project. As noted earlier, in late 1961 de Gaulle insisted that the EEC agree to his core principles for the CAP before proceeding to the second stage of implementing the customs union. The next time de Gaulle issued an ultimatum for the development of the CAP, in 1963, he explicitly threatened the very existence of the EEC. While repeating the general refrain that agriculture had to have a place in the common market, de Gaulle insisted on having a CAP that would unequivocally support French agriculture. In the face of approaching GATT negotiations, de Gaulle proclaimed that 'it will be necessary that the Common Market stand, complete and secured, *or that it disappear*' (De Gaulle 1970–1: vol. 4, 128–9, emphasis added). Having won a set of agreements in late 1963, de Gaulle again went on the offensive in 1964, as the Community tackled the key question of grain prices, which, as seen in Chapter 9, formed the basis of both farm incomes and consumer prices. De Gaulle insisted that French grain be privileged within the EEC, despite Germany's understandable preference for less expensive imports. He told the Germans that the lack of agreement 'endangered' the 'EEC itself'. Throughout the second half of 1964, de Gaulle went so far as to suggest in French government meetings that he would seek out Soviet markets if the Germans did not guarantee to buy French grain surpluses. Clearly, de Gaulle got Bonn's attention (Peyrefitte, 1997: 254, 261, 263, 268).[17] Ludwig Erhard, who replaced Adenauer as chancellor in 1963, reached an agreement in November 1964 that included price levels that would not penalize German farmers, who already received the highest prices throughout the EEC.

But it was de Gaulle's action in 1965 that sparked the Community's severest crisis. Having secured EEC markets for French produce, de Gaulle revisited provisional accords in 1962 that promised common financing of Community agriculture, a key French demand. Not only would the Germans have to give up American foodstuffs in favour of the more expensive French variety, but they would also have to subsidize French food production before being obliged to consume it (Dutch agriculture would fare tidily as well). Germany had agreed to this in principle in January 1962, with a more specific arrangement due to be worked out by 1 July 1965. As that date approached, the Six found themselves far apart on the question of CAP financing. A set of provocative Commission proposals in March, linking institutional and budgetary reform, even divided the Dutch and the French, who were otherwise united on most agricultural issues. In particular, the Dutch supported and the French opposed Commission proposals to transfer considerable budgetary authority to the European Parliament, away from the national parliaments.

The Six member states differed deeply on both questions (how to finance Community agriculture and how to control those finances). Most of the participants expected a marathon negotiating session extending beyond the stipulated deadline, as had happened in the past. Much to their dismay, de Gaulle instead withdrew France's highest representative to the EEC, claiming that his partners had dishonoured their promise in January 1962 to reach a new agreement by July 1965, even though France itself was one of the parties holding up a new accord. That was the beginning of the so-called Empty Chair Crisis, which de Gaulle had triggered ostensibly because of concerns about the CAP.

Yet word from Paris gradually highlighted the French president's overriding concern about the EEC's institutional arrangements, specifically his desire to curb supranationalism and promote intergovernmentalism. As it was, the Rome Treaty provided for the greater use of qualified-majority voting, an instrument of supranationalism, as of January 1966. The planned move to more majority voting became bound up in the Commission's proposals to strengthen the budgetary authority of the European Parliament and its own influence in the Community system. Hence de Gaulle's rather Delphic statement in his press conference of September 1965:

> What has transpired on the subject of the agriculture finance regulation, in Brussels on 30 June [when the Council of Ministers failed to reach agreement], shed light not only on the persistent hesitations of the majority of our partners concerning the entry of agriculture into the Common Market, but also on certain errors or equivocation of principle which figured in the treaties for economic union of the Six. That is why the crisis was, sooner or later, inevitable. (De Gaulle 1970–1: vol. 4, 377–81)

Was it really inevitable? Only if de Gaulle anticipated thwarting the treaty's mandate for more majority voting. The French president was seemingly telling his partners that even with an agreement on CAP finances, and even in the absence of the Commission's institutional proposals, he would have engineered a crisis within the EEC in order to protect national sovereignty through retention of the national veto.

The drawn-out resolution of the Empty Chair Crisis bears out that analysis: de Gaulle agreed to resume full French representation in the EEC when he and the others reached an accord on voting in the Council of Ministers, notwithstanding unsolved CAP financial questions. The French presidential elections of December 1965 do not seem to have altered de Gaulle's course, although middle-class protest voters rejected his European policies and shocked the General by forcing him into a second round of voting. Meeting in Luxembourg in January 1966, the Five agreed to the French demand that any member state could block progress in the Council of Ministers on points opposed to its 'very important interests'. This was the so-called Luxembourg Compromise. Only then, after the EEC resumed business as usual, did serious talks resume on financing the CAP, although they took only six months and no new dramatic threats to reach the previously elusive accord sought by Paris.

Both agriculture and institutions were important contributors to the Empty Chair Crisis. Even without the Commission's power grab, de Gaulle would probably have threatened the continuity of the EEC over the question of financing the CAP, which in effect meant massive German subsidies to French farmers. In May 1966, de Gaulle told his cabinet that the new agricultural accord, 'was the whole question. ... That was in the background of all the debates and all the difficulties. To succeed, everything counted, including the exits that we had to do' (Peyrefitte 2000: 185).

The previous January, however, de Gaulle's explanation of the crisis *per se* was institutional. 'Why had we broken things off? Because the Commission claimed an exorbitant role, [which the other member states] seemed ready to concede' (Peyrefitte 2000: 185, 183–4). Although the crisis may have made CAP financing easier and quicker to resolve in 1966, de Gaulle's own testimony confirms that it was rooted in the conflict over EEC institutions, between fledgling supranationalism and jealously-guarded intergovernmentalism. The Luxembourg Compromise encaged supranationalism before it could fly and strongly influenced the history of European integration for the next two decades.

The EEC between Britain and Germany

The financial accord of 1966 reflected some of de Gaulle's enduring concerns about the French and West German economies. He referred to the CAP as France's 'indispensable compensation for that which is risked in the industrial Common Market' with the Germans (Peyrefitte 2000: 185). De Gaulle knew that German industrial strength surpassed that of France. He relied on mercantilism and French food exports to maintain some economic balance.

But the General's concerns about Germany ran much deeper and occasionally took on some urgency. Erhard's fall from power in late 1966 gave de Gaulle pause. 'Germany is drifting ... precariously balanced. ... God knows where she might go. It is therefore necessary to remain in contact with her, to orient her towards peaceful paths, and to watch that she does not turn bad.' He was somewhat relieved to see familiar faces in Germany's new government, notably Chancellor Georg Kiesinger and Foreign Minister Willy Brandt.

In 1966 also, de Gaulle's views on the Soviet leadership were more nuanced than ever. He reported after a summit in Moscow that he saw the Soviets as 'peaceful', but American–Soviet hostility as dangerous. The minutes of the meeting reveal that de Gaulle pleaded Germany's case to Moscow. The Germans needed 'hope' for reunification, which would remove Germany as 'the object and the stakes of your [Soviet] conflict with the Americans'—as long as they accepted their postwar borders and renounced atomic weapons (Peyrefitte 2000: 197). De Gaulle then all but thanked the Soviets for providing a counterweight to the otherwise 'irresistible hegemony of the United States'. This was the same year, after all, in which de Gaulle withdrew French forces from the integrated Nato command and banished US forces from France, although he kept France in the Alliance itself. Still, de Gaulle now relied on his ability to escalate a hopeless conventional conflict into a nuclear one, thereby possibly forcing the engagement of American nuclear weapons in the defence of France (Vanke 2001a: 119–26).

At the next Franco–Soviet summit, in December 1966, de Gaulle promised to work with the Soviets to prevent the Germans from ever acquiring atomic weapons. Moreover, de Gaulle acknowledged that if any country were allowed to possess nuclear arms, then all countries in principle should be allowed to do so. For that reason, he continued, universal nuclear disarmament would be the best outcome. De Gaulle then re-emphasized his notion that European *détente* would enhance security so that Germany 'will no longer have vengeful ideas'. De Gaulle could see that post-Adenauer West Germany still offered well-meaning partnership for its neighbours. But he fretted about West German opinion if East Germany remained occupied, guns pointing towards the West. This combination of medium-term confidence and long-term concern motivated de Gaulle to urge Moscow 'to establish . . . normal relations between all European countries' (Peyrefitte 2000: 202–5).

Like Moscow and Bonn, London saw its position change as de Gaulle's tenure in Paris wore on. The new Labour government under Prime Minister Harold Wilson posed immediate challenges and opportunities with respect to the EEC. By early 1967, Wilson clearly wanted to pursue membership. Even though de Gaulle urged delay, Wilson proceeded with a formal application in May 1967 (Peyrefitte 2000: 261).

Although de Gaulle vetoed the second application even more swiftly than the first, he was more ambivalent this time around. If the English entered the common market, de Gaulle told his cabinet before the application was submitted, they 'would upset [its] results. They would become, for a thousand reasons, the dominant element'. The day after Wilson lodged the application, de Gaulle explained to his cabinet why Britain did not belong in the common market. While viewing 'this request with sympathy', de Gaulle observed that Britain would have to pay more for its food and buy from European producers. Britain did not seem prepared for this, nor for coordinated policies in capital movements and currency relations. While the English seemed to be moving 'towards Europe', and it was 'desirable that the day come when England can take its place in Europe, . . . this day has not yet come' (Peyrefitte 2000: 267, 269–70).

Within a week, however, de Gaulle revealed some doubts about his own position, as if he wished the British could transform themselves into the less challenging, more compliant partners that he insisted upon. 'We have long suffered from the insularity of the United Kingdom. If it turns to Europe, we do not have to reject (*repousser*) it.' But he continued to harbour suspicions, even certainty, that British membership would destroy the common market as he had shaped it, in part due to American infiltration through British membership. When the weakening British pound needed support in November 1967, Paris agreed to help. And even after France announced in December that it would refuse to consider British membership in the EEC, de Gaulle told his ministers, 'We will see if they make the necessary effort to be able to present their candidacy. I doubt it' (Peyrefitte 2000: 271, 273–4).

If de Gaulle's hidden tergiversations on Anglo–French relations in 1967 left some doubt about his evolving assessment of London, his surprising diplomatic gesture in early 1969 left none. Weakened by the tumult of 1968, when protesting French students and workers nearly toppled the regime, and spurned by Bonn when his own currency faced an unwanted devaluation, de Gaulle sounded out London about a possible change in French European policy that might even privilege Britain over an economically surging West Germany. This overture came in a lunch for Christopher Soames, British ambassador to Paris, at the French presidential palace. After years of rejection and animosity from Paris, London was not about to pursue this opening. To make matters worse for de Gaulle, the British publicly exposed his *démarche* in order to embarrass him, particularly in the eyes of Bonn. There was something unmistakably clumsy about de Gaulle's sudden offer of close collaboration with London, without consulting Bonn, after he had courted the latter against the former for more than a decade. Indeed, Couve de Murville, by that time de Gaulle's prime minister, later recalled that de Gaulle was not particularly 'proud' of the so-called Soames Affair, the fallout from which occasioned an extremely rare phone call from the President.[18]

Why did de Gaulle consider making Britain his primary European partner instead of Germany? Fear of Germany seems the most likely answer. Although Bonn then offered nothing more frightening than firebrand Franz-Josef Strauss in the government, the West Germans were increasingly asserting themselves in foreign policy, including foreign economic policy. For all his hostility and even spite towards the British, de Gaulle did not fundamentally fear them. Yet he always feared unchecked German strength. As the German government left French finances to work themselves out and pursued *rapprochement* with the East on its own terms, de Gaulle's France was increasingly sidelined. If de Gaulle had been more politically secure in France, instead of being weakened by the domestic events of 1968, and perhaps if he had been younger and more patient for opportunities to unfold, he might not have turned so brusquely from Bonn to London. That he did so revealed not a change in his long-standing goals of French strength through controlled European cooperation, but a lack of control of the balance of powers around him, a willingness to change tactics and strategies to meet his goals, and a long-term uncertainty about which European configuration would best suit France. Soon after, de Gaulle resigned from office.

Conclusion

What impact did de Gaulle have on the course of European integration? The years of wartime leadership did not offer General de Gaulle any significant opportunities to promote or obstruct the reorganization Europe, as victory and then recovery were the orders of the day. In opposition from 1946 to 1958, Citizen de Gaulle helped block the European Defence Community in 1954 but did not play a crucial role in that or any other stage of European integration. De Gaulle also opposed negotiation and ratification of the Treaty of Rome in 1957 but was unable to overcome the constellation of forces in favour of the EEC in Paris (and elsewhere).

Once in office in 1958, however, Prime Minister de Gaulle made France fit to participate in the common market, a task beyond the powers of previous prime ministers during the spiralling Algerian war. The newly-installed President de Gaulle then agreed to accelerate implementation of the customs union, but so did others, in France and elsewhere. In late 1958, de Gaulle blocked a British effort to subsume the EEC within a GATT-like regional trading organization, and in early 1963 he vetoed British membership in the EEC. It is quite possible that another French government would have torpedoed the proposed free trade area, but it is highly improbable that another French government would have rejected British membership. Indeed, within months of his departure from power in 1969, de Gaulle's Gaullist successor, Georges Pompidou, was offering EEC membership to London. One effect of Britain's early exclusion was that for a dozen years or so only six member states defined the EEC's patterns in trade, investment, and a broad range of other activities and expectations.

From 1961 to 1966, de Gaulle insisted that the EEC build a CAP that privileged intra-Community consumption (especially of French surpluses), that subsidized Community producers, and that subsidized surplus production for export to third countries. It is most unlikely that another French government, even a Gaullist one, would have obtained so much from its partners, especially because de Gaulle did so by threatening to leave the EEC, an anathema to most of the French political spectrum. Also, if another French government had allowed Britain to join earlier, de Gaulle's version of the CAP almost certainly would have been rejected by London.

In early 1966, as a result of the Empty Chair Crisis, de Gaulle secured a *de facto* amendment to the Rome Treaty by getting the other member states to grant veto rights when vital national interests were at stake. Although the Community lacked enforcement mechanisms and already fell short of full treaty implementation, it is hard to imagine that anyone among the Six, besides de Gaulle, would have secured so explicit a rejection of the treaty-mandated, qualified-majority voting system due to take effect at that time.

In summary, the four chief effects of de Gaulle on the EEC were: (1) prompt French participation in and a successful launch of the whole project; (2) the exclusion of the British and establishment of intimate working relations among the Six; (3) the construction of an extensive and expensive CAP; and (4) the Luxembourg Compromise, a brusque rejection of the Community's supranational principles and of one of its prescribed practices: qualified majority voting.

If de Gaulle's European policies sought to enhance French strength and independence, how did they fare? On defence, his withdrawal from integrated planning in Nato did nothing to change the fact that the Red Army possessed overwhelming conventional superiority in Europe. Yet his stewardship of France's atomic weapons programme ensured by 1963 that Paris could inflict serious pain on Moscow regardless of American hesitance to engage its own nuclear weapons.

On the economy, de Gaulle brought modernization of industry and services through exposure to moderate competition in the EEC. In agriculture, de Gaulle's record is mixed at best, even from a French perspective. He probably spared French consumers higher subsidy costs by passing the bill to Germany. To be sure, French farmers were a formidable lot, not easily chastened by de Gaulle, not to mention any other French leader. However, the maintenance of high consumer prices and the expansion of an open-ended subsidy regime in the EEC placed enormous burdens on non-farmers in France and elsewhere. On European institutions, de Gaulle's record is a matter of unceasing debate between those who believe that France would be better served by sharing sovereignty in Europe and those who advocate guarding as much sovereignty as possible, a matter that cannot be resolved here.

Finally, what prompted the General's various actions, tactics and strategies throughout his political career? De Gaulle was a French national idealist and a European pragmatist, although on the occasion of the Fouchet Plan, his national idealism briefly spilled over into foreign policy idealism for a project that he hoped to dominate. The virtue of de Gaulle's European policies was that, apart from considerations of cultural unity, he perceived a common European purpose for peace and prosperity, eventually including the Germans as partners. The problem with de Gaulle's European policies (rather than *policy*) was twofold: the CAP would tax the Community, including France, for decades; and the style and some of the substance of his negotiations severely damaged the kind of compromising and cooperative spirit that he believed necessary to ease perilous cold-war tensions and to bring Germany ever closer to France.

The complications of de Gaulle's European policies was not that they were reactive and mutable over the years, which of course they were. De Gaulle was neither the first nor the last statesman to contemplate abrogating an international treaty, in his case the Rome Treaty. Instead, the first complication was that French power in Europe was not enough to match de Gaulle's ambitions for it. Therefore, de Gaulle sometimes had to realign his concerns and priorities, just as Britain, Germany, and Soviet Russia did. The second complication was that de Gaulle's rhetorical appeal to the self-evident nature of his policy conclusions carried such force that any change seemed to mark capriciousness rather than flexibility. Such is the burden of a long-lived assertive statesman. Having attempted in the 1940s to dismember a hated Germany, by 1966 de Gaulle was suggesting to the Soviets that they should one day allow German reunification in order to encourage German trends towards peaceful stability within an integrated Europe, even though he avoided using the term.

It was easier for de Gaulle to possess a certain idea of France than it was for him to hold a steady and certain idea of Europe, as the constellations of European and world powers realigned even within a bipolar order. Given that de Gaulle's European policies reflected the potential and pitfalls of the powers that surrounded him, his policies necessarily evolved accordingly. De Gaulle pursued a united Europe to strengthen France and to preserve European peace and prosperity. The challenge was to maintain American security guarantees while maximizing French independence from the United States, to develop the French economy while boosting Germany as well, and to embrace Bonn and Moscow while keeping open a line of retreat to London and Washington. Due to the tensions between undeniable interdependence in defence and economics on the one hand and irresistible independence of action on the other, de Gaulle sometimes pursued European policies that were inconsistent in their means of coordinating European efforts but forever consistent in their ends of bolstering France through Europe.

Notes

1 Most of the documents cited from Jouve are speeches whose whole texts can be found in de Gaulle (1970–1).

2 Jouve notes that de Gaulle sometimes employed the word 'federation' during the war to mean confederation between sovereign states, perhaps because of the contemporary French definition of 'federation' as an acceptable synonym for 'confederation', as found for example in *Larousse* (Jouve 1967a).

3 Couve, interview with the author, May 1997. The impression of Couve's importance here is shared by those otherwise often in dispute with him, such as François Duchêne and Robert Rothschild; interview of the latter by the former, March 1986, Historical Archives of the European Communities, Interviews.

4 Jean-Marc Boegner to Seydoux, report of an unrecorded conversation between de Gaulle and Adenauer, 29 November 1958, France, Ministry of Foreign Affairs (MAEF), Cab. Couve 316.

5 Meeting on 10 June 1958, MAEF, Cab. Couve 316.

6 Bundeskanzler–Adenauer–Haus (BKAH) (Rhöndorf) III-3-a, p. 12.

7 De Gaulle note, 27 February 1961, Centre d'Histoire de l'Europe du Vingtième Siècle (CHEVS) (Paris), CM 7.

8 Summit meeting 20 May 1961, MAEF, Direction Europe, 1961–5, dr. 1961, pp. 3, 6, emphasis added.

9 Correspondence dated 22 December and 24 December 1961, in BKAH III-3-a.

10 Quotations from Adenauer's meeting with Paul Reynaud, 3 October 1960, Bundesarchiv-Koblenz (BA) N1351 Bd. 104. Adenauer–Blankenhorn meeting, 9 September, Adenauer–Couve meeting, 28 September, ibid., Bd. 103. Adenauer to de Gaulle, 8 October, BKAH III. 3. (a). Adenauer–Debré meeting, 10 October, ACDP I-010-19/4. Luns on Adenauer in Dutch cabinet meetings, 27 January 1961, 17 February 1961, ARA MR 5.

11 Report on Hallstein's meeting with Dutch diplomat Johannes Linthorst Homan, 17 October 1960, MBZ GS-55-64 1898.

12 20 May 1961, MAEF EU61-65 dr. 1961, emphasis added.

13 Luns report on Fouchet's comment, Luns to Paris embassy, 23 February 1962, MBZ GS-55-64 1896.

14 15 February 1962, MAEF Sec.-Gén. Entretiens 16.

15 8 November 1962, German government response to the French government memorandum of 19 September, MAEF AP Wormser dr. 1, 382–90.

16 20 May 1961, MAEF EU61-65 dr. 1961, pp. 8–9.

17 De Gaulle meeting with German Parliamentarian Eugen Gersteinmaier, quotation from diplomatic cable, 23 October 1964, PAAA B150 Bd. 39, 5472f.

18 MAEF AO 29, Couve de Murville, fourth interview, 30 September 1987, cassette 6.

Sources on de Gaulle and Europe

The best available understanding of Charles de Gaulle can be found in his extensive writings, interviews, and speeches cited in this chapter, along with the well informed commentary and contextualization of select biographies. The interviews documented in Alain Peyrefitte's three-volume *C'était de Gaulle* (1994, 1997, 2000), although not accessible to researchers in their original form, seem to be as reliable as they are requisite for any in-depth study of de Gaulle in the 1960s. Minutes of de Gaulle's meetings with foreign leaders and Foreign Ministers can be found in the archives of the French Foreign Ministry, series Secrétariat Général, sub-series Entretiens, a few of which are printed in the series, *Documents Diplomatiques Français*. A few important documents are found in Couve de Murville's papers, housed in Paris at the Centre d'Histoire de l'Europe du Vingtième Siècle. Among several good biographies, the most encyclopedic is Jean Lacouture's *De Gaulle* (2, vols 1990–2), also available (abridged) in English. Official French records for de Gaulle's two periods in office are supposed to be housed in the National Archives, in Paris and Fontainebleau, but especially for the period after 1958 these remain overwhelmingly closed until at least 2025. De Gaulle's private papers and what is presumably a large volume of official papers that he kept in his private possession (as is the norm in French politics) remain indefinitely inaccessible, subject to the de Gaulle family's wishes; those papers are reported to be massive in sheer physical size.

Further reading

The best primary source material in English is found in de Gaulle's memoirs (1955–60, 1972) and speeches (1947, 1967). Another collection is Cogan (1996). The most thorough biography is that of Lacouture (1990–2). Stanley Hoffman's (1964, 1974) analyses still count among the most persuasive.

Cogan, C. (1996), *Charles de Gaulle: A Brief Biography with Documents* (Boston: Bedford Books).

De Gaulle, C. (1955–60), *War Memoirs* 5 vols., (trans. J. Griffin) (New York: Viking Press).

De Gaulle, C. (1964), *Major Addresses, Statements, and Press Conferences, May 19, 1958–January 31, 1964* (New York: French Embassy, Press and Information Division).

De Gaulle, C. (1967), *Major Addresses, Statements, and Press Conferences of General Charles de Gaulle, March 17, 1964–May 16, 1967* (New York: French Embassy, Press and Information Division).

De Gaulle, C. (1972), *Memoirs of Hope: Renewal and Endeavor* (trans. T. Kilmartin) (New York: Simon and Schuster).

Hoffmann, S. (1964), 'De Gaulle, Europe, and the Atlantic Alliance', *International Organization*, 18/1: 1–25.

Hoffmann, S. (1974), 'De Gaulle's Foreign Policy: The Stage and the Play, The Power and the Glory', in Hoffmann (ed.), *Decline or Renewal? France since the 1930s* (New York: Viking Press), 283–331.

Lacouture, J. (1990–2), *Charles de Gaulle* 2 vols., (trans. P. O'Brian) (New York: W.W. Norton).

Part IV

From European Community to European Union

Chapter 8

A Dismal Decade?

European Integration in the 1970s

Richard T. Griffiths

Contents

Summary

The 1970s is often portrayed as a dismal decade in the history of European integration. Following a relaunch in the late 1960s in the wake of French President Charles de Gaulle's resignation, the European Economic Community (EEC) experienced severe turbulence as it digested British accession and was buffeted by the global economic downturn. A period of so-called Eurosclerosis—sluggish economic growth combined with institutional immobility—ensued. At the same time, however, the Community developed in important ways. The European Court of Justice generated an impressive body of case law; the Commission negotiated a new trade and aid agreement with a large number of African, Caribbean, and Pacific countries; national leaders launched the European Council (regular summit meetings) to give the EEC overall direction; and the first direct elections for the European Parliament took place in 1979. Equally important, the EEC adjusted to the international economic and financial turmoil that characterized the entire decade. Far from being a disastrous period for the EEC, therefore, the 1970s should be seen as a transitional decade between the launch of the Community in the 1960s and the acceleration of European integration in the 1980s.

Introduction

The European integration process is often presented in the academic literature as a 'stop-go-cycle' with spurts of rapid progress alternating with periods of stagnation. The first years of the EEC were marked by many significant advances. Internally, the EEC successfully completed the customs union, launched the common agricultural policy (CAP), and commenced the construction and operation of its own competition policy. Externally, it concluded preferential trading arrangements with former overseas territories, completed a round of international trade negotiations (the so-called Kennedy Round of the General Agreement on Tariffs and Trade (GATT)), and twice engaged in complex enlargement negotiations. The increasingly close cooperation among member states themselves, and between them and the Commission, led many to speculate that a 'United States of Europe' lay within reach in the not-too-distant future. When, in 1969–70, the EEC began a third attempt at enlargement and committed itself to achieving monetary union within the foreseeable future, it seemed as though a new period of rapid integration was about to start. However, despite the EEC's successful enlargement—some would say because of it—progress soon appeared to have stalled. As a result, the period from the 1970s to the mid-1980s is often depicted as the era of 'Eurosclerosis'—a hardening of the arteries that could ultimately prove fatal. Suddenly, member states appeared hesitant and unwilling to take further steps to deepen the integration process. More importantly, they took measures to restrict rather than advance supranational decision-making within the Community.

The European Court of Justice and integration

This lack of euro-enthusiasm did not stop the Community from expanding in areas that were initially unforeseen. In particular, the European Court of Justice (ECJ) continued to develop at a staggering pace. This led to the paradoxical situation whereby political analysts spoke of the EEC in terms of eurosclerosis and stagnation while jurists increasingly compared the EEC to a nascent federal state. It was the Harvard-based jurist, Joseph Weiler, who first highlighted the paradox of stagnation in supranational decision-making and progress in judicial supranationalism. Not only that, but Weiler postulated a direct causal relationship between the two phenomena by contending that the stagnation of European integration on the political front was the result of progress in the judicial field (Weiler 1981).

Weiler based his argument on two concepts that he drew from Albert Hirschman's classic study on organizational decay: voice and exit (Hirschman 1970). The concept of exit describes the process of organizational abandonment in the face of unsatisfactory performance. Applied to the EEC, it refers to the possibility that member states would default on the implementation of European decisions. The concept of voice describes the process of intra-organizational correction and recuperation. In the context of the EEC, it refers to the influence of national governments on political decision-making in the Community. To Weiler, the increasingly active role of the ECJ signified the impossibility—or at least the sharply reduced likelihood—of exit. The hardening of EC norms into binding law meant that member states could no longer evade their treaty obligations. The closure of exit increased the importance of voice: as it became more difficult to avoid the consequences of European decision-making, member states grew increasingly cautious during the decision-making process and became more determined to regain control over it.

Weiler developed his argument about the link between political and judicial developments even further. Crucially, he suggested that 'It would be wrong to consider the relationship in exclusively unidirectional terms. Instead, the relationship has been bi-directional and even circular' (Weiler 1990–1: 2426). The simultaneous processes of political sclerosis and judicial progress could be seen as antidotes to each other producing a certain balance by the cyclical interaction of the judicial-normative process with the political-decisional one (Weiler 1981: 292). In other words, while political sclerosis was the result of member state concerns over the growing influence of the ECJ, the increased activity of the Court was, in its turn, the result of stagnation on the political front.

A key question for historians is the plausibility of this argument. Community law had indeed experienced a dazzling development since the signing of the Rome Treaty. Initially, enforcement of Community law, like that of all international law, depended entirely on action by the national legislatures of the member states. By the mid-1960s it was already the case that a citizen of any member state could ask a national court to invalidate domestic laws found to be in conflict with directly applicable provisions of the Rome Treaty. A decade later, any citizen could do the same with any national law found to be in conflict with the self-executing provisions of legislation enacted by the Council of Ministers (Burley and Mattli 1993: 42).

It is also clear that the increasing importance of the ECJ was not anticipated by its political makers. Indeed, the political choice initially was to create a European court that was relatively weak. Potentially more effective models of legal systems had been considered during the negotiations and it would have been possible to make the Court's rulings enforceable from the start. Thus, the growing authority of the ECJ was due to its own jurisprudence and was not the result of political (re)considerations within the member states. It is also telling that while all national courts have accepted the supremacy of Community law, to this day no national judiciary has accepted the reasoning offered by the European Court as the legal basis of that supremacy (Alter 1996: 462).

That does not mean, however, that concerns over the activities of the ECJ were the direct cause of the political stagnation that set in during the 1970s. Weiler himself provides no clear hallmarks or legal cases that could be considered sufficiently important to spur political counteraction among the member states. On the contrary, the story of the growing importance of the ECJ could easily be seen as one of a slow evolution over time. At one point Weiler ascribes the success of the Court at least in part to the fact that its activities went largely unnoticed by the interpretative political communities in Europe (Weiler 1990–1: 2435). How, then, could it have raised sufficient concern within the member states so as to cause more than a decade of political stagnation?

Weiler's argument is suggestive but not easily verifiable. Moreover, historians looking at the 1970s do not have to tackle these arguments within the framework set by
Weiler himself. There are explanations for the supposed phenomenon of eurosclerosis that are both more plausible and more proximate. They include the disintegration
of the international monetary system in the early 1970s, the oil crisis of 1973 and the
'stagflation' that followed, and intensifying British obstructionism within the EEC as
successive governments sought to resolve the so-called British budgetary question.
These factors alone would be sufficient to explain the EEC's fluctuating fortunes in
the 1970s and early 1980s, with or without the added impact of an increasingly au-
thoritative and active European Court.

One could also question whether terms such as 'stagnation' or 'sclerosis' really capture the historical dynamics of that period. Historical determinism does not begin
or end at the decision-making moment. Almost all historical events are 'caused' by
factors operating over a longer time-span. Thus, the simple fact that nothing very
much seemed to have been decided in these years should not be taken to mean that
nothing at all happened. Indeed, one could argue that the developments of the 1970s
prepared the way for the renewed 'dynamism' of the Community later in the 1980s,
under the energetic leadership of Commission President Jacques Delors, which is examined in Chapter 10.

The Hague summit

The late 1960s and early 1970s started with a new sense of optimism about the future of the Community. The completion of the customs union in July 1968, eighteen
months ahead of schedule, and the initial successes of the CAP seemed to confirm
the dynamism of the common market. More important still was the sudden prospect
of progress on the political front, made possible by the resignation of French President Charles de Gaulle in April 1969 and his succession by the more pro-European and
less anglophobic Georges Pompidou. Finally, it seemed, the Community could decide
upon some issues that had lain dormant since the Empty Chair Crisis of 1965–6.

Although it was clearly not his main priority, Pompidou lifted the long-standing
French veto on British entry into the EEC. The French government was prepared to
accept British membership, but only in exchange for a permanent solution to the
budgetary question and only after the architecture of the CAP had been cemented
into place. The French made it clear that an arrangement for the financing of the
Community budget had to be made before Britain could enter the EEC.

The Hague summit of December 1969 was intended to launch the Community
firmly on a path of future development that could not be blocked or diverted once
enlargement had occurred. EEC leaders therefore called for completion, deepening, and enlargement of the Community, which some have seen as evidence of a
renewed surge towards a federal European state. 'Completion' meant, first and foremost, finding an arrangement that would provide the Community with its own
financial resources. It also involved the introduction of direct elections for the
European Parliament and an expansion of its budgetary powers. The goal of

'deepening' went much further. It meant 'moving forward the goal of a common market' by introducing a wide range of new Community policies. Before the summit only agriculture resembled anything approaching a common policy. Now, EEC leaders called for common policies in the areas of monetary union, foreign policy, fisheries, and regional development. The Commission, however, was not completely satisfied, as the national leaders had not tackled the issue of institutional reform. Indeed, the very prominence of the national leaders and the marginalization of the Commission during the two days of the summit threatened to tilt the political balance within the Community firmly towards the nation state (Ludlow 2003: 11–25).

The member states were more successful in attaining the aim of completion than they were in their attempts to deepen the integration process. By April 1970, negotiations among them had resulted in a permanent arrangement for the Community budget. Whereas hitherto the budget had been financed by direct contributions from the member states, which were renegotiated annually, the Community would now receive its own resources, comprising import levies on agricultural products and all other customs duties, as well as a small proportion (not to exceed 1 per cent) of national revenues from value-added tax (VAT). As part of the bargain, the European Parliament would have an opportunity to amend the annual budget but could only increase its overall amount within certain narrow limits.

Community financing was settled before the enlargement negotiations began in June 1970 (it was no accident that enlargement came *after* completion). Four countries had applied to join: the United Kingdom, Ireland, Denmark, and Norway (the latter withdrew its application following the negative outcome of a referendum held in September 1972). The applicants had not been consulted on the new financial arrangements, EEC leaders having decided at the Hague summit that the new member states would have to adopt the *acquis communautaire* (body of EEC rules and regulations) and endorse the political aims of the founding treaties. The steps taken towards 'completion' and 'enlargement'—the accession negotiations concluded successfully in 1971—demonstrated once more the speed with which the Community could act if all member states shared the same sense of urgency.

The more ambitious aim of 'deepening' proved harder to realize. Of course, the task of 'deepening' the EEC carried far wider implications than did that of 'completing' the existing arrangements. Clearly, deepening was politically more sensitive and harder to agree upon. Indeed, one could question whether some of the goals set by the heads of state and government at the Hague summit had not been too ambitious. For example, the aim of creating a common monetary policy envisaged the establishment of an economic and monetary union by 1980, under a plan drawn up by Luxembourg Prime Minister Pierre Werner. Similarly, the aim of extending cooperation in the political field to foreign policy soon raised the problem of finding an issue of foreign policy upon which the member states could actually adopt a common position. Two additional, mutually reinforcing problems complicated efforts to deepen the EEC. One was the changed international setting in which the Community had to operate in the 1970s. The other was the impact of enlargement. No sooner had the three new member states joined the EEC in January 1973 than the Community was confronted with the thorny issue of the British budgetary question.

British membership

The British had always had a complicated relationship with the EEC. The country's first membership application, in August 1961, had been abruptly terminated in January 1963. The second, in May 1967, had been even shorter lived. As seen in Chapter 7, both had ended with a French veto. If the original decisions to apply for membership had been hesitant and divisive, the manner of their rebuff had ensured that EEC accession remained highly controversial. Even so, the economic dynamism of the Common Market compared to the irregular progress of the stop–go British economy, and the Community's increasing importance as a market for British industrial exports, had convinced most politicians, albeit reluctantly, of the need to enter the EEC. Public opinion remained far behind. A Gallup poll in April 1970 revealed that 59 per cent of the electorate disapproved of the government's application for membership and only 19 per cent approved. This changed to a majority of support a year later. Nevertheless unlike Ireland, Denmark, and Norway, the United Kingdom did not hold a referendum on joining the Community—although France held a referendum on whether the EEC should enlarge (George 1998: 49).

After a six-day debate, the longest since the war, the House of Commons approved the terms of UK membership in October 1971. The motion passed only because sixty-nine Labour MPs voted with the Conservative government and twenty others abstained. The Labour dissidents outweighed the thirty-nine Conservatives who voted against and the two who abstained (Baker and Seawright 1998: 17). Opposition leader Harold Wilson had declared himself against membership 'on these terms', although he supported British membership in principle.

Besides the supranational features of the EEC, the British were mainly concerned about the CAP. In particular, they realized that the functioning of the CAP and the role of agricultural levies in the EEC budget would incur considerable costs for Britain. It might seem strange that agricultural policy lay at the heart of the British concerns over EEC membership, yet, as seen in Chapter 9, the CAP accounted for about three-quarters of the Community budget at the time of British entry and would continue to do so for a long time to come. Moreover, the mechanics of the CAP seemed to militate against British interests, with one notable exception: British farmers, who received generous subsidies from Brussels, soon learned to love it.

Britain had a small (but efficient) farm sector. As a result, Britain imported nearly half its food—far more than any other member state. British farm policy left prices to be determined by prevailing world markets (some seasonal import quotas notwithstanding) and compensated its farming community through direct income support. British consumers therefore benefited from low international market prices. The CAP was far less suitable for the British situation: a system that supported farm income by guaranteeing minimum prices of agricultural products simply did not make sense in a country that depended on cheap agricultural prices. Given that Community preferences lay at the heart of the CAP, it was anticipated that the direction of British food imports would turn towards higher priced Community suppliers. This would affect both the balance of payments and the level of inflation in Britain and, because of the way in which the EEC budget was financed, would have a negative impact on the national budget as well.

All this was known before membership. Indeed, because of the fundamental differences between the EEC and British farm policies, it had been possible to predict the impact of the CAP from the outset. First, the British would become net contributors to the budget. As they imported more agricultural products from outside the EEC, they would make a relatively large contribution to the budget (by turning agricultural levies over to Brussels). However, because subsidies from Brussels were linked to the size of the farm sector (and increasingly to the size of agricultural surpluses), Britain could expect relatively little in return from the EEC exchequer. Second, by shifting agricultural imports from the world market to more costly suppliers from within the EEC, the CAP would have a negative effect on Britain's balance of payments. Third, the CAP would increase inflation, as consumers would no longer be able to buy food at world prices and instead would have to pay higher EEC prices. Finally, the CAP would interfere with Commonwealth preferences (preferential access for Commonwealth products into the British market). This was seen more as a political cost that became less salient as the Commonwealth declined in importance for Britain.

The British government had made some estimates of the costs of Community membership. For instance, a 1970 White Paper estimated an increase in food prices of 18–26 per cent, which would contribute to a rise of 4–5 per cent in the cost of living. On the effects of membership on the overall balance of payments and on the budgetary contribution, the White Paper was less clear. The problem here was mainly that 'in the crucial area of our financial contribution to the [EEC budget], there is just not sufficient basis, in advance of negotiations, for making reliable assumptions either about its cost or our share of it' (White Paper 1970: Paragraph 44). The government did allege that the net cost to the balance of payments would be more than the 1967 estimate of £175–250 million annually, because of the devaluation of sterling and the increasing costs of the CAP. It is possible that the government was anxious not to get drawn publicly into too precise a definition of its position before negotiations started. This can be seen from the fact that the White Paper did not distinguish clearly between transitional and definitive budgetary arrangements (Young 2000: 36). The conclusion of the government on one point, however, was clear: the overall costs of membership would not be large and would be outweighed by the boost in exports that would follow freer access to the rapidly expanding EEC market. Thus, on the eve of membership, the economic benefits seemed obvious. Moreover, having apparently shaken off the balance of payments difficulties that had plagued it throughout the 1960s and seen the current account move into surplus, Britain had a renewed sense of economic optimism as it joined the Community in 1973.

This picture changed quite dramatically in the second half of 1973, with the onset of the first oil crisis. The rise in international commodity prices had broken the rhythm of postwar economic expansion and introduced a period of crises in which nearly all countries suffered from inflation, balance of payments deficits, and slower economic growth. Every member state experienced these problems, but none more so than Britain, which, in mid-1972, had launched a 'dash for growth' fuelled by deficit spending. The timing could hardly have been worse. The balance of payments plunged to a record deficit in 1974 and inflation soared higher that anywhere else in the Community, reaching 28 per cent in 1974 and over 30 per cent the following year. The economy experienced an unpleasant 'hard landing' with gross national product (GNP) falling 2.5 per cent in 1974 and unemployment climbing inexorably upwards and the budget lurching into deficit. The original estimates of the costs of membership had anticipated a negative impact on the balance of payments and inflation, but with so many variables moving out of control these 'costs' were no longer viewed with the same equanimity. Moreover, with the rest of Europe also in recession there were no longer any dynamic European markets for British industry to expand into. With the balance of payments steadily deteriorating, the budgetary costs of EEC membership required immediate attention.

The budget

Before opening the accession negotiations in June 1970, all parties had agreed that any problems of adjustment would be solved by transitional measures rather than by changes in existing rules. Budgetary arrangements were an exception to this. At the time, the leader of Britain's negotiating team had argued that the existing budgetary arrangements 'give rise to a problem of balance in sharing financial burdens' and that decisions taken in the EEC after 1969 had aggravated the problem. He warned that unless a fair and sound solution was found, 'the burden on the United Kingdom could not be sustained and no British government could contemplate joining' (Young 2000: 3).

It was not clear, however, what the British could do to ensure a fair solution. It was not coincidental that some of the most effective Community decision-making before 1973 had been spurred by the anticipation of British membership. With applicant countries having to conform to the *acquis* and political aims of the treaties, the original member states could impose their recently negotiated system on the prospective members. The only concession that the British obtained was an agreement on a five-year transition period during which they would not have to carry the full weight of budgetary contributions.

The situation changed with the fall of the Conservative government of Edward Heath in 1974 and the coming to power of a Labour government under Harold Wilson. The Labour party had rejected Britain's membership terms in 1973 with Wilson, then the leader of the opposition, branding them an 'intolerable and disproportionate burden on every family in the land and, equally, on Britain's balance of payments' (White Paper 1975: 5). There is little doubt that had he been prime minister, Wilson would have accepted the same terms that Heath had negotiated, but pressures within the Labour party had forced Wilson to take a more eurosceptical stance (Baker and Seawright 1998: 17). As a result, Labour had fought the elections with a commitment to renegotiate the accession treaty and hold a referendum on the result.

Some of Labour's demands had clearly been designed for the growing Eurosceptical group within the party and had no significance whatsoever for the negotiations. Labour's election manifesto had promised to retain a zero VAT rate on basic items, but EEC rules did not prevent this. Nor did the EC prevent Britain from protecting its balance of payments by limiting capital movements within Europe (Young 2000: 113). However, the four main demands that were accepted by the Council of Ministers as the basis of renegotiation were reasonable: lower agricultural prices; better access for third world (and Commonwealth) countries to the Community market; recognition of the United Kingdom's regional problem; and, most importantly, a new financial arrangement or refund for the budget contribution.

The renegotiations started in April 1974 and ended almost a year later, in March 1975. The outcome was a promise to review agriculture and trade policies; the negotiation of the Lomé Convention (a trade and aid accord between the EEC and numerous African, Caribbean, and Pacific countries); the creation of a regional fund; and the introduction of a corrective budgetary mechanism designed to resolve the problem of the excessive British budgetary contribution (the Lomé agreement and the establishment of the regional fund were not directly linked to the renegotiation, although the British government took credit for them in its 1975 White Paper). At first sight, these accomplishments seemed impressive. Not surprisingly, the government celebrated the outcome as a big victory for Britain in Europe. However, it was forced to allow dissenting cabinet members to campaign for a 'no' vote in the referendum. In the event, it mattered little. The 'yes' campaign was far better funded than the 'no' campaign and the result of the June 1975 referendum was a comfortable majority of 67 per cent in favour of continued British membership of the EEC.

It soon transpired, however, that the renegotiation had not met the most important British concern over Europe. The costs of the CAP continued to skyrocket and the British budgetary contribution followed in its wake. The correction mechanism agreed to by the member states in 1974 could do nothing to solve this problem and, in fact, was never triggered into operation (Swann 1988: 78). The idea behind the mechanism was that countries qualified for a rebate when they met all three of the following criteria: they were net contributors to the budget; they had a rate of economic growth that was not more than 120 per cent of the Community average; and they experienced a balance of payments deficit. The rebate would then be calculated as the gap between a country's percentage contribution to the budget and its percentage share of Community GNP. The problem was not that Britain paid too much into the EEC but that it received too little in return (see Table 8.1).

In terms of its GNP, and in comparison with the overall patterns of payments by the other member states, the British contribution was not excessively out of line. When the gross contribution is compared with gross receipts, however, the picture is completely different. Of the other member states, only Germany was in a similar position, though the discrepancy was not as great as it was for the United Kingdom. Table 8.1 relates solely to the sums of money that were paid into and received out of the Community budget. Although these accurately represent the Community system of budgetary transfers, they do not represent the whole transfer system between member states. From the British viewpoint, the situation became even worse when the 'food costs' as well as the 'budget costs' of the CAP were taken into account.

As already noted, before EEC membership Britain had paid for its food at world market prices, for which it had to pay in foreign exchange. As an EEC member state, Britain was obliged to pay its domestic producers the (higher) Community price. If it imported from outside the EEC, Britain charged a levy to bring the import price up to the EEC level, but instead of flowing to the British Treasury, such levies were transferred to the EEC budget, showing up as part of Table 8.1. However, if Britain imported from within the EEC, it paid other EEC producers prevailing EEC prices, for

Table 8.1 Financial costs and benefits of EEC membership

	Percentage share in Community GDP in 1977 at current purchasing power parity (PPP)	Gross contribution in 1980 as percentage share	Gross receipts in 1980 as percentage of total
Belgium/Luxembourg	4.3	6.1	11.9
Denmark	2.3	2.4	4.4
France	23.3	20.0	20.0
Germany	28.1	30.1	23.5
Ireland	0.8	0.9	3.8
Italy	15.7	11.5	16.8
Netherlands	5.8	8.4	10.5
United Kingdom	19.8	20.5	8.7

Source: Godley 1979: Tables 4.1 and 4.3

Table 8.2 Net national receipts estimated for 1980 (£ millions)

	Net budgetary receipt	Excess food costs	Total net cash receipt
Belgium/Luxembourg	557	−60	497
Denmark	188	244	432
France	−48	528	480
Germany	−724	−358	−1082
Ireland	289	173	462
Italy	491	−515	24
Netherlands	193	694	887
United Kingdom	−1203	−127	−1330

Source: Godley 1979: Table 4.4

which it had to pay in foreign exchange as well. This part of the CAP's operation fell completely outside the budget calculations, but because of the structure of UK trade it weighed particularly heavily on Britain's calculations of the costs of membership. It also weighed heavily on Germany, but Germany's balance of payments situation in the 1970s was far rosier than that of the United Kingdom. The major beneficiaries were France and the Netherlands, two large exporters of agricultural products to the other member states. The effects of these 'excess food costs' are shown in Table 8.2.

Britain had a point when it called the workings of the CAP unfair. It is noteworthy that two of the three losers to the CAP were among the poorest countries in Western Europe: both Britain and Italy had a per capita income far below the Community average and both lost out to the CAP. On the other hand, three of the four beneficiaries of the CAP had an average per capita income that was significantly above the

Community average. Of the 'poor' countries, only Ireland profited from the CAP. Instead of achieving an improvement in the relative position of farm income—and even that was questionable—the CAP resulted in transfers between individuals and between member states that in many respects were inequitable. Budgetary squabbles aside, this situation called for some kind of relief for the poorer countries. They received this in the form of a European regional policy.

Regional policy

One of the 'deepening' aims of the Hague summit had been the creation of a regional policy to reduce economic imbalances within the Community. After the CAP, regional policy was supposed to become the most significant Community policy. As it happened, it would take regional policy quite some while even to approach the CAP in size and importance.

The preamble to the Rome Treaty had already established that member states were 'anxious to strengthen the unity of their economies and to ensure their harmonious development by reducing the differences existing between the various regions and the backwardness of the less favoured regions' (Allen 1996: 212). To that end, the European Investment Bank (EIB) had been created. The EIB raised resources largely by borrowing on national and international capital markets and either made loans to individual investment projects or guaranteed loans made by other financial institutions. The main logic behind the creation of the EIB was a fear that regional problems might destabilize the Community and undermine its long-term political goals. One effect of removing intra-Community tariff barriers, for example, would be increased competition for traditional industries in many relatively weak regions. It was possible that those regions would not be able to survive the competition and, faced with such a prospect, future governments would become reluctant to implement Community policies (Pinder 1983: 16).

The idea that the EEC itself should be an active participant in regional policy first surfaced in 1969, for two reasons. The first was that moves towards economic and monetary union (EMU) by 1980 could increase the disadvantages of backward regions by making it impossible for national governments to increase their country's competitive edge in international markets by means of currency devaluations. EMU, therefore, could have far-reaching implications that would have to be offset in part by the creation of a regional policy (Williamson 1975). The second reason was Britain's dissatisfaction with the EEC budget and the hope that expenditure on backward regions, with which the United Kingdom was relatively well endowed, would increase its share of EEC expenditure, especially if regional policy became an important expenditure item. As one of the poorer members of the Community, Britain could expect large direct transfers through a regional fund.[1] Britain therefore aimed for a regional policy that would overtake the CAP as the most important Community policy (George 1998: 56).

The question of establishing a regional fund became a major issue for Britain, Ireland and Italy during the enlargement negotiations. Because of its economic size and because it lacked many poor regions of its own, Germany would become the major contributor to the proposed new fund, which therefore depended for its existence on Germany's support.[2] The Germans finally gave their consent at the Paris summit of

October 1972, where EEC leaders decided to create a European Regional Development Fund (ERDF). All that remained for Britain to do was to make sure that the ERDF would be as large as possible. It was then, however, that lightning struck.

The second half of 1973 was dominated by the first oil crisis, when Arab produc-ers quadrupled the price of oil in the aftermath of the Arab–Israeli war. The en-suing economic crisis increased Britain's concern over its budgetary contribution to the EEC and dashed British hopes of establishing a regional policy sufficiently gener-ous to resolve the issue. The stumbling block took the form of strong German anti-pathy towards the fund. Having reacted to the oil crisis by implementing a forceful deflationary policy entailing deep budget cuts, Germany was reluctant to endorse an expansionist regional programme at a European level. Moreover, as the prospect of establishing EMU by 1980, if at all, receded fast, part of the rationale for the Fund also disappeared. Perhaps the most important reason, however, was Germany's irrit-ation with Britain's 'nationalistic' oil policy. When the oil crisis broke out, both the British and the French sought bilateral deals with oil-producing Arab states, arguing that no Community norms had been broken because energy policy lay outside the Community system. Nevertheless, Britain's rush for national security played badly in Germany, where the government became reluctant to make concessions in other areas.

Between July 1973 and November 1974 individual governments and the European Commission proposed no less than fourteen different arrangements for the ERDF. Only the threat by Italy and Ireland to withdraw from the December 1974 summit if agreement were not immediately forthcoming averted a deadlock. The result was the creation of a regional fund on an experimental three-year basis, which was later prolonged for a second three-year period.

The ERDF was not successful at either alleviating the budget problem or contrib-uting to the reduction of regional income discrepancies. First, the sums involved were relatively small. The ERDF never claimed more than 8 per cent of the EEC budget—less than 0.08 per cent of EEC gross domestic product (GDP). As long as the ERDF was a temporary arrangement, it was difficult to establish a claim to a larger share of the Community budget. Moreover, the EEC had a legal obligation to fund the CAP, whatever the cost, and this was a period when the cost of buying and stockpil-ing surpluses began to soar out of control. Second, what was instituted was a com-mon fund, not a common policy. The existing development map of each member state defined the areas qualifying for funds, which were to be used only for develop-ment purposes. Later even this minimum requirement was abandoned when the UK Treasury openly used the fund as a budgetary transfer.

The budgetary question would dominate relations between Britain and the other member states for quite some time to come. During the 1979 election, the Labour and Conservative parties took highly aggressive stances towards the EEC, which Margaret Thatcher was able to translate directly into government policy, with a vengeance. The demands for equitable treatment came to dominate EEC decision-making until the issue was eventually resolved at the Fontainebleau summit in June 1984 (Baker and Seawright 1998: 20–1).

The break-up of the monetary system

Of the all the proposals for 'deepening' made at the Hague summit, the goal of establishing EMU by 1980 was by far the most ambitious. The EMU would change the face of the EEC dramatically, as it would transfer to the supranational level the control and implementation of a core instrument of state power. Indeed, the supranationalism involved in EMU was certainly far more than de Gaulle would ever have been willing to accept. It is interesting to note, therefore, what brought this sudden interest in EMU to the fore.

Many contemporary observers suggested that just as the customs union and the CAP had been the main driving force of integration in the 1960s, so would EMU become the main driving force in the 1970s. The comparison did not end there, as EMU was also seen as crucial to the survival of both the customs union and the CAP. The background to this was the growing amount of foreign exchange speculation in the late 1960s and, more specifically, the resulting Franco–German exchange crisis of 1968–9. If exchange rates fluctuated wildly, it would be difficult to maintain the CAP's system of uniform intervention prices throughout the Community and keep trade open. As seen in Chapter 9, the short-term response, later to become almost institutionalized, was to introduce a cumbersome system of 'green currencies' — in effect, a system of subsidies and rebates on trade in agricultural products. The danger to the customs union took the form of higher transaction costs generated by exchange rate uncertainties. In the event, these fears were exaggerated as, over time, forward trading developed and reduced these costs considerably. Thus, only the need to 'save' agricultural policy became a major factor in promoting EMU. What this implied was significant interference in a major area of domestic economic policy-making in order to alleviate a problem in a policy area (the CAP) that was still taking shape. This fit the goals and strategy of some 'Europeanists', turning a problem into an opportunity for further integration.

In short, EMU was not only promoted as the new driving force towards further integration but also as an instrument crucial to the survival of the Community as a whole. It is no wonder that, as monetary cooperation began to unravel and the goal of EMU to recede, many commentators regarded the Community as being in an acute state of crisis. That view was rather exaggerated. First, although it did not achieve EMU by 1980, the Community did succeed in creating the European Monetary System (EMS) by 1979, a regional currency arrangement that perhaps better answered Europe's needs at the time than a complete EMU would have done. Second, one could question whether, or at least for how long, the ultimate goal of EMU remained a serious aim of the Community. Tsoukalis has suggested that the convergence of interests following the Franco–German crisis of 1968–9 quickly dissipated (1977: 169). Already at the Hague summit in December 1969 the French government had made clear that it no longer accepted the desirability of a complete monetary union.

Most explanations of the failure of the Werner Plan for EMU start with the disagreement between 'monetarists' and 'economists' over the strategy to be adopted during the transitional period. At issue was whether fiscal and monetary policy should converge before beginning to 'lock' exchange rates (the economists' position) or whether to move early with exchange rate convergence in order to force states to adopt appropriate policies (the monetarists' position). More important for the fate of EMU, however, was an inconsistency between the goal of the European currency bloc and its relationship with the Bretton Woods system of quasi-fixed exchange rates against the dollar. On the one hand, the decision to achieve EMU was motivated by concern over the growing instability of the Bretton Woods system; on the other hand, the steps taken towards EMU took the Bretton Woods system for granted. In other words, EMU depended on the system to which it was supposedly a response. The inconsistency was there from the start. Thus, the Werner Report proposed reaching complete EMU in three stages: stage one, beginning in 1971 and lasting three years, would achieve a 'concentration' of national macroeconomic policies with a goal of narrowing exchange rate fluctuations among member countries; stage two would create a European Monetary Cooperation Fund, which would evolve into a European central bank managing a common currency in the final stage; stage three, involving the irrevocable fixing of exchange rates, would begin by 1980. Unfortunately, unlike the Delors Plan of 1990, which underpinned the Maastricht agreement on EMU, there were no specific policy targets or criteria. In the event, international developments forced the member states to postpone the implementation of the first stage of the Werner Plan.

In August 1971 the Bretton Woods system collapsed. European policy concentrated on restoring the international monetary system while at the same time reinforcing regional currency stability. In response to the decision taken at the Smithsonian conference of December 1971 by the Group of Ten major industrial countries to increase the margins against the dollar from 1.5 per cent to 4.5 per cent (allowing a total swing of 9 per cent), the EEC decided in March 1972 to restrict the margin of fluctuation of its cross-rates to 4.5 per cent. Together the European currencies moved as a 'snake' (within a range of 4.5 per cent) within the 'tunnel' (of 9 per cent) against other currencies (a system known as the 'snake in the tunnel').

Although it brought about more realistic exchange rates, the Smithsonian agreement did nothing to remove the underlying causes of exchange rate diversity. The US budget deficit continued to pump dollars into the system and this, together with the acceleration of raw material prices, fuelled inflation. As countries responded differently to these challenges, confidence in the viability of the new exchange rates evaporated and the system finally collapsed in March 1973. The oil crisis, at the end of the year, killed off any lingering hopes that it could be revived. By that time the United Kingdom, Ireland and Italy had decided to give priority to domestic policy aims and had abandoned the snake. France followed suit in January 1974, though it rejoined briefly (for nine months) in mid-1975. What remained of the snake was a small core made up of Germany, the Benelux countries, and Denmark, with Austria, Switzerland, Sweden, and Norway as associate members (Padoa-Schioppa 1994: 241–2). Obviously, it was Germany that orchestrated the arrangement, not the European Monetary Cooperation Fund envisaged by the Werner Report. Despite these developments, the goal of EMU was never officially revoked. While denying its feasibility in the medium term, member states kept paying lip service to it. One example was the United Kingdom's affirmation of its commitment to EMU immediately after floating the pound in June 1972 (Oppenheimer 1974: 23). However, as the 1970s progressed, it became increasingly clear that the Community could not

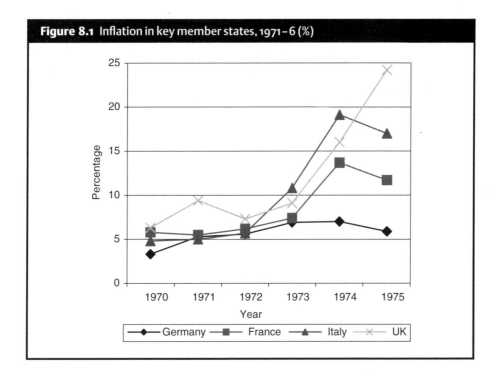

Figure 8.1 Inflation in key member states, 1971–6 (%)

even agree on the establishment of the next step: a regional scheme of fixed but adjustable parities (the so-called 'floating peg' system). Indeed, all attempts at reform were doomed as long as the member states disagreed on how to react to the economic turmoil dubbed 'stagflation'.

The reaction to the economic crisis of the 1970s varied from member state to member state. Faced simultaneously with the problems of high inflation and low economic growth, the German authorities gave preference to the maintenance of price stability. The Bundesbank (German central bank) adopted a restrictive monetary policy and was prepared to accept the consequence: economic recession (Marsh 1992: 192). Other countries aimed instead at maintaining high growth but had to bear the inflationary consequences. As shown in Figure 8.1, whereas at the beginning of the 1970s the inflation levels of France, Germany, Italy and the United Kingdom were similar, by the mid-1970s they had diverged considerably.

With differences of that magnitude, any attempts to re-establish monetary cooperation on a Community basis were unlikely to succeed. When it was launched in 1969, on the back of a decade of economic convergence and international monetary stability, European monetary cooperation had seemed straightforward. A decade later, this was no longer the case. Yet the conviction grew that it was necessary to do something about monetary instability.

Towards the end of the 1970s, it became increasingly clear that German macroeconomic management had been more successful than that of the other leading European countries. The German export sector experienced a renewed boom and both inflation and unemployment were among the lowest in the Organization for Economic Cooperation and Development (OECD). By contrast, the other leading

European countries had witnessed a sharp erosion of their competitive positions and experienced both higher inflation and higher unemployment. In 1977, France, the United Kingdom and Italy all cautiously implemented stabilization programmes directed primarily against inflation. The Modell Deutschland (German model) served as their main example (Story 1988: 399; Ungerer 1997: 149).

It was no accident, therefore, that European monetary cooperation was suddenly 'in the air' again or that concern over the dollar served to trigger a new initiative. The Germans were particularly concerned about a renewed slide of the dollar that had started in the second half of 1977. A new scheme was launched at a meeting of the European Council in March 1978 and was presented as a Franco–German initiative. This time, the EEC was more cautious than it had been a decade earlier. The aim of EMU was replaced by a 'zone of monetary stability' in which participating member states could operate. This proved difficult to achieve, as it was hard to agree on an arrangement that responded to the varying demands of all Community members. At the start of the negotiations, inflation rates within the Community still varied by as much ten percentage points. The French, especially, insisted that the new arrangement had to be sufficiently different from the existing snake, calling it an 'animal de la préhistoire monétaire européene' (Ludlow 1982: 3). They feared, once again, that the monetary system would be dominated by Germany.

EEC leaders finally agreed on the establishment of the EMS, which would start formally in March 1979. To accommodate French concerns, a parallel European currency unit (ecu) was created. This basket currency, comprising specific weightings for each currency in the exchange-rate mechanism of the EMS, would be used to calculate the margins of fluctuation within the system. However, the essence of the intervention system would remain the same as in the snake. It did not take long, therefore, for the system to become known as another 'German mark zone', just as the earlier snake had been (Heisenberg 1999; Loedel 1999). To accommodate members with initially high inflation rates, large intervention bands of 12 per cent were envisaged instead of the 4.5 per cent agreed upon by participants with lower inflation rates. Even so, the British government, emerging from a protracted period of labour unrest (the strike-ridden 'winter of discontent') and facing elections, eschewed membership in the system's exchange-rate mechanism (ERM).

The EEC had little success with the timing of its monetary schemes. Just as the Werner Plan had almost been derailed by the first oil crisis, so the launch of the EMS coincided with the second oil crisis. As wave upon wave of speculation buffeted the European currencies, regular crisis meetings and periodic realignments preserved the fiction that there was anything like a stable system. By March 1983, the German mark had appreciated by a little over 15 per cent against the ecu, while the French franc had slumped by 11.15 per cent and the Italian lire by 14.25 per cent. Although this caused some satisfaction among detractors of the scheme, and no little concern among those trying to make it work, there was little else to be done. As long as inflation rates continued to diverge or, more to the point, as long as the government priorities and policies that lay behind them continued to diverge, there was no realistic alternative. However, a structure was in place and pressures were growing that would form a new consensus among EEC member states on macroeconomic policy options.

Slower growth

Many of the problems confronting the member states and affecting their propensity and ability to cooperate can be traced directly to the economic slow-down of the 1970s. The immediate aftermath of the first oil crisis (1974–5) had been a shock for the Community. For most countries, for the first time in the postwar period, output actually contracted, and quite sharply too. The Keynesian analysis suggested that the oil producers had removed a chunk of demand from the economy and that governments should step in to plug the gap. However, the recession was accompanied not only by rising unemployment on a scale not previously experienced in the postwar years but also by very strong inflationary pressures (Aldcroft 2001: 188). The phenomenon of 'stagflation' had arrived, and with it 'the crisis of economics'.

The inherited wisdom from Keynesian economics was that when the economy threatened to slow down and unemployment to rise, governments should increase their expenditure in order to make up the shortfall in demand. It was assumed that the downturn would relieve any inflationary pressures in the economy and that the inflationary impact of government intervention would be negligible, or at least containable. On the other hand, if countries faced inflationary pressures and, with fixed exchange rates the rule, a subsequent deterioration in the balance of payments, a sharp dose of monetary and fiscal deflationary medicine was required. The arrival of stagflation presented governments simultaneously with the challenges of recession and inflation, whereby solving one problem would merely aggravate the other. Governments were now faced with policy choices that they had not earlier confronted. Gone were the days when one policy instrument, depending on how it was used, could solve all problems.

The crisis of economics, however, went one level deeper. Critics now levied charges that Keynesian demand management had never worked properly. First, the time-consuming process of planning, approving and executing changes in expenditure had meant that instead of being counter-cyclical in their impact, as intended, demand management tended to be pro-cyclical. Second, critics suggested that government expenditure had a greater impact on inflation than had been assumed and was relatively ineffective in raising demand. What these critics advocated was the use of monetary policy as the main tool. The problem with monetarism, the Keynesians argued, was that it worked no better than their own prescription and that changes in the money supply were ineffective in promoting growth. Nonetheless by the end of the 1970s most countries had adopted some form of control of monetary aggregates, together with fiscal policies designed to stabilize or lower public sector deficits (Aldcroft 2001: 206–7). However, as governments tried to use monetary instruments, it transpired that money, as a variable, was neither easy to define nor to use. But what really plunged economics into a crisis was the fact that monetarism offered no way out of the policy dilemmas posed by the coincidence of low growth and high inflation.

It was at this point that another element entered into the debate. If oil dependence had been the cause of the recession, then Japan should have been on its knees. Although Japanese super-growth belonged to the past, Japan had recovered strongly from the oil shock and was expanding faster than the European economies. Moreover, the so-called Asian tigers—Korea, Taiwan, and Singapore—were also surging ahead. Eventually, European policy-makers began to see the problem not as one that required a choice between policy instruments (Keynesian or monetarist) or between conflicting goals (inflation or growth), or even as a question of economic management, but as one of adaptation to structural change.

A group hitherto considered on the right of the political spectrum now began to dominate the debate: the so-called supply-siders, whose most famous exponent was University of Chicago economist Milton Friedman. Supply-side economics suggested that the undermining of the market, by government, lay at the heart of Europe's problems. By neglecting the long-term growth in economic capability and competitiveness, conventional demand management had weakened the microeconomic base in return for small, temporary gains in the level of employment (Cairncross 1992: 6). Governments made choices that consumers would not necessarily make for themselves and charged for their services in ways that did not reflect their true costs.

Moreover, governments themselves were monopoly suppliers of many services and were a generous 'banker of last resort' to underwrite any losses. Government spending had increased substantially over the past decades. By the mid-1980s, government outlays averaged over 50 per cent of GDP as against 32 per cent in 1960. More significant was the change in the composition of government spending. By the late 1970s, European governments were spending more on transfer payments to individuals than on purchases of goods and services (Boskin 1987: 18). Finally, even in areas where the government was not a supplier, it was a regulator, restricting and distorting market incentives with swathes of social and environmental legislation. Not surprisingly, given its antagonism to government spending and regulation, supply-siders found ready allies among monetarist economists and policy-makers. Monetary caution, combined with deregulation and privatization, began to assume an ever more central role in the policies of EC member states. Germany, a late convert to Keynesianism, was an early and ultimately successful proponent of monetary constraint. The Keynesian experiments in Italy and the United Kingdom in the early 1970s were wrecked on the rocks of International Monetary Fund (IMF) relief schemes. In the United Kingdom, the Conservative victory in 1979 ushered in the Thatcherite revolution.

The second oil shock of 1979 marked the final break with conventional postwar policy-making. Recessionary impulses would normally have triggered a move towards expansionary policies, but a host of unresolved problems stemming from earlier shocks, such as inflation, budgetary deficits and wage pressures, made sure that governments could no longer afford to contemplate accommodating external shocks as they had done in the past. The main exception remained France, where the election of the socialist François Mitterrand as president in 1981 led to the last great Keynesian experiment in Europe. A mixture of expansionist policy and social reform, engineered by his finance minister, Jacques Delors, would light the way to a different future. Two years later, battered by currency speculation, a depreciating currency and a deteriorating balance of payments, Mitterrand abandoned the experiment (at Delors's behest). Thereafter France, too, committed itself to the primacy of low inflation and fiscal prudence.

Conclusion

From the mid-1970s onwards, contemporary observers almost universally used terms such as 'eurosclerosis' and 'europessimism' to describe the state of the EEC. By 1980 some academics warned about the possible disintegration of the EEC and even leading members of EC institutions openly spoke of the dismal state that Europe was in. At the twenty-fifth anniversary of the Rome Treaty, in 1982, the president of the European Parliament compared the Community to a 'feeble cardiac patient whose condition is so poor that he cannot even be disturbed by a birthday party' (Lagerfeld 1990: 66).

This chapter first questioned the accuracy of this picture by suggesting that throughout the 1970s integration continued, but less through the taking of bold new decisions at Council of Ministers' level than through the inexorable extension of Community law. However, the chapter rejected a specific link between these two phenomena. Governments did not become hesitant to make decisions because they realized that those decisions would indeed be binding. If governments did become more restrained, it was more likely because having seen the demise of Gaullism in France, the EEC was soon faced with a British variant of it, which would eventually reach its apogee in Thatcherism. At the heart of this new obstructionism lay the workings of the budget and the CAP, or rather their impact in an economic environment where the key variables of budget, inflation and the balance of payments were deteriorating fast.

This chapter also suggested that the apparent absence of important decision-making moments should not be taken to imply that nothing noteworthy was happening, or even that what was happening was moving the EEC in the wrong direction. The EEC persisted with some initiatives despite an unfavourable environment. At the same time, shifting national preferences in other areas might have hindered short-term decision-making but opened perspectives for more dramatic moves in the future. Instead of seeing the ambitious slate of initiatives realized or launched under the Delors presidency as an outcome of favourable developments in the 1980s, it might be worth tracing their roots to the 1970s, as argued also in Chapter 10.

First among the achievements of the 1970s, the goal of enlargement, agreed to at the Hague summit, had been realized. It was true that in the case of the United Kingdom this was not without difficulty, but both Denmark and Ireland slipped without too many difficulties into the Community system. One could postulate that, had it not been for the oil crisis, the United Kingdom might have created fewer problems but, those difficulties notwithstanding, the first enlargement did not deter the EEC from further rounds of enlargement, embracing Greece in 1981 and Spain and Portugal in 1986.

Second, the continuous hammering (primarily by the British) on the need for reform of the CAP and increasing reluctance by the Germans to keep underwriting its costs did lead in 1984 to the first moves to restrain agricultural expenditures. The milk quotas introduced at the Fontainebleau summit in June 1984 (the same meeting of the European Council that resolved the British budgetary question) seemed a timid step at the time but paved the way for more ambitious moves culminating in the CAP reforms of 1992 that allowed the European Union to conclude the Uruguay Round of trade liberalization in the General Agreement on Tariffs and Trade (see Chapter 9). Third, reform of the CAP, in turn, made room for expenditure increases in other directions, notably on economic and social cohesion (mostly on a regional basis). The ERDF, born under such inauspicious circumstances and initially so cynically deployed, had served to point out the new direction. Under the guise of the structural funds, introduced in 1986, it was to grow to account for over 20 per cent of the EEC budget by 1990 and closer to 35 per cent a decade later.

The events of the 1970s were to presage two further moves of possibly even greater significance. First, in 1986, the member states signed the Single European Act (SEA), a major revision of the Rome Treaty that underpinned completion of the single market (the so-called 1992 programme). Member states might not have been able to agree on the SEA without the lessons learned over the previous decade. One area of special concern had been Europe's competitive position in the high-technology field. By the 1980s it had become clear that the Community was suffering from a loss of competitiveness on world markets. The policy of national champions had led to a considerable fragmentation of markets at a time when research and development costs were escalating and product life was shortening. It was increasingly apparent that firms even as large as Philips (in the Netherlands) and Siemens (in Germany) could no longer afford to develop the next generation of products on their own: their markets were just too small to rationalize start-up costs (Holmes and Kempton 1999: 302). In 1981 the Commission urged the Council of Ministers to develop a framework for intensive collaboration in the field of research and development, which emerged in the mid-1980s in the form of programmes such as Eureka and Esprit. Those initiatives were nevertheless deemed insufficient to regain competitiveness. Thus, the Commission suggested a complete removal of barriers to trade within the Community in order to generate greater efficiency through competition and scale economies. Already beginning to target domestic market impediments, EEC member states were ready for a European initiative and willing to accept a suspension of unanimity in decision-making to realize it (see Chapter 10). This commitment to completing the common market required the long gestation period and the paradigm shift of the 1970s.

Second, in 1992 the Maastricht Treaty (or Treaty on European Union) marked the largest leap forward in European integration since the Rome Treaty. Central to its aims was the achievement of EMU, with the introduction of a single currency, a single monetary authority, and a single monetary policy. This would have been impossible to contemplate had the member states not persisted in the 1970s with their experiments in closer exchange-rate management. It would have been easy, after the obvious failure of the Werner Plan, to have accepted the fact that the regime of floating currencies was the most appropriate, on both a global and a regional level. It would have been easy, as the newly constructed EMS seemingly limped from crisis to crisis, to have bowed before the apparent inevitability of market forces and to have acknowledged the frailty of institutional constructions to avert them. Yet, having weathered three years of almost continuous battering, in 1983 the EMS entered into calmer waters and oversaw a long period of exchange rate stability among its members—long enough to adopt monetary policy as a major part of the agenda for deeper European integration when the occasion arose.

Notes

1 A report in 1973 on the Regional Problems of the Enlarged Community (the so-called Thompson Report) concluded that even the most prosperous region in the United Kingdom lay below the Community average.

2 Under the Commission's plans Germany would contribute 28 per cent of the cost in return for only 8 per cent of the benefits.

Further reading

The existence of a thirty-year rule for archive access means that archive-based research on the events covered in this chapter has barely started. One exception is the Hague Conference, at which the decision was taken to open membership negotiations with the United Kingdom, and which has been covered in a special number of the *Journal of European Integration History* (2003). Lord (1993) analyzes the course of the negotiations themselves and two excellent textbooks, by George (1998) and Young (2000), describe the further history of Britain's relations with the EEC. Simonian (1985) describes the development of the much-vaunted Franco–German axis in the 1970s. A recent, if rather eclectic, view of the EEC's developments in the 1970s against the economic backdrop is provided by Gillingham (2003) while the EEC's response to the disintegration of the international monetary system is dealt with by Coffey (1987).

Coffey, P. (1987), *The European Monetary System: Past, Present and Future* (Boston: Kluwer).

Gillingham, J. (2003), *European Integration 1950–2003: Superstate or New Market Economy?* (Cambridge: Cambridge University Press).

George, S. (1998), *An Awkward Partner: Britain in the European Community*, 3rd edn. (Oxford: Oxford University Press).

Journal of European Integration History (2003), 9/2.

Lord, C. (1993), *British Entry to the European Community under the Heath Government of 1970–4* (Aldershot: Dartmouth).

Simonian, H. (1985), *The Privileged Partnership: Franco–German Relations in the European Community, 1969–1984* (Oxford: Clarendon Press).

Young, J. W. (2000), *Britain and European Unity, 1945–1999* (Basingstoke: Macmillan).

Websites

There are three main links to original documentation. The European Navigator (http://www.ena.lu/mce.cfm) has its own collection of mostly French documents, audio and video fragments, the latter often accompanied by transcription. It also contains bibliographies, glossaries and a photo album. The University of Pittsburgh's Archive of European Integration (http://aei.pitt.edu) also contains a rich collection of written documentation of European integration history. The main feature of Leiden University's EU History (http://www.eu-history.leidenuniv.nl/) is its links to a large selection of historical documents, as well as audio and video fragments on the postwar history of European integration, mostly in English. It also has a separate collection of federalist documents and a guide to electronic resources on European integration.

Chapter 9

European Integration in the Image and the Shadow of Agriculture

Ann-Christina Lauring Knudsen

Contents

Summary

Wine lakes, butter mountains and an uncontrollable budget fed an unflattering image of the common agricultural policy (CAP) that haunted the European Community (EC) by the mid-1980s, at a time when Brussels was seriously trying to boost the EC's ability to compete globally in industrial and technological products. The European project has always been more about agriculture than most would admit and the CAP has cast a long shadow over other key activities such as financing, enlargement, and external commercial relations. The CAP can only be understood in political rather than economic terms as a redistributive welfare policy and as a continuation of national agricultural welfare regimes. Nevertheless the soaring cost of the CAP as well as the policy's pernicious international impact generated tremendous pressure for reform. Recent concerns about the environment and food safety, and about the possible impact of European Union (EU) enlargement into Central and Eastern Europe, have further fuelled the reform movement. Given the political importance of supporting farm incomes, however, the CAP is likely to endure in some form or other.

Introduction

The common agricultural policy holds a special place in the history of the European Union. Measured in terms of size—of the budget, of administrative effort and of legislative output—the CAP is impressive. Yet many observers are highly critical of the CAP, often because of their failure to understand why the policy exists. Economists generally dislike the CAP because it does not easily suit a liberal market order into which they want to place the European integration project. For example, the editorial line of the influential *Economist* magazine has always been strongly critical, as when it famously characterized the CAP as the 'single most idiotic system of economic mismanagement that rich western countries have ever devised' (*The Economist*, 29 September, 1990). Indeed, economists and journalists have frequently joined forces in mocking the CAP, ridiculing the many hours spent by ministers and bureaucrats in Brussels discussing premiums for suckler cows, common European grain prices or butter export subsidies. There is no doubt that most people are oblivious to the CAP's technicalities. Nevertheless a relentlessly negative approach has left the public wondering why the political leaders of the EU—a successful club of the world's richest states—have, during its entire history, spent half or more of the EU's budget on a single sector which, ironically, has been in constant socio-economic decline throughout the period.

This chapter seeks to explain the fundamental puzzle of why the CAP exists. The characterization of the CAP as 'Europe's most illustrious accomplishment and its prodigal son' (Koester and Bale 1994) is more in line with this chapter's approach than the quote from *The Economist* above. The chapter argues that the CAP should not be viewed from an economic angle, but from the perspective of the political purpose that it serves. The ultimate objective of the CAP is to provide income support for a sector vital to the daily functioning of society, something that could not be obtained—so it is assumed—through market mechanisms alone. The core policy instruments of the CAP, chosen in the first half of the 1960s, remained unaltered for three decades. Indeed, the so-called MacSharry reform of 1992 and subsequent reforms have remained faithful to the farm income support goal.

The political emphasis on welfare therefore holds the key to understanding the CAP. The welfare objective of the CAP is fully in line with the welfare state goals and policies that have characterized Western European countries since the early twentieth century. From that perspective, it is clear that the CAP suits the political leaders of the EU much better than they are willing to admit during occasional heated debates about it. The chapter therefore focuses on the internal and external repercussions of maintaining the welfare goal of the CAP throughout the history of the EU. Accounts of the preferences and behaviour of individual governments and supranational actors in the literature on European integration have generally overlooked the continuity of goals and interests in the conduct of the CAP (Lindberg 1963; Moravcsik 1998).

The European agricultural welfare state

The EU did not invent agricultural policy. Rather, the CAP is built on strong policy traditions that have existed in all the member states for decades. In fact, by the time that the Rome Treaty was signed, in March 1957, agricultural welfare states were entrenched throughout Western Europe (Milward 2000; Sheingate 2001; Tracy 1989). In the post-1945 period the trend in agricultural policies was first to stabilize and then to increase farm incomes, as a result of which farming had become the most regulated sector of the economy. This section of the chapter provides an overview of the development of the European agricultural welfare states with a view to showing how the CAP emerged in that image.

Agriculture as a special sector

The authors of the Rome Treaty demanded that the new Community should take account of 'the particular nature of agricultural activity' (Article 39.2 EEC). This implied a continuation of the particularly close relationship between the state and the agricultural sector that already existed in all the member states, in contrast to the more liberal tone that rang through most of the treaty. Prominent people like Ludwig Erhard, German economics minister and later chancellor, criticized this exception for agriculture (Wünsche 1989). But he was overruled by a majority in his Christian Democratic Party, which was a firm promoter of the German (agricultural) welfare state. In turn, the Deutsche Bauernverband (DBV)—the major agricultural interest group with a membership of around 90 per cent of German farmers—was a key supporter of the party. The agricultural welfare state had become an important part of the successful political configuration of the Federal Republic, and throughout Western Europe similar policies were created. The obvious question is why agriculture, a sector in constant decline in industrial societies, was able to claim and maintain this special position.

The first part of the answer pertains to the basic fact that food is necessary for human survival, and that a constant and adequate food supply is fundamental for political stability. Yet food supplies are subject to natural, unpredictable factors such as weather, climate, and soil conditions. Political leaders everywhere are fully aware of the need to ensure the food supply to the greatest extent possible, notably through close relations with farmers and farm groups. Such relations emerged especially in the second half of the nineteenth century, during the nation-state building process.

In the space of a relatively short time in the twentieth century, Europe endured two devastating wars. Fertile farm areas were turned into battlefields, bottlenecks of food distribution appeared, food rationing became necessary, and temporary starvation loomed. Political leaders were forced to reconsider their food supply strategies. Food production in Western Europe was restored, and was increasing for almost a decade by the time the Rome Treaty was signed, yet wartime memories were never far away. This explains the insertion into the Rome Treaty of the objective of assuring the 'availability of [agricultural] supplies' (Article 39(d) EEC).

There was little doubt, then, that the special position of agriculture nationally would have to be replicated in the CAP for reasons of food security. In the political process of creating the CAP in the early 1960s, securing supplies was always mentioned at the top of each policy document. But food security never became a problem again, as marginal productivity rates increased steadily due to the technological revolution in the sector, and the EC never needed specific productivity targets as countries in Central and Eastern Europe did. It is highly likely that the potential threat of cold-war conflict was an additional factor in the political justification of special treatment for agriculture in the EC, though Community documents bear no direct evidence of this.

Since the second half of the nineteenth century, political leaders in Europe have systematically built links—formal and informal—between state institutions and representatives of the farming sector. It is striking, however, that agriculture was able to exert political influence beyond the socio-economic importance of the sector into the postwar period. One reason is that the farm vote goes beyond the farmer, as it is generally expected that people in rural communities are likely to have similar political preferences. This considerably enlarges the potential political constituency for farm representatives (Keeler 1996; Self and Storing 1962; Sheingate 2001).

Moreover, the farm sector had a particularly high degree of unionization—generally higher than, say, the industrial sector—that made such network-building possible. As Keeler has noted, 'this is one of the more important "secrets" behind the farm lobby's disproportionate clout' (Keeler 1996: 134). For the farmer, the importance of membership of a farm group is clear, and transcends political affiliation, simply because it is often the only way to access technical services such as specialized credit facilities or advice on new production techniques.

As World War II came to an end, farm groups were drawn into the reconstruction of political institutions in Western Europe (Milward 2000). The formal and informal networks that farm groups presided over went into even the remotest corners of the state, and were useful not only for assuring the adequate food distribution but also for re-establishing political stability in rural areas. This, in turn, gave farm groups and rural communities considerable political leverage in the decades to come. As a result, most major political parties appealed to broad farming constituencies by pledging support for the agricultural welfare state (Hendriks 1991; Keeler 1996).

The farm income gap

The Rome Treaty also stipulated that the CAP should seek 'to ensure a fair standard of living for the agricultural community, in particular by increasing the individual earnings of persons engaged in agriculture' (Article 39(b) EEC). In the decades following the war, general income levels and standards of living were rising, but less so in agriculture. Farm interest groups throughout Western Europe angrily protested this income gap (Knudsen 2001b; Peterson 1979; Tracy 1989). Postwar welfare states broadly focused on improving the incomes of those disadvantaged by the market; farmers' income gap campaigns fitted nicely with this, and so were highly successful. From the late 1940s, so-called farm income parity legislation became the norm throughout Western Europe, with the aim of bringing farm incomes into line with those of other sectors. Interwar agricultural policy instruments, including the organization of agricultural markets to obtain political control over the level of prices, continued to be applied. National market organizations included the guarantee of minimum prices to farmers and trade protection to fend off unwanted external pressures on domestic markets. Market organizations supported all producers, who received additional sector-specific benefits such as tax rebates, fuel subsidies, and favourable loan schemes.

Postwar farm income parity legislation as the basis for the agricultural welfare state rested on similar assumptions throughout Western Europe. Foremost was the assumption that the unacceptable income gap was largely due to market deficiencies and that product prices determined farmers' incomes. This, however, was not entirely correct. Although parity income legislation was usually based on the assumption that all farmers faced similar problems, and granted all farmers similar benefits, the farm sector was not homogeneous. Historically, income levels always differed dramatically between small and large farmers and among regions. Farm income depended also on a variety of factors other than producer price such as location, climate, conditions of ownership, market access and education. Some farmers did well, but many throughout Western Europe were simply not able to cope with the modernization process and seemed destined to have a low standard of living no matter what the level of state support. Moreover, the cultural notion of the small farmer and the family farm was linked in many countries, and was used rhetorically to obscure the problem of hidden unemployment in the countryside where too many people—the whole extended family—lived off the farm. The family farm as a cultural unit was often not viable economically, but postwar governments dared not risk the wrath of dominant farm groups and others by saying so publicly.

The nature of agricultural production is such that productivity increases tend to manifest themselves slower in agriculture than in industry. For instance, the purchase of a tractor may bring about a significant technological improvement in daily routines on a farm, but it is not likely to produce a marginal productivity increase comparable to the introduction of an assembly line in a car factory. In addition, factors such as the immobility of land, rural conservatism, and economic illiteracy among farmers contributed to low incomes in the agricultural sector (OECD 1964, 1965). Nevertheless the national market organizations continued to support all producers—rich and poor farmers alike—on a universal basis. In this way, painful political choices were avoided. The assumption of the direct price–income link was a policy legacy from the days when the profession was more primitive, although in the postwar period many farmers themselves were not interested in preserving a peasant way of life. Even before the CAP there was an obvious misfit between the core instrument of agricultural policy and the realities prevailing in the sector. However, the continued strength of the cultural notion of the family farm throughout much of Western Europe meant that the myths underlying agricultural policies lived on, and that the policy objectives could not be questioned but could not be plausibly attained either.

In reality, factors other than prevailing prices were important in the final calculation of farm incomes. These included access to credit facilities with an eye to updating production equipment, access to pension schemes, management skills of the farmer, tax breaks, and other special benefits. Governments adopted national structural policies to supplement national market policies. The bill for all these policies and preferential programmes soared towards the end of the 1950s. Because the policies did not attain their goals, however, farm groups continued to campaign for income support into the 1960s and beyond.

The original CAP framework

The prevailing national policies inspired the choice of policy objectives and instruments for the CAP. Policy-makers decided on the original framework between 1958 and 1964, although they extended it continuously until the early 1970s. In a process largely guided by the European Commission and accepted by the Council of Ministers, the policy principles of common market organizations and common price levels were put in place by 1962. So was the notion of common financing by the European Agricultural Guidance and Guarantee Fund (EAGGF). Only the policy framework existed at that moment: technical details such as the common price level for farm products—that is, the main policy instrument, notionally, for reaching the income objective—had yet to be decided.

During the early policy process, it quickly became clear that a policy focusing on the organization of the six national markets and the fixing of a common price would constitute the core policies of the CAP. This was essentially the sum of agricultural policies operating in the member states; the highest common denominator prevailing. Despite the fact that they had failed to achieve their goals nationally, the very same policy instruments were built into the CAP. In their eagerness to create the CAP as the first major EC common policy, politicians and officials never actually called for a thorough analysis to establish the real extent of the income gap.[1]

The main point of contention, therefore, was not whether to create the CAP or what its objectives and main policy instruments should be, but the level at which the common price for grains should be fixed. Because grains are at the centre of the food chain, grain prices usually determine the prices for practically all other agricultural products. The problem within the new EC was that national price levels differed greatly: Germany, Luxembourg and Italy had relatively high national prices; France and the Netherlands had low prices; and Belgium was somewhere in the middle.

High price countries were unwilling to lower their prices towards the average EC grain price level, as this would signal the willingness of their governments to dilute the income basis for their farmers. Hence the DBV's campaign against fixing a common grain price lower than what already existed in Germany. German farmers' hostility began as early as 1960, three years before the Commission ever submitted common grain price proposals, and caused repeated deadlocks in EC negotiations in the years to come. The problem was not resolved until the German government and the Commission joined forces in the autumn of 1964 and offered transitional compensation to farmers in countries where the grain price would be lowered as a consequence of the introduction of the common price. Compensation was to be paid jointly by the EC and the relevant member state. Ironically, in the midst of this contentious political process the Council never discussed the actual common price level for grains, which was set instead at exactly the level proposed by the Commission. The long-drawn process of creating the common grain price left politicians, such as French President Charles de Gaulle, impatient with Community decision-making.

The common market for around 90 per cent of the EC's agricultural production took effect in 1968; common market organizations and common minimum prices were created for grains, sugar, milk, beef, pork, and a number of fruits and vegetables. Thus a central part of the national agricultural welfare state was surrendered to the EC. The original CAP focused narrowly on supporting the income of agricultural producers, paid for from the common budget, and so the first major EC policy was essentially a redistributive one. In effect, dual welfare systems now existed. The remaining parts of the agricultural welfare state stayed within the national spheres of authority: policies for structural development of agricultural infrastructure, tax rebates, and general and special social benefits to the sector. Studies have shown, however, that such national income supports often turned out to be more important to the marginal level of farm income than the product prices. The generosity of the national welfare systems differed greatly among member states and made it practically impossible to get a comprehensive view of farmers' incomes throughout the EC (Hill 2000). Yet, the original CAP proved to be durable as the policy instruments chosen in the first half of the 1960s remained in place for the next three decades.[2]

The first commissioner for agriculture, Sicco Mansholt, was instrumental in the process of creating the CAP (Freisberg 1965; Knudsen 2001b; Peterson 1979). A farmer himself, Mansholt was minister for agriculture in the Netherlands from 1945 until joining the Commission in 1958. Such a long tenure was unusual for any minister who has to deal with powerful farm lobbies. Mansholt was also a committed European federalist who had argued on many occasions for the creation of one European agricultural policy rather than many individual ones (Noël 1988; Thiemeyer 1999). Mansholt strove to combine important features of national agricultural policy and political traditions with the Community method of decision-making. He was a socialist who never hid his belief in the necessity of strong state involvement in running the sector.

Shortly after joining the Commission, Mansholt invited the main farm groups in the member states to form an EC-level interest group. As a result, the Comité des Organisations Professionnelles Agricoles (COPA) was established in Brussels in early 1958. Other professions quickly followed this example, but rarely matched COPA's size and influence. In the process of drafting proposals for the CAP, Mansholt held many consultative meetings with COPA, and also managed to incorporate the organization into the political system of the EC by creating a committee structure comprising interest groups, national agricultural ministries and the Commission (Knudsen 2001b). In turn, close contacts with COPA and other important groups served to legitimize the Commission's work.

The Council of Ministers was informed of these contacts on various occasions, and generally did not object. Although COPA was too fragmented in the 1960s to come up with a collective opinion on important issues such as the level of the common grain price (Knudsen 2001b), by the 1970s COPA enjoyed 'unmatched power' over a number of crucial technical decisions on CAP prices (Grant 1997: 148). In any event, all the main national farmers' groups supported the notion of creating the CAP, expecting that EC policy would be more beneficial for them than national agricultural policies. Indeed, the widespread view that the DBV opposed the CAP outright is wrong. The DBV was working actively for the creation of the CAP, though on its own terms (Freisberg 1965; Hendriks 1991; Knudsen 2001a, 2001b).

The Special Committee on Agriculture (SCA), created by the Council in May 1960, was an additional feature of the EC's agricultural political system. Made up of senior agricultural experts and agricultural attachés, the SCA resumed the role played by the Committee of Permanent Representatives in other EC policy areas. What emerged, therefore, was a complex political system as the basis for the fusion of national and EC executives in the field of agriculture. A parallel system of consultation for farm groups, at the national and European levels, also came into being.

It is clear that the personality of the relevant Commissioner played an important part in shaping the CAP (Cini 1996; Grant 1997; Tracy 1989). Throughout the EU's history, practically everyone holding the post has had considerable high-level expertise in the field, giving them an important advantage in the EC's agricultural political system. However, a final analysis focusing only on the power of the farm lobby, individual member states or the particular Commissioner would be inadequate. CAP decision-making soon came to resemble policy-making in other pluralist political systems involving many actors at multiple levels, making it difficult to determine who exactly was responsible for the eventual outcome. At the same time, CAP decision-making mainly took place in a highly compartmentalized political space reserved for agricultural experts, making it difficult to break the path dependency of the policy.

The not-so-common CAP

The CAP is not as *common* as the name suggests. The framework of the CAP, with the common price level at the centre, is the original core policy. A number of other policies have developed around this. Often anchored nationally, their purpose is to help meet the objectives of the CAP. For instance, the agreement on the common grain price in December 1964 was made possible only by allowing supplementary national compensations in order to support farm incomes. Following successive EC enlargements in the 1970s and 1980s, agriculture became an even more difficult area in which to reach agreement. Agriculture and rural populations played important socio-economic roles in five new member states—Ireland, Denmark, Greece, Portugal, and Spain—and still held a significant political position in Britain.

Each new member state placed particular agricultural issues on the table, the sum of which added to the complexity of the farming sector and production in the EC as a whole. As a result, the mismatch of the CAP's original policy instruments became more apparent. These problems were often overcome in the accession negotiations by allowing special agreements on agricultural policy between the new member state and the EC, frequently with joint EC and national administrative responsibilities

(Griffiths 2002). Once inside the EC, a new member state was better positioned to get new special arrangements. By the time of the Iberian enlargement in 1986, the administration of the agricultural policies looked so complex—a medley of common and national rules that embraced practically every activity of the farming industry and its surroundings—that the CAP earned its reputation of 'Byzantine complexity' (Rieger 2000: 190).

The following sub-sections illustrate two important aspects of the uncommonness of the CAP: the so-called green monetary system and the development of rural policies.

Green money

It might seem ironic that, after a decade spent establishing a common price regime for key agricultural products, around which EC institutions and procedures were built, it took only a couple of years for the common price regime to disintegrate on the margins. The notion of a common price level for agricultural products was obviously an abstraction in a system with several independent national currencies. The constant challenge, given such a constraint, was to bridge the gap between abstraction and reality, given that farmers received payments in their respective national currencies. Initially, the Commission created an artificial, supranational currency for accounting purposes as early as 1962, the unit of account (UA), to which each national currency had a fixed relationship (exchange rate). The UA was set at parity with the gold–dollar convertibility rate to which all EC currencies were anchored in the 1960s. Agricultural support prices were fixed in UA and subsequently converted into national currencies. This was a relatively straightforward device in times of currency stability, which therefore 'lulled most of the negotiators into a false sense of security' (Tracy 1989: 268). When the economic climate changed at the end of the decade, the UA encountered serious, unforeseen problems with regard to common agricultural prices. As most observers admit, the solution was a prolonged technical, administrative and financial nightmare.

The problems began when the French franc was devalued and the German mark revalued in the autumn of 1969. Subsequently, both governments imposed temporary national measures to avoid negative effects on national farm incomes, believing that this would not affect the functioning of the CAP. France introduced compensatory amounts for agricultural trade in the form of levies on exports and subsidies on imports. Germany followed suit, giving subsidies to compensate farmers for the anticipated loss of 1,700 Deutsche Marks in annual EC revenue. The German government eventually gave 800,000 farmers an average of 8,100 marks each over a four-year period as a national measure to avoid negative income-related repercussions of the exchange rate turbulence (Swinbank 1978: 19).

The second serious blow to the common price system came in the wake of the international monetary turmoil of 1971, after the decision of the Nixon administration to abolish dollar–gold convertibility. Following detailed discussions, member states decided formally to acknowledge the system begun by France and Germany as a temporary measure in order to continue to fulfil the objectives of the CAP. Member states were thus allowed to continue to provide 'green money'—officially called monetary compensatory amounts (MCAs)—supposedly as a temporary measure. The only alternative to MCAs, it seemed, was the demise of the CAP, the central pillar of the EC in the 1970s. As no one really wanted that to happen, the financing of the MCAs was moved into the EC budget to secure their continued existence. Paradoxically, the acceptance of MCAs demonstrated that national governments saw domestic price stability as more important than the maintenance of common prices.

The UA later became linked to the European currency snake, but the floating currencies of the 1970s meant that it was difficult to stabilize the green currencies, which therefore became entangled in the floating currencies scenario. This also meant that 'common' agricultural support prices were allowed to diverge in the member states, so much so that the gap between them at times was larger than what had existed before the common EC price regime. Some member states repeatedly took advantage of this by devaluing or revaluing their green rates, thereby directly affecting the prices that farmers received in national currencies. As a British expert noted at that time, the 'so-called "common policy" consists of seven different price zones separated by a confusing array of compensatory amounts' (Swinbank 1978: 9, 13).

Community financing of the MCAs was expensive. When it was agreed in 1971 to transfer the cost of financing MCAs from the member states to the EAGGF guarantee fund, it was expected that the MCAs would soon be phased out (Pearce 1981: 37–45). That did hot happen. In 1975, the MCA system alone amounted to 9 per cent of EAGGF expenditure; by 1977 it had risen to 12 per cent (Fearne 1991: 50). In effect, the MCAs were devised to shelter farm incomes from currency turbulence, but the cost was very high. As Tracy notes, 'the green rates and the resulting MCAs could be regarded as the inevitable consequence of not having monetary union among the Member States: so long as substantial currency adjustments were liable to occur, the agri-monetary system provided a necessary buffer' (Tracy 1989: 311). Effectively, this had overvalued agricultural prices in the Community. Subsequently, as Tracy notes, 'when the ECU [European Currency Unit] was introduced in 1979 [as part of the European Monetary System], common prices in ECU had initially to be fixed 21% higher to avoid a corresponding reduction in national prices' (Tracy 1989: 311). This obviously had an important knock-on effect on the national price levels (see Table 9.1).

By the early 1980s, the MCAs had become a complex affair. A notional reform of the agri-monetary system was agreed upon in 1984, in conjunction with the British budgetary deal, where a new green ECU was introduced. This was based on the strongest currency in the European Monetary System (EMS), the Deutsche Mark, instead of the whole basket of currencies. But to get to that point, a series of new correcting devices was introduced. As Grant notes: 'The old joke that only six people in Europe fully understand the operation of the CAP had to be changed, to revise downward the figure used' (Grant 1997: 88).

Another attempt at phasing out the remaining MCAs was made in conjunction with the single market project in the second half of the 1980s. This looked promising for a while. However, the effort to align all support to the ECU was obstructed by the currency turbulence of 1993 and instead opened a new set of green currency problems. The collapse of the exchange-rate mechanism of the EMS in August 1993 triggered a new green currency crisis just as the MCAs were supposed to be abandoned. It became clear that the immediate budgetary effect of ending this system without harming farm incomes considerably would be far higher than the

Table 9.1 Increases in common agricultural prices following the Council decisions of June 1979 and the changes in the green rates in April and June 1979 (%)

	Average increase in prices in ecu	Average increase of prices in national currency (after application of green rates)
West Germany	+1.2	+0.4
France	+1.4	+8.7
Italy	+1.5	+11.5
Netherlands	+0.9	+0.6
Belgium	+1.3	+0.8
Luxembourg	+0.9	+0.6
United Kingdom	+1.1	+12.0
Ireland	+1.1	+1.4
Denmark	+1.3	+1.3
EC–9	+1.3	+6.4

Source: European Commission (1980*b*)

EC's budget could bear. However, the prospect of additional enlargement, together with monetary union, meant that a solution to the complex green money became ever-more pressing.

Towards a more holistic approach

In the autumn of 1958, Commissioner Mansholt was invited to speak at the DBV's annual meeting. His message was that several million farmers throughout the EC were redundant and would have to leave the sector in the next decade. Needless to say, his speech was not received with great enthusiasm and may have laid the foundation for the strained relationship between Mansholt and the DBV in the years to come. Given that the Commission had not yet had much time to prepare its proposals for the CAP, it is highly likely that Mansholt revealed only his personal vision of the CAP in this speech. In view of the hostile reaction to it, however, Mansholt adjusted his approach and did not speak about structural reforms in the EC for the next decade, until *after* the CAP had become reality, by which time the member states had surrendered the core of their agricultural policies to the EC.

Structural problems in EC agriculture in 1958 were exacerbated by many small and fragmented farms producing inefficiently at too high a cost. All member states had, to different degrees, their own structural policies to deal with such problems, modernize their farm sectors, and strengthen economic cohesion. Often structural policies had the additional purpose of improving conditions for certain farm communities to keep the land populated and avoid more migration than the cities could absorb. Structural policies were often the largest item of national expenditure on agriculture (Hill 1984: 28), yet they seemed largely inadequate for creating a modern farming sector in the near future (Tracy 1989: 232f.).[3]

A structural policy within the framework of the CAP was only discussed sporadically during the early 1960s. Funding for a common *guidance* policy (i.e. structural policy) was included when the EAGGF was created in 1962, though expenditure on it remained marginal for the following decade. Such a policy would most likely demand a more complex administration of programmes than anyone was prepared to face at the time. Moreover, farm lobbies made closing the income gap through the price remedy their main demand. From the perspective of the political leaders, price support had the advantage of providing short-term results whereas structural policies took longer to be effective.

Mansholt relaunched the debate over structural problems in EC agriculture just eighteen months after the common price came into effect in 1968. In the so-called Mansholt Plan, he argued that the original CAP framework would never attain its objective without a concerted process of modernization (Communauté Européenne 1969). Mansholt claimed that roughly 5 million people should leave the sector, in addition to the 5 million who had already left since 1958, and suggested using incentives such as retirement schemes and re-schooling for those who wished to go. He also advocated that the EC should offer retraining programmes to help those staying on the land to practise modern farming and should encourage mergers of holdings to create larger farming units. With more efficient production, Mansholt argued, it should be possible to lower Community support prices and hence cut the cost of the guarantee section of the EAGGF.

The Mansholt Plan provoked 'violent opposition among farming circles' (Tracy 1989: 267). Farmers reacted predictably, dubbing Mansholt a 'peasant killer' and protesting loudly after publication of the plan. Yet, Mansholt had launched an important debate, which the whole EC agricultural political system soon took up. Farm organizations were primarily concerned about the implications for farm incomes of the suggested moderation in EC common price levels (Fennell 1997: 210), not the future number of farmers. But the proposals seemed so radical that no government wanted to face the storm at home and the plan was shelved for a while. Nevertheless, the Mansholt Plan provided the intellectual stimulus for the first EC structural programmes for agriculture, adopted in 1972 and financed under the EAGGF. Primarily, these offered Community co-financing of national programmes. Hence, they were not 'common' policies, as the original CAP was, but were framework programmes adding to national initiatives, primarily under local management (Hill 1984: 40 ff.). The programmes covered modernization, retirement, advice, and training. Their overall effect was expected to be a reduction in the number of farmers; during the first decade of operation they assisted about 600,000 elderly farmers to give up the land. One in three French farms was merged as a result (Clout 1984: 81).

A 1975 Council Directive went in the opposite direction. By then it was recognized that decades of rural exodus had resulted in depopulation of certain areas and caused negative economic and cultural consequences there (see Table 9.2). Small communities were dying. Italian mountain areas, for example, lost an average of 30 per cent of their inhabitants between 1950 and 1980 and village population declined by half in some stretches of the Apennines (Clout 1984: 35f.). Another problem was that the younger generation was more inclined to migrate in large numbers from 'less favoured areas' where farming did not pay off. It was estimated that about a quarter of the Community's area, and about 20 per cent of all farming, was 'less favoured'. With the

Table 9.2	Rural exodus: percentage of the working population employed in agriculture in the EC, 1958–99			
1958	1970	1980	1990	1999
26	13.5	9.6	6.5	4.5

Source: European Commission, *The Agricultural Situation in the European Union* (Luxembourg: Office for Official Publications of the European Communities).

aim of avoiding total depopulation of certain areas, maintaining peasant culture and promoting economic cohesion, the Community therefore launched co-financed programmes from 1975 onwards to sustain farming in less favoured areas. The accession of Britain and Ireland greatly increased the political support for such programmes, although all member states benefited from them.

The improvement of farm income continued to justify the financing of structural policy under the EAGGF guidance fund, but the 1975 initiative was contrary to Mansholt's modernization ideas. In conjunction with the core of the CAP and the MCAs, it had the effect of keeping more people on the land than would otherwise choose to stay there. Community spending on structural programmes remained well below 5 per cent of total CAP expenditure until the 1980s, which left many observers unimpressed (Grant 1997: 72). But it should be remembered that the Community programmes were merely co-financed national initiatives and that Community framework projects tended to encourage local initiatives that might not have been launched otherwise. The accession of Mediterranean countries in the 1980s added to the demand for further aid to unfavourable rural areas as well as for modernization programmes. During the Greek accession negotiations, a number of measures were agreed specifically for the Mediterranean regions, which, not surprisingly, Italy strongly supported. A few years later, Greece went so far as to approve Spanish and Portuguese accession subject to extending these measures into the so-called Integrated Mediterranean Programmes, from which southern France also benefited (Tracy 1989: 307, 328). A special agricultural development programme was created for Portugal during the accession negotiations.

As Tracy observed:

> Before long almost every Member State had obtained EAGGF aid for regional schemes of one kind or another. Often these measures were introduced in response to a political need, with little prior analysis of the economic requirements of the region and little or no consultation at the regional level. Some such schemes were hastily concocted as makeweights in the context of annual price reviews, to enable particular Ministers to subscribe to a package arrangement. (Tracy 1989: 329)

Still, the CAP became the platform for the development of a more holistic rural policy in the EC, on which the cohesion policy adopted with the single market programme was built.

The global context

All states that can afford to do so subsidies their farmers in one way or another. It may seem ironic that the more industrialized a state becomes the more it tends to support its ever-smaller farm sector. By international comparison, the CAP is prominent but not exceptional. Japan, Switzerland, Norway, Iceland, and South Korea all subsidize their farmers more than the EU does.[4] The United States and Canada subsidize agriculture on average a little less than the EU does, but their state involvement in the running of the agricultural economy remains intense. Only New Zealand unilaterally, and rather successfully, decided to quit farm subsidies in the 1980s. Indeed, the Organization for Economic Cooperation and Development (OECD) estimated that in 1986, which is seen as a peak year, state subsidies in its member states amounted to $13,000 per full-time farmer, or the equivalent on average of $167 per hectare of farmed land (*The Economist*, 6 September, 2001). The OECD's grim judgement is that agricultural policies 'impose costs on consumers and taxpayers, reduce economic efficiency, distort production and trade, impede growth in developing countries, and may damage the environment'.[5] At the turn of the millennium, the annual state payments to farmers in OECD countries exceeded Africa's entire gross domestic product (GDP) and domestic support to the agricultural sector in the United States, Europe, and Japan accounted for about 80 per cent of the world's total (*The Economist*, 6 September, 2001).

Despite general international agreement that agricultural subsidies distort international trade, free trade in agricultural products has never really existed since the emergence of a true world market in the mid-nineteenth century. It is difficult to determine whether the creation of the CAP made the member states on balance more or less protectionist and whether world trade became more or less distorted as a result. It is clear, however, that the formation of the CAP gave EC member states new leverage in world agricultural affairs as they began to speak with one voice. The EC became the world's largest food importer and competition for access to the EC's agricultural markets intensified. The EC also became the world's second largest agricultural exporter of main food products. The international conflicts that ensued took place primarily in the context of the General Agreement on Tariffs and Trade (GATT) and the World Trade Organization (WTO).[6]

Agriculture in the GATT and the WTO

The close connection between external agricultural trade barriers, the special domestic position of agriculture, and the welfare objectives of stability of farm prices has made agriculture one of the most difficult areas to negotiate in the international context. When the GATT was created in 1948, the United States had the strongest economy in the world and was determined to keep its privileged position as an agricultural exporter. Western European states were in the process of reconstructing their agricultural sectors after the war, largely through US-sponsored Marshall aid. By 1950, agricultural output had reached prewar levels, and from then on productivity increased steadily. The privileged position of the United States meant that it was not interested in discussing agricultural trade liberalization, but this changed with the creation of the EC's common market. In 1962 the United States launched the Trade Expansion Act and pushed for talks on agriculture with the Community in the Kennedy Round of the GATT (1963–7) (Andrews 1973: 61–8). By then the EC was reluctant to enter talks and politically was probably not ready to reduce its barriers in agriculture because the common grain price and agricultural levy had barely been settled. The Kennedy Round included an agreement on grains but did not address the fundamental issue of agricultural support policies employed in all the industrial countries. The EC gradually moved on to a level playing field with the Americans but avoided such negotiations for the next two decades.

Meanwhile, technological progress made EC agriculture very successful and the EC became a leading exporter. By the early 1980s, the EC was a net exporter of such important commodities as grains, sugar, wine, beef, and veal. Thereafter, the list of bitter complaints about EC protectionism and unfair trading practices, such as dumping of foods at subsidized prices on the world market, grew ever longer. Agricultural export strategies were becoming fiercer in order to maintain market shares and the number of international agricultural trade disputes grew steadily (Patterson 1997: 136). Supported by a number of less developed countries (LDCs), the Cairns group of net agricultural exporting countries, led by Australia, demanded that agriculture be taken seriously in the Uruguay Round, which began in 1986. In addition, by the mid-1980s several international meetings of political leaders began addressing the need to end the distortion of world agricultural markets. In 1987, OECD ministers recognized for the first time the need for the organization's members 'to refrain from actions which would worsen the present situation, in particular by avoiding measures that would tend to dispose of the stocks built up' (Fennell 1997: 165f.).

The EC's willingness to go along with this was furthered by the internal budgetary restraints that it faced and the embarrassingly huge food surpluses in storage. However, the EC entered the negotiations with the rhetorical line that the CAP would not be altered. Much changed inside the EC during six years of Uruguay Round negotiations, prompting it finally to review its position. Progress was made only after the collapse of the negotiations over agriculture in 1990, which threatened to invalidate the whole Round.

The final compromise included three areas of international agricultural trade: market access, export subsidies and domestic support. The most significant impact of the agricultural agreement on the CAP was that the EC agreed to change its price policy. Reductions in price levels were agreed, including a 29 per cent reduction in grains. The agreement had an equally important impact on another fundamental instrument of the CAP, agricultural import levies, which had never been questioned before (Charvet 2001; Fennell 1997: 135). The EU agreed to convert most of these into tariffs and reduce them by about one-third. Moreover, countries acknowledged for the first time during the Uruguay Round that domestic politics were legitimate concerns of international trade talks. This became a point of departure for the subsequent set of international trade talks in agriculture: the Doha Round (Michelmann et al. 2001). In spite of frequent criticism of the results reached in the international arena, however, nobody truly believed that agricultural trade barriers would be wiped away in one stroke.

Achievements and unintended consequences

The CAP is a complex affair and is not easily assessed definitively in terms of success or failure. Nevertheless, this section develops some of the main achievements and unintended consequences of the first three decades of the CAP.

Achievements

The CAP has been remarkably successful by practically any measure. Of course the question of why the CAP has loomed so large in the history of the EC begs the question of why other policies have remained so relatively insignificant until recent years, for instance monetary union and common security. The fact that the CAP preoccupied the EC for its first twenty-five years must be ascribed to the success of the agricultural political system described above. The Council of agricultural ministers spent more hours discussing the CAP than any other sectoral Council. It met on average once a month, sometimes more, often for several days at the time. By contrast, ministers dealing with the internal market met seven times in 1990—a peak year—and ministers for industrial affairs met four times (Hix 1999: 67; Van Schendelen 1996). More meetings between national experts were held in the area of agriculture than any other area, pioneering the fusion of national- and European-level institutions by the early 1960s. And more legislation was passed in this area, accounting for more than half of the *acquis communautaire*.

Taking into account the enormity of national agricultural administrations in terms of personnel and legislation, and considering that agricultural ministers were notoriously turf-protecting, this was a stunning political achievement. The EC-level farm lobby became a model for other interest groups in Brussels—Keeler notes that while most European-level interest groups employ only one or two officials, COPA has a full-time staff of forty-five (Keeler 1996: 133; see also Averyt 1977; Peterson 1979). The Commission's directorate-general for agriculture was by far the largest, until gradually overtaken in the late 1990s by the external affairs directorate-general, due primarily to Central and Eastern European enlargement.

These institutional successes can only be understood in light of the historical importance attached by political leaders to the creation of the CAP, despite agriculture's

Table 9.3 EC trade in agricultural products, 1968–85 (millions of ecu at current figures)

	1968 (EC–6)	1985 (EC–10)
Intra-EC trade	4384	58633
Imports from third countries	8822	48812
Exports to third countries	2950	31138

Source: European Commission (1987)

steady socio-economic decline. The EC farm sector successfully integrated technological improvements into the production process. Agricultural output grew on average by 3 per cent or more annually from the 1960s to the mid-1990s, and exports grew by more than double that amount. Trade in agricultural products grew considerably both within the EC and with the outside world. This enabled the EC to become a dominant exporter of agricultural goods, while the constant demand for foreign foods within the EC made it possible to maintain its status as the world's leading importer (see Table 9.3).

Unintended consequences

There is a long list of consequences unintended by the architects of the CAP. The term 'unintended consequences' refers here to the outcomes often observed with path-dependent public policies. For instance, the environmental damages linked to practices of intensive farming encouraged by high price supports became an important issue in the late 1980s in creating a highly negative public image of farming and the CAP. Another example is that fraud involving CAP funds became a serious problem. The sheer complexity of the CAP opened many opportunities for those who wanted to abuse the system. It is difficult to measure the full extent of fraud, given that only recorded cases can be counted. Several enquiries into the problem in the 1990s suggested that perhaps as much as 10 per cent of the EC's budget was wasted either by fraud or other kinds of improper use of Community funds (Fennell 1997: 166f.; Grant 1997: 10). Although there has been a tendency to discover more fraud in the south than in the north, cases have been found throughout the EC. This section details three other significant areas of unintended consequence: income distribution, surplus production and the budget.

Income distribution and the welfare goal

The CAP affects every person in the EC, as food prices have a direct impact on people's disposable incomes. By 1990, it was estimated that the CAP inflated Community food prices by 7 per cent above the level that they would have been without price subsidies to farmers (Keeler 1996: 127). This is a particularly sensitive issue because high food prices affect low-income households, which have to spend a larger proportion of their disposable income on food than high-income households. Although most EC member states already had inflated farm prices before the CAP, the creation of the high common price level cemented these for decades to come. Ironically, consumers did not seriously attempt to gain influence over CAP decision-making until they became (marginally) represented in the EC agricultural political system in the late 1990s, a development that was unrelated to the price effects of the CAP.

The political justification for maintaining the original CAP was to raise farm incomes. After three decades, this had only succeeded to a certain extent. It is true that real incomes in agriculture had increased by an average of around 2.8 per cent from 1968 to 1980, an increase similar to that in other main sectors of the economy (Hill 1984: 107). However, such figures tell little about the real situation within the sector (Hill 2000). The price policy of the CAP meant that farmers received support in proportion to how much they could produce; no limits were initially set. The more that farmers could produce, the more support they would receive. As a result, the CAP generally supported large producers more than small ones. In the 1980s, the '80:20 ratio' (80 per cent of EC price support going to 20 per cent of farmers) became a 'stylized fact' (European Commission 1991: 5; Grant 1997: 78).

Historically, large inequalities had always existed within the agricultural sector, but the fact that the key instrument of the CAP exacerbated such inequalities was seen by many as detrimental to its purpose. Nonetheless, it has also been estimated that the social costs of removing the CAP would be very high (Keeler 1996: 132). Although farm incomes are difficult to measure exactly—average incomes do not really exist (Hill 2000)—experts agree that the situation was highly unsatisfactory (Tracy 1989: 301f.). In 1991, the Commission explicitly acknowledged that '[t]he existing system does not take adequate account of the incomes of the vast majority of small and medium-sized family farms. The per-capita purchasing power of those engaged in agriculture has improved very little over the period 1975–89' (European Commission 1991: 9).

The regional distribution of CAP support similarly remained unjust. The fact that different types of crops received different levels of support reflected strongly on the overall income of certain regions. In the name of efficiency, the CAP encouraged specialization, for instance the production of olives in Mediterranean regions. But the switch to monocultural production was not necessarily advantageous in the long run and such regions became more vulnerable to changes in the common price level. A close correlation exists between average regional agricultural income and the CAP support received within the region; during the 1970s, the incomes of rural areas receiving CAP support actually widened (Pearce 1981: 52f.). In certain parts of the EC, large-scale industrial farms thrived. But the regions where farming was not viable saw negative developments, with many farmers choosing to leave the land, often at high personal cost, especially as the farm had often belonged to the family for generations.

In the same vein, another phenomenon developed: part-time farming. This meant staying on the farm but generating additional income from non-farming activities. An estimate from 1980 suggests that 64 per cent of EC farmers were part-timers (Hill 1984: 107). Historically, of course, members of the family farm have often supplemented the farm's income through non-farming activities such as hunting, crafts, or the provision of local services. The new dimension was that in a period of increased professional specialization many farmers were forced to seek revenue outside their profession, although they had never before had such high public income support. A recent OECD report confirmed that part-time farming is a continuing trend in the EU essentially because agricultural support policies are not as effective as they could be (OECD 2003a). Farm household incomes are now on average closer to those of other households than they have been in the postwar period, but this is only because non-agricultural revenue makes a significant contribution to the total farm household income. This suggests, once again, that the core instrument of the CAP was ill chosen to fulfil its goal.

Butter mountains and wine lakes

The initial objective of creating self-sufficiency in food products in the EC was soon achieved. Rapid technological progress helped to increase yields and marginal productivity at a hitherto unseen rate. Production increased fast, despite mass migration out of the sector, diminishing the number of production units considerably. The market and price policy at the centre of the CAP had created an almost risk-free environment in which the EC guaranteed to purchase at a high price all that could be produced. By 1968, farmers in the EC produced more grains, sugar and dairy products than could be consumed, and many fruits and vegetables were periodically massively over-supplied (Tracy 1989: 267). During the 1970s surpluses of wine, olive oil, beef and veal followed. In the period 1973–88 agricultural production increased by 2 per cent annually, but internal consumption grew only by 0.5 per cent annually (European Commission 1991: 9). The EC market was saturated and the world market was being bombarded with EC agricultural surpluses.

These surpluses, frequently characterized as butter mountains and wine lakes, were not foreseen in the early 1960s when the CAP was created and growth in agricultural output was highly desirable. It was difficult to anticipate the impact of the technological revolution in farming before it actually happened. The farming profession was often criticized for this, but it seems unfair to fault individual farmers for attempting to make the most of their business, as other businessmen would do, by taking advantage of new technologies and selling their products at a guaranteed high price. The Commission summed up the flipside of the production miracle in agriculture:

> Success had led to the costly storing of food surpluses. We have 20 million tonnes of cereals in intervention [i.e. storage] and that is predicted to rise to 30 million tonnes. We have almost one million tonnes of dairy products in stock. We have, also, 750,000 tonnes of beef in intervention which is rising at the rate of 15,000 to 20,000 tonnes a week. As no markets can be found for these products, they are being stored at taxpayers' expense; and we have run short of storage space. Clearly the continuation of such a policy is not sustainable physically or from the point of view of the budget. The *status quo* cannot be defended or maintained. It is also important to point out that even with a 30% increase in the farm budget, from 1990 to 1991, farmers' incomes in all Member States are set for further decline. (European Commission 1991: 5)

Budget crisis

Initially, no ceiling was set on CAP expenditure, and from the 1970s onwards EC policy-makers faced severe financial hangovers from the open party invitations of the early 1960s. The ensuing budget crisis threatened in the 1980s to bring the EC to the 'brink of bankruptcy' (Fennell 1997: 165f.). It was increasingly difficult to justify high expenditure on a policy that created such obvious negative consequences. It was politically impossible to raise the EC's budget ceiling by much, although the total budget was relatively small (Laffan 1997). The budget crisis was not solely caused by the CAP, but agriculture comprised such a large share that it attracted the primary attention and criticism. From all sides there was agreement that CAP expenditure had to be brought under control. Even the agriculture commissioner repeatedly warned about the possible collapse of the CAP, which could easily bring the EC to the brink of failure (Clout 1984: 181).

The response came in a series of partial reforms beginning in the early 1980s, in the form of production restrictions and expenditure ceilings. The issue was linked to the British budgetary question and to early discussions about completing the single market. The European Council agreed in Fontainebleau in June 1984 that agricultural spending would not be allowed to increase by more than 2 per cent a year. However, as the agreement did not include instruments to control production, it had no practical effect. Instead, agricultural spending rose by more than 18 per cent in the coming year (Patterson 1997: 145). The next step was to try to control expenditure by curbing production through the imposition of controls. Dairy products and grains were the most out-of-control areas of expenditure, yet both were politically difficult to address.

Because milk production can take place on relatively small farms throughout the EC, large numbers of dairy farmers in all member states benefited from the current regime. Milk surpluses in the EC had begun to appear in the mid-1960s and the Commission had initially tried to set the common milk price at a level low enough to discourage production (Hill 1984: 32f.). This was overruled in the Council, where visions of poor, small dairy farmers swayed government ministers. The Commission published a report in 1980 entitled 'Milk: Problem Child of European Agriculture' (European Commission 1980a), which the national political leaders practically ignored. Ultimately, the high price for dairy was triggered by domestic concerns about small farmers' incomes: 'While economists agree that policies to curtail excess milk production are needed, politicians are loathe to adopt a policy that could reduce farmers' income' (Koester and Bale 1984: 41). Because price reductions touch a raw nerve in CAP politics, the proposed solution was not to cut prices but instead to create milk quotas, with the aim of reducing production by 6 per cent (European Commission 1984). Reaching this solution took up much time and energy and necessitated torturous, drawn-out negotiations that saw a staged walk-out from the European Council by the Irish prime minister. The milk quotas were generally successful in spite of the difficulty of applying them in certain member states. For instance, in Britain the government allowed farmers to sell their quotas to other farmers, creating a 'grey' market for quotas, which largely defeated their purpose. Italy did not fully implement the scheme until 1995, more than a decade after its introduction.

Another attempt at reform involved grain production. This sparked a battle with the large grain farmers, who were highly influential in certain member states as well as in COPA. In 1985, the Commission painted a gloomy picture: if current trends continued, carry-over stocks of grains would rise to over 80 million tonnes by the early 1990s, corresponding to nearly half of annual production. It was clear that such surpluses could never be sold anywhere (Fennell 1997: 325f.). Massive food surpluses that could only be destroyed were already an embarrassment to the EC, especially at a time when pictures of starving children in Africa filled the media.

The proposed solution was simply to take land out of production (so-called set-aside) in return for compensation. However, the initial scheme was feeble and based on voluntary participation. The Commission was hostile to it because it would add yet another layer of complicated administration to the CAP and require investment in expensive monitoring equipment (Tracy 1989: 324). It was difficult to explain to the public that farmers were being paid *not* to farm. The effect of the first set-aside scheme was miniscule at first. A year into its application, barely 1 per cent of total arable land had been taken out of production. This amounted to 'no more than an exercise in containment' (Fennell 1997: 168).

Unlike state budgets, the EC budget is not allowed to go into deficit. Yet, experts estimate that 'concealed through clever accounting, this actually happened in 1987 by 4–5 billion ECU' (Patterson 1997: 146). Price supports, financed through the guarantee section of the EAGGF, had run out of control. The situation was unsustainable and was affecting the EC's activities in other policy areas. At the same time, statistics showed that average farm income was still declining. This unacceptable financial situation flew in the face of ambitions plans for the EC's single market programme and provided ample incentives for budget reform. The eventual solution had to include budgetary discipline without harming the incomes of important domestic farm groups, not least because 1988 was an election year in several key member states (Patterson 1997: 145 ff.). The so-called Delors I package, finally agreed to in 1988 after seven months of intense negotiations, imposed rules for budgetary discipline on the CAP. It also included an expansion of funds for less developed parts of the Community (the structural funds) and allowed for an increase of own resources to the Community's coffers (Laffan 1997: 10).

The so-called stabilizer reforms agreed to in relation to the CAP set production ceilings for all major crops and penalties for producers (so-called co-responsibility levies) if they exceeded them. In addition, the Council decided to extend the voluntary set-aside scheme, with part of the cost being absorbed by national budgets. The Commission once again did not back this particular aspect and therefore decided not to make a thorough analysis of its broader impact. As with the other budgetary reforms, the stabilizer package was patchy, complicated, and did not attack the root of the problem. In a melancholy vein, Tracy observed that:

> The Community seems to have embarked on the business of paying farmers not to produce for the wrong reason, as an alternative to a realistic pricing policy; without adequate prior analysis; and without assurance that the scheme can be adequately implemented and policed. It is a sad comment on the inadequacy of the policy-making process. (Tracy, 1989: 325)

The partial reforms of 1984–8 reduced the CAP's share of the budget: it fell from 75 per cent of the total in 1985 to 65 per cent at the end of the decade. By 1993, it had dropped to around 54 per cent (Grant 1997: 76). At the same time, however, spending on other policies, such as cohesion, grew considerably and benefited many rural areas. Another effect was that administratively the CAP became more complex than ever. Farmers were swamped with ever-more complicated forms to complete in order to receive support. By 1991, the income situation had again deteriorated and the Commission talked forthrightly of a 'crisis of confidence' in the EC (European Commission 1991: 11).

The new CAP

In the 1980s and 1990s, the CAP faced a number of challenges from outside the EC which led to real reform and a new emphasis in the policy. The so-called MacSharry reform of 1992 was the first to alter the core instruments of the original CAP. A subsequent food crisis, resulting from the outbreak of 'mad cow' disease, led to more awareness of food safety and producer concerns in the CAP. As a result, the CAP has changed shape radically but still maintains its original objective of farm income support.

The MacSharry reform

The MacSharry reform of 1992 was the first true reform of the original CAP because it targeted the policy's core instruments. Leading agricultural experts described the reform as 'an absolutely remarkable achievement, and a major departure from earlier attempts at reforming the CAP' (Tangermann 1998: 13). Given the circumstances described in the sections above, the timing of the reform was not surprising. The budgetary problem was still not resolved, but that was not sufficient incentive for a genuine CAP reform and was not the centrepiece in the reform discussions either. If excessive expenditure was the main problem, the CAP would have been reformed earlier. Nor do embarrassing surpluses explain the timing of the reform.

Instead, it was the deadlock in the Uruguay Round that provided the trigger and the immediate opportunity for launching CAP reform (Rayner et al. 1993). Towards the end of the 1980s, the mode of policy-making in the CAP had changed. With a number of increasingly important policies, such as environment and trade, overlapped with the CAP, an opportunity arose for a wider set of experts to have a say in agricultural policy-making. At the same time, there was more willingness to push for reform within the EC as the political scope was broadened from the narrow purview of producers.

Ray MacSharry, the Irish commissioner for agriculture, introduced an important dynamic into the reform process. He appreciated the extent of the pressure emanating from the international environment, having seen the GATT negotiations collapse over agriculture in 1990 (Grant 1997: 151 ff.; Tangermann 1998: 25f.). MacSharry argued that the only viable, long-term option was to have a competitive price policy that would also lower the incentives to over-produce and would take into account environmentally friendly ways of production. Yet the objective of the CAP should remain the same as before. MacSharry therefore recognized 'the need to compensate farmers for price cuts and quota restrictions' (European Commission 1991: 5f.). The Commission set out a comprehensive reform proposal in 1991, with the Council reaching agreement on it in May 1992. The reform targeted all CAP sectors, but above all grains, the prices for which were cut according to the agreement reached in the GATT (29 per cent over three years). Beef support and butter prices were also cut according to GATT. In addition, the export subsidy reductions and levy conversions on the table in the GATT talks were incorporated into the reform. As farmers stood to lose revenue and suffer a fall in income, the MacSharry reform would probably never have passed the Council without some other measure of financial support for farmers.

The novelty of the reform was a switch from price guarantees to the introduction of direct income compensations to farmers. The reform therefore expanded the set-aside scheme, making it compulsory for large-scale arable producers, who would receive compensations in return for lost production on set-aside land. The change meant that EC support to farmers became partially de-coupled from production—the terminology this time was compensatory (deficiency) payments and, later, de-linkage. Leading agricultural experts have often advocated such an approach, a form of which is used in the United States and was used in Britain before it joined the EC. In the GATT context, de-coupling was not seen as a direct trade barrier and was less trade-distorting than price guarantees.

Moreover, the reform tried to move away from the '80–20' provision of aid towards a better distribution for smaller farmers. MacSharry insisted that the 'agricultural budget should then become an instrument for real financial solidarity in favour of those in greatest need' (European Commission 1991: 12). Needless to say, this element, called modulation, was strongly contested by larger farmers. The final reform did not introduce modulation levels as high as the Commission initially had proposed. Nevertheless the extent of the modulation eventually introduced moved the CAP closer to integrating a rural development perspective and reversed the trend away from support of super-size farmers to the maintenance of smaller farmers. The reform also included a series of 'accompanying measures', such as financial incentives for the use of certain agri-environmental production methods.

Praise for the MacSharry reform outweighed the inevitable criticism of it. On the whole, the reform seemed like a 'major philosophical change and a moral victory for the Commission' (Patterson 1997: 159). By 2002, direct payments constituted around 60 per cent of the EAGGF's guarantee fund and the trend was upward. Another reform initiated at the end of the 1990s under Agriculture Commissioner Franz Fischler followed in MacSharry's footsteps. The overall thrust was to cement the general consensus among political leaders that the EC was equipped to deal with welfare aspects and would remain a redistributive policy, albeit now in a more direct way.

Mad cows, food safety, and farming as a common good

The CAP was not responsible for the outbreak of bovine spongiform encephalopathy (BSE)—better known as mad cow disease—that erupted during the 1990s, but the crisis had important implications for the CAP and significantly influenced legislation on food products and the treatment of public health issues in the EU. The media coverage of the scandal and the subsequent public outcry affected consumer choices in all member states (Charvet 2001: 18). Beef and veal consumption plummeted, with disastrous consequences for all cattle farmers. Politics and science became mixed up with emotional 'eat national foods' campaigns. There were some human fatalities and millions of cattle were destroyed. The first case of BSE was identified in Britain, but it was not until the number of known cases had reached 15,000 that the Commission placed a partial ban on British exports of live cattle (excluding certified BSE-free cattle). Later other countries faced their own BSE cases. This sub-section is not concerned with the complicated political epic but only with the consequences of the crisis for the CAP (Carson 2003; Neyer 2000).

EC food legislation has often been ridiculed by consumer groups for being concerned with the size and shape of fruits and vegetables and with addressing national trade barriers and regional pride rather than focusing on food quality and safety, the labelling of food products, human health or animal welfare (Carson 2003: 18 ff.). The BSE crisis brought these issues to the top of the agenda and made them an integral part of the CAP reform debate. The controversies over so-called 'Frankenstein foods' contributed to this as well. New groups, such as the European Consumers' Organization (BEUC), took centre-stage. Even the World Health Organization called for food safety regulations.

The Commission responded to widespread concern by establishing a directorate-general for consumer policy and health protection in 1995. By including a reference to food safety and public health in the Amsterdam Treaty, member states acknowledged that these were not merely national concerns. The lack of political accountability in such issues was also highlighted, with the European Parliament being given greater oversight responsibilities. Moreover, the creation of the European Food Safety Authority (EFSA) was an important institutional change reflecting Community-wide public health concerns. Its establishment formed part of a strategy towards restoring confidence in the CAP and in the safety of food products coming from within and outside the EU (Carson 2003: 14). In 2000, the Commission introduced an integrated food safety strategy ('From the Farm to the Fork'), involving several directorates-general.

After several years of dramatic discussions of these issues, the agricultural community managed to turn a potentially disastrous situation to its advantage. Fischler repeatedly argued that:

> We should not forget that the production methods required for [safer food] often entail higher costs or lower yields, which up to now have not always been adequately compensated by the market. Therefore it is right that only producers who are willing to sign up to [new] quality rules should continue to benefit from public funding. (Fischler 2003)

By winning widespread acceptance of the view that both *food* and *the countryside* are common goods in the EU, Fischler managed to swing the debate towards a justification of continued support for farm incomes. At the same time, farmers have managed to claim compensation for complying with EU environmental restrictions, which is contrary to the 'polluter pays' principle applied in other industries.

Fischler argued in addition that the millions of city-dwellers who go on holiday in the countryside each year should be willing to pay for sustainable small-scale peasant farming and the preservation of beautiful landscapes. Portraying farmers as custodians of the countryside is part of the move towards *multifunctionality*, the latest buzzword in CAP reform. Earlier, MacSharry had argued that '[t]here is no other way to preserve the natural environment, traditional landscapes and a model of agriculture based on the family farm as favoured by the society generally' (European Commission 1991: 12). The OECD supported this view in a series of studies, advising that 'it is more efficient to pay directly for public services such as maintaining an agreeable countryside, and to charge those whose activities pollute the environment. Payments for a public service would contribute to rising farmers' incomes' (OECD 2003*b*; see also OECD 2001). If these developments are realized, the CAP will finally have managed to square the circle between consumers and producers. Romantic urban visions of the countryside have not been so prevalent for centuries, and the CAP stands to benefit from them.

Conclusion

The farm income support objective of the CAP has been remarkable tenacious and long-lived, placing welfare as a central concern of the European integration process. The CAP is a continuation of the agricultural welfare state, yet the literature on European integration has generally ignored the centrality of agricultural welfare policies. The mismatch of policy instruments chosen from the outset—the common market and the price policy—has proved equally enduring throughout the history of the EU. Subsequently, the CAP was never fully able to live up to the political expectations, which were mostly out of touch with the socio-economic realities of the sector. Yet, it may also be argued that the member states continuously confirmed their commitment to the maintenance of the CAP, for instance during the annual price reviews. Many parties involved in the agricultural political system feared that a thorough reform would jeopardize the core objective of the CAP. Attempted reforms from the 1960s to the 1980s were therefore patchy and incomplete. These included MCAs, set-aside, production, and budget ceilings, and the development of supplementary rural policy programmes. Due to the compartmentalized form of policy-making that existed for decades, the CAP was not capable of reform from within. As one of Europe's leading agricultural experts noted, 'The long and multifarious history of the CAP could easily be written up as a history of attempts at reforming this policy—mostly failed attempts, one should say' (Tangermann 1998: 12).

The focus on the market policy to attain the objective of the CAP led to the assumption that competition with agricultural products coming from outside the Community could have a harmful effect on EC farmers' incomes, and so should be blocked or at least politically controlled. The protective agricultural regime of the CAP led to much frustration in the world trading community. As is usual with welfare policies, however, possible external effects were not discussed during the establishment of the CAP. The merging of six agricultural regimes into one gave the EC important leverage in international agricultural affairs, although it is doubtful that international agricultural trade would have been liberalized had the EC not existed, for the simple reason that international trade in agriculture never has been free.

Undoubtedly, political leaders would design the CAP differently today from the way they did in the early 1960s. At least, they would probably adopt different policy instruments and would choose a broader definition of 'agriculture'—embracing consumers and the food industry—as opposed to the narrow focus on producers that characterized the CAP for most of its life. The income support objective is still alive, as seen in the Commission's *Agenda 2000* proposals to reform and prepare the CAP for Central and Eastern European enlargement.

One of the biggest challenges of the marathon enlargement process of the late 1990s and early 2000s was preserving the CAP without destroying its purpose, given that the agricultural sector throughout Central and Eastern Europe suffered from severe structural deficiencies. Extending the instruments of the CAP directly to the new member states would have had serious distorting effects: by Central and Eastern

European standards, direct and indirect CAP transfers at the rate prevailing in Western Europe were so high that an extension of them would likely have caused a disincentive to modernize. One problem rarely addressed in the enlargement process was that Central and Eastern European states generally did not have national welfare systems similar to those in the 'old' member states. The lack of such domestic support for Central and Eastern European farmers could have created yet another difficulty for the CAP to achieve its objective. Regardless of the special provisions in the accession treaties for agricultural policy, the CAP is likely to receive much of the blame for the painful transformation to modern farming that these countries are facing. If so, European integration will probably continue its course between the image and the shadow of agriculture.

Notes

1 For a detailed historical analysis of this political process, see Knudsen (2001b).

2 For a broad introduction to the mechanisms of the CAP, see Fennell (1997), Grant (1997) and Tracy (1989).

3 Dutch structural policy was often seen as the most advanced, but its concentration on water management made it an unsuitable model for the EC to adopt.

4 Subsidization is measured in terms of producer support estimate (PSE), which indicates the state subsidy percentage of value of gross farm receipts. For a good comparison, see the annual reports of the OECD, *Agricultural Policies in OECD Countries: Monitoring and Evaluation.*

5 http://www.oecd.org/EN/home/0,, EN-home-1-nodirectorate-no-no–1,00. html

6 For the international situation concerning less developed countries, see, for instance, Charvet 2001; Hoffmeyer 1982; Lingard and Hubbard 1991; Lister 1988.

Further reading

Agriculture is one of the most thoroughly studied areas of EU policy. The best general texts include Fennell (1997), Grant (1997) and Tracy (1989). On the history of the common agricultural policy, see Knudsen (2001b) and Noël (1988). Moravcsik (2002a, 2002b) presents a provocative thesis about the centrality of the CAP in French President Charles de Gaulle's policy towards the European Community. Keeler (1996) is extremely insightful on the politics of the CAP, especially in relation to the Uruguay Round negotiations of the General Agreement on Tariffs and Trade.

Fennell, R. (1997), *The Common Agricultural Policy: Continuity and Change* (Oxford and New York: Oxford University Press).

Grant, W. (1997), *The Common Agricultural Policy* (Basingstoke: Macmillan).

Keeler, J. (1996), 'Agricultural Power in the European Community: Explaining the Fate of CAP and GATT Negotiations', *Comparative Politics*, 28/2: 127–49.

Knudsen, A.-C. (2001b), *Defining the Policies of the Common Agricultural Policy: A Historical Study* (Florence: European University Institute).

Moravcsik, A. (2000a), 'De Gaulle between Grain and Grandeur: The Political Economy of French EC Policy, 1958–1970 (Part 1)', *Journal of Cold War Studies*, 2/2: 3–43.

Moravcsik, A. (2000b), 'De Gaulle between Grain and Grandeur: The Political Economy of French EC Policy, 1958–1970 (Part 2)', *Journal of Cold War Studies*, 2/3: 4–68.

Noël, G. (1988), *Du pool vert à la politique agricole commune: Les Tentatives de Communauté agricole européenne entre 1945 et 1955* (Paris: Economica).

Tracy, M. (1989), *Government and Agriculture in Western Europe*, 3rd edn. (New York: New York University Press).

Chapter 10

From Deadlock to Dynamism

The European Community in the 1980s

N. Piers Ludlow

Contents

Summary

In the course of the mid-1980s, the European Community (EC) went from being a seem-ingly moribund entity to a rapidly developing success story. The launch of the single market programme revitalized the EC, helped it overcome long-standing institutional paralyses, created onward pressure for yet more integration, and forced the rest of the world to pay heed to the European integration process once more. This chapter ex-plores the origins of the transformation, looking at a number of rival explanations be-fore concluding that the most important factor was the emergence of a new degree of consensus among economic and political leaders about what 'Europe' should do. The chapter then explains how the apparently narrow target of establishing an internal market within the Community encouraged multiple other efforts to integrate Western Europe more closely.

Introduction

The second half of the 1980s was arguably the most active and dynamic period of the European integration process since the early 1960s, when the customs union was put in place. From 1985 onwards, the European Community recaptured the momentum that it was perceived as having lost twenty years earlier and generated a head of steam that endured at least into the early 1990s and arguably to the present. In the process, the EC set itself one major target, the creation of a single market by the end of 1992, which in turn necessitated multiple pieces of European legislation, altered its institutional workings so as to facilitate the enactment of these new laws, and created a whole series of pressures that do much to explain its subsequent course. This chapter therefore poses a number of key questions: Where did the new momentum come from? Why did it take the form that it took? What exactly did it entail? Where did it lead?

Before tackling these questions, however, it is important to sketch out the economic and political background. For one of the most remarkable aspects of the 1980s *relance* (relaunch) was that it emerged out of a period during which both Western Europe in general and the EC in particular appeared to have lost their way. The gloomy state of Europe in the early 1980s needs to be recalled, if only to throw into sharper contrast the sudden surge forward in the latter part of the decade.

Deadlock

To a large extent, the difficulties that the EC faced between 1980 and 1985 were the prolongation of the economic difficulties of the 1970s, which are examined in Chapter 8. The early 1980s was thus a time of unacceptably high unemployment, sluggish growth—if not outright recession—and high inflation. Indeed, the co-existence of these last two—low or negative growth and inflation—led economists who had previously regarded them as incompatible to coin a new term for the phenomenon: stagflation.

To compound the situation, Western Europe appeared to be performing much worse than its principal competitors. During much of the 1970s, struggling European governments could at least take comfort from the fact that, if the state of their own economies was poor, that of their main external competitor, the United States, was even worse. By the 1980s, however, this solace ceased to be available. Under Ronald Reagan the US economy began a remarkable run of recovery and rapid growth, fuelled by technological advance, which was to persist (with a few brief interludes) throughout the 1980s, the 1990s and into the early 2000s. The longevity of the US boom was not, of course, known at the time, but it was already clear that US economic dynamism had returned and that the world's largest economy was growing significantly faster than that of Western Europe.

Furthermore, the early 1980s was also when the Japanese economic challenge most clearly imprinted itself on the European mind. Up until the mid-1970s, the countries of the West (including the United States) had been remarkably complacent about Japan's spectacular postwar growth, dismissing Japanese manufacturers as purveyors of cheap and imitative goods that might challenge bargain basement products but would never compete head on with premium goods. To put it in automotive terms, Toyotas and Datsuns (later Nissans) might compete with Ladas (unreliable Russian cars) or possibly some of the cheaper Fiats, but they would never rival Volkswagens, let alone BMWs or Mercedes. By the late 1970s and early 1980s, this was manifestly not the case (if it ever had been). Japanese cars, electronic products and other consumer goods were clearly as good as, if not better than, their European counterparts. Worryingly for European manufacturers, they tended to be less expensive and more reliable. It is not coincidental that the two consumer products that most symbolized the early 1980s—the video cassette recorder and the Walkman—were primarily associated with Japanese producers.

Western Europe therefore faced the prospect not only of the United States reestablishing an economic lead over its competitors, but also, more troublingly, of the Japanese grabbing second place in the world economic table, a place that Western Europe had long taken for granted. All of this contributed to the invention of another term widely used in the political debates of the time: Eurosclerosis. The contrast with the Euro-dynamism of the 1960s could not have been greater.

Alongside such economic problems were profound political difficulties, both within individual Western European states and at the international and Community levels. Domestically, the 1980s was a time of increasingly bitter left–right polarization. Although the danger posed by the extreme left-wing terrorism of the late 1970s had faded somewhat—despite the fact that the Red Brigades and the Red Army Faction had not disappeared entirely—the day-to-day politics of Europe's major countries went through a peculiarly hard-hitting phase. The uproar caused in Britain by Prime Minister Margaret Thatcher's right-wing economic policies, following the Conservative Party's victory in the 1979 general election, and by the ascendancy of the far left within the opposition Labour party, was matched by acrimonious exchanges in France between the right-wing Gaullists and the newly-united political left. In Germany, meanwhile, huge controversy over the stationing, under Nato auspices, of intermediate-range nuclear missiles, in response to a similar deployment on the other side of the Iron Curtain by the Soviet Union, generated a massive peace movement and caused deep social and political divisions.

The so-called Euromissile crisis was a dramatic manifestation of a period in East–West relations sometimes dubbed 'the second cold war', when the temporary thaw of the 1970s came to an end as the two superpowers lurched into ever more aggressive stances towards each other. A succession of crises in Afghanistan, Poland, El Salvador and Grenada underlined just how frosty superpower relations had become. Renewed East–West tension spilled over into West–West rows, with Western Europe and the United States differing markedly in their analysis of how dangerous the Soviet Union really was and, more importantly, of which tactic—confrontation or ongoing cooperation—would prove most effective in dealing with it.

Within the EC itself, the successful launch of the European Monetary System (EMS) in 1979—examined in Chapter 8—could not conceal the wider problems that the integration process appeared to be facing. First and foremost, Western Europe's sluggish economic performance could be seen as a direct rebuke to the EC, which, having taken credit for the remarkable economic advance of the 1960s, could not escape some of the blame for the limping performance of the 1970s and early 1980s. Indeed, sluggish economic performance threatened to erode the EC's early accomplishments as governments and industries looked for salvation through protectionism, state subsidies, and other measures designed to favour domestic producers over and above outsiders.

Second, the EC's institutional system seemed especially hard hit. The optimism surrounding the first enlargement of the early 1970s, when Britain, Denmark and Ireland joined, had given way to irritation, with the newcomers angry at their relative failure to shape the EC in their own image, and the founder members cross with the way in which the new arrivals appeared to slow progress. Particular acrimony surrounded the British, who followed their abstention from the EMS, the Community's most exciting recent project, with the launch, under their new and abrasive prime minister, of a determined campaign to correct a budgetary anomaly whereby Britain, then one of the EC's least prosperous member states, contributed a disproportionately large share of the Community budget. Most other member states were willing to concede that Britain had a case, but the manner in which Thatcher pursued it generated huge resentment and annoyance. The diaries of Roy Jenkins, the President of the European Commission and a former British finance minister, are particularly revealing of the depth of anger caused by what he called the BBQ—either the British Budgetary Question or, less charitably, the Bloody British Question (Jenkins 1989: 545). Such political discord seemed to bode ill for the national governments' chances of getting their act together and using their new collective body, the European Council, to map out the way forward. Instead, European Council meetings came to be dominated by ill-tempered exchanges about the Community budget, food surpluses generated by the common agricultural policy (CAP), or the complex and lengthy talks to admit Spain and Portugal into the EC (Greece had joined relatively easily and unobtrusively in January 1981).

The European Commission, an alternative source of dynamism within the EC, seemed at an equally low ebb, especially once Jenkins, a relatively strong president, was succeeded in 1981 by Gaston Thorn, a former prime minister of Luxembourg. The 1970s had been a particularly morale-sapping decade for the Brussels institution—a time of weak leadership when the vast majority of its initiatives appeared to have fallen on stony ground. The appointment to its helm of a politician from the EC's smallest member state, barely able to control the competing 'barons' among his fellow Commissioners, let alone impose his will on national leaders, raised little prospect of the early 1980s being a time of change for the better.

Finally, the European Parliament, which amid much excitement had been directly elected for the first time in 1979, seemed initially unable to fulfil the hopes of those who had placed great faith in this development. A large number of high-profile European politicians had put their names forward in the first direct elections, trusting that their collective appearance in Strasbourg might herald a giant and immediate advance for parliamentary influence and power. But when nothing much happened, in the short term at least, many of the political heavy weights stopped turning up in Strasbourg, adding a serious problem of absenteeism to the lengthy list of the European Parliament's difficulties.

The Community of the early 1980s, therefore, did not appear to be on the threshold of a major step forward. On the contrary, the prevailing mood was strikingly captured by *The Economist*, which not only decided to close its Brussels office during this period but also marked the passing in March 1982 of Walter Hallstein, the Commission's first president, with a front cover featuring a gravestone on which was written: 'EEC. Born March 25, 1957. Moribund March 25, 1982. *Capax Imperii Nisi Imperasset.*' This quotation from Tacitus, which *The Economist* itself translated as 'it had seemed capable of ruling, until it tried to rule', seemed to sum up the extent to which the EC had fallen short of its founders' aspirations.

Dynamism

Given this gloomy backdrop, where did the *relance* come from? Or, to put it another way, why was *The Economist* so wrong? The traditional answer centres on the appointment of Jacques Delors as Commission president in January 1985. Delors's arrival in Brussels was, according to the standard account of the 1980s revival, the catalyst for a major change in both the pace and focus of European integration (Grant 1994; Ross 1995).

The single market programme

Delors's first key contribution was to identify a new target for the Community process, thereby ending a period when the EC seemed to be drifting aimlessly, unsure of the direction in which it needed to go. The goal selected was the internal market project: the idea of building a truly barrier-free Western Europe-wide market by the end of 1992 (hence its other name in English: the 1992 project). Implementing the so-called single market programme would require a systematic campaign to rid Europe of the nefarious non-tariff barriers that had clogged up the common market, established in the 1960s with the removal of tariffs and quotas.

Non-tariff barrier (NTB) were legal and/or administrative arrangements ostensibly designed for innocent purposes (health and safety, equal rights, financial transparency, etc.) but in reality often intended to make it harder for European rivals to sell products or to do business at the expense of home-grown companies or firms. It was quite common practice, for example, for national governments to set the exact specifications needed to produce, say, fireworks, that 'coincidentally' corresponded with the norms of domestically produced fireworks and equally 'coincidentally' were rather different from those prevailing in other European countries. This would lead to a situation whereby one European country, Italy for example, was able either to block the import of German or French fireworks altogether, ostensibly on safety grounds, or oblige the German and French manufacturers to alter their product so as to conform to Italian norms. Conforming to another set of norms could cost a lot of money and time, resulting in the erosion of the price advantage that the Germans or French had initially enjoyed over the Italians. Italian producers would hence be effectively protected from outside competition.

Aware of the pernicious impact of NTBs, member states had agreed in the Rome Treaty to try to harmonize rules governing product standards, testing and certification. That proved to be a laborious process, with Commission proposals for harmonized measures becoming bogged down in the Council of Ministers' decision-making machinery, especially as governments responded to industry pressure for protection. Unable to protect their ailing domestic industries by means of tariff or quota barriers—to have done so would have violated the Treaty of Rome—governments turned instead to more underhand methods to obstruct their European competitors, blocking efforts at harmonization in the Council of Minister or, worse still, introducing new NTBs.

By the early 1980s, the problem had become acute. The much-vaunted 'Common Market', supposedly in existence since the late 1960s, was in fact broken up into numerous national markets, all with somewhat different norms and regulations obstructing the entry of products from other member states. In deciding to spearhead a campaign aimed at the abolition of NTBs, Delors therefore chose a target that was likely to capture the enthusiasm of a new breed of European leaders eager to break away from the beggar-thy-neighbour practices of the recent past.

The Commission based much of its approach to the removal of NTBs on a seemingly obscure 1979 ruling by the European Court of Justice: the so-called *Cassis de Dijon* case. This established that Germany had been acting illegally in banning the sale of a French liqueur whose alcoholic content did not meet German standards. The Court ruled that a product suitable for sale in one member state should be cleared for sale in the rest of the Community as long as it met basic health and safety requirements. The principle of *mutual recognition*, upon which the Court based its decision, gave the Community an extremely powerful way of avoiding having to draw up new regulations for most European products, a truly Sisyphean task that had brought EC decision-making to a halt in the 1970s. Thanks to the Court's ruling, the Commission was able to insist that most products should be covered by mutual recognition, with the task of devising new legislation being limited purely to those products whose norms were so divergent that mutual recognition was impossible to accept.

The 1992 programme would nonetheless require a considerable amount of legislative activity, which in turn acted as a catalyst for overdue reforms of the EC's decision-making procedures. According to Lord Cockfield, the British Commissioner entrusted by Delors with the task of identifying the non-tariff barriers to be replaced, 297 pieces of Community legislation would have to be passed before the single market could become a reality. Given the halting progress of EC legislation in the 1970s and the first part of the 1980s, such an ambitious legislative agenda was bound to concentrate the member states' minds on the issue of institutional reform, notably a decisive move towards greater use of qualified-majority voting, something the Commission had hoped to see become widespread early in the EC's history but that had been held up by the Luxembourg Compromise of 1966.

Apologists for Margaret Thatcher often say that the prime minister supported the single market programme because it was meant to be about deregulation, not re-regulation. If that was the case, Thatcher was being naïve or disingenuous. The

Commission did not suggest that member states abandon the practice and principle of product regulation, only that the numerous national norms in force at the outset of the process be replaced by fewer European norms. Often this involved devising a new piece of regulation from scratch so as to please all the member states. Hence Cockfield's estimate of the legislative programme necessary to establish a true single market. If Thatcher really was surprised, she may have been guilty of not having read the texts to which she put her name—not something that she was normally accused of.

Thatcher was on firmer ground in suspecting that a rediscovery of purpose and institutional vitality in the EC would serve as a platform for other, far-reaching ambitions harboured by Delors. The full scope of Delors's aspirations would only become clear once the 1980s drew to a close, but even without subscribing to a Delors-centred explanation of the EC's revival, there is little doubt that the Commission president entertained hopes of pushing Europe much more decisively and radically in a federal direction.

Pressure from big business

An alternative, rather more subtle and less personality-centred explanation of the acceleration of European integration in the late 1980s, places great importance on an alliance of interest that developed between the Commission and European big business (Sandholtz and Zysman 1989: 95–128). According to this reading, the roots of the *relance* could be traced to a mounting dissatisfaction, in Brussels and in corporate headquarters across Europe, with the industrial strategies followed by European countries during the 1970s and early 1980s. These strategies had erred in two fundamental ways. First, they were too protectionist, fracturing a unified European market into multiple sub-markets by means of non-tariff barriers. Second, they placed undue reliance on so-called national champions: big, often nationalized industries that governments deemed vital to the country's economic health, and had therefore subsidized and pampered so as to avoid the ill-effects of the downturn. Examples included British Leyland (before Thatcher), Fiat, Renault and Phillips.

As a result of these misguided policies, the argument went, Europe had become steadily less productive, less efficient and less inclined to innovate technologically than either America or Japan. Trapped in their small, semi-protected national markets, Europe's principal firms had neither the incentive to invest enough to modernize nor the means to achieve the economies of scale open to their Japanese and American counterparts, both of whom benefited from a much larger domestic market. It followed, therefore, that if the EC could break down the barriers sundering its potential marketplace, Europe's firms would be able to realize the benefits of deeper integration and catch up with the US and Japanese pace-setters (the combined population of the EC, after all, was bigger than that of either the United States or Japan).

The Commission had tapped into these sentiments in the early 1980s when it sought to develop a programme to encourage European companies to invest in high technology. The so-called Esprit and other programmes mattered less for what they achieved directly than for the network of contacts that they helped forge between Europe's business leaders and the Commission. It was out of this network that the idea of the single market programme emerged.

Both the Delors and the big business explanations have their attractions. Delors's personal impact was certainly significant, doing much to restore the battered morale of the European Commission. That he came to embody the European project also testifies to his remarkable publicizing skills. Undoubtedly, at crucial times his energy and capacity to persuade member state governments of the importance of his goals was vital. In particular, his mastery of the often highly complex dossiers surrounding each aspect of the integration process enabled Delors to play a much more central role at gatherings of EC leaders than most of his predecessors had done. Being the man to whom all eyes turned as soon as technical questions arose greatly enhanced Delors's influence.

It was also useful for the Commission to be able to find support within the business community for many of its ideas. One of the remarkable features of the early years of European integration was the weakness of the ties between industry and the Commission compared, for instance, to the ties that grew up between the Commission and national farmers' organizations (as seen in Chapter 9). That Commission–industry ties belatedly started to develop in the early to mid-1980s is thus of some significance. And given the influence that business leaders are able to exercise on government, particularly when parties of the centre-right are in power, the development of an alliance of interest between the Commission and senior European industrialists was likely to have had some effect on the course of events.

The primacy of national governments and the European Council

Both explanations fall down, however, in one important regard: neither the Commission nor big business ultimately ran the Community. Any complete explanation of why the EC changed its spots in the mid-1980s therefore needs to start with those who had the real ability to effect such a change, namely the member state governments. For it is national ministers, meeting collectively in the Council of Ministers, and national leaders assembled in the European Council, who do most to determine the direction of European integration. Accordingly, it is necessary to explain why these national politicians rediscovered the utility of 'Europe' in the mid-1980s.

The key lies in an emerging policy consensus among member states about the economic need for greater liberalization in Europe. By the early 1980s, most of Western Europe was ruled by parties of the centre or centre-right: Christian Democrats in Germany, Italy, Belgium, the Netherlands and Denmark; Conservatives in Britain. These governments believed that the state-centred recovery strategy followed by their left-of-centre predecessors in the 1970s had been a disaster, as Europe's lagging competitiveness clearly showed. In their view, any European recovery needed to start with an ambitious programme designed to free up both the individual national economies and the European market, which was far too weighed down by national barriers. Furthermore, they were largely in agreement that the EC should pursue the key economic virtues that had seen Germany through the 1970s, namely low inflation, sound government finances, a strong currency and export-led growth. Again, such targets could be most realistically reached were the entire European marketplace to be liberalized. Thus, there was a growing consensus about what Europe's economic goals should be and about the first steps necessary to reach them.

The problem, as it had been for so much of the 1960s, was France. Since 1981, when François Mitterrand became president, France had been led not by the centre-right, but by the left. Mitterrand's government included not only the Socialist party that he had led back from the political wilderness, but also the Communists. Economic liberalization, therefore, was not high up on its agenda. On the contrary, the whole French economic programme upon which the left had come to power was based on domestic state measures designed to reflate the economy and combat the high unemployment of the early 1980s. Public spending and deficit financing, two staples of Keynesian economics, were central to such an approach.

Yet such a course collided head-on with the country's European commitments. The central difficulty was none other than the EMS. For the policies pursued by Mitterrand's first government guaranteed that the French franc fell much further and faster against other European currencies than was permitted under EMS rules. Within a year of the new government taking office France had had to devalue the franc twice, but even this was not enough as money flooded out of the country, putting great downward pressure on the French currency in the process. By early 1983, Mitterrand faced a stark and painful choice: either abandon the economic policy upon which he had been elected or withdraw from the EMS, thereby compromising France's whole European strategy, based as it was upon close cooperation with Germany. As the relevant chapter in a recent biography of Mitterrand puts it, the decision was 'le socialisme ou l'Europe' (socialism or Europe) (Lacouture 1998: 67–101).

A fierce argument ensued within the French government. In favour of defying the EC were several senior ministers like Jean Pierre Chevenement and Pierre Beregevoy, plus a number of major French industrialists, who advocated a total break with all of France's European commitments and the establishment of a new industrial policy based upon a much higher level of protection. Taking the opposite line were most of Mitterrand's economic advisers and the French finance minister, who was none other than Jacques Delors. And it was Delors and the cause of Europe that won. In March 1983, the French government undertook an economic U-turn, abandoning its attempt to achieve Keynesianism in one country in favour of loyalty towards its European attachments.

Having done so, France in general and Mitterrand in particular acquired a strong incentive to see the EC deliver; after all, it would be pointless to accept such humiliating change if the EC were to remain economically stagnant. France therefore changed from being the country most obstructive to European reform of a liberal kind into a strong champion of deeper European integration. The French president admittedly continued to harbour doubts about too much economic liberalization, but he was a shrewd enough politician to realize that if the Community could be revitalized, albeit initially around a programme somewhat alien to his core beliefs, a whole variety of other more palatable European opportunities would open up in the medium term. It would also become possible to build a closer relationship with Chancellor Helmut Kohl of Germany, thereby revitalizing the Franco–German axis so crucial to European politics during the 1960s and 1970s. Furthermore, if the route to economic salvation did not lie through a national strategy, France was determined to seek it through a European one.

The birth of the consensus so vital to Europe's *relance* thus required a combination of electoral outcomes between 1979 and 1983, which brought mainly centre-right parties to power, and the EMS-induced crisis of French economic policy-making in 1983, which obliged the most powerful exception to this right-wing trend—Socialist-led France—to conform to the European norm. Also important was the solution, for the time being, of the long-running British Budgetary Question. This was achieved by the European Council at its meeting in Fontainebleau in June 1984, by means of a complicated rebate deal which would ensure that Britain received back some of the money that it paid into the EC budget. With Thatcher temporarily appeased in her quest, as she put it, to 'get her money back', one of the issues that had done most to sour European Council meetings during the early 1980s was resolved before the launch of the single market programme.

Two further elements were necessary to complete the recipe for the EC's *relance*. The first was an awareness that the Community would soon be enlarged to include Spain and Portugal, both of which had been negotiating to join since the late 1970s. With that in prospect, member states appreciated that a failure to sort out their institutional paralysis *before* enlargement occurred would make it still harder to decide anything in the enlarged EC. Just as it had at the end of the 1960s and would do again thirty years later, the imminence of enlargement spurred institutional reform. The second element was the way that the constant economic and political squabbling between Western Europe and the United States helped create a temporary sense of solidarity among European leaders. The range of transatlantic disputes—from the row over the laying of a pipeline in Western Europe to import gas from the Soviet Union to the multiple trade flare-ups of those years—ensured that not even countries like Britain and the Netherlands, normally loyally Atlanticist, were entirely immune from the appeal of doing more at a collective European level in order to counter American influence. As with the launch of the EMS, a small pinch of anti-Americanism proved a useful ingredient in the political mixture necessary to get Europe moving again.

Finally, reference ought to be made to the European Council, the forum in which the key decisions were taken. For again like the EMS, the single market programme and the accompanying Single European Act (SEA) were fundamentally products of the European Council, whose various summit meetings were milestones along the road to the EC's revival. It was thus the Brussels European Council of March 1985 that first approved the 1992 target date for completion of the single market. The Milan European Council of June 1985 not only endorsed the Commission's White Paper detailing the legislative steps necessary to achieve the single market, but also decided to convene an Intergovernmental Conference to negotiate decision-making reform. Controversially, this step was taken as the result of a vote that saw Thatcher and her Greek and Danish counterparts placed in a minority. The Intergovernmental Conference was brought to a successful conclusion by the European Council in December 1985. Each of the breakthroughs that helped transform the EC could thus be linked to one or more meetings of Europe's most senior political body.

The SEA itself marked the first significant revision to the Community's treaty texts since the merger of the three communities' executive bodies in 1965. Of particular importance was the alteration in the voting procedure. Qualified-majority voting, which had been sparingly used despite being officially allowed by the Rome Treaty, became the norm for most decisions relating to the single market (although in practice many matters were settled without a vote). In addition, the European Parliament was given a much greater role in the legislative process. That increase in Strasbourg's influence, wrongly anticipated in 1979, was thus belatedly achieved in 1987. But also important in the new treaty text was the recognition of the European Council's place within the Community structure. Although the institution had existed since 1975, the vagueness of its legal links with the rest of the EC had stood in ever more striking contrast to its obvious centrality to the European integration process. By recognizing that regular meetings of the heads of state and government were part of the Community's institutional structure, a long-standing legal and political anomaly was corrected.

Overall, it thus seems much more convincing to opt for an explanation of the EC's *relance* that focuses primarily on the role of the member states. Delors and the Commission certainly played an important part. Moreover, Delors ably exploited the revival of interest in European integration in order to become the most high-profile member of the European Commission since Walter Hallstein two decades earlier. But whereas it is possible to imagine a less able Commission president exploiting the re-emergence of a consensus among the member states about what Europe should do collectively, it is certain that no Commission leader, however dynamic, would have been able to accomplish much in the teeth of member state indifference, hostility or total division. The change of heart in national capitals rather than the change of personnel in Brussels therefore lay at the root of the EC's revival.

Such an explanation also highlights how the Community's new achievements were solidly grounded in the recent past. Without the EMS, the emergence of the European Council, and key rulings of the European Court, all of which dated from the supposedly dark days of the 1970s, it is difficult to imagine Delors's scheme for the *relance* of Europe being nearly so effective. Similarly, the change in the European Parliament's powers that were included in the SEA would have been difficult to imagine had the Parliament not been directly elected since 1979. No periodic gathering of nominated national parliamentarians (as the European Parliament was composed before direct elections) would have been granted the level of influence over single market legislation that Strasbourg acquired through what became known as the co-operation procedure. A careful reading of how the Community recaptured its rapid forward movement in the mid-1980s therefore raises a number of questions about the standard and almost uniformly gloomy reading of the preceding decade. As seen in Chapter 8, although the 1970s may not conjure up an image of great European progress, many of the institutional and policy developments that occurred at that time were to prove central to the EC's subsequent revival.

Impact

Regardless of its provenance, the single market programme and the SEA revitalized the EC. The goal of complete market integration captured enthusiasm at government, business and even popular levels. Among business it triggered a wave of European take-overs and mergers, as companies scrambled to become big enough to compete in the single market. And among ordinary people, European integration once more became a visible process, albeit one that many regarded equivocally.

The single market programme also captured considerable attention from outside the Community. This applied to the Americans, who had seemingly lost interest in the process of European integration they had earlier supported so ardently. It was true also of the Japanese. And crucially it was the case for multiple European countries, including some of the remaining West European states that had earlier chosen not to join the EC. The relaunch of the mid-1980s therefore became an important factor in the decisions of Austria, Finland, and Sweden to seek EC membership (they finally joined in January 1995), although for all three the end of the cold war in the late 1980s would do much to remove the potentially insoluble problem of reconciling EC membership with their status as neutrals in the East–West conflict.

The long-term impact of the EC's revitalization would have been decidedly limited, however, had the process been restricted to achieving a single market. For all the economic importance of the four freedoms that stood at its heart—free movement of goods, labour, capital, and services—it is difficult to generate enthusiasm around a process of economic liberalization. But just as in the 1950s and 1960s, integration in one area soon led to pressure for related advances elsewhere. The neo-functionalist notion of 'spill-over', famously proclaimed dead by Stanley Hoffmann in the mid-1960s, appeared to have risen from the grave (Hoffmann 1966).

The most straightforward case of spill-over was the way in which the success of the 1992 programme revitalized certain long-standing policy areas of European integration that had become moribund. Examples include competition policy, which suddenly became much more important, and even glamorous, in view of all the transnational merger activity now taking place on a European scale. Similarly, external commercial relations assumed a new prominence as countries once more flocked to the Community's door seeking special commercial arrangements and trying to involve the EC in complex international-level bargains to prevent their goods being locked out of what some dubbed—rather unfairly—'Fortress Europe'. Regional or cohesion policy was another area that experienced a knock-on effect through the use of the Community budget to spread money from the wealthier to the poorer parts of the Community. This strand of Community policy-making had existed since the 1970s, but the size of the budgetary transfers carried out by the EC increased massively with the advent of structural funds, the pay-off demanded by the poorer countries in return for their acceptance of the single market project. Indeed Delors, who saw the structural funds as an integral aspect of European integration, always regarded the single market programme, the SEA, and the budget agreement of 1988, which boosted the structural funds substantially, as indissolubly linked.

There were links as well between the single market programme and closer intergovernmental cooperation among EC member states. For instance, the Community's entry into the area of justice and home affairs, later a vital pillar of the European Union, was related to how the 1992 programme was meant to abolish border controls. For if these were removed (or even just scaled down), each member state's capacity to stop criminals fleeing abroad, prevent the entry of illegal immigrants, or control the influx of drugs would be correspondingly reduced or removed. The only answer was to do more at the European level. Likewise, the pressure to coordinate European foreign policy increased. With the EC once more becoming an international player of note economically, it became ever more anomalous that member states, able to negotiate jointly in the General Agreement on Tariffs and Trade (GATT), were incapable of formulating a unified stance on the major foreign policy questions of the day. This process was further accentuated by the enthusiasm of the administration of the first President Bush (1989–93) for the emergence of a genuine European partner.

Finally, there is the connection between the single market programme and economic and monetary union (EMU), the centre-piece of the Maastricht Treaty, the next major milestone in the history of European integration. There are two ways of explaining the link. The first is simple, if inadequate. It posits that the removal of all other barriers to trade across Europe made the persistence of currency barriers ever more strikingly aberrant. It was therefore totally logical to seek to remove this last, major, non-tariff barrier. A second, somewhat more complicated argument, highlights the way that the removal of exchange controls and restrictions on cross-border capital movements—part of the internal market process—knocked down one of the major props upon which the EMS rested. As a result the whole long-term stability of Europe's monetary situation was cast into doubt and the EC faced a choice between either returning to the monetary instability of the 1970s or advancing towards some rather tighter form of monetary integration, reliant on greater monetary policy convergence rather than central bank intervention (Padoa-Schioppa 1987: 72–88). Understandably in the circumstances, member states opted for advance rather than retreat, with the notable exception of Britain under Thatcher and her successor, John Major. As seen in Chapter 11, from 1988 onwards monetary union was back on the EC's agenda, although it was not until 1999 that it would become a functioning reality.

Conclusion

In conclusion, it is worth pointing out that among the cluster of factors that was to lead from the SEA in the mid-1980s to the much more ambitious Maastricht project of the 1990s, there lurked a development that helps to explain popular resistance to the emerging European Union. For the single market project, while greeted with moderate public enthusiasm, brought the integration process down to a level that affected, or threatened to affect, the day-to-day lives of ordinary Europeans in a way that had not occurred previously. Implementation of the single market programme in the late 1980s therefore triggered a rash of scare stories about how some or other tradition, product, or procedure was likely to be harmed by meddling bureaucrats in Brussels, and a smaller number of cases where such harm was actually done. This contributed greatly to the mood of public doubt that did so much to sour the reception of the Maastricht Treaty. Both the contents of the Maastricht Treaty and the difficulties encountered during the ratification crisis in 1992 can therefore be linked to the *relance* of European integration in the 1980s.

Further reading

Historical writing about the EC during the 1980s is still very much in its infancy. Archival access to the documents that most historians prefer working with is still patchy and the period is also too recent for the sense of perspective that many seek. As a result the field is largely left to a combination of journalists, political scientists and participants. Much of their output can be very useful. It is, however, very different in both its tone and its source base from the type of literature from which earlier chapters in this volume have been able to draw.

The most stimulating of the political science analysis of the 1980s is that by Moravcsik (1998). His argument is never less than forceful and often contentious, but his views are impossible to ignore and the theories that he advances to explain the whole of the EC's development since 1958 fit much better with the events of the 1980s than they do with any other decade. Much less satisfactory, but widely read is Gillingham (2003).

These overviews can be supplemented with texts focusing either on one particular policy area or one particular player. On monetary integration the best texts are Gros and Thygesen (1998) and Szasz (1999); on the single market programme, Sandholz and Zysman (1989) and the recollections of one the key protagonists, Cockfield (1994); and on the underlying transformation of Europe's legal status, Weiler (1999). Also useful are Ross (1995) on Delors, Friend (1998) on Mitterrand, and Corbett (1998) on the role of the European Parliament. The story can then be taken up to the Maastricht Treaty with Dyson and Featherstone (1999) and Mazzucelli (1997).

Cockfield, A. (1994), *The European Union: Creating the Single Market* (London: Wiley Chancery Law).

Corbett, R. (1998), *The European Parliament's Role in Closer EU Integration* (Basingstoke: Macmillan).

Dyson, K., and Featherstone, K. (1999), *The Road to Maastricht: Negotiating Economic and Monetary Union* (Oxford: Oxford University Press).

Friend, J. (1998), *The Long Presidency: France in the Mitterrand Years, 1981–1995* (Boulder, CO: Westview Press).

Gillingham, J. (2003), *European Integration, 1950–2003: Superstate or New Market Economy?* (Cambridge: Cambridge University Press).

Gros, D., and Thygesen, N. (1998), *European Monetary Integration: From the European Monetary System to Economic and Monetary Union*, 2nd edn. (Harlow: Addison-Wesley Longman).

Mazzucelli, C. (1997), *France and Germany at Maastricht: Politics and Negotiations to Create the European Union* (New York: Garland).

Moravcsik, A. (1998), *The Choice for Europe: Social Purpose and State Power from Messina to Maastricht* (Ithaca, NY: Cornell University Press).

Ross, G. (1995), *Jacques Delors and European Integration* (Cambridge: Polity Press).

Sandholz, W., and Zysman, J. (1989), '1992: Recasting the European Bargain', *World Politics*, 42/1: 95–128.

Szasz, A. (1999), *The Road to European Monetary Union* (New York: St. Martin's Press).

Weiler, J. (1999), *The Constitution of Europe: 'Do the New Clothes Have an Emperor?' and Other Essays on European Integration* (Cambridge: Cambridge University Press).

Websites

There are a number of websites that contain materials relating to European integration in the 1980s. The two best sites on European integration history generally are based in the University of Leiden and in Luxembourg. They can be found at http://www.eu-history.leidenuniv.nl/ and http://www.ena.lu/mce.cfm. Each contains a mixture of documents, multimedia resources, bibliographies and links. Also useful are the links listed on a US-based website: http://library.byu.edu/~rdh/eurodocs/ec.html. The EU's own web-pages only really come into their own for those seeking very recent documentation. They do, however, contain a fairly sketchy overview of the Union's past at http://europa.eu.int/abc/history/index_en.htm, the most useful feature of which is a facility which allows you to look up the most significant European integration-related developments in any given year since 1950.

Chapter 11

From the Single Market to the Single Currency

Dorothee Heisenberg

Contents

Summary

The launch of the euro in January 1999 as a virtual currency (notes and coins followed in 2002) was one of the greatest achievements in the history of European integration. It was the culmination of a process that began in the mid-1980s when France, concerned about German dominance of the European Monetary System (EMS), launched various proposals to strengthen its voice in European monetary policy-making. Germany's political leaders sympathized with France and were eager to deepen European integration. However, the satisfaction of the Bundesbank (German central bank) with the *status quo* tempered the politician's fervour for a new monetary policy initiative. The active participation of the Bundesbank's president in a committee (the so-called Delors Committee) to develop a plan for economic and monetary union (EMU) helped to reconcile the Bundesbank to the idea, which was quite advanced by the time that the Berlin Wall came down in November 1989. The sudden prospect of German unification had little direct impact on EMU, which formed the centrepiece of the Maastricht Treaty of 1992. One of the most surprising aspects of European integration in the 1990s was the determination of most national governments to participate in Stage 3 of EMU (the launch of the single monetary policy and the single currency) despite the lack of public enthusiasm for the venture and the unpopularity of the budget cuts sometimes necessary to meet the convergence criteria. Although EMU was almost entirely a political project, there were hopes that the euro would generate economies of scale, price transparency, lower prices and other economic benefits. To date these benefits have not materialized, especially in Germany, the eurozone's biggest economy. Nor have the large member states of the eurozone stuck to the terms of the Stability and Growth Pact, which was intended to strengthen the fiscal foundations of EMU.

Introduction

The creation of the new European currency, the euro, on 1 January 1999, marked the completion of one of the greatest feats of European integration since the Treaty of Rome. Confounding critics, who believed that the political will to complete this historic project was absent, eleven of the then fifteen member states of the European Union (EU) fixed their currencies irrevocably together and, on 1 January 2002, replaced them with shiny new euro coins and colourful crisp bills. The history of how this milestone of European integration happened is an essential element in understanding the dynamics of European economic and political integration.

This chapter focuses on the significant individuals, ideas and institutions that made the single currency a reality. The creation of a European currency, mirroring European integration generally, has been very much an elite-driven, top-down, politically insulated phenomenon. The 'permissive consensus' (Lindberg and Scheingold 1970) that had prevailed in the European Community throughout the 1960s, 1970s and 1980s was in evidence throughout the negotiations on EMU that ended at the Maastricht summit of December 1991. However, after the Treaty on European Union, or Maastricht Treaty, had been signed, a new era of mass public–elite relations about European matters began. The story of the EU after Maastricht is one of new popular participation in heretofore elite decision-making, a development that the statesmen did not always welcome.

If the signing of the Treaty on European Union marked the highpoint of Europhoria, the post-Maastricht years of painful fiscal austerity and the popular perception of a democratic deficit in all European institutions signalled a new euroscepticism that persists to the present. Yet citizens in the eurozone are proud of the creation of the euro, with 66 per cent of them agreeing that the adoption of the new currency will remain one of the major events in the EU's history (European Commission 2002). Moreover, despite fiscal austerity, slowing economies since the creation of the euro, and the initial weakness of the euro's value relative to the dollar, 54 per cent of eurozone citizens believed that the adoption of the euro strengthened their countries for the future. However, uncertainty remains about whether the United Kingdom, Denmark and Sweden will eventually join the eurozone, when the EU's new member states will join, and how successful the euro will be in creating the conditions for growth and prosperity that were promised at the inception of the plan.

This chapter examines the choices and events that led to the signing of the Maastricht Treaty in December 1991, which committed all member states except the United Kingdom to relinquish their monetary sovereignty by 1999 at the latest. Denmark only received its opt-out in response to the referendum of June 1992, in which a narrow majority rejected the Maastricht Treaty. The history of monetary union does not end there, however, as many of the political dynamics between 1991 and 1999 generated significant doubts about whether the member states would actually go through with the plan or whether it would flounder as had the Werner Plan, an earlier scheme for monetary union (see Chapter 8). Finally, the chapter examines the period since the creation of the euro, analyzing its successes and failures, as well as prospects for the future.

From the EMS to Maastricht, 1987–91

In order to understand the negotiations on economic and monetary union, one must be absolutely clear about the *status quo* in 1987. The European Monetary System, launched almost a decade earlier (see Chapter 8), had provided reasonably stable exchange rates among currencies participating in its exchange-rate mechanism (ERM) (see Gros and Thygesen 1998; Heisenberg 1999; Ludlow 1982; McNamara 1988). The central feature of the ERM was an adjustable peg, which meant that participants could periodically realign the parity rates (+/− 2.25 per cent of the central peg) between all the currencies as their economies diverged, but only on the basis of consensus. Because of its historical record of no devaluations, Germany had become the *de facto* anchor of the system. This proved particularly advantageous to Germany, which could run a monetary policy congenial to its economic situation and still have quasi-fixed exchange rates *vis-à-vis* its major European trading partners. In the design of the ERM, the French had tried to make the intervention obligations more symmetrical than they had been in the earlier exchange rate regime, the so-called 'snake'. France and the other weaker currency countries had ultimately been disappointed that the ERM did not turn out to be more beneficial to the needs of their economies. Although President François Mitterrand had made a radical policy choice (the '*franc fort*' strategy) in May 1983 to remain in the disinflationary ERM despite his electoral promises, the French were not satisfied with the workings of the ERM and continued to press for the 'institutional progress' that had been promised in the original EMS agreement.

The *status quo* implied that France and other participants in the EMS would be favourably inclined towards a monetary union as this would give them at least a small say over their monetary policy, while Germany, which had a superior position within the EMS, would resist any moves towards a different system. Therefore, it is more difficult and important to understand why Germany would agree to join a monetary union.

By 1987, businesses, politicians and academics generally judged the EMS a success. The number of realignments among currencies in the ERM had begun to fall and European economies were (for the most part) converging towards similar inflation rates. In Britain, Prime Minister Margaret Thatcher was under pressure finally to join the successful regime. Unbeknown to her, the chancellor of the exchequer (finance minister) had been shadowing the EMS since March 1987 in order to bring monetary stability to the British economy as well (Thatcher 1993). From an economic perspective, the ERM was very successful in limiting exchange rate fluctuations among the participating countries.

French and German preferences

The diplomatic perspective was less rosy, however. The French were frustrated by the fact that they remained second-class citizens in the regime, despite the success of Mitterrand's *franc fort* policy. Inflation was at German levels, but whenever the German mark (Deutsche Mark or DM) appreciated (as it did, for example, in January 1987) because of sudden international currency inflows seeking a safe haven, the French central bank (Banque de France) had to intervene with scarce reserves in order to prevent the franc from falling below its DM floor. Germany, on the other hand, did not have to intervene until France crossed the band, and then only with a weaker currency. Moreover, German exporters did not have to bear the trade disadvantages of an appreciating currency. From the point of view of the entire French political class, these asymmetries had to be remedied.

Over the course of 1987, three different solutions were proposed:

1. Changes to the EMS in the form of the Basle/Nyborg Agreement.
2. A Franco–German Economic and Financial Council.
3. economic and monetary union.

The Basle/Nyborg Agreement, signed in September 1987, was an attempt to create some of the financing mechanisms for intervention that had been promised in the original EMS agreement, but that had been stymied by the German central bank in the influential Monetary Committee of the EU, which advised the Council of Economic and Finance Ministers (Ecofin). The agreement attempted to make intra-marginal intervention by both currencies the norm, rather than waiting until the 2.25 per cent bands had been crossed before intervening. Ultimately, however, the Basle/Nyborg Agreement did not result in the kinds of changes that France had been hoping for, as the Bundesbank's and the Banque de France's interpretations of their obligations differed significantly and the facilities for intervention remained small (Dyson 1994; Heisenberg 1999). Moreover, the Basle/Nyborg Agreement included the recommendation that more active reliance should be placed on interest rate changes than on interventions in the currency markets, placing the onus primarily on the countries whose currencies were under strain due to the DM's strength.

French attempts to have a greater say in monetary policy were also evident in proposals for the Franco–German Economic Council. Timed to coincide with the twenty-fifth anniversary of the Franco–German Treaty of Friendship (the Elysée Treaty of 1963), France proposed the council as a means of promoting closer coordination of interest-rate policy between the two countries. German Chancellor Helmut Kohl and

Foreign Minister Hans-Dietrich Genscher welcomed the initiative, but the Finance Ministry and the Bundesbank opposed the implicit right contained in the proposal to set international obligations before domestic stability concerns (Dyson 1994; Heisenberg 1999). The interventions of the Bundesbank and the German Finance Ministry resulted in a memorandum being added to the proposed agreement stating unequivocally that the Council would be a consultative rather than a decision-making body. French efforts to have an input into monetary policy had been thwarted again.

It became clear on 'Black Monday', the day in October 1987 of the largest (percentage) fall in the US stock market history, how limited the Basle/Nyborg reforms really were. As investors moved their funds into safer currencies, the DM began to appreciate and, through no fault of their own, the other ERM currencies approached the bottom of their respective bands against the DM. In the aftermath of the currency upheavals, French Finance Minister Edouard Balladur sent a new proposal to the Germans in January 1988, elaborating an entirely new currency regime with fixed exchange rates and joint monetary decision-making among all participants. It should be noted that the French had sent several similar proposals to the Germans that had all fallen on deaf ears (Dyson and Featherstone 1999). This time, some Germans were more receptive to a *relance européenee* in the area of monetary union.

Genscher had a strong incentive to appease the French because Franco–German diplomatic relations had been severely strained by the resistance of the Bundesbank to lowering interest rates significantly after the October stock market crash. The German foreign minister also had a genuine preference for greater European federalism. Moreover, because the Bundesbank was independent of the German government, any greater integration of monetary policy would not come at the expense of the German government at all. Finally, having just taken over the presidency of the Council of Ministers for the first six months of 1988, Genscher was interested in initiating a large European project to showcase Germany's European ambitions. Monetary union could provide just that goal.

Chancellor Kohl's reaction to Balladur's monetary union proposal was more reserved. Although also favourably disposed towards European initiatives, keen political instincts alerted Kohl to the potential domestic conflicts that such a proposal might engender. Indeed, Germany's finance and economics ministries were pessimistic that such a proposal would be good for the German economy and, privately, the Bundesbank strongly opposed any changing of its competencies (Heisenberg 1999). Kohl nevertheless allowed Genscher to place the matter on the agenda of Germany's Council Presidency and undercut domestic (notably Bundesbank) opposition to the plan by announcing that 'the longer-term goal is economic and monetary union in Europe, in which an independent European Central Bank, committed to maintaining price stability, will be able to lend effective support to a common economic and monetary policy' (*Financial Times*, 23 June 1988).

The Delors Plan

Once the Germans had decided to put monetary union on the agenda, the next question was who would flesh out the vague ideas and make concrete proposals on how best to move forward. The issue was important because if it were left to the economists, too many roadblocks would be foreseen and the project would quietly be shelved. Yet if it were left to the politicians, too many technical problems would be ignored and the project could fail. European leaders spent the first evening of their June 1988 summit in Hanover trying to find the right balance of political and economic interests. The summit concluded with the decision to establish a committee of central bankers (one from each member state in an *ex officio* capacity) and three academics, plus Commission President Jacques Delors, to 'study and propose concrete stages leading to the progressive realization of economic and monetary union' (European Council 1988).

The so-called Delors Committee met over the next ten months to formulate a plan to achieve monetary union. There were significant differences of opinion among committee members over the timing of the transitions and the degree of economic convergence required to reach that goal (Cameron 1992: 48). In effect, the committee's deliberations replicated those of the Werner Committee in 1971 (see Chapter 8). Then, the divide had been between countries that wanted a speedy transition to monetary union in order to facilitate economic convergence (notably France), and those that wanted significant economic convergence as a precondition for monetary union (notably Germany). In the Delors Committee, the participants agreed to a three-stage process, with new institutional structures to be created at every stage. One of the key questions dividing the participants was whether to set firm deadlines for each stage or to make the stages contingent on sufficient economic convergence, as they had in the Werner Report. France's representative argued that the Delors Plan would meet the same fate as the Werner Plan if strict deadlines for transitions were not made, but the representatives of Germany, Britain, and the Netherlands all insisted on convergence and slower transitions before responsibility was handed to the new monetary institutions.

The Delors Report was released in April 1989 and served as the blueprint for EMU. Although approved unanimously within the committee, the report itself 'contained a lot of German thinking'. Indeed, Bundesbank president Karl-Otto Pöhl, who initially was sceptical of EMU, expressed satisfaction with the outcome. The other representatives were well aware that the Bundesbank had *de facto* veto power over monetary union if the plans were not in accordance with Germany's preferences. In the end, all of the committee's participants understood that Germany's participation in EMU was essential for the success of the venture (Heisenberg 1999: 106).

Meeting in Madrid in June 1989, the European Council devoted considerable time to the Delors Report. On the one hand, France, Italy, Spain, Belgium, and the Commission wanted a fast track to monetary union with firm commitments to a strict timetable. On the other hand, Germany, Britain, the Netherlands, and Denmark argued against an immutable timetable. At issue was a paragraph in the Delors Report stating that 'the creation of an economic and monetary union must be viewed as a single process ... the decision to enter upon the first stage should be a decision to embark on the entire process' (Committee for the Study of Economic and Monetary Union 1989: 31).

The timing of the intergovernmental conference (IGC), which was required to negotiate the proposed treaty changes, was a second point of contention between Germany and France. Kohl wanted the IGC to start after the federal election in December 1990, in which an extreme right party that could benefit from the German public's anti-EMU feelings was expected to do well. By contrast, Mitterrand wanted the IGC to start as soon as possible after the launch of Stage 1 of EMU, which was due to begin on 1 July 1990.

German unification

It is important to note that it was Chancellor Kohl who salvaged a compromise at the European Council in Madrid, in June 1989. In exchange for Kohl's agreement to the launch of Stage 1 in July 1990, and for instructing the relevant committees to begin planning the IGC, the European Council concurred that the Delors Report represented *a* process, not *the* process for the realization of EMU, and that the beginning of the IGC and of Stages 2 and 3 would be decided only after 'full and adequate preparations' were completed. If Kohl had wanted to prevent monetary union, he would not have struck this compromise to enable EMU go to forward. As it was, Kohl set in motion the process almost exactly as it would unfold, nearly five months before the fall of the Berlin Wall and before anyone thought that German unification was even a remote possibility. It is therefore incorrect to argue that Kohl agreed to monetary union in exchange for German unification.

The fall of the Berlin Wall on 9 November 1989, nonetheless changed some of the negotiating dynamics at the European level. For instance, during a meeting between Mitterrand and Kohl in December 1989, Kohl agreed to start the IGC in December 1990, immediately after the German elections, rather than in 1991 as he had originally wanted in order to allow time to plan the parallel IGC on political union. However, as Dyson and Featherstone indicate, Kohl had already conceded this point when Joachim Bitterlich, head of the chancellor's office, indicated to French presidential adviser Elizabeth Guigou at a meeting on 12 October 1989 that:

> Kohl shared Mitterrand's enthusiasm for setting a firm date for an IGC on EMU. . . . In fact, agreement on this issue seemed so obviously in sight [at the December 1989 Strasbourg European Council] that the date of the IGC did not figure in the Franco–German summit at the beginning of November. . . . The main uncertainty related to the lack of a firm date for the German elections. (Dyson and Featherstone 1999: 76)

The possibility of German unification did not affect the EMU negotiations in any real fashion, but it lessened German pressure on France to make equally significant progress in the concurrent negotiations on political union. After November 1989, the discussions on political union, in which Kohl had been extremely interested, became more pro forma than real. The Maastricht Treaty ultimately reflected these facts.

The year 1990 was marked by the immense and overwhelming changes in the East–West German (and indeed Eastern–Western European) relationship. As Kohl and Genscher struggled to stay ahead of events in East Germany, Mitterrand and the other Western European leaders were largely spectators of the German–American–Soviet drama. Although technically France and Britain had a veto over German unification, any theoretical leverage they might have had was gone by April, when the EU convened a special European Council meeting in Dublin formally to endorse German unification (among other things).

Negotiating EMU

Because the European Council had agreed in Strasbourg in December 1989 that the IGC on EMU would begin the following December, 1990 became the year of the technocrats. In each of the relevant ministries in all of the member states, position papers and drafts of the new treaty were quietly forged. At meetings of key EC committees, such as Ecofin and its preparatory Monetary Committee, the focus on details was evident. Two of the most important issues for the Bundesbank were the statutory independence of the proposed European Central Bank (ECB) and the role of the ECB in setting exchange rate policy (Dyson and Featherston 1999: 210). Moreover, the Bundesbank wanted the Committee of Central Bank Governors to draft the statute of the ECB so as to ensure that political compromises would not be made on the priority of monetary stability. The Bundesbank was also concerned that there should be central control over budget deficits and that no new institutions be given monetary policy responsibility until the single currency came into being.

In a working paper published in August 1990, the Commission proposed 1 January 1993 as the date for the beginning of Stage 2, a proposal that the Dutch, British and Germans rejected immediately. The Bundesbank countered with a suggestion that the next stage could begin by January 1994 if strict criteria had been met (*Financial Times*, 8 October 1990). Kohl agreed to that date at the meeting of the European Council in Rome in October 1990. Within a month, the Committee of Central Bank Governors had already finished its work on the ECB statute. Thus, when the two IGCs began in December 1990, many of the institutional questions relating to EMU had already been settled. The most divisive part of the ensuing negotiations revolved around questions of a possible 'two-speed' EMU and how to ensure that fiscal power, which would remain at the national level, would be consonant with monetary policy set by the ECB.

The 'two-speed' issue was difficult because such an arrangement would be setting a precedent for European integration: having a common policy without all member states joining at the same time. The European Council had agreed in Rome in October 1990 to a finite period between the beginning of Stages 2 and 3. Given the Bundesbank's insistence that economic convergence had to occur before monetary union, it was likely that some member states would join EMU before others.

EMU would also set another precedent for European integration: the existence of an 'opt-out' from a common policy. As the IGC negations wore on during the Luxembourg Presidency in the first six months of 1991, it became obvious that Britain, though now led by the apparently less europhobic John Major, was not going to accept monetary union under any circumstances. Accordingly, Ecofin agreed in May 1991 that no member state could be forced to enter the single currency and, conversely, that no member state could prevent the others from forming EMU.[1]

As the Committee of Central Bank Governors was finalizing the ECB's statute, the national governments presented their treaty drafts at successive monthly IGC meetings. Holding up progress was the question of when the ECB would be created. The European Council had stipulated in October 1990 that 'at the start of the second phase, the new community institution will be established' (European Council 1990), but the Bundesbank was adamant that monetary policy-making authority would not go to the new institution until economic convergence had been accomplished, that is, at the beginning of Stage 3. The compromise eventually reached between Kohl and Mitterrand was that France would accept strict convergence criteria if Germany would allow the creation of an embryonic central bank at the beginning of Stage 3. Thus, the European Monetary Institute, comprising the heads of each member state's central bank, would be created on 1 January 1994, but would not take over responsibility for monetary policy until the beginning of Stage 3.

The Monetary Committee was charged with negotiating the convergence criteria and the excessive deficit procedure. The German and Dutch governments wanted tough criteria to ensure economic convergence. The Italians and the Commission argued instead that a degree of flexibility was essential (Dyson 1994). Not surprisingly, Germany's perspective prevailed and the Committee eventually developed five convergence criteria:

1. A maximum 3 per cent budget deficit (of gross domestic product (GDP)).

2. A maximum 60 per cent government debt (of GDP).

3. Inflation no higher than 1.5 per cent above the average inflation of the three best-performing countries.

4. Long-term interest rates no more than 2 per cent above the three best-performing countries.

5. Two years of membership in the EMS without devaluing.

In the years following the signing of the Maastricht Treaty, the first and last convergence criteria would prove to be the most important.

The 3 per cent deficit limit, which was later institutionalized in the Stability and Growth Pact (SGP), was a number seemingly chosen at random, with more political than economic rationale behind it. Some argue that the French took the ratio from Mitterrand's public commitment in 1983 during the French Socialists' policy U-turn (Dyson and Featherstone 1999: 215). Others suggest that the reference point was selected to be low enough to ensure that Italy would not be in the first group of EMU participants.[2] Adding to the political nature of the reference point was the precise wording of the final convergence criteria text which stated that if a member state's ratio had declined 'substantially and continuously' and had reached a level that 'comes close' to the 3 per cent figure, the member state in question would be allowed to join. Thus, although the convergence criteria drafted by the Monetary Committee appeared to be very strict and in line with German preferences, in practice, they were much more flexible and, in the event, were not interpreted strictly by the Commission. 'Flexible interpretation' also proved to be a recurring theme of monetary union when it came time to enforce the SGP.

During the IGC, the inclusion of seemingly tough convergence criteria created the negotiating space for France and Italy to include a specific date for the beginning of Stage 3. For France, it was essential to make Germany's EMU commitment irreversible. This was done in a creative arrangement to which Kohl agreed, on the eve of the Maastricht summit, without consulting other members of the German negotiating team. The final formula was that if a majority of member states met the convergence criteria in 1996, EMU would begin on 1 January 1997. However, if—as seemed likely—there was not a majority in 1996, only those countries that met the convergence criteria in 1998 would enter monetary union on 1 January 1999. Thus, monetary union was assured even if it were to encompass only France and Germany, which were expected to meet the convergence criteria without great difficulty. With the benefit of hindsight, given the domestic opposition to EMU in several key member states in the late 1990s, it seems clear that EMU would not have been possible had the 1999 date not been enshrined in the treaty.

The EMS crises and the road to EMU, 1992–8

The Maastricht Treaty was rightly hailed as a highpoint in EU history. Never before had such an ambitious programme been advanced at the supranational level. However, the fact that all this had been done without much domestic debate in even the traditionally Europhile member states would come back to haunt the politicians over the next few years. The first casualty was the EMS, which had functioned so well to reduce inflation and stabilize exchange rates among European countries over the course of the 1980s. In the early 1990s, however, the ERM was under severe strain because of German unification, coupled with French and British obstinacy. Kohl's decisions to finance German unification with government borrowing rather than tax increases and to exchange the East German mark for the Deutsche Mark at a one-to-one ratio generated inflationary pressure in Germany while the rest of Europe verged on recession. When the Germans discretely canvassed the other Europeans for a realignment of the ERM in early 1991, the French were unwilling to break their hard-fought link to the DM lest it send the wrong signals to the markets.

Similarly, when Thatcher finally decided, in October 1990, to include the British pound in the ERM, her government unilaterally announced the rate at which it would enter instead of negotiating the parity with the other EMS partners as had been the usual practice (not least because there were intervention obligations on the part of all currencies). Many ERM participants publicly worried even then that the pound's rate was unrealistically high. As a result of all of these factors, by early 1992 the pound and the French franc were beginning to draw currency speculators' attention.

The EMS crises

The EMS crises of September 1992–August 1993 have been cited to show that EMS-like currency arrangements are bound to fail because they are inherently unstable (Eichengreen and Wyplosz 1993). However, if one examines the causes of the EMS crises, the more accurate conclusion is that using the EMS as a criterion for joining monetary union makes the arrangement unstable because it disables the system's traditional safety valve, that of political agreement on a comprehensive realignment. It is essential to remember that the fifth EMU convergence criterion was participation in the EMS for two years without a devaluation. The fact that economic differentials could no longer be corrected by means of realignments meant that German unification essentially undermined the EMS just as it was set to become a measure of economic convergence.

For the currency markets, the triggers for all-out speculation on the franc and the pound were the referenda on the Maastricht Treaty in Denmark and France. The Danish referendum, obligatory under Danish law, took place in June 1992. President Mitterrand, whose political popularity was flagging, scheduled a referendum for September 1992, hoping to harness his political star to the presumed acceptability of the Maastricht Treaty. Unfortunately, rather than Maastricht's popularity helping Mitterrand's political fortunes, the reverse occurred. As the entire treaty was difficult to read, anti-Maastricht groups in Denmark, France and other member states were able to portray it as an enormous power-grab by the European institutions of member states' sovereign rights. Accordingly, the Danes voted against the Maastricht Treaty by a margin of 50,000 votes and opinion polls in France showed that anti-Maastricht groups might also win there. The currency markets, which seized on this situation as an indicator that the ERM participants might not maintain their punishingly high interest rates for the sake of EMU, began selling off weaker European currencies.

During the summer of 1992, currency markets reacted to the fact that the Bundesbank did not lower interest rates despite economic signals that the German economy itself was beginning a downturn and that the other EMS members desperately needed lower interest rates to stimulate their economies. When, in September, the Bundesbank president suggested that a realignment was inevitable, the intervention obligations on the UK Treasury grew too onerous for John Major, whose government became the first ever to leave the ERM. Italy, which had devalued 7 per cent the previous week to no significant effect, followed Britain out of the ERM on 16 September, the day known as 'Black Wednesday'.

France, which had survived the currency turbulence leading up to the country's Maastricht referendum by means of a line of credit from the Bundesbank, continued to lobby for lower German interest rates throughout the next year. However, to demonstrate to the currency markets its independence from political interference, the Bundesbank obstinately refused to lower interest rates significantly (the Bundesbank's show of independence was all the more striking given that its own analysis of German inflationary pressures pointed to a significant slowing of the economy). Germany's intransigence on interest rates caused the EMS to disintegrate in all but name in August 1993, when the parity bands were widened to +/−15 per cent.

Different member states drew different lessons from the EMS crises. For French and German politicians, the lesson was that monetary union had to be accomplished expeditiously so that European currencies would no longer be at the mercy of speculators. For Britain and Denmark, the lessons of 1992–3 were that currency union would undermine their ability to protect their own economies from the policies of the others and thus should be avoided at all costs. The Danish 'no' had provided the opportunity to amend the Maastricht contract; in the revised version Denmark secured an 'opt-out' from monetary union.

Getting to Stage 3

In the other member states, the primary preoccupation of governments was to cut budgets and debts in order to be in the first wave of EMU. Indeed, the pace of progress on most other EU business essentially stopped in 1993–7 as domestic manoeuvreing to meet the Maastricht criteria took centre-stage. Many member states, including the traditionally high-deficit prone economies of Italy, Portugal and Spain, made it a domestic priority to be in the first wave of EMU entrants. In France, governments changed from left to right, and back again, but the essential budgetary policies remained constant. By 1994 it was fairly clear that the earlier date for EMU (1997) was unlikely to be met. Nevertheless, most countries wanted to avoid being perceived as laggards by not being able to join the final stage in 1999.

There were complaints by fiscal stalwarts that some countries were resorting to 'creative accounting' to meet the criteria. Italy was most often mentioned in this context (for example, by introducing a European 'tax' that would be collected up until 1997—the year the statistics would be used to calculate the convergence ratios—and then refunded, keeping lists of 'informal' spending commitments, and suddenly 'finding' money in the Treasury). Yet both France and Germany also tried to use unusual accounting devices to ensure that their 1997 deficit ratio was below 3 per cent. Ironically, Germany had itself placed the primary emphasis on the deficit criterion by mentioning it again and again as the most important element not to be fudged. Thus, although all of the member states ultimately made tremendous progress towards getting their deficits below 3 per cent by 1997 (Italy, for example went from a deficit of 6.7 per cent in 1996 to 2.7 per cent in 1997), there was far less convergence on public debt ratios. For example, Belgium had a public debt of 122 per cent in 1997, twice the convergence criterion's reference value, but was allowed to join EMU in the first wave anyway. Italy rejoined the ERM (still with its +/−15 per cent wide bands) in November 1996 and received a waiver for not being in the EMS for two years without devaluing to make it eligible to join EMU in the first wave. In short, in the final interpretation of the five convergence criteria, there was a great deal of leeway afforded to most countries in order to make possible the entry of eleven of the twelve member states who wanted to join on 1 January 1999. Britain, Denmark and Sweden chose to remain outside the eurozone initially, whereas Greece failed to meet the convergence criteria.

The foregoing discussion of the convergence criteria is important to bear in mind when analyzing the importance of the SGP, which member states appended to EMU in the 1997 Amsterdam Treaty. The genesis of the pact was Germany's fear that profligate countries would 'slim down' their deficit spending during the crucial year of 1997 and then resume their spending patterns once in the monetary union, destabilizing the union and calling into question the ECB's 'no bailout' clause. In early 1995, the Bundesbank and the German Finance Ministry began discussing a 'stability pact' that would automatically punish countries with a deficit over 3 per cent. Initially, the idea emanating from the Germans was that countries running a deficit would lose some of their regional aid, but over the next year the proposal was opposed by almost all other member states and had to be changed significantly. Opposition to the proposal focused on the stipulation that the penalty would be 'automatic' and that the disciplinary procedures would begin as soon as a deficit existed. The other member states wanted to take action only if an excessive deficit persisted, a position that was ultimately incorporated into the final pact, albeit with time limits delineating how long a state would have to rectify its problems.

The problem of the automaticity of fines was not as easily resolved: the French wanted some kind of political intervention that would allow a degree of flexibility with respect to when countries would be fined. Yet this political flexibility was exactly what Germany wanted to avoid. However, during the final negotiations at the Dublin summit in December 1996, Kohl was isolated politically and forced to choose between having a looser SGP than his government had wanted and having no pact at all. Unsurprisingly, he settled on the existing arrangement. The SGP incorporated in the Amsterdam Treaty used the system of peer pressure as the primary mechanism to ensure compliance, supported by draconian fines that were unlikely to be imposed because of their severity.

The inclusion of the SGP in the monetary union was considered a victory for the German 'stability first' negotiators. The French had obtained a step towards more political discretion in the implementation of the pact, but it was rather far from the larger hope of the French government, which was to create a *gouvernement économique* of the eurozone. The French view was that a political counterweight to the ECB needed to be created to ensure that growth was given enough weight in the monetary–fiscal policy mix. The French proposed the creation of the Euro-X Group (with the X standing for the number of countries in the eurozone) to discuss economic policies to promote growth. Renamed the Eurogroup at the beginning of the French Presidency in July 2000, it never lived up to the hopes of the French as a political counterweight to the ECB.

By and large, many of the decisions about the implementation of monetary union made between 1993 and 1998 incorporated German preferences more often than those of the other member states. The deference to Germany was no accident: public opinion there about monetary union was extremely negative and passage of the Maastricht Treaty had been difficult. The opposition in Germany's parliament eventually agreed to EMU only after the government had agreed that parliament would have the right to vote on whether the convergence criteria had been met before Germany substituted the euro for the DM. Thus, with every post-Maastricht decision, Germany's partners were faced with the question: would the German parliament use its power to block the country's adoption of the euro if the decision in question did not incorporate Germany's preferences? In addition, the entry into force of the Treaty on European Union was delayed by almost a year because the German constitutional court had to rule on the constitutionality of certain provisions of the treaty.

Final steps

The popularity of monetary union was falling not only in Germany but also in many other member states in the period 1993–7. The reality of budget cuts, taken in order to meet the budget deficit criterion, had made even pro-integration member states like Belgium and Italy less positive about the benefits of currency union. In 1995, incoming French President Jacques Chirac had supported his prime minister's significant public sector cuts, resulting in strikes by 1 million workers in December. The cuts continued in 1996 and Chirac decided to call parliamentary elections to shore up political support in advance of more budget cuts in 1997. In what was considered a huge losing gamble, Chirac discovered that the voters preferred as their new Prime Minister Lionel Jospin, the socialist opposition leader, who had promised less austerity. Despite his electoral promises, however, Jospin was as effective at wielding the budgetary knife as the conservative government before him had been.

The French case is elaborated here as an example of government policy continuity in the face of significant electoral opposition. This was the case in other member states as well (Jones et al. 1998). The overriding imperative of the governments of most EU countries was to obtain membership in the first round, once the decision had been made (in June 1995) that a majority of states would not meet the convergence criteria in 1996. Almost all other major EU business, including institutional reform and enlargement, took a back seat to the race to meet the convergence criteria.

In March 1998, the Commission released a report on the eligibility of member states to participate in Stage 3 of EMU. The Commission included Italy and Belgium among the eligible countries, despite the fact that both had more than double the allowable government debt (the Commission interpreted generously the 'significant progress made' phrase in the convergence criteria). Greece was the only member state that had wanted to join but was deemed not ready (Greece subsequently joined on 1 January 2001, on the basis, it was later discovered, of false figures). Sweden, Denmark and the United Kingdom, where public opinion was significantly against EMU, elected not to join, but left open the possibility of later participation (European Commission 1998). The Bundesbank was asked to write a report recommending which countries had met the convergence criteria in advance of the German parliament's key vote on monetary union. It seconded the slate of countries recommended by the Commission, and the German parliament gave its assent.

The European Council of May 1998 was supposed to have been a triumphal moment for the EU. Instead, the summit became bogged down over the appointment of the new ECB president. Dutch Central Bank President Wim Duisenberg had made his appointment as head of the European Monetary Institute in 1996 contingent on his selection by the national governments as the first ECB President. President Chirac had not given his approval then, but Jean-Claude Trichet, Governor of the Banque de France, had sent a note of support. In November 1997, Chirac formally announced that he wanted Trichet to become the first president of the ECB instead of Duisenberg. Many thought that this was simply a bargaining chip in France's attempt to create a *gouvernement économique* alongside the ECB but Chirac dug in his heels. Only a last-minute intervention by the British prime minister salvaged the summit. A compromise was reached whereby Duisenberg agreed to step down 'voluntarily' mid-way through his term in office, without stipulating a precise date. In the event, Duisenberg's early retirement came much later than expected because Trichet had become mired in a legal investigation in France and could not assume the ECB presidency until November 2003.

The experience of EMU

The creation of the virtual euro in January 1999—notes and coins were not introduced for another three years—was largely uneventful. Although technically all eleven participating national currencies were locked together, the currency union was not as visible as one might have expected for such a major event. Sixty-eight per cent of the population in the eurozone countries knew that the value of the euro had been fixed against their currency, but the domestic transitions were not as dramatic as they would be when euro coins and notes were introduced on 1 January 2002 (European Commission 2000).

European policy-makers were chiefly preoccupied with the external value of the euro, especially *vis-à-vis* the US dollar. When the currency was introduced, one euro was worth $1.1667. In the first year, the euro fell 15 per cent in value relative to the dollar. Within Europe there were large differences of opinion as to whether this was relevant in any meaningful way. The newly created ECB claimed that the external market value of the euro did not matter as long the new currency was stable. For some politicians, the external value mattered more concretely. Not only was Europe's prestige diminished but also, more importantly, the falling value of the euro implied that investors did not want to hold euros.

In Germany, Oskar Lafontaine, finance minister in the newly-elected Social Democrat–Green coalition government, allied with his French counterpart at a G7 meeting to propose a target range of the euro against the dollar. Although the United States immediately rejected any notion of tying the dollar's value to a target range, and Lafontaine was forced to resign in March because of political and economic differences with Chancellor Gerhard Schröder, there were many in Europe who remained concerned as the euro's value continued to decline against the dollar.

The euro's nadir came in October 2000, when the new currency was worth only $0.82. Although the euro had recovered to its initial trading range by May 2003 and indeed rose to $1.35 by January 2005, the 'lack of confidence in the euro' argument caused a great deal of finger pointing between national governments and the ECB Governing Council. For their part, the representatives of the ECB blamed low eurozone growth rates, especially in Germany, the eurozone's largest economy, on the lack of structural reforms. National governments, however, blamed low eurozone growth rates on inappropriately high interest rates, citing as an example the US Federal Reserve's willingness to cut interest rates as soon as the US economy weakened.

Clearly, the way that interest rate decisions were made by the ECB's governing council was partly to blame for the so-called '*status quo*' bias of the ECB. Although the ECB's statute called for decisions to be made by simple majority, with each member state casting a vote, Duisenberg immediately announced that the ECB's decision-making would be consensual. The result was that significantly more members of the Governing Council had to be persuaded to change interest rates than under the treaty-prescribed method. In December 2002, the ECB proposed an asymmetrical rotation of voting rights, partly in anticipation of the EU's enlargement to twenty-seven member states (including Bulgaria and Romania) and partly to give greater voting weight to the larger eurozone economies (Heisenberg 2003).

The ECB also received a great deal of criticism for a lack of transparency in the decision-making process. Although Duisenberg could have released minutes of key meetings in order to make the bank's decisions clearer to the markets (and hence smooth the foreign exchange market functioning), he decided in 1998 that there would be no information beyond the ECB president's statement after a meeting (and answers to reporters' questions) to explain the ECB's monetary outlook. The relative lack of information made the markets very dependent on Duisenberg's statements, but he had not mastered the fine art of 'central banker speak' and in the first two years there was a great deal of miscommunication with market participants.

The low external value of the euro, criticism of the ECB, low growth rates in the eurozone, and traditional sovereignty concerns did not make those EU member states not yet in Stage 3 of EMU (the so-called 'outs') inclined to join as soon as possible. UK Prime Minister Tony Blair was perhaps the best example of procrastination because of popular opposition to membership. When he was first elected in 1997, Blair held a pro-EMU position but was keenly aware that 59 per cent of Britons opposed monetary union. He therefore vowed to take Britain into the euro only after a referendum, but not before the end of his first term and only when five rather vague tests (posed as questions) had been met:

1. Are business cycles and economic structures compatible so that Britain could live comfortably with euro interest rates on a permanent basis?

2. If problems emerge, is there sufficient flexibility to deal with them?

3. Would joining EMU create better conditions for firms making long-term decisions to invest in Britain?

4. What impact would entry into EMU have on the competitive position of the United Kingdom's financial services industry, particularly the City's wholesale markets?

5. Would joining EMU help to promote higher growth, stability, and a lasting increase in jobs?

In June 2003, the UK Treasury released a report stating that only one of the tests had been met and that the conditions were not (yet) right for Britain to participate fully in EMU. Although Blair maintained that he still intended to bring Britain fully into EMU, there were no indications that he would propose a referendum before the end of his third term in office, which began in May 2005.

The pro-euro movement in the UK was not helped when the two other outs, Denmark and Sweden, held referenda that resulted in decisive rejections of the euro. The Danish referendum, held on 28 September 2000 (exactly a month before the euro reached an historical low point against the dollar) failed to garner enough support: 53 per cent opposed adopting the euro and 47 per cent voted in favour, with a record 87 per cent turnout. Similarly, a Swedish referendum held on 14 September 2003 also failed: 54 per cent against; 46 per cent in favour; with a turnout of 80 per cent.

Implementing the Stability and Growth Pact

Anti-EMU groups in Denmark, Sweden, and the United Kingdom made much of the fact that the SGP seemed like an enormous intrusion into a sovereign state's affairs. The pact was designed as a multi-step process arbitrated by Ecofin. The Commission was responsible for surveillance of the member states' medium-term budgetary positions and would notify the Council of any excessive deficit. Ecofin would then decide by qualified-majority vote (of all member states, not just those in the third stage of EMU) whether an excessive deficit existed. If the Council decided that an excessive deficit existed, it would make policy recommendations to the country concerned to correct the deficit within ten months. If the deficit persisted, the Council could decide, again by qualified majority, whether to impose a fine on the member state with an excessive deficit. The fines called for in the treaty were extraordinarily heavy, amounting to 0.2 per cent of GDP plus 10 per cent of the budget deficit in excess of the 3 per cent reference point (not to exceed 0.5 per cent of GDP).

It did not help the popularity of the SGP that the smaller member states perceived it as being strictly applied to them and fudged for the larger member states. Ironically, the first member state singled out by the Commission and the Council of Ministers for censure was Ireland in 2001. Ireland was one of only two eurozone countries with a budget surplus and robust growth, yet the Council opined that a tax cut proposed by the Irish government 'was not consistent with the broad guidelines of the economic policies as regards budgetary policies' (Council for European Union 2001). The Irish government carried on regardless, without fear that the EU would be able to punish a country that did not have a deficit. Portugal, on the other hand, did receive a warning in 2001 for having a deficit of 4.2 per cent.

The history of the SGP became significantly more contentious in 2002–3. In 2002, the Commission flagged Germany, Portugal, and France for their excessive deficits. By 2003, France, Germany, and Italy all had budget deficits over 3 per cent and were in danger of being fined for not bringing their budgets under the deficit ceiling. Given that their fellow finance ministers would be voting on whether to impose draconian fines on the largest member states, the German and French finance ministers felt relatively confident that they could simply propose budgets that were moving in the right direction (towards the 3 per cent reference point) without risking fines. Moreover, sentiment was running against enforcement of the pact because fiscal stability was not perceived as trumping economic growth in the sluggish eurozone environment. In October 2002, Commission President Romano Prodi openly called the pact 'stupid' and in June 2003 the French finance minister refused to change his expansionary budget, saying that growth and employment were more important than the pact. In July 2003, President Chirac suggested that the member states should agree to a 'temporary softening' of the pact. Accordingly, Germany and France convened an informal meeting to discuss possible changes.

The problems of the SGP highlighted two hallmarks of European policy-making: some countries' opinions matter more than other countries' opinions and informal agreements to enforce or not to enforce certain obligations were standard operating procedure. The smaller 'outs'—Denmark and Sweden—wondered whether the pact would have been enforced if they had been the fiscal delinquents, and countries like Austria and Belgium, which had made considerable efforts to reduce their budget deficits in accordance with the Commission's medium-term budgetary surveillance, thought it unwise to let the larger countries avoid having to make the same difficult decisions.

Controversy over the SGP came to a head in a lengthy meeting of Ecofin in November 2003, when Hans Eichel, Germany's finance minister, refused to cut his country's 2004 budget by another €6 billion. France, which had also been told to cut an additional €6 billion, followed suit. Rather than imposing fines on Germany and France, however, the member states agreed to suspend the pact's sanctions mechanism (with Spain, the Netherlands, Austria, and Finland opposed) because there were not enough votes to push through the sanctions. In response, the Commission took the member states to the European Court of Justice for failing to implement the framework on mutual budgetary surveillance as set out by law.

Clearly, the Commission was acting not out of fear that the euro was in danger of collapsing (the euro was at its historical high against the US dollar when the Commission announced its intentions), but because it wanted to set a clear precedent that large member states could not shirk their EU obligations. In the heated debate at the December 2003 meeting of the European Council about the modalities of qualified majority voting in the new constitutional treaty, the SGP was cited as a reason not to give France and Germany relatively greater voting power. As before, developments in EMU created new dynamics in European integration.

Conclusion

The launch of the euro and of the ECB to manage the common monetary policy was one of the most ambitious developments in fifty years of European integration. The roles of Germany and France in the drama of this development deserve to be highlighted because they represent the epitome of the so-called Franco–German motor. Monetary union was something that Chancellor Kohl was willing to pursue with his friend President Mitterrand for the sake of the European project, even if it was against the interests of Germany, as perceived by almost every party, interest group and citizen.[3] Ultimately, France achieved a measure of influence over European monetary policy, but the institutions of EMU that were established in order to obtain the Bundesbank's approval sharply circumscribed France's ability to bring about a different monetary policy environment.

There can be no doubt that the creation of the single currency was a success: there were no technical glitches either with the introduction of the euro in 1999 or the massive exchange of national currencies for euro coins and bills in 2002. The euro has become a widely held staple of international portfolios, and although its value fluctuated 35 per cent in the first six years against the dollar, this is not outside the variations of individual national currencies before 1999. The ECB Governing Council has made complex policy decisions on such matters as whether to incorporate more inflation targeting or improve the management of monetary policy with up to twenty-seven member states. Perhaps most surprising of all, Europeans are now largely supportive of the venture, as reflected in opinion polls.

It is also clear that the introduction of the euro has coincided with a significant slowdown of the European economies. Apart from technical questions, the best (and ongoing) measure of the euro's success must be whether the economies of participating countries thrive. Although it is widely acknowledged that the single currency was entirely a political, not an economic, project, there were hopes that the euro would generate economies of scale, price transparency, lower prices, and other economic benefits for the eurozone. To date these benefits have not materialized, especially in Germany, the eurozone's largest economy.

The German economy had never been a high-growth economy, but in the first five years of EMU its output fell and hovered on the verge of recession. It is thus unsurprising that 52 per cent of Germans (the highest percentage in the eurozone) polled in November 2002 said that the adoption of the euro was disadvantageous overall and would weaken their country. Fully 68 per cent (again the highest percentage polled) said they were 'quite' or 'very' unhappy that the euro had become their currency (European Commission 2002). Here popular opinion mirrored what experts also observed. In 'A Half-Serious Proposition', *The Economist* newspaper applied the United Kingdom's five tests to Germany and found a better case for Germany quitting the euro than for Britain adopting it (*The Economist*, 12 June 2003).

If the first years in the euro were disproportionately bad for Germany, it begs the question whether German policy-makers were naïve about the effects of the single currency on their economy (relative to the *status quo*) or whether other considerations overrode their qualms. The history of the EMU negotiations suggests the latter explanation: Kohl, always more a politician than an economist, seized the opportunity to strengthen federalism at the European level and worked towards that goal despite opinion polls against monetary union and the warnings of economists and his own government ministers that EMU would be a great risk. For France, Italy, and the other member states, the single currency would be a risk, but as the EMS already obligated them to a monetary policy that did not necessarily suit their domestic economies, the upside risk of the euro outweighed the downside risk. France had to suffer the fact that the ECB was created in the image of the Bundesbank, but at least it was being run after November 2003 by a French official. Italy might have been marginalized in the negotiations on monetary union, but its citizens no longer paid enormous inflation premiums on their extensive government bond issues. Regardless of its economic impact, however, it remains to be seen if EMU will live up to Kohl's political vision of it as a stepping stone to a more federal Europe.

Notes

1 The Nice Treaty of February 2001 institutionalized this approach to integration as 'enhanced cooperation'.

2 Author's interview with a Bundesbank official, November 1993.

3 Moravcsik (1998) argues that EMU was in Germany's economic interest, but Heisenberg (1999) disagrees.

Further reading

A good reference book about the European Central Bank and the euro is Padoa-Schioppa (2004), which provides a short historical overview of monetary union, and discussions about problems of economic coordination and monetary policy strategy. De Haan et al. (2005) focus on the problems of monetary policy-making and institutional reform of the central bank. A highly detailed (859 pages!) historical account of the creation of monetary union is Dyson and Featherstone (1999). On the origins and emergence of the European Monetary System, see Ludlow (1982), and, going further back in time, on the first attempts at monetary union, see Tsoukalis (1977). For more information on the stability and growth pact and its implications, see Brunila et al. (2001).

Brunila, A., Buti, M., and Franco, D. (eds.) (2001), *The Stability and Growth Pact:* *The Architecture of Fiscal Policy in EMU* (Basingstoke: Palgrave Macmillan).

De Haan, J., Eijffinger, S., and Waller, S. (2005), *The European Central Bank: Credibility, Transparency, and Centralization* (Cambridge, MA: MIT Press).

Dyson, K., and Featherstone, K. (1999), *The Road to Maastricht: Negotiating Economic and Monetary Union*, (Oxford: Oxford University Press).

Ludlow, N. P. (1982), *The Making of the European Monetary System: A Case Study of the Politics of the European Community* (London: Butterworths).

Padoa-Schioppa, T. (2004), *The Euro and Its Central Bank: Getting United after the Union* (Cambridge, MA: MIT Press).

Tsoukalis, L. (1977), *The Politics and Economics of European Monetary Integration* (London: Allen and Unwin).

Websites

For more information on the ECB as well as working papers and statistical information, go to the ECB official website at www.ecb.int. A very comprehensive listing of other good websites about the euro is available at http://www.eurunion.org/infores/euroweb.htm. University of Rome economist Giancarlo Corsetti has set up a website with information about the Euro at http://www.iue.it/RSCAS/Research/Eurohomepage/.

Chapter 12

The European Union, the Soviet Union, and the End of the Cold War

Jeffrey J. Anderson

Contents

Summary

Just as the outbreak of the cold war in the late 1940s shaped the contours of (Western) European integration, the end of the cold war in the late 1980s had a profound impact on the European Union (EU), notably by triggering an avalanche of applications from the neutral states and from the newly-independent countries of Central and Eastern Europe. For much of its history the EU had little interaction with the Soviet bloc, although the acceleration of European integration as a result of the single market programme and the Single European Act may have hastened the reform movement in Central and Eastern Europe and ultimately the collapse of the Soviet Union itself. The relationship between Western European integration and Eastern bloc disintegration across political, economic and security dimensions may be tenuous but is nonetheless noteworthy.

Introduction

For all its economic justifications and ambitions, the European integration project emerged in response to two closely linked geopolitical challenges in the postwar period. The first was to ensure that Germany would be bound ineluctably to its Western European neighbours, and as such have little or no opportunity to plunge the continent into war as it had done repeatedly over the past 100 years. The second was to establish and maintain a zone of stable prosperity that could serve as a bulwark, both real and symbolic, against the advances and encroachments of the emerging Soviet threat. Openly encouraged by the United States, the founders of what became the European Community (EC) kept those twin objectives firmly in mind as they crafted their momentous undertaking in regional integration during the 1950s.

As such, it can be plausibly argued that the Soviet Union, by extending its sphere of influence into Central and Eastern Europe and into the heart of the vanquished Third Reich, contributed to the formation of a unique regional initiative that now bears the title European Union. The timing of the two developments—the formation first of the Eastern bloc and then of the West European bloc—as well as the openly expressed perceptions of key decision-makers, supports this proposition. A somewhat more rigorous test might involve the use of a counterfactual: had the Soviet-dominated Eastern bloc not emerged, would West European elites have moved with the same pace and direction towards a common market with supranational political aspirations? This avenue of enquiry is unlikely to yield much added value; imagining the post-1945 geopolitical landscape as unchanged with the sole exception of the expansion of the Soviet sphere of influence into Central and Eastern Europe strains the imagination.[1] Therefore, although we may not be in a position to assess the precise level of importance of this causal variable, we can say that it mattered a great deal to postwar European integration.

Flash forward four decades: the relaunch of the European project in the form of the Single European Act; reform communism emanating from Moscow and pulsing throughout the Eastern bloc; the collapse of the Berlin Wall; German unification; the end of the cold war; the demise of the Soviet Union. How (if at all) were these seismic events and processes connected? More precisely, did the acceleration of European economic and political integration in the 1980s play any part in the unravelling of the Soviet empire? Did postwar history come full circle—having been brought into being in part because of the Soviet threat, did ever-closer union precipitate the end of the threat itself? In turn, did the weakening and then abrupt disappearance of the Soviet Union shape the trajectory of the European project as it sought to intensify integration? If so, how, and with what consequences? This chapter addresses these questions.

First, it examines the development of relations between the EC and its member states, on the one hand, and the Eastern bloc countries centred on the Soviet Union, on the other, through the mid-1980s (the eve of the almost simultaneous emergence of systemic reform drives within both the Soviet Union and the EC). The next section explores the interactions between European integration and Eastern bloc disintegration across political, economic and security dimensions. The chapter concludes with an assessment of the overall relationship between process and outcomes across the Western and Eastern halves of Europe, and provides some reasoned speculation about the future trajectory of this increasingly integrated and unified continent.

East–West relations in Europe, 1945–85

As seen in Chapter 2, international relations in Europe after World War II quickly assumed the form of bloc rivalry. As the US commitment to Western Europe's future strengthened after 1947, reactions from the other side of the new continental divide were swift and decisive. In the military realm, the creation of the North Atlantic Treaty Organization (Nato) over the course of the 1950s was paralleled by the emergence of the Warsaw Pact alliance in the East. Economically, the Council for Mutual Economic Assistance (CMEA, also known as Comecon) was formed in 1949 at Moscow's initiative as a political response to the Marshall Plan, and its organization and activities were endowed with renewed emphasis yet again after the creation of the European Economic Community (EEC) in 1957.

The CMEA's main purpose was to coordinate central plans among the Soviet bloc states (including three non-European members: Cuba, Mongolia and Vietnam), particularly as regards trade, and to assist in the setting up of common economic projects and joint ventures. Unlike the EC, the CMEA did not rest on an explicit or even implicit principle of supranationality, entailing the pooling of sovereignty; CMEA members guarded their prerogatives in the negotiation and implementation of international economic agreements vigorously and jealously, in stark contrast to the security realm. Clearly, the active presence and leadership of the Soviet hegemon at the centre of the CMEA limited the extent to which other members could exercise true sovereign latitude on economic matters. Nonetheless, this was not a supranational integration project in the Western European sense.

The waxing and waning of military tensions between the United States and the Soviet Union is the subject of a deep and well-known literature. To the extent that Europe was a factor in the unfolding of superpower conflict and competition, the key role was played by the Federal Republic of Germany. A complex mixture of security interests and domestic politics drove West Germany's foreign policy towards the Soviet Union and its Eastern bloc satellites, and they took a major turn in 1970. *Ostpolitik*, launched by the Social Democrat–Free Democrat coalition government, sought to establish a sturdy regional *détente* capable of withstanding the vicissitudes of superpower relations and to promote the cause of unification by drawing East Germany into ever-deepening ties (*Wandel durch Annäherung*) (Garton Ash 1993; Hanrieder 1989). West Germany was often out front of its fellow EC partners on the question of relations with the Eastern bloc; lacking the capability to formulate common foreign economic objectives, the EC did not seek to stand in for its member states in their evolving economic relations with the Soviet Union and its satellites.

Owing to the greater latitude granted the European allies by the United States on economic matters, there was considerable movement in relations between Western and Eastern Europe. Given the nature of the twin events beginning in the mid-to-late 1980s—Western European integration and Eastern bloc disintegration—this is clearly worth a closer look.

View from the East

Up through the early 1970s, relations between the EC and the CMEA were distant, to say the least; from the vantage point of the CMEA, the view was openly hostile. This flowed from the internal assessment, derived from a relatively unvarnished reading of Marxist doctrine, that this economic union of capitalist states was a temporary phenomenon. Collapse, the product of internal contradictions, was inevitable. '[Far] from recognizing the [European] Community, the CMEA countries declared their non-recognition and attempted to block EC participation in international organizations and conventions' (Nello 1991: 18). The EC responded with inaction and perhaps even indifference, absorbed as it was with the implementation of the common market and, increasingly, the common agricultural policy (CAP). Moreover, the fact that none of the EC members, with the possible exception of Germany, held any great stakes in East–West trade, served to reinforce the tendency to look anywhere but eastward for trading partners and initiatives.

Beneath the CMEA's official stance of hostile non-recognition, however, a slow process of reappraisal was taking place within the Soviet Union and its Eastern satellites. This came about both in response to the successful consolidation of the Community, which undercut the confident predictions of Marxist doctrine, and as a result of domestic changes in Eastern Europe. In 1962, official reports and speeches issued at the highest levels in Moscow acknowledged the EC as 'an economic and political reality'. Scholars interpreted this policy change of heart as an attempt on the Soviet Union's part to use the example of the EC as a means of convincing recalcitrant allies in Central and Eastern Europe of the wisdom of deepening the CMEA's level of integration to embrace more muscular forms of supranational planning. As such, the Community's influence was indirect—a demonstration effect that dovetailed with the economic objectives of the Soviet hegemon (Marsh 1978: 25–70). Although these ambitions eventually came to naught, the reversal of perception and rhetoric endured.

A second and more consequential factor in bringing about a formal shift in the East's approach to Western European integration was the spread of economic and political reform initiatives within the Communist bloc countries. Confronted with irrefutable evidence of economic inefficiencies and a widening development gap with respect to the Western democracies, members of the Soviet bloc began to experiment with reform socialism, with a view to improving production efficiency via the introduction of new techniques and, where consistent with the basic modalities of the command economy, market mechanisms. These reform initiatives were widespread, reaching all the way to the centre of the Communist bloc in Moscow, but they differed in intensity and outcome. Countries such as the German Democratic Republic undertook only modest, even grudging, attempts at reform, whereas others, like Hungary, plunged in enthusiastically. Where economic reform efforts spilled over into calls for political liberalization, the outcome was often tragic, as in the case of Czechoslovakia in 1968.

Achieving economic reform depended on access to advanced technology as well as to information on new production and management techniques, all of which necessitated opening up to the EC—the most proximate source of these valuable and, from the standpoint of the CMEA members, scarce commodities. Foreign trade and economic cooperation with the capitalist enemy trumped doctrinal qualms. It is perhaps natural to assume that the orders came from the top; in other words, that this initiative was spearheaded by Soviet authorities. In fact, the most insistent demands for a reorientation on foreign trade and economic cooperation with the West, and principally the EC, came from the reforming Central and Eastern European countries. Marsh, for example, describes the Czech press, in the 1960s, expressing open criticism of trade relations with the country's CMEA partners and advocating a return to prewar trade relations with its Western European neighbours (Marsh 1978: 30–1).

Although the Soviet Union ultimately responded to the Czech challenge with tanks, this was not a feasible general solution to the larger issues of political cohesion and economic reform in the Communist bloc, including its home economy. In the end, Moscow offered its satellites a quid pro quo: in exchange for a major initiative intended to improve political and economic relations with the West, the Soviets asked for and received a strengthening of the ties between and among the CMEA members. Many Central and Eastern European countries saw this in positive terms. In order to extract the greatest possible level of benefits from any new economic relationship with the West, the CMEA had to improve its level of internal coordination so as to exercise maximum leverage at both the negotiation and implementation phases. The result was to solidify, at least for a time, the regional blocs in Europe.

Soviet-led efforts at greater economic integration led to the adoption of a formal plan of action in 1971. During these negotiations, the EC surfaced repeatedly as a template or model for emulation, particularly in discussions over the extent to which the revamped CMEA should rely more on market mechanisms of exchange. Internal CMEA discussions focused not so much on emulating specific policies or institutions of the EC as on adapting fundamental market-based principles and practices to the needs of advanced socialism (Marsh 1978; Nello 1991; Timmermann 1990: 103–29).

Growing interest among Eastern bloc countries in a new foundation for regional trade relations was mirrored in the West, albeit for different reasons. The volume of economic interactions between EC members on the one hand and CMEA countries on the other began to grow markedly towards the end of the 1960s as Western firms, aided by their governments, sought new markets in a context of increased international competition and economic instability (see Table 12.1). Some of this took the form of trade in goods and services and rested on a wide array of credit and subsidy programmes erected by EC members to support trade with Soviet bloc trading partners, who generally lacked the requisite levels of convertible currency. Moreover, the Soviet Union and its Central and Eastern European partners began to express a preference for modalities of economic cooperation that involved not simply traditional trade, but rather technology transfer, turn-key plants, and joint ventures. Western firms and their national governments began to compete fiercely for business in the East.

Table 12.1 Total EC trade with Central and Eastern Europe (million ecu)

	1958	1960	1965	1970	1975	1980	1985	1987	1989
USSR									
Exports	386	604	563	1,415	5,064	7,808	12,509	9,189	12,592
Imports	477	706	1,066	1,554	4,064	11,382	20,710	13,128	15,511
CMEA									
Exports	550	788	1,387	2,550	7,118	9,422	11,029	10,029	13,150
Imports	609	818	1,436	2,430	5,076	9,120	13,262	11,350	14,509

CMEA figures exclude trade between West and East Germany.
Source: Nello (1991: 78)

The EC's response

Both of these trends, the one in trade and the other in economic cooperation, drew the attention of the European Commission which, beginning in the late 1960s, sought to harmonize policy in this area. Given its responsibility for the development of a common commercial policy, the Commission could no longer afford to ignore growing Western European economic involvement in the Soviet bloc. Lacking the relative economic might, to say nothing of tanks, available to the Soviet Union, the Commission had to rely on its powers of persuasion, backed by the Rome Treaty, to convince the member states of the wisdom of greater coordination in this area of policy. By the early 1970s, in a context of economic crisis, mounting concerns about the EC's weak hand in negotiations with the United States and Japan, and bitter experience with the ability of CMEA members to play one Western investment suitor off against another, the member states consented to a greater degree of coordination on commercial policy, including that directed at the CMEA.

Two ultimately intersecting developments in the early 1970s strengthened the possibility of coordinated, collective action *vis-à-vis* the CMEA countries. First, EC member states put in place European Political Cooperation, a mechanism designed to improve foreign policy coordination. The linear ancestor of the Common Foreign and Security Policy of the 1990s, European Political Cooperation emerged out of internal tensions generated by Germany's *Ostpolitik* and gave EC member states a modest but nonetheless enhanced capacity to conduct something resembling a European foreign policy.

The second important development was the convening of the Conference on Security and Cooperation in Europe, in 1974. While preparing for the conference during the previous two years, member states made full use of the new political cooperation mechanism. The principal focus was on foreign policy and security, although the conference also dealt with economic issues within the framework of an *ad hoc* group. The final agreement, which came to be known as the Helsinki Accords, 'established the legitimacy of human and minority rights in Europe and provided indirect support and inspiration to the political dissident movements in Poland and Czechoslovakia, allowing them to move forward once [Soviet President Mikhail] Gorbachev opened the possibilities for reform [in the 1980s]' (Wallander 2003: 169). Preparations for the conference, along with the multiple stages of the negotiations, brought EC member states together on a regular basis with representatives from the Eastern bloc nations and served to reinforce consensus-building among the member states themselves about the advantages of a more structured economic relationship with the East. Not only were there material gains to be realized, which required coordination, but there was also the possibility of effecting incremental, desirable changes within the Eastern bloc. This position came to be known by the slogan 'Change through Trade', which was especially prominent in West Germany but attracted fervent adherents throughout the EC (Jacobsen 1990: 101).

In mid-1974, the EC Council of Ministers approved a plan to introduce a notification and consultation procedure covering economic cooperation and trading agreements with state-trading (i.e. CMEA) and oil-producing countries. The purpose of the initiative was to regulate uncontrolled, competitive bidding among EC members for contracts with partners in these regions, with the Commission having responsibility for implementation and oversight. By year's end, the Commission had put several procedures and guidelines in place, putting flesh on the skeletal set of responsibilities defined earlier in the year. Viewed in broader perspective, this initiative was part of a larger set of policy initiatives that endowed the EC, and specifically the Commission, with greater powers of coordination in the area of trade policy.

The EC's new approach to the Eastern bloc was predicated on relations between the EC and individual members of the CMEA, not the CMEA as a collectivity. This resulted from a combination of principle and practicality. In the first place, the EC was opposed to any approach that institutionalized 'bloc relations', and in the process strengthened the Soviet Union's control over its East European satellites, thereby frustrating the EC's attempts to exert economic and political leverage in the region. Second, the EC took note of the fact that the CMEA did not seek to manage the economic relations of its members with countries like the United States and Japan, and saw no reason to be treated differently. Finally, the CMEA, in spite of its attempts to deepen the level of integration among its members, did not possess the necessary legal authority and policy instruments to function as a capable negotiating partner on matters of trade and economic cooperation.

Needless to say, the EC's approach met with considerable mistrust and even outright opposition within the CMEA, especially from Moscow, which saw the initiative as a thinly disguised Western attempt to divide and conquer. In many respects this was already happening. According to Marsh, 'Hungary, Poland, and Bulgaria were reported to have made informal contacts [with Brussels] in order to raise problems concerning the CAP, whilst Romania had actually gone as far as joining the Community's Generalized Preferences scheme for developing countries' (Marsh 1978: 53).

The Soviet Union sought to parry the thrust of the EC's emerging common commercial policy by insisting that the development of East–West economic relations would have to be predicated on bloc-to-bloc negotiations and interactions, spearheaded by the EC and the CMEA acting on behalf of their respective memberships. The opposing positions represented by the CMEA and the EC led to several years of wrangling, marked by repeated and ultimately unsuccessful attempts to finalize a set of formal principles and policies governing the relationship between the two regions.

Working in the EC's favour was the actual development of the common commercial policy towards the Eastern bloc. It is no exaggeration to say that it became increasingly difficult and expensive (in terms of opportunity costs) for the individual CMEA members to shun the EC. This was by no means a linear process; the Commission was mired in difficult discussions with individual member states over the extent to which it could claim to regulate national policies in this area and its hand in negotiations with CMEA members was often undercut by centrifugal forces at home. Nevertheless, a breakthrough occurred in early 1976 when Romania bucked the official CMEA line and entered into formal negotiations with Brussels over textile import quotas. Poland followed suit less than a year later on the same issue. Later expanding to include detailed talks between individual CMEA members and the EC's Common Fisheries Policy in 1977, East–West economic relations continued to move in a direction favourable to the Commission's long-term goals, although no overarching formal agreement was forthcoming.

East and West, 1985–90

The 1980s, a decade of ferment and creative reform in both halves of Europe, actually witnessed a decline in trade and other forms of economic cooperation between EC and CMEA countries, despite a considerable warming of CMEA attitudes towards the EC (Nello 1991: 21–2). For the Western countries, trade with the East grew less significant as a percentage of total trade as compared to the pre-1972 period. For the Eastern bloc countries, the accumulation of external debt over the preceding decade—ironically, the by-product (and literally the price) of closer economic ties with the West—coupled with their inability to compete in global markets for manufactured goods, led to a steady fall in their share of Western imports. In response, these countries cut imports from the West (Hanson 1989: 58–9).

Western European integration took a major stride forward in the mid-1980s, with the ratification of the Single European Act (SEA) in 1987. The SEA established the now famous deadline of 31 December, 1992 for completion of the internal market and introduced procedural innovations—notably an extension of qualified-majority voting in the Council of Ministers, coupled with a 'cooperation procedure' for the European Parliament—that heralded a break with the principle of consensual decision-making set out in the Luxembourg Compromise of 1966. Despite the contentious tone of the scholarly debate over the origins and implications of the SEA, contributors agree that the initiative was driven by elites and that the impetus for the far-reaching internal reforms came largely from beyond the European continent. Specifically, Western Europe reacted to the competitive challenges posed by the changing relative power positions of Japan and the United States (Sandholtz and Zysman 1989: 95–128). The cold war logic, and embedded within it the issue of politico-economic relations with the Soviet Union and its Eastern bloc satellites, played no discernible part in the unfolding of single market programme.

Perestroika

The story line developing in the East during the same period reads very differently. Reform movements and initiatives in Poland, Hungary, and even the Soviet Union itself, unfolded in a larger context shaped by the undeniable achievements of Western capitalism. The stimulus for Gorbachev's programme of *perestroika*, or economic reform, came from abroad, in much the same fashion as did the stimulus for completing the single market. 'The rapid development of the third industrial revolution in the United States, Western Europe, and Asia have demonstrated that the USSR [Union of Soviet Socialist Republics] is increasingly falling behind in the economical [*sic*] and technological field. This dealt a psychological shock of immense intensity to the Soviet elite' (Timmermann 1990: 104).

Gorbachev and the Soviet leadership publicly acknowledged the economic and political power centre emerging in Western Europe and undertook a diplomatic campaign in the mid-to-late 1980s to forge closer ties with countries in the region, above all with West Germany. At a time when Europe's future seemed to be growing more open-ended, the Soviet-led initiative emanated from several overlapping and reinforcing concerns. Most prominent, the Soviets hoped to sway European public opinion on issues like conventional disarmament and the stationing of short-range nuclear missiles, issues that went to the heart of East–West relations and over which there were significant differences of opinion between the United States and its European partners. In reaction to the hardline stance adopted by the Reagan administration *vis-à-vis* the Soviet Union, the EC's nascent European Political Cooperation framework provided an internal forum for developing a distinctive foreign policy profile (Nuttall 1997: 22).

Gorbachev's repeated public references to a 'common European home' went hand-in-hand with more practical attempts on the part of Moscow to reorient perceptions on the continent. Indeed, the new thinking of the Soviet leadership sought to unleash a process of normalization in Europe and the eventual reunification of the continent on terms that transcended the cold war divide (Sobell 1990: 61). Gorbachev stressed the need for comprehensive domestic reforms in Central and Eastern Europe, suggesting that 'the Soviet Union was not eager to prop up regimes that could not survive on their own terms and that did not meet the needs of their countries' (Wallander 2003: 152). These overtures and pronouncements found a receptive audience in many parts of Western Europe.

A strong developmental rationale also permeated Soviet initiatives designed to strengthen ties with the EC and its member states. *Perestroika*, which aimed at nothing less than the complete modernization of the socialist economy, depended on improved access to and utilization of Western technology. Observing the ambitious single market initiative from the outside, Soviet leaders feared that 'in [the] future Europe's efforts may not be directed at constructing the "common house", but on the contrary, at the division of Europe into a prospering EC Western Europe and a crisis-prone and decaying CMEA Eastern Europe' (Timmermann 1990: 106).

Soviet overtures elicited a divided response in Western Europe. Germany reacted with the greatest enthusiasm, seeing in Gorbachev's reforms a clear path to a reduction in East–West tensions and new modalities in inter-German relations

(Mayer 1977: 721–37). The British government, led by Margaret Thatcher, reacted with acute mistrust and openly speculated that the Soviet Union was up to its old tricks of sewing divisions within the West. The French worried about the Germans and the possibility that they would forsake Western Europe for a chance at eventual reunification. In short, Western Europe exhibited anything but a unified response to the evolving situation in Moscow and the rest of the Eastern bloc, and so was hardly in a position to channel, shape and manage (Allen 1997: 219–35).

German unification

Events in the two Germanys best exemplified the tenuous connection between integration in the West and disintegration in the East, and as such are worthy of closer scrutiny. Over the course of 1989, West Germans observed the great drama unfolding across the Elbe with interest and hope, but little ability to influence events. The building confrontation between the East German regime and its domestic opponents took on added urgency in Bonn, the West German capital, as the number of East German refugees (not to mention ethnic Germans from Eastern Europe) entering West Germany swelled into the hundreds of thousands, each entitled by law to citizenship. In early November, Chancellor Helmut Kohl issued an extraordinary appeal to East Germans to remain in their country and work for change (Jarausch 1994: 23).

Domestic externalities were less significant in concentrating the minds of West German politicians than emerging ramifications at the international level. Bonn had to walk a fine line. On the one hand, the government could not remain silent as demonstrators, chanting 'We are the people!' and demanding basic human rights, were brutalized by East German security forces. On the other hand, Bonn could ill afford to do anything that might precipitate a lethal crackdown by the East German regime. Nor could it openly raise the prospect of unification, even indirectly, as this would threaten Gorbachev's already precarious political position in Moscow.

On 8 November, in a state-of-the-nation address to parliament, Kohl called for an all-German dialogue and pledged a comprehensive assistance package if the East German Communist Party relinquished its monopoly on power, allowed the formation of independent political parties and groups, and provided for free and fair elections. West German politicians on both the left and the right consistently framed any possible road to unification in terms of the self-determination of the East German people within a pan-European settlement of the cold war.

With the unexpected but definitive collapse of the Berlin Wall on 9 November 1989, the issue of German unification leapt to the top of the East–West agenda. For the West Germans, a gradualist approach to unification seemed especially wise in light of unease and uncertainty about Moscow's reaction. Yet by the end of November, developments in East Germany unexpectedly began to force an acceleration of Bonn's timetable, provoking disquiet and even outright opposition from within the Soviet leadership and even West Germany's EC partners.

The failure of gradualism lies ultimately in the virtually preordained failure of East Germany's reformers both inside and outside the official apparatus to develop a socialist alternative to the Federal Republic. The abortive search for a 'Third

Way'—alternately described as socialism with a bottom line or capitalism with a human face—was intended to stave off unification by salvaging unique and valued components of the East German economic model and, it is no exaggeration to say, of East German identity: solidarity, community, security, equality (Jarausch 1994: 99–112). In the end, the attempt to chart a path between Western capitalism and Eastern communism grossly misjudged the wishes of average citizens, who were interested not in abstract critiques of capitalism but in tangible, rapid improvements in their standard of living. East German reformers failed to win a West German commitment to underwrite what officials regarded as a play with no clear script, ending or purpose.

The Bonn government, confronting a relentless flow of East German refugees into the country and sensing that the international window of opportunity could come crashing down at any moment, was soon compelled to adopt a more direct approach to the reopened German question, an approach that gained in confidence and direction as the reform movement in East Germany faltered and the regime began to collapse. Kohl seized the political initiative on 28 November with his 'Ten Point Plan for German Unity'. The plan elicited worried statements from abroad, scepticism from important figures in the East German Communist Party, and outright opposition from the Greens, who seemed especially enamoured of socialist experimentation in East Germany (Markovits and Gorski 1993). Kohl's statement resonated with East German citizens, who stepped up their demands for rapid change.

In early February 1990, Bonn received firm indications that Moscow would not insist upon neutrality as the price for German unification. Kohl threw himself into the task of forging a political mandate for unification, with his eye on the first ever democratic national elections in East Germany, held on 18 March. The Chancellor and his ministers successfully transformed the March elections into a referendum on unification. East Germans voted unambiguously for markets, democracy and unification: 'a ringing endorsement for the social market economy' (Jarausch 1994: 127). No longer was it a question of whether unification would take place, but when and how. On 1 July 1990, German economic, social, and monetary union came into effect. Three months later East Germany dissolved and five new *Länder* (states)—Brandenburg, Mecklenburg–West Pomerania, Saxony, Saxony–Anhalt, and Thuringia—plus East Berlin acceded to the Federal Republic of Germany.

All along, Moscow held the key to unification.[2] The EC, however, was not an irrelevancy. The Bonn government confronted two challenges linked to its Community membership and associated obligations: first, to allay the concerns of its EC partners about unification and its implications for stability in Europe; and second, as rapid unification became a virtual certainty, to secure EC accession for the soon-to-be former East Germany in a timely and mutually acceptable way. In a manner that echoed its domestic agenda for unification, Bonn sought to signal and secure the maximum amount of continuity in its relationship to the EC.

West and East Germans alike could hardly be faulted for wondering why their Western European neighbours did not share their elation about the prospect of unification. British Prime Minister Thatcher cautioned against a 'rash' resolution of the German question, while French President François Mitterrand described German unification as 'a legal and political impossibility' (Görtemaker 1994: 155). European reactions were especially pointed after Kohl's surprise announcement of his Ten-Point Plan. Sceptical foreign actions and statements, which continued into 1990, were received with anger and consternation in Bonn. In response, political elites both in and outside the Federal Republic sought refuge in deeper European integration.

East and West since 1990

Bonn's emphasis on the European dimension of unification dovetailed with the designs of actors elsewhere on the continent: specifically, Jacques Delors, President of the European Commission, and key member states such as France, eager to secure from Germany an irreversible commitment to further integration. The communiqué issued at the conclusion of the Strasbourg summit in December 1989 expressly linked the further deepening of European integration and German unification, which appeared even at that early date all but certain (European Parliament 1989). In March 1990, Kohl announced his government's unwavering support for the goal of the economic and monetary union (EMU) which, as seen in Chapter 11, was already being pursued in the EC. One month later, he and Mitterrand called for the convening of an intergovernmental conference (IGC) on political union to run parallel to formal discussions over EMU, which would chart a course towards a stronger, more democratic Community, a common foreign and security policy, and intensified cooperation on justice and home affairs—all made more urgent by the unfolding transformation of East-West relations in Europe. The eventual outcome was the Treaty on European Union, signed at Maastricht in December 1991 (Baun 1996; Sandholtz 1993: 1–39). Thus, in the face of deep-seated domestic unease about the risks of EMU, the chancellor committed his country to the twin objectives of economic and political union.

Throughout, Germany played a central role—often constructive, on occasion disruptive—in debates and discussions over the development of a common European foreign and security policy that took account of developments in the East. The repercussions of the Gulf War in early 1990 gave a significant push to the German commitment to a common EC foreign policy. The failure to secure a coordinated response to the crisis, for which Germany certainly bore a good share of the responsibility, led to intensified efforts on the part of Germany, France, and the European Commission to move the Community beyond the tepid framework of European Political Cooperation. The results at Maastricht, which were accompanied by a slew of self-congratulatory statements issued by the national governments, fell well short of expectations in the press, academe, and even among the member states themselves, who saw the need to include a provision in the treaty calling for a follow-up IGC in 1996 to revise and reform what had been accomplished at Maastricht (De Schoutheete de Tervarent 1997: 41–66).

The Yugoslav débâcle

In the midst of these halting deliberations, the Yugoslavian crisis erupted. Casting a nervous eye on the Soviet Union and the Baltic republics, EC member states stressed the desirability of a peaceful resolution to the conflict and the preservation of national unity. The Community offered to serve as a broker between the central government in Belgrade and breakaway republics, sending a delegation of three foreign ministers repeatedly to mediate the conflict. With the cooperation of the United States, the EC's then twelve member states also activated the Conference on Security and Cooperation in Europe (CSCE) crisis consultation mechanism established earlier in 1991.

A crack appeared in the EC's common front during the first week of July 1991, when the German government signalled that the Community would have to consider accepting the independence of Slovenia and Croatia if the strife continued to worsen and mediation efforts proved ineffectual. Sensitive to the potential repercussions, German officials were quick to stress that acceptance did not equate with full diplomatic recognition of independence, and justified their position as consistent with the principle of self-determination for national and ethnic groups. Although this represented a clear break with the EC's declared position, the Germans reiterated their pledge to work with other member states to effect what they saw as potentially necessary adjustments. The French foreign minister warned that any softening of the EC's position could exacerbate the volatile situation among Eastern Europe's ethnic minorities. EC member states with separatist problems of their own, like Britain, Spain, and France, were adamant about maintaining the territorial integrity of Yugoslavia. Nevertheless, the majority of member states signalled their intention to reconsider their support for Yugoslav unity if fresh violence occurred. On 8 July, an accord was struck between the Yugoslav central government and the Yugoslav republics, with the EC assisting in the process. Slovenia and Croatia agreed to suspend the implementation of their declarations of independence for three months, during which time the Yugoslav federation would be reorganized in negotiations mediated by the EC. The pledge to maintain a cease-fire was to be overseen by a contingent of 150 unarmed civilians acting under EC auspices.

While the agreement held in Slovenia, the situation in Croatia quickly degenerated into a vicious cycle of violence and exposed along the way the limits of effective EC intervention. European efforts to mediate the conflict failed in early August and Brussels turned to the CSCE for support. The French raised the idea of sending in an armed buffer force organized by the Western European Union (WEU) to separate the insurgents in Croatia, which drew a discouraging response from the Soviets, who warned that any foreign intervention in Yugoslavia could lead to full-scale European conflict. Germany, ever sensitive to Soviet objections, pushed for a solution involving peacekeeping forces under CSCE auspices. Bonn also threatened Serbia with economic sanctions if it continued to block progress on a settlement. On 8 August, Yugoslavia agreed to accept additional international observers from both the EC and other CSCE member countries, who were to monitor any accord reached between Croatia and Serbia. These arrangements were quickly swept aside by fresh rounds of violence.

Within a few short days of the Maastricht summit, Bonn announced that it would formally recognize Slovenia and Croatia by year's end, even if this meant breaking ranks with the majority of its EC partners, the United Nations (UN), and the United States. Ultimately, this display of foreign policy muscle pulled the EC in its wake. However, the appearance of unity in Brussels was purchased at a high price, as Bonn's unilateralism embittered many other member states. While Germany's decision did not violate the letter of the Maastricht Treaty, it was interpreted by many in and outside Germany as violating the spirit of the agreement. German politicians were motivated largely by domestic political factors—they believed that the diplomatic isolation of Serbia would stem the flood of Yugoslavian refugees into Germany, which had tripled in 1991 over the previous year. German policy-makers also believed that the string of diplomatic failures by the EC, the UN, and the CSCE was undermining domestic support for these international institutions and for Germany's pledge to work within them to achieve a solution to the crisis.

Post-cold war enlargement

Events in the aftermath of the failed August 1991 coup in the Soviet Union also spurred developments in EC foreign policy-making circles. Up until the break-up of the Soviet Union in December 1991, EC member states officially pursued a policy of maintaining the *status quo*—placing all their eggs in Gorbachev's basket. Once the break-up became inevitable, they quickly changed tack. German concerns centred on the security of the former Soviet nuclear deterrent, the observance of existing treaties such as the Helsinki Accords and arms control agreements, the servicing of the Soviet foreign debt, and measures to ease the process of economic and political liberalization. While Bonn was quick to establish bilateral contacts with the increasingly assertive and independent republics, above all Russia, it relied heavily on international institutions to manage what it interpreted as positive though not entirely risk-free developments.

Germany reaffirmed the indispensability of the 'political parallelogram' consisting of Nato, the CSCE, the EC, and the WEU. It even proposed the creation of joint embassies for EC member states in each country of the Commonwealth of Independent States (CIS), a loose association of former Soviet republics. Important figures within the foreign policy establishment also called upon international institutions to adapt to the rapidly changing circumstances on the continent. Foreign Minister Hans-Dietrich Genscher pushed successfully for the inclusion of all CIS states, including those in Asia, into Nato's North Atlantic Cooperation Council and the CSCE. He also called upon the EC to negotiate a treaty with the CIS as well as separate treaties with each of the CIS members, again including those lying wholly in Asia. These proposals, however, touched off a heated debate in the German foreign policy establishment and met with a chilly reception in Brussels and from particular member states, above all Britain and France.

Already by 1990–1, the gravitational pull exerted by the EC's single market initiative, combined with the dissolution of cold war, prompted clear signals from Central and Eastern Europe that Brussels could expect a lengthy queue of applicants for membership (Baun 2000; Michalski and Wallace 1992; Nugent 1992: 311–328). Germany, the most consistent advocate of enlargement in the 1970s and 1980s, gave enthusiastic support to the applications from members of the European Free Trade Association, three of whom (Sweden, Finland, and Austria) eventually joined in January 1995. Germany also backed the accession of the newly-independent Central and Eastern European states. Extrapolating from their own experiences with national democratic consolidation and supranational integration in the 1950s, German political elites believed that the prospect of membership would facilitate the path of the Central and Eastern European countries to democracy and capitalism, thereby contributing to political stability and economic prosperity in the region. The German government spearheaded the creation of EC assistance programmes such as PHARE (Pologne-Hongrie Actions pour la Reconversion Économique) and TACIS (Technical Assistance for the CIS). It also provided much of the impetus for the string of 'Europe Agreements' negotiated with Poland, Hungary, the Czech and Slovak Republics, Bulgaria, Romania, the Baltic republics, and Slovenia, which were viewed as precursors to formal membership (Kramer 1993: 213–44).

Although conceived as a formal prelude to enlargement, these various agreements and treaties with the emerging democracies in Central and Eastern Europe filled out the skeletal framework of the common foreign and security policy agreed at Maastricht. The EU's approach projected a set of values that 'underpinned the whole EC project—namely, democracy, soft-edge capitalism, a zone of peace between the member states, and diplomatic mediation between third parties designed to undercut the causes of major conflicts [in Europe]' (Hill 1997: 87). The framework of agreements, which towards the latter half of the 1990s led to formalized negotiations over the terms of accession, also served to structure and channel relations with the countries of the region as Western governments grew more wary of a fast track to enlargement (see Chapter 13).

As the anticipated costs of Eastern enlargement began to weigh more heavily on member states like France, Germany helped to sustain political momentum behind the initiative, most notably at the Essen summit of EU leaders in December 1994. However, the Kohl government's ostensibly unbounded enthusiasm for Eastern enlargement began to ebb, albeit subtly and gradually, as the debate about the level of German contributions to the EU budget sharpened during the latter half of the decade.

In July 1997, the Commission published *Agenda 2000*, which set out its vision of the Union's enlargement process. The report recommended that accession negotiations commence immediately with six countries deemed best qualified to join: the Czech Republic, Estonia, Hungary, Poland, Slovenia, and Cyprus. The Commission identified a second group of applicants—Bulgaria, Latvia, Lithuania, Romania, Slovakia, and Malta—that would have to demonstrate further progress on economic and political liberalization before negotiations with the EU could commence. Acknowledging the budgetary concerns of many current members, principally Germany, the Commission maintained that enlargement could be financed without increasing the overall budget ceiling of 1.27 per cent of EU gross domestic product. *Agenda 2000* proposed an extension of the current financing arrangements up to 2006, with reform of the CAP and the structural funds—specifically, tighter eligibility requirements for aid recipients—generating the necessary savings.

The poorer members of the EU, led by Spain, greeted the Commission's budgetary proposals with open scepticism. Their reactions turned angry when, in September, the Germans and the Dutch stepped up demands for a new financing formula that would reduce their countries' net contributions to the EU. In March 1998, German officials openly threatened to derail the package of policy reforms contained in *Agenda 2000* if a commitment to 'substantial and permanent' cuts in Germany's net contributions to the EU was not forthcoming. Soon thereafter, the German government expressed reservations about reform of the CAP and structural funds, as this could end up increasing Germany's net contributions to the EU and would almost certainly harm east German interests in the process. The Spanish government stated categorically that the accession of poor, farm-intensive members from Central and Eastern Europe could not be financed on the backs of those in the EU most vulnerable to enlargement and least able to afford it. Amid the growing dispute over the costs of enlargement, France, Belgium, and Italy demanded that unresolved questions pertaining to institutional reform of the EU be settled before commencing accession talks with the first wave of applicants. Thus, in an ironic twist, Germany's budget goals increasingly conflicted with the country's wider objectives.

Generally speaking, the approach adopted by the EU revealed that the prospects for eventual membership drove the common foreign and security policy *vis-à-vis* the East. This 'membership driven' *Ostpolitik* gelled in 1997, when the EU and Nato, in separate decisions, undertook formal steps to open negotiations for eventual enlargement with a certain number of Central and Eastern European countries. This brought tangible consequences for the continent:

> A process began of separating Europe into 'insiders' and 'outsiders'. For no matter how frequently NATO and EU officials say that they do not intend to redivide Europe, and no matter how many 'partnership' agreements they offer to non-members, it is inevitable that admitting some countries to full membership of the two organizations and excluding others will produce 'insiders' and 'outsiders'. . . . Being 'outside' affects the way people perceive themselves and their environment. It also affects their relationships with both 'insiders' and fellow 'outsiders'. . . . The perception of exclusion, therefore, has important consequences for the domestic and foreign policies of outsider states. (Light et al. 2000:)

Chief among the outsiders was Russia, especially after the EU finally enlarged in May 2004 to include ten Central and Eastern European countries, with Bulgaria and Romania due to follow within three years.

Conclusion

The end of the cold war brought about a major transformation of Europe. Viewed from the perspective of 'bloc mentality' and the deep-rooted antagonisms that permeated continental relations after 1945, integration and ascendance in the West coincided with disintegration and decline in the East. The preceding analysis has shown the tenuous yet mostly indirect causal links between these two complex phenomena. Early on in the post-World War II period, Western Europe's approach to the Eastern bloc became predicated on the dual principles of containment and co-existence, but within that, a unified, coherent common foreign policy was never really in evidence.

To point out the shortcomings and gaps in the EU's foreign policy *vis-à-vis* the East over the years is not to suggest that European integration had no effect on the transformation of the region: '. . . [F]ar more important than what the West did was what it was: free and prosperous' (Gati 1990: 188). Writing about the demise of the Soviet Union, Wallander concludes that 'the West played a role through the growth of its own economic and technological strength—the standard against which Soviet performance was measured. But this was not in itself a matter of Western policy; the mere existence of the West was what mattered' (Wallander 2003: 150). These 'milieu' effects, however indirect, were critical in shaping the choices made and foregone in Moscow and elsewhere in the Soviet bloc.

For its part, the break-up of the Eastern bloc forever altered the course of European integration. Here, the effects were even less intentional than those flowing in the West to East direction, as outlined above. Breaking free of Soviet domination, Central and Eastern European countries immediately looked to the EU for orientation and anchoring. Their overwhelming desire to rejoin if not Europe, which they had never left, but the community of European democracies could not be blunted, given the way in which the ideology and rhetoric of European integration had developed over the four decades since the EC's inception. Thus, indirectly but no less tangibly, the disintegration of the Soviet sphere of influence placed an indelible imprint on the trajectory of the European project. As a result, the continent is much closer to being 'a common European home' than Gorbachev could possibly have envisioned in the mid-1980s, but it is a home built on very different foundations and one whose reach ends more or less where Russia begins.

Notes

1 The counterfactual fails the 'co-tenability' requirement. See Fearon (1991).

2 There are several comprehensive accounts of the '2 + 4' negotiations that resulted in German unification, including Pond (1993) and Zelikow and Rice (1995).

Further reading

This chapter focuses on the intersection of three voluminous literatures: European integration, the rise and fall of the Soviet Union, and the cold war. As such, a good understanding of each of these three areas would be a valuable starting point. Readers can now choose from a number of excellent historical overviews of European integration: see Milward (2000), Gillingham (2003) and Dinan (2004). For a thorough overview and analysis of the inner workings of the European Union, see Wallace, Wallace and Pollack (2005). Suny (1998) offers a concise and informative history of the Soviet Union; the Gorbachev era is ably discussed in Brown (1996). On the subject of the cold war, three works in particular offer excellent overviews: Gaddis (1997), Painter (1999) and McMahon (2003).

Brown, A. (1996), *The Gorbachev Factor* (Oxford: Oxford University Press).

Dinan, D. (2004), *Europe Recast: A History of European Union* (London: Palgrave).

Gaddis, J. L. (1997), *We Now Know: Rethinking the Cold War* (Oxford: Oxford University Press).

Gillingham, J. (2003), *European Integration 1950–2003: Superstate or New Market Economy?* (Cambridge: Cambridge University Press).

McMahon, R. (2003), *The Cold War: A Very Short Introduction* (Oxford: Oxford University Press).

Milward, A. S. (2000), *The European Rescue of the Nation State*, 2nd edn. (London: Routledge).

Painter, D. (1999), *The Cold War: An International History* (London: Routledge).

Suny, R. (1998), *The Soviet Experiment: Russia, the USSR, and the Successor States* (Oxford: Oxford University Press).

Wallace, H., Wallace, W., and Pollack, M. (eds.) (2005), *Policy-Making in the European Union*, 5th edn. (Oxford: Oxford University Press).

Websites

Readers interested in learning more about European integration can browse the EU's official website at http://www.europa.eu.int/. Links to scholarly analysis and discussion of integration are available at the European Union Studies Association (EUSA) website at http://www.eustudies.org/. Contemporary cold war studies, which have benefited from the release of official documents on both sides of the former Iron Curtain, can be surveyed at the following sites: Cold War International History Project (http://wwics.si.edu/index.cfm?topic_id=1409&fuseaction=topics.home); The Harvard Project on Cold War Studies (http://www.fas.harvard.edu/~hpcws/index2.htm); and The Parallel History Project on Nato and the Warsaw Pact (http://www.isn.ethz.ch/php/).

Chapter 13
The Enlarging European Union

Anna Michalski

Contents

Summary

Enlargement has had a profound impact on the process of European integration. Having enlarged almost constantly since the early 1970s, the European Union (EU) has extensive experience of conducting accession negotiations and integrating new member states. Yet each round of enlargement is unique and has its own political dynamic, based in part on the special characteristics of the applicant states. The EU and its member states have established over the years an enlargement doctrine based on a number of principles, such as accepting the Union's *acquis communautaire* (body of rules and regulations), refusing to grant derogations or permanent opt-outs, and allowing transitional periods of only a limited scope and time. In the most recent enlargement, which brought in the countries of Central and Eastern Europe, plus Cyprus and Malta, the EU added the so-called 'Copenhagen criteria' to the requirements for accession, thereby extending the process to cover the candidates' democratic credentials and economic competitiveness. In an effort to cope with the challenge of diversity posed by enlargement, the EU has developed a panoply of strategies to deal with growing differences among the member states' levels of socio-economic development as well as their policy needs and aspirations without (as yet) formally resorting to a division of its membership in concentric circles, core and peripheral groups, or alternative frameworks.

Introduction

From its inception in the early 1950s, the European Union has been tightly linked to the question of enlargement. Seen in historical perspective, the successive enlargement of the EU to include the vast majority of European countries is a natural solution to the unnatural division of Europe caused by the cold war. But the unification of Europe was not always perceived as an obvious end-goal, nor was the choice of the form of integration that came to characterize the EU clear from the outset.

Despite the existence of very different visions of the nature and objective of European integration, the EU has over the years exerted considerable pull on neighbouring countries. Even before its main policies had been properly put in place, the United Kingdom, Ireland, Norway, and Denmark applied for membership in 1961 with the hope of participating in and possibly shaping the development of key policy areas, such as external trade and agriculture. Why the EU has attracted (and still attracts) all European countries, some of them very hesitant about membership in a supranational entity, holds the key to understanding the dynamics of European integration.

Whereas the pull of integration has profoundly affected neighbouring countries, pressure from them to find a suitable relationship with the EU has had a direct impact on the course of European integration. The dynamic released by the debate on the widening and deepening of the EU has pushed integration forward, sometimes with unexpected outcomes. It is probably true to say that more than any other factor, enlargement has had a major impact on the political dynamics, institutional structure, and policy mix of the Union. Every round of enlargement has brought into the EU the special characteristics of the acceding countries, resulting in a readjustment of the existing pattern of cooperation and integration. Officially, however, the EU's doctrine on enlargement is clear: membership entails a total acceptance of the Union's *acquis communautaire*, composed of the treaties, secondary legislation, political commitments, and policy doctrine (such as in the area of external relations). The discrepancy between the official, technical aspect of enlargement and the non-official, political dimension has complicated every round of accession, tossing up problems and ruffling political sensitivities, but also producing quick solutions once the political 'settlement' of enlargement, among new and old members, has been struck.

It is equally true to say that every acceding country has experienced a drastic transformation to its political system as well as to its economy and socio-economic regime. Some countries have deliberately sought to anchor their political, economic and societal development within the Union and have therefore accepted the impact of integration; others have experienced a more difficult adaptation process with important (and not always welcome) changes to their socio-political structures.[1]

Principles, conditions, and instruments of enlargement

The treaties

'Any European state may apply to become a member of the Community.' With such concise wording in the Treaty of Rome (1957), the founding fathers imagined the enlargement of the European Economic Community (EEC), leaving it up to European and national officials in the early 1960s to organize the legal basis, content, and conduct of the accession negotiation when the United Kingdom, Ireland, Denmark, and Norway first applied to join. Later, the Single European Act of 1986 added to the original requirement of consensus among the member states in the Council the assent of the European Parliament to the enlargement of the European Community (EC). At the time, no further consideration of potential new members' democratic credentials or socio-economic model was thought necessary, given that the prevailing geopolitical situation (the continuing cold war) precluded large-scale enlargement. The existing member states shared the same democratic values and norms and their economic and social systems were built on similar models; differences between them were of degree rather than of principle.

In view of possible enlargement following the end of the cold war, however, the member states agreed to specify the conditions of accession in the Maastricht Treaty of 1992. The new provision clarified the fundamental principles of the Union, namely those of 'liberty, democracy, respect for human rights and fundamental freedoms and the rule of law', which any new entrant would first have to fulfil. Other new measures to ensure the application of these principles were added in the Amsterdam Treaty (1997), such as the possibility to suspend the rights of a member state found to be in serious and persistent breach of these principles. The unratified Constitutional Treaty (2004) elaborated even further the fundamental values of the Union by adding human dignity and equality and by specifying that these values are common to member states 'in a society of pluralism, tolerance, justice, solidarity and non-discrimination'. It also made the application of the provision of suspension more workable by adding a preliminary stage in which the risk of a serious breach is established and hearings with the member state in question are undertaken before the European Council proceeds to suspend the rights of that state. Finally, the Constitutional Treaty introduced another novelty by providing for the possibility of a member state withdrawing from the EU.

The *acquis communautaire*

As the treaties gave only general indications of the criteria that countries aspiring to membership should fulfil, the EC institutions and member states developed a more detailed enlargement doctrine that did not change much during the first four rounds of accession (see Table 13.1). The principal condition of membership was the candidates' total acceptance of the *acquis*, often in the form of a pledge given in the formal application for membership. The *acquis* is normally defined as the treaties and the subsequent legislation enacted in the framework of the Union—amounting to some

Table 13.1 Rounds of enlargements		
Number	**Year**	**Acceding countries**
First	1973	Britain, Denmark, Ireland
Second	1981	Greece
Third	1986	Portugal, Spain
Fourth	1995	Austria, Finland, Sweden
Fifth	2004	Cyprus, Czech Republic, Estonia, Hungary, Latvia, Lithuania, Malta, Poland, Slovakia, Slovenia

80,000 pages of legislative text at the time of the fourth enlargement (1995). The *acquis* also includes the political obligations of membership. As French President George Pompidou announced in 1969 when he lifted the French reservation on UK entry into the EC, these include subscribing to the founding fathers' vision of an ever closer union among the peoples of Europe.

Besides sharing the objectives of integration, the *acquis*'s political dimension also includes commitments taken in the framework of intergovernmental cooperation among the member states. In the early days of the EC, political cooperation amounted to only a few concrete obligations. Later, various 'unofficial' criteria were added, such as Nato membership in the case of Spain, and with respect to all candidates: no border disputes with neighbours; membership in organizations such as the Council of Europe and the Organization for Economic Cooperation and Development (OECD); and being a signatory to certain international treaties such as the European Convention on Human Rights (ECHR). With the launch of the common foreign and security policy (CFSP), the European Security and Defence Policy, cooperation on Justice and Home Affairs and, in a different manner, the Lisbon process for economic modernization and reform, intergovernmental treaty obligations, political commitments and other undertakings have become an important part of the political *acquis*. Thus, in order to show their good will, the Central and Eastern European countries associated themselves with the EU in diplomatic *démarches* and political statements even before they were accepted as official candidates for membership.

The principle of the total acceptance of the *acquis* implied that accession negotiations were really about the length of transition periods, not permanent opt-outs or derogations to established rules. Transition periods were applied also in reverse, prompted by the demands of existing member states that provisions of a certain policy not be applied to the new entrants before domestic stakeholders had time to adjust to the new competitive situation (restrictions on the applicability of the common agricultural policy in Spain and on the free movement of workers from the new Central and Eastern European member states come to mind). In the first four rounds of enlargement the principle of sticking to the *acquis* was followed almost without exception (although the EU was sometimes tolerant of certain national sensitivities with a limited overall impact). Where it was necessary to accommodate potential new member states, rather than reforming existing policies, the EU adapted those policies (for instance, by adding a new 'objective' to the structural funds when Finland and Sweden joined) or invented measures to help entrants cope with the economic and political pressures of integration (such as launching regional policy to accommodate the United Kingdom in 1974 and, almost twenty years later, launching the cohesion fund to help Spain and other poorer countries). Only with the fifth accession did the question of policy reform surface. Instead of far-reaching reform, however, based on a discussion of the kind of policies that would be appropriate in the EU of twenty-five countries, the existing member states once again adapted those policy regimes likely to be put under stain (chiefly financial) as a result of enlargement. Partial and piecemeal reforms have meant that the *acquis* has remained fairly constant throughout successive enlargements.

The Copenhagen criteria

For a long time, therefore, the only criterion for membership beyond the treaty's 'European' requirement was the total acceptance of the *acquis* with its official, largely economic, content and its more obscure political content. With the prospect of an unprecedented enlargement to include the countries of Central and Eastern Europe, which were pursuing a gradual transformation from totalitarian regimes with centrally-planned economies to democratic regimes with free-market economies, the EU member states decided to spell out the conditions for membership more explicitly in order to protect the Union framework from a dilution of objectives, a fragmentation of policies, and a breakdown of institutional structures. To that end, the European Council agreed in Copenhagen in June 1993 to accept the Central and Eastern European countries' membership aspirations provided that the future applicants fulfilled certain requirements:

> [the] stability of institutions guaranteeing democracy, the rule of law, human rights and respect for and protection of minorities, the existence of a functioning market economy as well as the capacity to cope with the competitive pressure and market forces within the Union. Membership presupposes the candidate's ability to take on the obligations of membership including adherence to the aims of political, economic and monetary union. (European Council 1993)

These conditions—to which the European Council later added good neighbourly relations among the candidates as well as between candidate and non-candidate countries, the adjustment of administrative structures, and a stable economic and monetary environment—became the new basis for accession on which the candidate countries' readiness would be evaluated. Not surprisingly, the Union was criticized for raising the bar to membership and demanding the fulfilment of criteria that had not been asked of any other candidate before, even where it might have been justified. Moreover, the political criteria posed a dilemma for the Union, whose own democratic credentials were far from satisfactory, and posed a conundrum for the Commission services which were to carry out the evaluation of the candidates. The economic criteria also posed some difficulties as they referred to a qualitative condition that necessitated continuous economic analysis rather than a comparison of rules and regulations in force. The same was true of the criteria concerning the candidates' institutional capacity. Overall, the Copenhagen criteria required continuous monitoring and regular assessment to a degree that had not been practised in the previous rounds of enlargement.

Instruments of enlargement

There are no treaty-based provisions regarding the instruments at the disposal of the EU institutions for either the conduct of negotiations or the integration of new member states. In fact, most of the legal and procedural instruments that are used have grown out of practice and have become increasingly sophisticated over time. The formal status of the accession negotiation is a bilateral intergovernmental conference with the member states of the EU on one side and the candidate country on the other. Legally binding instruments are therefore based on international law; other instruments are either procedural or financial.

Of the few instruments of a legal nature, the accession treaty and the national ratification instruments are the most significant. Each country (member state or candidate) needs to decide which type of ratification is the most appropriate according to its traditions and constitutional requirements. In many cases a parliamentary endorsement suffices, but given the importance of the decision and the intense public interest that EU membership arouses, ratification by referendum has become increasingly common (in the fifth enlargement eight out of ten countries held referenda). An existing member state may also hold a referendum on whether to enlarge the EU, the precedent being set by France in 1972 (France has promised to hold a referendum as well on Turkish accession). Such referendums are often more the result of a political strategy or tactics to deal with domestic concerns than a genuine intention to let the citizens pronounce themselves on the question itself.

The accession treaty is based on international law and can therefore in theory be the subject of revision if the two parties want that. However, because very little of the real content of membership (the *acquis*) is negotiable, the accession treaty is a brief document with little in terms of substantive (policy) provisions. Moreover, experience shows that the EU is extremely reluctant to renegotiate the conditions of membership, regardless of the strength of the new member state's complaints (a point borne out by the United Kingdom's 're-negotiation' of its terms of accession in 1974–5). In any case, countries that enter the EU resentful of their terms of membership are more likely to play it tough once inside, in an effort to readjust the existing policy regimes to suit their interests.

In terms of procedural and financial instruments, the EU institutions, in particular the Commission, have developed a panoply of reporting instruments to accompany the process of integration into the EU. The Commission's opinion on a candidate's readiness to join remains the foremost of these reports. It is directed to the Council and forms the basis for the decision to open negotiations. The Commission has issued opinions on all candidates since the first applications for membership were presented in the early 1960s. Not until the fifth enlargement, however, did the Commission opinion form the basis for a programme (the so-called 'pre-accession strategy') to assist the candidate countries to adjust to membership before the formal date of entry and in no previous accession round did the Commission issue regular reports on the candidates' progress towards membership. Indeed, the fifth enlargement was accompanied by a full range of monitoring and reporting requirements that was unheard of in previous rounds. It distinguished itself by the comprehensive system of regular up-dating and reporting on the candidates' progress and by the sophistication of the instruments that were put in place to help the candidates to adopt the *acquis*. These instruments range from the regular reports, composite papers (of which the most important was *Agenda 2000* (European Commission 1997)), the pre-accession strategy with its dedicated financial instruments such as Phare, SAPARD (agricultural instrument), ISPA (instrument for structural policies), the twinning programme with existing member states to strengthen the candidates' administrative capacity, TAIEX (Technical Assistance Information Exchange Office), and on the side of the candidates, the National Programmes for the Adoption of the *Acquis*.

Conduct of accession negotiations

The process of accession starts with the potential candidate state handing in a formal application for membership to the EU, most often to the foreign minister of the country holding the Council presidency. Once this application has been formally acknowledged by the EU, the Commission evaluates the candidate country's readiness to assume the obligations of membership and identifies areas and issues that might pose problems during the negotiations.[2] This is an important phase for the candidate countries, as the assessment of the Commission of the state of affairs in different sectors of the national economy and the over-all ability of the country to assume and correctly apply the *acquis* sets the tone not only for the ensuing negotiations but also for any agreement of pre-accession assistance from the EU. In the first enlargements, the Commission concerned itself mainly with the socio-economic situation in the candidate countries, but with the widening of the EU's own policy scope and the formulation of the Copenhagen criteria, the Commission has also analyzed the political situation, the state of democracy, the robustness of the institutional infrastructure, the state of the economy, the candidate's position on the world stage, and relations with neighbouring countries.

Throughout the years, the Commission has only twice recommended that the Council reject an application for membership. First, in 1976 the Commission recommended that the Greek application be put on hold in order to let the Greek economy be brought into line with the EC. The Council, which primarily for political reasons wanted Greece to join quickly, rejected the Commission's opinion and decided to open accession negotiations. The Commission issued a favourable opinion in 1979. Second, in 1997 the Commission recommended that accession negotiations not be opened with Slovakia, which did not fulfil the political conditions because of the instability of its institutional structures and shortcomings in the functioning of its democracy. The Commission had this time coordinated its position with the member states, who endorsed it with the understanding that as soon as the political situation changed for the better the EU would reconsider its decision. The Commission can also chose to recommend membership in principle but at the same time argue that the opening of the actual negotiations be deferred to a later stage when the candidate has completed economic and/or democratic reforms (this was the case with five of the Central and Eastern European countries and with Turkey).

Once the Commission has presented its opinion, the European Council may decide when to start the accession negotiations. As mentioned above, the formal status of the negotiations is an intergovernmental conference between the member states and the candidate state. In the early 1960s, the Commission's involvement was not a foregone conclusion as some member states preferred to exclude it altogether (Kitzinger 1973). However, the growing complexity of the *acquis* along with the necessity for the member states to reach a common position among themselves has made the Commission's good offices essential. The Commission has ever since played an important role in bringing the negotiations to a successful conclusion. From an organizational point of view, during the first four rounds of enlargement the accession negotiations were quite straightforward, involving the following steps:

(1) The *acquis* was first divided into chapters.

(2) The candidate country presented a position paper on its political and economic situation, including the status of the transposition of the *acquis* (were applicable) and requests for transitional periods, and an explanation of how and when they would be faded out.

(3) With the assistance of the Commission, the member states agree on a Common Position for each of the chapters.

(4) The Council presents the Common Position to the candidate state. The ensuing negotiations essentially deal with the length and terms of the transition periods.

(5) As the negotiators reach agreement on a chapter, it is provisionally closed, and the attention focuses on the following one.

(6) The accession negotiations conclude when all chapters have been successfully agreed to.

All accession negotiations follow in large part this somewhat simplified structure even though political considerations and outside events inevitably have an impact on the conduct of negotiations. The fifth enlargement, however, witnessed the introduction of a number of new procedures and reporting and monitoring instruments which changed the character of negotiations quite substantially.

(1) This enlargement was seen more in terms of a process than solely hard negotiations on the terms of entry. Integration of the candidate states into the EU was a concern from the beginning of the process and a number of instruments were conceived to steer their economic and political transition in the right direction. Foremost among them was the pre-accession strategy based on bilateral accession partnerships and the National Programmes for the Adoption of the *Acquis*, which directed EU assistance to the candidates in the form of financial, technical, and institutional-building support. The candidates also participated in Community agencies and in important EU developments such as the Lisbon strategy, the Broad Economic Policy Guidelines, the Convention on the Future of Europe, and the intergovernmental conference that led to the Constitutional Treaty.

(2) The candidates' progress in socio-economic transition and democratization, along with their adaptation to the criteria for membership, was subject to continuous monitoring and reporting. The Commission issued yearly country reports and a composite paper (later a strategy paper) to give the over-all progress of negotiations and highlight particular issues or problems to which the EU should pay attention.

(3) Fearful of unravelling its policy regimes and rules and regulations, the EU put particular onus on the candidates to prove not only that they had transposed the *acquis* but also that they were capable of applying it. In previous accessions, the EU had left the actual implementation of the *acquis* to the applicant country itself. Nor had the EU judged if a candidate's institutional structure was capable of meeting the obligations of membership. This time, such evaluations were ongoing and seen as a common concern of the EU.

Roles and responsibilities

The member states are represented in the *Council of Ministers*. The foreign ministers, meeting in the General Affairs and External Relations Council, have over-all responsibility for enlargement. They meet regularly (typically once a month) to negotiate enlargement-related issues both among themselves and with the candidates. Much of the negotiations, however, take place among their senior officials: the permanent representatives in the case of the existing member states and the ambassadors to the EU in the case of the candidates. Council working groups discuss technical issues within their respective areas of responsibility. The country holding the presidency plays an important role in setting the agenda, pushing for the conclusion of various chapters or reaching agreement on particularly difficult problems that stretch over several policy areas. The presidency chairs the meetings and, with the assistance of the Commission, tries to reach compromise solutions or package deals. Although member states defend their national interests, they do not want to bring a new member state into the EU on terms so disadvantageous that it will doggedly try to regain what it lost in a 'bad' accession deal.

Since the early 1990s, enlargement has been a recurring point of the agenda of the *European Council*, which retains the ultimate responsibility for directing the process and, when necessary, finding solutions to difficult problems that more often than not involve disputes among existing member states over the terms to offer the candidates in a specific policy or over the impact of enlargement on the Community budget. Assisted by the Secretary-General of the Council, the European Council (which includes the Commission president) sets the political framework in which enlargement takes place, smoothes any concerns that are raised by neighbouring countries, and acts as the Union's public face, in particular *vis-à-vis* the EU's citizens.

The *Commission* is at the centre of the negotiations. In previous enlargements it set up a dedicated taskforce that dealt exclusively with the preparation, conduct, and follow-up of the negotiations. In the fifth enlargement, the Commission established a directorate-general to steer the process. The Commission does not negotiate with the candidates in formal terms but, because it engages in early dialogue with the applicant country, acquires extensive expertise and knowledge about the situation in various sectors. Throughout the process, the Commission conducts technical discussions with the candidates' administrations and various stakeholders in society. Through its delegations in the candidate countries, the Commission collects information, distributes Community aid and keeps up a continuous dialogue. Due to its privileged position the Commission has come to play an essential role in the negotiations by proposing the draft common positions as well as possible compromise solutions. The paramount aim of the Commission is to protect the integrity of the *acquis*, including ensuring a workable application of the *acquis* after accession. The Commission's nightmare is an accession on terms that make the new member states unwilling or unable to implement the *acquis* or contribute to the functioning of the Union's various policies.

The *European Parliament* has no role in the negotiations *per se* but, through its formal right of assent, has a veto power over the whole undertaking. It therefore closely monitors the enlargement process and is quick to pronounce when it thinks that the negotiations are not proceeding in the right direction. The Parliament sets up committees to debate progress on enlargement and passes resolutions on the various documents released by the Commission and on the situation in the candidate countries. It also sets up joint parliamentary committees with parliamentarians from the candidate states to discuss matters of common concern. The aim of the Parliament is to defend the objectives of integration and the values of the Union, but Parliament is extremely reluctant to deny entry into the Union for a country struggling hard to fulfil the conditions for membership if the alternative would be a backlash on the road towards modernization and democratization.

The *candidate country* applies to join an existing club whose rules make up a carefully balanced contract among existing members. It therefore has little choice but to accept the *acquis* and procedures of the Union. Because the *acquis* stretches over a great number of sectors the candidate has to carry out an analysis of the necessary changes to existing policies and structures. The amount of technical detail involved in the process requires a great deal of interdepartmental coordination in the candidate country and the setting up of numerous fact-finding working groups with representatives from the Commission. Once the negotiations get under way the candidate is represented by a chief negotiator and a negotiation team often with a truly interdepartmental composition, sometimes dominated by officials from the foreign office with technical expertise provided by other ministries.

The experience of enlargement

The EU has thus far experienced five rounds of enlargement, all carried out on the basis of the principles and procedures analyzed above, but each with its distinctive nature and dynamic, depending on the special characteristics of the candidate country.

The first enlargement: Britain, Denmark, and Ireland

The first enlargement of the then EEC started as early as 1961 when the British government of Prime Minister Harold Macmillan applied to join. Britain's application raised three sensitive areas: the Commonwealth, the common agricultural policy (CAP) and the European Free Trade Association (EFTA). Britain's application spurred applications from three other countries: Ireland (July 1961), Denmark (August 1961) and Norway (April 1962).

At the time, the EEC and Euratom had been in existence for only three years and the Community was in the middle of difficult internal discussions on the development of the CAP, Community financing, and the conduct of the Common Commercial Policy, especially in view of the Dillon Round of the General Agreement on Tariffs and Trade (GATT). The United Kingdom, which had chosen not to join the three communities in the 1950s and had been a driving force behind EFTA, revaluated its situation in the early 1960s for both political and economic reasons (Audland 1993).

Five of the existing member states strongly supported Britain's application but, as seen in Chapter 7, France had strong reservations, based largely on President Charles de Gaulle's fear that Britain might push the Community in an Atlanticist direction and therefore undermine its independence *vis-à-vis* the United States. De Gaulle also suspected that British economic interests, in particularly in agriculture and towards the Commonwealth, would change fundamentally the nature of the Community's nascent policy regimes, to the detriment of French interests (Moravcsik 1998). Finally, there was a feeling that the carefully crafted political balance among the existing member states would be upset, again to the detriment of French claims for leadership.

Accordingly, de Gaulle broke off the negotiations in January 1963 during a press conference in which he declared that Britain's very different production, consumption and trading patterns were not compatible with those of the Six and that Britain's foreign policy preferences would risk turning the EEC into a large Atlantic Community (De Gaulle 1963). This *de facto* veto also put a halt to the negotiations with Denmark, Norway and Ireland, which were not then in a position to join the EEC without Britain. The negotiations had been organized in such a way that the Six always met first with the United Kingdom and only then with the other candidate countries so that if the British negotiations ended in failure, the other candidates would be able to withdraw from the conference table as well. In May 1967, British Prime Minister Harold Wilson lodged a second application for membership of the EEC, this time without any conditions attached. Once again, Denmark, Ireland, and Norway followed suit, and once again, de Gaulle vetoed British entry, questioning Britain's motives and possible impact on the Community (De Gaulle 1967).

Not until The Hague summit of December 1969, shortly after de Gaulle's departure, did the Six reach agreement among themselves to resume the accession negotiations with the four candidate countries, thanks to an announcement by the new French President, George Pompidou, that Britain's entry into the EEC was acceptable in principle to France. At the decisive summit, Pompidou spelt out the famous triptych of completion, deepening and enlargement. Completion referred primarily to the adoption of a new financial regulation, on which the CAP depended. Deepening referred to further economic integration, including close coordination of national economic and monetary policies. Once these provisions were in place, the EEC would be ready to include new members (Pompidou 1969).

The negotiation process started in the first half of 1970 with preparatory talks between the Commission and the candidate states, during which time the member states established among themselves the Community's common position on the various negotiating chapters. The formal negotiations began in June 1970 and were conducted on a different basis from the negotiations some eight years earlier. Those negotiations had been based on a conference between the member states (collectively) and the candidate states (one at a time), which had led to criticism that Britain had been able to divide the member states. This time the Community was represented by the country holding the presidency (the other member states acting as silent observers), which, with the help of the Commission, negotiated with the candidate states one at a time. Although the negotiations were supposed to advance in parallel, Britain tried to reach an agreement first with the Community, which was then presented to the other candidates. If one of the other applicants raised a major reservation and the Community concurred, the negotiations had to start again with Britain (as with the other candidates), resulting in long marathon sessions of up to 48 hours at a time (Kitzinger 1973).

The negotiations lasted roughly one year with agreement being reached between Britain and the Community by the summer of 1971. The issues that had posed the greatest difficulties were the transition period for the CAP; the transition period for the common commercial policy (including the common external tariff), in particular regarding sugar imports (Britain sought to protect the interests of the developing Commonwealth countries); Britain's budget contribution; and the transitional period for phasing out unrestricted New Zealand diary exports to the United Kingdom. Because of Britain's small agricultural sector and external trade pattern (Britain imported large quantities of food from around the world), the agreed-upon budget contribution was higher than Britain's per capita gross domestic product (GDP) warranted. This came to haunt Britain's relations with the other member states for a long time. As seen in Chapter 8, some of those concerns were met soon after accession by the creation of the European Regional Development Fund and, later, the negotiation of a British budget rebate. However, the issue recurs every time the member states discuss the financial framework for the EU budget.

The other candidate countries generally followed the United Kingdom's lead. Both Denmark and Ireland depended heavily on access to the British market (roughly 50 per cent of Danish agricultural exports went to the United Kingdom and Ireland had a free trade agreement with Britain). All three of the other candidates had one thing in common: accession to the EEC without the United Kingdom was unacceptable both for internal and external reasons. Although, in comparison to the United Kingdom, their entry into the EEC was a fairly easy affair (apart from the issue of Norwegian fisheries), they approached the EEC very cautiously. As members of EFTA, Norway and Denmark had already reaped many of the benefits of free trade in industrial goods, but the prospect of having their most important single export market united with continental markets was a very attractive proposition. In the case of Denmark, the negotiations did not throw up any unexpected difficulties (Danish farmers were eager to benefit from the CAP and Danish industry had undergone the necessary transformation during the long waiting period in the 1960s). As a result, Denmark did not ask for any transitional provisions. Nato membership placed Denmark and Norway in a favourable foreign policy position, having given both countries long-standing contacts with other Western European countries. In the case of Norway, concern about the Community's fishing regime resulted in tough negotiations with the Six, the outcome of which eventually played an important role in the domestic debate before the referendum in 1972, no doubt contributing to the narrow rejection of the accession treaty.

Ireland saw the EEC membership as essential for the economic expansion it needed so badly and as a way to assert itself politically *vis-à-vis* the United Kingdom (Hillary

1993). Ireland's main concerns were in the area of agriculture, where it wanted to be covered by the CAP as quickly as possible; in fisheries, where both sides reached an acceptable agreement after protracted negotiations; trade links with Britain, which were allowed to develop as foreseen by the Anglo-Irish free trade agreement; and the country's relatively poor level of economic and social development, for which special funds were established (EC Bulletin 1972). The issue of Irish neutrality, one of the central themes in the subsequent referendum debate, was not raised in the negotiations as the *acquis* contained no references to foreign and security policy and as Ireland's narrow understanding of neutrality was not considered in any way problematical for the other member states.

The referendum in Ireland in May 1972 resulted in a resounding 'yes' to membership (83 per cent in favour). In Denmark, in October 1972, 63 per cent voted in favour. But in Norway, in September 1972, 53.3 per cent rejected EC membership. After a difficult debate in the House of Commons, the British government won a vote in favour of accepting the treaty of accession. Accordingly, Britain, Denmark, and Ireland joined the Community in January 1973.

Southern enlargement: Greece, Spain, and Portugal

The Greek and Iberian enlargements are normally considered separately, even though they share some important characteristics. First, all three countries had only just emerged from right-wing dictatorships when they applied for membership. Despite their differences, the authoritarian regimes in these countries had frozen economic, social and democratic development. The EEC presented a much needed anchor for the young and fragile democracies. Second, decades of economic difficulties and backwardness posed a dilemma for the new political regimes which knew that democracy depended on social and economic modernization in order to achieve the full support of the population and the national elite. The EEC offered open markets for industrial products and much needed dynamism for a corporatist business sector and state-owned companies. Membership also opened possibilities for migrating workers to find jobs in Western Europe as well as a generous agricultural regime that could support the modernization of the domestic farming sector while simultaneously protecting farmers from international market forces. For the existing member states, the southern enlargement was primarily a political step. The democratization and economic modernization of these countries was of outmost importance not only in terms of the ongoing cold-war conflict but also for regional security.

Greece signed an association agreement with the EEC in 1962 that anticipated a Greek membership application by 1984 at the latest, upon completion of a customs union. That was too long for Greece to wait. Accordingly, in 1975, a year after the restoration of democracy, Greece applied for membership. As mentioned earlier, the Council disregarded the Commission's negative opinion and decided that accession negotiations should begin as soon as possible with Greece. The negotiations lasted until April 1979 and the treaty of accession was signed in Athens the following month (Greece became the tenth member of the EEC in January 1981). During the negotiations, the issue of transition periods, in particular for the agricultural sector, posed the greatest problem. These were finally fixed at five years for most sectors while in a few areas, notably the free circulation of workers, a seven-year period was applied.

The strain of economic adaptation to the EEC was alleviated by transfers from the regional and agricultural funds. From the first year of membership, Greece was to become a net recipient of Community funds (which later stabilized at about 5 per cent of the country's GDP). The most significant impasse in the negotiations occurred when certain groups within the Community pushed for the simultaneous accession of Greece, Spain, and Portugal, which would have delayed Greek entry. Subsequently, the Greek government did everything possible to convince the member states to keep the negotiations separate, which the Nine agreed to do (Contogeorgis 1978).

The larger political framework did not affect the negotiations directly, but it was clear that Greece saw Community membership as a means of strengthening its position *vis-à-vis* neighbouring countries, in particular Turkey, which was not a member. Turkey felt side-stepped by the Community as it also had an association agreement with the EEC dating from 1963, which included a pledge of eventual membership. With Greece already in the EEC, it would be much more difficult for Turkey to join. Greece also hoped, through its membership of the Community, to be able to distance itself from the influence of the United States, whose support for the military regime had made it very unpopular among the population (Ioakiminidis 1993).

After accession, which coincided with an economic recession, the Greek Socialist Party (PASOK) came to power, with Andreas Papandreou as prime minister. PASOK had long opposed Greek membership of the EEC. Once in government, it set out to obtain better terms, just as the British had done. To placate the Greek government, the EEC established the Integrated Mediterranean Programmes. In operation between 1985 and 1992, these sought to alleviate the effects of Spanish and Portuguese accession on Mediterranean regions in existing member states by helping them to diversify their economies from a heavy dependence on agriculture.

In 1977, Portugal and Spain applied for membership. The following year the Commission delivered favourable opinions on both countries, despite pointing to serious difficulties that would arise in relation to agriculture, fisheries, the industrial sector and the free movement of workers. By refraining from recommending a pre-accession period as it had done two years earlier in the case of Greece, only to be turned down by the Council, the Commission took the view that appropriate solutions to these problems could be found in the framework of the negotiations and that lengthy transition periods should be fixed accordingly.

Predictably, this round of negotiations, in particular those between the EEC and Spain, were protracted, with stalemates, public demonstrations, and diplomatic wrangles spread over a six-year period. The main difficulties emerged between Spain and France on the question of the integration of Spanish fruit and vegetables into the CAP and over Spain's access to fishing waters off the French coast. There were also concerns among existing member states about an influx of migrant workers from Spain and Portugal, and the likely strain on Community funds caused by two new member states whose needs were great, thanks to their high levels of unemployment and low productivity in the agricultural and industrial sectors. The period of economic slow-down throughout Europe caused by the effects of the second oil shock in 1979 further aggravated the internal bickering over the Community budget and institutional reform and compounded the substantive problems posed by the Iberian accession.

A final political settlement between the Ten and Spain (the Portuguese negotiations had in effect been concluded over a year earlier) was not reached until March 1985, when the Spanish negotiators accepted the transitional periods offered by the Community (EC Bulletin 1985). The assessment at the time was that Spain had reached reasonably favourable terms for its industrial sector (to dismantle quotas and other barriers to trade) and for migrant workers (a seven-year transition period was imposed on the right to work in other member states). In the fisheries sector, Spain won the right to double the national catch of hake in French fishing waters. However, in the agricultural sector, where the Community bowed to demands from French interest groups, the outcome was less favourable for Spain, with a ten-year transition period for fruit, vegetable, oil, and wine. During the first four years of the transition period, Spain would be on a par with non-member states that did not have preferential trade agreements with the EEC. Moreover, Spain and Portugal were not included in the Integrated Mediterranean Programmes, despite the obvious need for modernization of the Iberian economies.

On the political level, the member states' reticence in practice, if not in principle, to Iberian enlargement led to acrimonious relations in particular between Spain and France, where, in addition to clashes between farmers and fishermen on both sides of the border, the presence of Basque separatists on French territory led to heated diplomatic exchanges between the two countries. Moreover, successive Spanish governments were uneasy about the link made by EEC member states between EEC and Nato membership. Spain's accession to Nato in 1982 reverberated in the domestic political debate about Community membership.

After their accession to the Community in 1986, Portugal and Spain set out to offset the unfavourable terms of accession by demanding that the Community bear some of the burden of adjusting to the single market and to economic and monetary union. The Iberian countries were able to negotiate compensatory mechanisms in the financial frameworks known as the Delors I (1988–92) and Delors II (1993–9) budget packages through the introduction of the cohesion fund and other additions to the structural funds in exchange for agreeing to the Single European Act, the Maastricht Treaty, and the accession of Austria, Finland, and Sweden. Since becoming Community members, the Spanish and Portuguese economies have undergone a profound transformation in which the *acquis* and the financial transfers from the Community have played an important part. For instance, the divergence of Spain's per capita GDP relative to the EU average was 74.2 per cent in 1980 and 81 per cent in 2000, while for Portugal it was 55 per cent in 1980 and 74 per cent in 2000. The structural funds have contributed to this convergence by making up a substantial part of public investment, rising to 42 per cent in 1996 in Portugal and 15 per cent in Spain (Royo 2004).

The EFTA enlargement

In the second half of the 1980s, the prospect of being excluded from the economic dynamics of the single market programme led the EFTA countries (Austria, Norway, Finland, Iceland, Switzerland, Sweden, and Lichtenstein) to seek a preferential agreement with the EC. With membership in the Community still considered improbable for geopolitical or domestic reasons (although Austria applied to join in 1989), the EFTA countries sought to establish a structured relationship with the EC that would give them access to the European market without having to accept all the obligations of membership. Commission President Jacques Delors responded by proposing the European Economic Area (EEA), a unified European market covering the whole of Western Europe. The EFTA countries readily agreed and negotiations soon began to adapt the *acquis* of the four freedoms (goods, capital, services and people) and certain flanking policies (such as research, environment, and social policy) to the needs of the EEA.

The ensuing agreement, however, turned out to be less favourable than the EFTA countries had initially thought, mainly due to institutional challenges which proved impossible to overcome.[3] At the same time, profound geopolitical changes were taking place in Europe following the end of the cold war and Soviet dominance over Eastern Europe. The end of the East–West conflict in Europe radically changed the strategic position of a number of neutral or non-aligned EFTA countries, notably Austria, Finland and Sweden. Together with a feeling that the EEA would not give them satisfactory long-term access to the emerging European market, this put the question of EC membership in a new light. Accordingly, Finland, Norway, and Sweden followed Austria in applying for EC membership. Switzerland applied in May 1992, but put its application on hold after the negative outcome of a referendum on EEA membership in December 1992. Given its dependence on fishing, Iceland decided that EC membership, which stipulated the sharing of resources, was not in its interest.

Following positive opinions from the Commission on the applications of Austria, Finland, Norway and Sweden, the accession negotiations began in early 1993 and lasted for a little more than twelve months (European Commission 1994). Difficult issues included fisheries for Norway, road transit through the Alps for Austria, Artic farming for Finland and Sweden and mountain farming for Austria, the right to uphold more stringent rules in the area of environmental protection for all candidates, and financial contributions to the Community budget. Despite that, the negotiations preceded rapidly, for a number of reasons:

1. All candidates were modern market economies, with good track records (often better than in the existing EC member states) in areas such as social cohesion and consumer and environmental protection. Their long-standing democratic traditions and well-functioning institutions, together with their reputations for being model countries in terms of socio-economic cohesion, made their integration into the EC attractive.

2. The candidates were to become net contributors to the EC budget which offset the concerns of the Mediterranean countries about increased competition in the internal market.

3. The fact that these countries had already adopted about two-thirds of the *acquis* as a result of their membership in the EEA speeded up the accession negotiations considerably.

Initially, the member states had not wanted the accession negotiations to begin before ratification of the Maastricht Treaty, but after the negative outcome of the referendum in Denmark in May 1992 it was important for the EC to be able to claim a success in the accession process with the EFTA candidates. The European Council therefore decided in December 1992 to open the accession talks and aim for a speedy conclusion. The question of institutional reform lingered on, however. First, the Maastricht Treaty called for an intergovernmental conference in 1996 to discuss the functioning of the new intergovernmental pillars, a date that the candidate countries did not want to miss. Second, some member states, in particular the United Kingdom and Spain, worried about the consequences of integrating the new member states into the existing institutional architecture as their inclusion would make it harder for the existing member states to form a qualified majority in the system of weighted voting used in the Council of Ministers. Faced with the threat of an institutional stalemate, member states adopted the so-called Ioannina Compromise—a convoluted political agreement on the calculation on blocking minorities devoid of any legal value (EC Bulletin 1994).

Another reason why the member states had wanted the Maastricht Treaty to be ratified before starting the accession negotiations was the possible negative impact on the nascent common foreign and security policy of the entry into the EU of neutral member states. In the event, the EU did not force the candidates publicly to renounce their stance on neutrality and the candidates had no particular problems accepting the terms of the Maastricht Treaty, especially as the *acquis* at the time was not fully elaborated and alluded only to the possible extension of cooperation to the defence area. Moreover, the formulation in the treaty was sufficiently flexible for the candidates to argue that they would not be forced to accept provisions in the field of security and defence against their will.

The candidate countries had to conduct difficult domestic campaigns before their respective referenda on enlargement. In Austria, EU membership was accepted in June 1994 with 66.4 per cent in favour; the vote in Finland in October was also positive (56.9 per cent in favour); in November, Swedes voted in favour of EU membership by a small majority (52.2 per cent); while in Norway, accession to the EU was rejected (52.2 per cent against membership).

The Central and Eastern European countries, Cyprus, and Malta

In May 2004, eight Central and Eastern European countries (the Czech Republic, Hungary, Estonia, Latvia, Lithuania, Poland, Slovakia and Slovenia), plus Cyprus and Malta, joined the EU, thus increasing the number of member states to twenty-five. That left only Romania and Bulgaria still negotiating membership. Ever since the fall of the Berlin Wall, the EU had been fretting about an enlargement to the East, which it knew it was morally and politically obliged to undertake. However, the prospect of letting into the club so many countries still in the process of transforming into fully-fledged democracies was daunting.

The EU's first step was to negotiate Europe Agreements with the potential applicants. These agreements were meant to give the newly independent countries a framework for their relationship with the EU that would assist them in their economic, social, and political transformation. However, those agreements did not correspond to the needs of the countries concerned because important sectors, such as agriculture, steel, iron, coal, and textiles, in which these countries would have been able to compete with producers in the West, were excluded (Michalski and Wallace 1992: 136–40).

Moreover, informal soundings-out in the early 1990s about the acceptability of a 'political' membership in order to let the Eastern economies transform before integrating into the internal market were turned down for the reason that the discipline of the Community regimes was exactly what these countries needed to keep their transformation processes on track.

Meeting in Copenhagen in June 1993, the European Council decided that the Central and Eastern European countries would in principle be allowed to become members provided that they fulfilled a number of criteria (see above) and that the EU itself was ready to include new members in terms of its policies, institutional structures, and financing. A string of membership applications followed between 1994 and 1996, adding to those of Malta and Cyprus in 1990.

Because of the complexity of this enlargement (the number of countries and their status as transition economies, the nature of the conditions, the capacity of the candidates to adopt the *acquis* and the readiness of the Union itself), the Commission undertook to produce a document that would present a vision of an enlarged EU. Thus *Agenda 2000* proposed a framework for the Central and Eastern European countries' progressive integration into the EU based on a series of in-depth evaluations of the candidates' readiness, a reinforced pre-accession strategy that would address some of their main weaknesses, an evaluation of the development of the Union's policies in view of enlargement, and a new financial framework for the period 2000–6 (European Commission 1997). Despite declaring that none of the candidates was fully ready for membership, the Commission recommended the opening of accession negotiations with Hungary, Poland, the Czech Republic, Slovenia, Estonia and Cyprus in 1998 while the others would be included in a broader enlargement process before their accession negotiations could begin. Besides dividing the candidates into two groups, *Agenda 2000* made other controversial assumptions about the integration of new member states which later formed the basis of the EU negotiation positions:

1. The EU's overall budget in the coming financial framework would not exceed the 1.4 per cent of the EU's GDP ceiling set by the Delors II package, thus effectively stating that enlargement would not cost member states extra as the necessary financial means would have to be found within the current framework, at least until 2006.

2. The new member states would not be covered by the direct payments to farmers that had been agreed to as part of the 1992 reform of the CAP.

3. The structural funds would be progressively applicable to the new member states but a total redirection of the funds to the East was not recommended.

4. A ceiling of 4 per cent of GDP should be put on the amount of transfers that a candidate country would be allowed to receive from the EU.

Based on *Agenda 2000*, in December 1997 the European Council decided to open negotiations with six countries. Soon thereafter the screening of the *acquis* began with all candidate countries and in November 1998 negotiations were officially opened with countries in the first group. Two years later, in December 1999, the Union abandoned the strategy of enlargement in successive waves. Instead, each candidate would progress towards accession on the basis of concrete achievements.

Subsequently, accession negotiations were opened with the remaining five Central and Eastern European countries and Malta. Meeting in Copenhagen in December 2002, the European Council reached agreement on the financial arrangements for enlargement which paved the way for settlement of the outstanding chapters, notably agriculture, regional policy (including the structural funds), and the financial contribution of the new member states. Earlier, the EU and the candidate states had reached agreement on the free movement of workers, which involved a seven-year transition period. Other difficult chapters included nuclear safety (existing member states had demanded the closure of unsafe nuclear plants in Lithuania, Slovakia, and the Czech Republic) and competition policy (the candidate states had given tax breaks to companies investing in their countries that were in breach of EU law). Issues not directly related to the negotiations, such as Russian concerns about Kaliningrad, its enclave wedged between Poland and Lithuania, were also settled in time for the formal accession of the ten candidate countries in May 2004.

The negotiations followed in broad terms the well-known principles of accession, with some important new instruments and procedures (discussed above). The sheer complexity of the process, stemming not only from the number and diversity of the candidates but also from the uncertainty caused by their simultaneous social, economic, and political transformation, triggered fears that the candidates' institutional infrastructure would not cope with implementing the *acquis* correctly. There were also concerns that the EU's policy regimes would prove unsuitable for countries in desperate need of economic growth after having been excluded for years from the process of gradual socio-economic modernization that characterized the development of the modern welfare society in Western Europe. In technical terms these fears proved unsubstantiated and the framework put in place to sustain negotiations over a number of years delivered a reasonable degree of fairness and efficiency.

Apart from the negotiations, the broader political context played a fundamental role in setting the terms of the candidates' EU membership. This enlargement, more than ever before, pushed the Union to adapt its own structures, policy regimes, and political dynamics to allow for the integration of the new member states. These reforms covered the funding arrangements for the Union after enlargement and therefore the shape of the most costly policy regimes: the CAP and the structural funds. They also covered the EU's institutional structure and capacity to manage common policies and other programmes. Clearly, there was a need to maintain some of the privileges of the existing member states while offering an acceptable minimum compromise to the candidates. The results were not always satisfactory. Hence the inadequate agreement on institutional arrangements and decision-making mechanisms in the Nice Treaty; the half-hearted reform of the CAP and the structural funds and the discriminatory provisions for the candidates' gradual inclusion into these policy areas; the half-hearted reform of the Commission and the Council of Ministers; and the conduct of the intergovernmental conference in 2003–4 that resulted in the Constitutional Treaty. Only time will tell if these measures are sufficient to keep the Union functioning efficiently and equitably with a much larger membership or if the current situation is an unstable equilibrium in which new and old member states will struggle to shape and reshape the Union according to their interests and needs.

The challenge of diversity

Throughout the history of European integration, enlargement has fuelled a debate about diversity or, to be more exact, about how great a difference among the member states is sustainable before the Union framework cracks or breaks up. There are two types of diversity: one that concerns the fundamental values of Europe, whereby diversity is seen as something natural and positive, a characteristic inherent to European culture as it has evolved throughout the centuries and that makes it distinct from other societies where the melting-pot principle or cultural dominance have prevailed. Diversity in this sense is enshrined in the Charter of Fundamental Rights (2000) and the Constitutional Treaty (2004). The other type of diversity arises from concerns about preserving the institutional structures, policies, and political dynamic of the Union given the inevitable impact of new members on established European regimes. These concerns, which often arise from existing members' vested interests, have been voiced before each enlargement and are often unduly alarmist.

Nevertheless, it is undeniable that the diversity arising from accession has changed the Union, adjusting or adding new dimensions to the integration process. Before and during accession, and despite the doctrine of the total acceptance of the *acquis*, the Union has reformed its institutions and/or the way in which they operate, extending rather than reforming existing policy regimes and accommodating the existing financial framework to make enlargement possible. After accession, new member states have almost invariably sought further changes in the policy regimes in order to make the terms of their membership better suited to their needs and interests. They have also introduced their own ideas about efficiency and justness to the activities of the Union and tried to influence policy-making and governance accordingly. The process of adjustment, despite being piecemeal and incremental (and never following any agreed upon master plan) has changed the Union profoundly.

In institutional terms, the inclusion of new member states and the perceived negative impact on the Union's decision-making efficiency prompted calls to extend the policy areas governed by majority voting and transfer new competences to the Union level. The reforms undertaken in the Single European Act, the Maastricht Treaty, the Amsterdam Treaty, and the Nice Treaty included provisions to that effect. In view of Central and Eastern European enlargement, concerns were raised about the composition and functioning of the institutions—the previous approach of incremental adjustment being deemed untenable. Member states responded with the Nice Treaty and later the Constitutional Treaty. Enlargement has also triggered reforms to improve the functioning of the institutions outside the framework of the treaties, in particular through internal reform of the Council and the conclusion of inter-institutional agreements, such as the one in 2003 on better law-making. Governance reform and improved cooperation between European institutions could be seen as an attempt to prevent Union decision-making from becoming bogged down in the face of reluctant member states and a means of managing policy regimes efficiently in spite of increased diversity on the ground.

Flexibility as a treaty-based provision was formally introduced in the Amsterdam Treaty and further elaborated upon in the Nice Treaty. It broke with one of the main principles of integration, namely that all members should apply the totality of the *acquis* of the Union. Instead, it became possible for a number of member states (the triggering majority has decreased with successive treaty reforms) to create among themselves new areas of cooperation making use of the framework and institutions of the Union. There are certain conditions which these countries need to fulfil, for instance that the cooperation must not harm the non-participating member states' interests or any Community policy regime, such as the internal market, and that the cooperation must remain open to all member states. Member states have been extremely reluctant to put these provisions to use as their implications are quite profound, but possible areas in which enhanced cooperation could be invoked include defence, economic policy, and justice and home affairs.

Enhanced cooperation, however, was nothing new for the EU as member states had already made such arrangements in various areas outside the treaty framework. One such area was monetary policy cooperation under the European Monetary System, before the Maastricht Treaty introduced precise rules on the conditions that had to be fulfilled by member states that wanted to adopt the euro. When the EU enlarged in 2004, only twelve of the twenty-five member states were in the eurozone; the others were either not yet ready or did not want to adopt the euro. Flexibility was also institutionalized in the areas of foreign and security policy: all EU member states participate but they may chose not to take part in activities with security and defence implications, by making use of 'constructive abstention'. Some member states are more active than others in developing the European Security and Defence Policy. In the area of border control management, the so-called Schengen system for a frontier-free EU follows its own rules concerning conditions for participation (subject to the approval of the Schengen Executive Committee) and has an atypical membership structure. Thus, countries not in the EU, such as Norway and Iceland, are signatories to the Convention and participate fully in the policy regime, whereas Britain and Ireland do not.

Diversity has also been met at a different level through the principle of subsidiarity, which stipulates that the Union shall not take action unless local and/or national action is inadequate to reach the objectives of the treaties. The burden of proof of the necessity for action on the European level falls on the EU institutions, in particular the Commission, which has to justify any new policy initiative on the grounds of subsidiarity. The Constitutional Treaty gave national parliaments the right to challenge action by the Union on the basis of subsidiarity, but this may not be implemented for some time to come. Finally, with the Lisbon process, the latest addition to the Union's over-arching policy processes, the absence of treaty-based commitments and legislative competences on the European level have resulted in disappointing progress on jointly agreed policy objectives. As there are few possibilities to enforce measures against the wishes of member states, progress depends on the political will of individual member states.

As the Union gears up to deal with the implications of the fifth enlargement, which inevitably resulted in an increase in diversity among member states, not only in their economic, social, and environmental situation but also in their historical and cultural experiences, commentators are beginning to ask whether the objectives of integration as they have hitherto been defined still satisfy a membership with diverging policy needs and political aspirations. The European institutions have started to reform the way in which policies are conceived, executed, and enforced, but as yet there has been no meaningful debate on what policy goals the Union should be pursuing and hence what kinds of competence should belong to the European level and to the national or regional levels. It is an open question whether the necessary trust and sense of common commitment among member states exists in order to open such a fundamental debate or whether diversity will prevent them from forming a meaningful community of interest. Also, with the introduction of flexibility in the treaty and the prospect of further enlargements, including the possible accession of Turkey, the question of alternatives to full membership has arisen yet again.

Conclusion

Since the 1950s the EU, created by a small number of like-minded Western European countries, has, through successive enlargements, come to encompass almost the whole of Europe, forming the largest economic entity in the world and arguably the most fascinating political project in history. The integration of new member states has been an ongoing process; with each accession, the original 'contract' between member states has been reshaped to reflect a new situation. The initial objectives of integration have remained largely unchanged, as have the basic contours of the institutional structure and policies of the Union, despite numerous reforms to make them more efficient and relevant. As the Union has moved its borders further east and south-east, enlargement has become one of its most potent foreign policy instruments. In particular, the prospect of membership has become a powerful motivation for modernization and democratization in countries that would otherwise have to undergo painful transformations without the anchor of an externally imposed regime. There is, however, a limit to how far the EU can extend its membership before the very reasons for its attractiveness to neighbouring countries disappears. Integration depends on a high degree of trust among member states and on their long-term commitment to common goals. Without these two elements the Union's special kind of polity will become difficult to sustain. Therefore, the question of where the Union's borders should finally be established is becoming increasingly relevant. It is one that member states will have to face up to in the near future.

These kinds of consideration are uppermost in the debate about Turkey's possible accession. In December 2004, the European Council gave a somewhat hesitant approval to start negotiations with Turkey (and with Croatia as well), provided that the country fulfils a number of preconditions, including officially recognizing the Republic of Cyprus. The EU retained the right to suspend negotiations if Turkey was found in breach of fundamental democratic rights and liberties. It also pledged to delay Turkey's possible accession until after 2014, when a new framework for the EU budget will take effect. In addition, individual member states may call for permanent safeguard clauses in sensitive areas, such as the free movement of workers. The European Council soberly recalled that the aim of the negotiations is indeed accession, but if a candidate country (such as Turkey or Croatia) is not in a position to assume in full the *acquis*, alternatives to membership will be sought.

Notes

1 On the impact of EC membership on Denmark, see Michalski (1995).

2 The EC rejected Morocco's application for membership in 1987 on the seemingly self-evident grounds that Morocco was not a European country, without the Commission ever having issued an opinion.

3 Delors had proposed an institutional 'osmosis' between the EC and EFTA. This was unacceptable to the European Parliament because it threatened the EC's independence and institutional integrity. When the European Court of Justice upheld the view of the Parliament, the Commission and the member states had to go back to the negotiating table to find a new institutional set-up for the EEA, one that turned out to be less advantageous to the EFTA countries.

Further reading

On the process and impact of enlargement generally, see Zielonka (2002) and Mair and Zielonka, eds. (2002). Kitzinger (1973) provides a lively account of the European Community's first enlargement; Tsoukalis (1981) and Royo and Manuel, eds. (2004) assess the EU's Mediterranean enlargement. Michalski and Wallace (1992) examine the importance of enlargement in the post-cold war period. Avery and Cameron (1998), Mayhew (1998), Amato and Batt (1999), and Cameron (2004) focus on the road to and implementation of Central and Eastern European enlargement.

Amato, G., and Batt, J. (1999), Final Report of the Reflection Group on the Long-term Implications of EU Enlargement: The Nature of the New Border (Florence: The Robert Schuman Centre for Advanced Studies, European University Institute, with the European Commission Forward Studies Unit, Italy (November).)

Avery, G., and Cameron, F. (1998), *The Enlargement of the European Union* (Sheffield: Sheffield Academic Press).

Cameron, F. (2004), *The Future of Europe: Integration and Enlargement* (London: Routledge).

Kitzinger, U. (1973), *Diplomacy and Persuasion: How Britain Joined the Common Market* (London: Thames and Hudson).

Mair, P., and Zielonka, J. (2002), *The Enlarged European Union: Diversity and Adaptation* (London: Frank Cass).

Mayhew, A. (1998), *Recreating Europe: The European Union's Policy towards Central and Eastern Europe* (Cambridge: Cambridge University Press).

Michalski, A., and Wallace, H. (1992), *The European Community: The Challenge of Enlargement* (London: Royal Institute for International Affairs).

Royo, S., and Manuel, P. C. (eds.) (2004), *Spain and Portugal in the European Union: The First Fifteen Years* (London: Frank Cass).

Tsoukalis, L. (1981), *The European Community and its Mediterranean Enlargement* (London: Allen and Unwin).

Zielonka, J. (2002), *Europe Unbound: Enlarging and Reshaping the Boundaries of the European Union* (London: Routledge).

Part V

Historiography

Chapter 14

The Historiography of
European Integration

Desmond Dinan

Contents

Summary

The federalist narrative of European integration dominated teaching and thinking about the subject from the late 1940s to the late 1970s. According to this account, the Hague Congress of 1948 and the European Defence Community (and with it the European Political Community) of the early 1950s were great opportunities lost; the nation state was in long-term decline; and the European Coal and Steel Community (ECSC) and the European Economic Community (EEC) presaged the eventual emergence of a United States of Europe. At the same time, scholars and analysts of the European Community presented a more realistic picture of the process of European integration that foreshadowed the revisionism of Alan Milward in the 1980s. The Milwardian view of European integration—that it is driven by national economic and social interests and that the nation state and the supranation are not only compatible but also mutually reinforcing—has since dominated. More recently, greater access to national and other archives and the increasing political salience of European integration have contributed to a spurt of historical scholarship on the European Union (EU). So has the work of Andrew Moravcsik, a political scientist whose theory of liberal intergovernmentalism rests on specific case studies in the history of European integration. John Gillingham, one of the foremost historians of the EU, sees the process of European integration as an epic struggle between statism and market forces.

Introduction

It is hard to resist beginning a chapter on historical interpretations and explanations of European integration with the following quotation from Alan Milward, the most influential historian of the process:

> The historiography of European integration is dominated by legends of great men. Many histories emphasize the role of a small band of leading statesmen with a shared vision. For the [European] Community's supporters they have become saints, men who held fast to their faith in European unity and through the righteousness of their beliefs and the single-mindedness of their actions overcame the doubting faithlessness of the world around them. Monnet, Schuman and Spaak are honoured above others in the calendar, although Adenauer and de Gasperi stand in almost equal rank. Their photographic icons decorate the walls of the [Commission's headquarters in Brussels], while cheap coloured reproductions of the arch-saint Monnet adorn the desks of their faithful servants on earth. (Milward 1992: 319)

The tone and content of that sweeping statement, the opening paragraph of a chapter provocatively entitled 'The Lives and Teachings of the European Saints' in Milward's hugely significant book, *The European Rescue of the Nation State*, helps to explain why Milward is a thorn in the side of the supposed acolytes of the European project, those who revere the so-called founding fathers. Little wonder that Milward is widely regarded as the leading revisionist historian of European integration, someone who almost single-handedly reversed the prevailing view of the emergence in the 1950s of the ECSC and the EEC, which posited that the new supranational entities heralded the fall of the nation state and the rise of a federal Europe.

Yet this assessment of Milward's impact and of the historiography of European integration is somewhat misleading. Indeed, the founding fathers had more than their fair share of disciples. Jean Monnet, who in fact was irreligious, had the largest and most vocal following. Apart from a relatively few hagiographers, however, from the very beginning (the immediate postwar years) European integration attracted a host of chroniclers, commentators, analysts and observers, who produced a huge quantity of material, of varying quality and usefulness, on the emerging European Communities. Early accounts of European integration ranged from the worshipful—the kind easily and amusingly caricatured by Milward—to the factual—the kind that Milward drew upon to substantiate some of his supposedly revisionist claims.

Moreover, the historiography of European integration really began only in the 1980s. For the mass of material on European integration produced in the preceding decades was not the work of historians or, to be more precise, was not historical work, given that the full range of raw material for the study of European integration only began to become available in the late 1970s with the declassification of most government documents covering the early postwar years (under the standard 'thirty-year rule'). Strictly speaking, only as the ensuing archival-based research was disseminated at conferences and in publications did the historiography of European integration truly commence. And when it did, it was dominated not by the legends of great men, as Milward claims, but by the Milwardian view that integration was a response by astute politicians and perceptive civil servants (including the founding fathers) to the needs of the nation state at a critical juncture in European history.

Most of the early historians of European integration—the groundbreakers of the 1980s—were disciples of Milward, not of Monnet, many having worked with Milward at the European University Institute in Florence. Milward put his stamp on the historiography of European integration not so much with *The European Rescue of the Nation State*, which appeared in 1992, but primarily with *The Reconstruction of Western Europe*, which appeared in 1984 and contained many of the points upon which he later elaborated. Far from being a revisionist, Milward was a pioneer whose state-centric rationale for European integration immediately became the accepted view, at least among professional historians, and has remained so ever since.

This chapter begins by outlining the federalist narrative of the development of European integration in the early postwar years, a narrative that dominated official and popular accounts of the European project until the early 1980s. Coexisting with the federalist narrative, however, was a wealth of information on the European Communities and insights into the dynamics of European integration provided by astute academic and other observers, whose contributions are examined in the next section. The accumulation of such information and insights gradually eroded the credibility of the federalist narrative and laid the groundwork for the Milwardian assault on it. Following an assessment of Milward's seminal contribution to the historiography of European integration, the chapter provides an overview of recent scholarship, including the work of Andrew Moravcsik, whose blend of history and political science has had a major impact on the field of EU studies, and John Gillingham, a foremost historian of the EU.

The federalist narrative

The idea of European integration was never more popular than in the immediate aftermath of World War II. The experience of the interwar years (when virulent nationalism was on the rise), of the World War, and then of the early cold war strengthened popular sentiment in Western Europe (Eastern Europe being under tight Soviet control) in favour of new arrangements for international relations. There was much talk (at public meetings, in books and pamphlets, and in the media) of replacing the traditional system of relations among European states with new federal or confederal arrangements. Various proposals floated around, involving some degree of shared sovereignty among participating states and the establishment of supranational European institutions. Public figures and political pundits on both sides of the Atlantic outdid themselves in their advocacy of European federation, which was rarely precisely defined. Words such as 'integration', 'union' and 'supranationalism' were bandied about as panaceas for Europe's ills. This gave rise in the late 1940s to the European movement, a loose collection of individuals and interest groups ranging across the political spectrum from the non-communist left to the discredited far right.

Interest in European federation culminated in the Congress of Europe, a glittering gathering of over 600 influential Europeans from sixteen countries held in The Hague in May 1948. The participants, who included leading European politicians, readily agreed on the desirability of European unity but could not agree on what they meant. They decided nonetheless to establish an international organization, the Council of Europe, which would include a parliamentary assembly. Ardent federalists, such as the Italian Altiero Spinelli, wanted this to be a constituent assembly charged with drafting a constitution for the United States of Europe.

The ferment and legacy of the European movement spawned a dedicated group of writers who promoted an interpretation of European integration that gained considerable currency in the decades ahead. In their view, the Congress of Europe was a great opportunity lost. Instead of producing the institutional architecture for a future European federation, the Congress resulted in an ineffectual organization, the Council of Europe, that did little more than facilitate an exchange of ideas and information among its member states on social, legal, and cultural matters.

As Richard Mayne, a prominent member of the European movement, recalled:

> Bliss was it in that dawn to be alive. Looking back across the yellowing, dusty archives of barely thirteen years ago [from 1962], it is hard to write without irony or bitterness of so many disappointed hopes. In 1949, faith—and public pressure—seemed to have moved mountains: an official Assembly of parliamentarians from ten countries had been established: excitement was in the air: the possibilities seemed boundless. ... [But soon] it had become clear that the reality of the Strasbourg [Assembly] was a pale shadow of its founders' aspirations. (Mayne 1962: 81–2)

The evil of intergovernmentalism

In the federalists' opinion, the fault lay with intractable intergovernmentalism, epitomized by the United Kingdom and personified by Britain Foreign Secretary Ernest Bevin and former Prime Minister Winston Churchill, politicians on opposite sides of the political divide (Bevin was a social-democrat, Churchill a conservative). Bevin had made no secret of his disinterest in European federalism, but Churchill had flirted with the idea. First, in June 1940, when France was on the verge of military collapse, Churchill had proposed an Anglo–French Union. Second, Churchill had called in a speech in Zurich in September 1946 for a 'United States of Europe'. Given his stature after the war as Europe's leading statesman, Churchill's speech had attracted considerable attention and buoyed the hopes of European federalists.

When it came to putting words into action, however, Churchill would not subscribe to a Council of Europe with federal ambitions. Nor would Bevin countenance such an organization. Both politicians, and probably a majority of Britons, wanted cooperation among European states to be organized solely along intergovernmental lines. In other words, national governments would have to remain firmly in control and not cede authority or sovereignty to supranational institutions. The inclusion of a ministerial body in the Council of Europe reflected their preference and doomed the assembly to ineffectualness.

Churchill's incorrigible intergovernmentalism could hardly have surprised the European federalists. After all, the former prime minister was an avowed British nationalist. Such were the high hopes of European federalists, however, that they deluded themselves into thinking that the offer of Anglo–French Union in June 1940 was more than merely a desperate effort to keep the French army in the fight (Churchill wanted France to carry on the war from North Africa) and that the Zurich speech was a clarion call for a New Europe.

The federalist narrative of European integration depicts the failure of the Congress of Europe as a major turning point. European federalism had been building steam for decades, even centuries. Its origins lay in 'a continual hankering after some kind of European unity' (Mayne 1962: 35), notably since the glorious days of Charlemagne, who became Holy Roman Emperor in 800. Nostalgia for the Holy Roman Empire is a recurring theme in European federalism, despite Charlemagne's mixed legacy (Barbero 2004; Becher 2003).[1] European federalists fondly cite the calls for European unity made by such Christian intellectuals and politicians as Pierre Dubois (a French pamphleteer who lived in the late thirteenth and early fourteenth centuries), Richard Hooker (a Renaissance English preacher in the late sixteenth century), the Duc de Sully (chief minister to Henry IV in the early seventeenth century), William Penn (the English Quaker and founder of Pennsylvania in 1682), Baron von Leibniz (a German philosopher in the late seventeenth and early eighteenth centuries), the Abbé de Saint Pierre (author of *Le Projet de paix perpétuelle* in 1713), and Henri de Saint-Simon (the French social theorist who wrote *Nouveau Christianisme* in 1825). Little wonder that Christian Democracy, a post-World War II political movement, embraced the idea of European unity.

European federalism includes a rich literature espousing Christian ideals and emphasizing the duration and strength of the so-called European idea. Proponents include Bernard Voyenne (1954), Denis Hay (1957), Denis de Rougemont (1961), Hendrik Brugmans (1966), and R. C. Mowat (1973).[2] Brugmans was the first president of the Union of European Federalists and rector of the College of Europe in Bruges from 1950 to 1972 (he also won the Charlemagne Prize). The College of Europe originated in the Congress of Europe when Salvador de Madariaga, a Spanish writer in exile, proposed the establishment of a postgraduate programme on European integration for students from different countries. A group of citizens from Bruges, a beautiful medieval city about fifty miles from Brussels, lobbied successfully for the college to be located there. During his long tenure as rector, Brugmans was an unrelenting proponent of European federalism, although most of the students at the College evinced a greater interest in conducting transnational love affairs and landing lucrative positions in the institutions of the European Communities.

The spiritual dimension of European federalism gave many of its proponents a 'holier than thou' attitude. In the long march of history, federalism seemed to them to have a better lineage and be a worthier cause than modern nationalism, which had brought Europe to such chaos and disarray in 1945. Many federalist writers anticipated the sudden demise or gradual withering away of the nation state and its replacement by a federal association of states. It was axiomatic for them that supporters of traditional political arrangements and international relations were naïve (at best) or malevolent (at worst).

From Spinelli to Monnet, Schuman, Spaak and Delors

If Bevin and Churchill were the villains (so far) of the federalist narrative, Spinelli was the hero. Here was someone who had suffered at the hands of Benito Mussolini, Italy's fascist leader, had thought deeply about Europe's future and had pushed hard for a federal Council of Europe. Spinelli advocated a 'big bang' approach to European integration, wanting to reconstitute Europe along federal lines while the European state system was still malleable, or so he thought.

The failure of the Council of Europe left the federalists in the doldrums. Spinelli slunk back to Italy, not to reappear on the European scene for another two decades, when he became a member of the European Commission and then, in 1979, a member of the first directly elected European Parliament. There he would revive the federalists' hopes by authoring and pushing through parliament the Draft Treaty Establishing the European Union, a revered federalist text.

In the meantime, Monnet had come to the fore. Monnet was an awkward character for many federalists to embrace. Although a proponent of European unity, Monnet took an unheroic, low-key approach to European integration, the exact opposite of Spinelli's. He was a backroom boy, preferring to move piecemeal towards a European federation via the unglamorous path of functional economic integration. Nor was he religious, let alone a Christian Democrat (neither was Spinelli, for that matter). He was not a politician either, but a prominent national and (before that) international civil servant.

Almost alone among influential Europeans at the time, Monnet had not bothered to go to the Hague Congress. His absence was due not to doubts about European unity but to disdain for the populism of the European movement and its constituent parts. Monnet was an elitist and a pragmatist. He preferred to pursue functional economic integration. Close cooperation between countries in specific economic sectors, Monnet believed, held the key to overcoming national divisions and ultimately achieving European federation. Decisions to implement functional economic integration would be taken not by 600 delegates at the Congress of Europe but by powerful politicians in the privacy of their government ministries.

Monnet's elitism and absence from the Hague Congress are usually missing from federalist accounts of the history of European integration. Such accounts instead emphasize a note that Monnet wrote in August 1943 to the French Committee of National Liberation in Algiers, in which he argued that there would be no peace in Europe 'if States reestablished themselves on the basis of national sovereignty with all that this implies by way of prestige politics and economic protectionism'. Instead, Monnet asserted, 'the States of Europe must form a federation or a "European entity," which will make them a single economic entity' (Monnet 1978: 222).

This note is generally cited as conclusive evidence of Monnet's early and abiding commitment to European federalism. Federalist accounts of European integration generally gloss over Monnet's postwar role as head of the French national plan for economic modernization, which was unabashedly nationalistic in nature, except to claim that the so-called Monnet Plan was a precursor for the decisive Schuman Plan, which heralded the ECSC.

In the federalist scheme of things, Monnet provided the necessary link between the setback of the Council of Europe and the advance, however unprepossessing, of the ECSC. Just as federalism appeared to be faltering in the late 1940s, or so the federalist narrative would have it, Monnet produced, like a rabbit out of a hat, the proposal for a Franco–German coal and steel pool, under supranational control and open to other European countries, with which he would forever be associated.

Nevertheless the proposal bore not Monnet's name but that of French Foreign Minister Robert Schuman. Schuman was no mere political frontman for Monnet's audacious plan. Undoubtedly his role was truly pivotal for the success of the scheme. That said, Schuman was ideally cast for the federalist narrative of European integration. Coming from the disputed province of Lorraine and having grown up in German-occupied territory, Schuman sought above all to promote reconciliation between France and Germany. He was not only a Christian Democrat but also a devout Catholic—celibate and saintly.

In the standard federalist narrative, the Schuman Declaration had all the elements of high political drama. France was under intense diplomatic pressure from the United States to abandon its punitive policy towards Germany and come to terms with the existence of the new Federal Republic. Monnet and Schuman wanted to oblige but were unable to square French fear of Germany with French vulnerability to American pressure, especially in the context of the deepening cold war. The solution (the proposed ECSC) hit Monnet like a bolt of lightening during a hiking holiday in April 1950. Constrained by the climate of retribution towards Germany that pervaded postwar France and by a natural reserve and inhibition, Schuman had hitherto refrained from taking any conciliatory steps in the direction of the erstwhile enemy. Now, emboldened by Monnet's novel idea, Schuman floated the fateful proposal with secrecy and speed.

As well as winning the approval of his government colleagues, Schuman needed the support of German Chancellor Konrad Adenauer. Using one of Monnet's contacts as a go-between, Schuman let Adenauer into the secret. According to the federalist narrative, Adenauer responded enthusiastically because, like Schuman, he had a strong personal yearning for Franco–German reconciliation. A more compelling reason surely was Adenauer's awareness that, in the prevailing climate of deep distrust towards Germany, shared sovereignty was the sole means of achieving Germany's international rehabilitation. Only by integrating closely with neighbouring countries could Germany hope to remove the remaining controls on its domestic and foreign policies. Federalists generally ignore such a realist explanation, focusing instead on Adenauer's supposed European idealism and Christian Democratic principles. Federalists also add to the mix Italian Prime Minister Alcide de Gasperi, another Christian Democrat and *bone fide* European idealist, who nonetheless played only a marginal role in the development of European integration and whose motives owed as much to concerns about the growing strength of the Italian Communist Party as to a burning desire for a federal Europe.

For all the excitement surrounding the Schuman Declaration, the ensuing ECSC was a letdown for European federalists. The proposed common market in coal and steel was a far cry from the much sought-after European federation. Federalists' hopes soared again with the proposal (also engineered by Monnet) for a European Defence Community (EDC) and the accompanying plan for a European Political Community. Federalists' hopes correspondingly plunged when the French parliament refused to ratify the EDC treaty in August 1954, thanks to the concerted opposition of the communists on the left and Gaullists on the right, two avowed enemies of European federalism. According to the federalists, the failure of the EDC and with it the European Political Community ranks alongside the stunted development of the Council of Europe as the greatest setback in the history of the European integration, greater even than the political crisis in the EEC provoked by French President Charles de Gaulle in 1965–6.

The indefatigable Monnet produced yet another plan to reinvigorate European integration, this time for a European Atomic Energy Community (Euratom). A separate plan for a common market in industrial goods, based on an earlier Dutch proposal, also surfaced. While paying due homage to Monnet for helping to 'relaunch' European integration in the mid-1950s, the federalist narrative cannot disguise the fact that Monnet backed the wrong horse (Euratom) and was no longer a major political player (he had lost all influence in Paris and had resigned as president of the ECSC's High Authority, the forerunner of the European Commission). Nevertheless, federalists emphasize (and arguably exaggerate) the role of Monnet's lobby group for further European integration, the Action Committee for a United States of Europe.

The new hero, in the federalists' view, was Belgian Foreign Minister Paul-Henri Spaak, who engineered the successful outcome of the Messina meeting of foreign ministers in June 1955, which resulted in the intergovernmental conference in Brussels in 1956–7 that brought about the EEC and Euratom. But Spaak is not as compelling a character in the federalist narrative as is Schuman or possibly even Monnet. Without doubting his commitment and contribution to European integration, many federalists were discomfited by his socialism and anti-clericalism. In the pantheon of European federalists, Spaak is a lesser deity than Adenauer, Schuman, and de Gasperi.

Walter Hallstein, the first president of the European Commission, arguably occupies a position slightly below Monnet, and possibly below Spaak as well, in the federalist pantheon. Like Monnet, Hallstein was a senior government official before becoming involved in the movement for European integration (he was State Secretary in the German Foreign Office). Hallstein was a zealous federalist who, as Commission president, sought to assert the EECs' political character. That brought him into conflict with de Gaulle, who soon became the greatest scoundrel in the federalist narrative (much greater than Bevin or Churchill, who at least had made the famous Zurich speech). What seemed to some federalists like a titanic struggle between two great leaders, one (Hallstein) representing the future of Europe and the other (de Gaulle) clinging to the past, was in reality an unequal battle between a powerful national leader and the head of an emergent European institution with political pretensions. Although de Gaulle may have opposed the strengthening of supranationalism in the nascent EEC under any circumstance, Hallstein played into the French president's hands and alienated other national leaders by using every opportunity to push European integration along federal lines and enhance the Commission's power.

The so-called Empty Chair Crisis and the ensuing Luxembourg Compromise of January 1966 contributed to a political malaise in the EEC that stretched into the early 1980s. The economic recessions of the 1970s made matters worse. These were the dark ages for European federalists, a time when European integration seemed stagnant or even regressive. Salvation came in the form of Jacques Delors, who was appointed Commission president in January 1985 and oversaw the single market programme later in the decade. By that time, the federalist narrative of European integration enjoyed wide currency among those who thought about the EEC or were taught anything about it. This was a story of opportunities lost and gained, of a few far-sighted statesmen struggling for Europe's soul against atavistic nationalists, of supranational institutions embodying the ethos of European federalism and constituting an embryonic European government, of brave Eurocrats in Brussels, Luxembourg, and Strasbourg, many of them forged in the federalist College of Europe, carrying the torch of European unity. It was the story put out by the EEC itself in glossy brochures and colourful posters in Schuman Circle, at the heart of the 'European district' in Brussels.

The standard or official view of European Community history received a boost with the publication of Monnet's memoirs, first in French in 1976, then in English in 1978 (Monnet 1976, 1978). By that time Monnet was a very old man, as concerned about the financial security of his wife as about his political legacy. He wrote his memoirs with both in mind, although the book was more successful politically than commercially. It reminded people of Monnet's existence at a time when the European Community appeared to be stalled. The European Council, a recent innovation, helped to keep the Community ticking over but was overtly intergovernmental, involving regular get-togethers by national leaders, initially without the Commission president. Nevertheless Monnet, always willing to flow with the tide, gave his blessing to it.

Monnet's memoirs chronicled a long and varied life that included many international adventures well before he hatched the Schuman Declaration in 1950, when he was already in his early sixties. Not surprisingly, his story of the Schuman Plan, the ECSC, and the Action Committee validated the prevailing and preponderant federalist version of events. The reviewers were generally kind, paying tribute to a man who, if not at the epicentre of European history, had undoubtedly helped to shape its contours in the twentieth century. Monnet's death soon after his memoirs appeared reinforced the general deference to his and the other federalists' view of the European Community's early years. It would have been churlish of anyone in the late 1970s to question the accepted wisdom.

Walter Lipgens

Walter Lipgens, professor of history at the European University Institute (EUI) in Florence from 1976 to 1979, certainly would not have done so. On the contrary, he lent considerable academic credibility to the federalist narrative. A convinced federalist himself, Lipgens embarked on the monumental task while at the EUI and later at the University of Saarland, until his death in 1984, of attempting to collect and publish every speech, statement, and scrap of documentary evidence, country by country, from the resistance movement and subsequent European movement in support of European integration, together with a commentary by professional historians.

According to the British historian D. C. Watt, who did not participate in the project, Lipgens insisted that his collaborators in the EUI and elsewhere 'subscribe to a collective declaration on the advisability and inevitability of the establishment of a federal united Europe'. This was too much for some of his colleagues. The British representatives, in particular, 'already aware that in certain moods Professor Lipgens could lapse into a somewhat Zoroastrian attitude to his faith in which Ernest Bevin … was cast as the Prince of Darkness, resisted the idea as both inappropriate and limiting in that it would enable the … exclusion of themes, incidents, ideas and fields … which were certainly germane to the study of European development, but which Professor Lipgens regarded as heretical' (Watt 1990: 392). The apostates were allowed to participate regardless.

Lipgens's Herculean effort did not bear the abundant fruit that he had hoped for. Nor did he live to see the results—three edited volumes (Lipgens 1985, 1986; Lipgens and Loth 1988). The shortest of these was over 800 pages long, but that was a considerable reduction in size compared to the original proposal. Nor was the work evenly spread among European historians, with German scholars (perhaps reflecting Lipgens's primary contacts) predominating. The volumes may also have had the contrary effect from that intended by Lipgens. For the contrast between the weight of documentary material contained in them and the actions of European politicians was striking. Why had so many speeches, policy papers and other pronouncements on European integration borne such relatively paltry results?

Lipgens's project at least brought together a set of useful documents on the early years of European integration. It also brought together a group of historians of postwar Europe, many of whom resented the restrictions that Lipgens had attempted to place on their work. They were deeply dissatisfied as well with the prevailing federalist narrative. With the opening of national archives covering the immediate postwar period, in keeping with the general rule that restricted access to government papers for thirty years, historians were finally able to explore the dynamics of national decision-making on issues ranging from the Marshall Plan to the ECSC. They also had a vehicle, the Commission-funded EC Historians Liaison Committee, to help them to do so.[3]

Alan Milward, a brilliant economic historian, was one of those sceptical scholars. Beginning with *The Reconstruction of Western Europe* (1984) and culminating in *The European Rescue of the Nation State* (1992), his work largely discredited the federalist narrative and established a new orthodoxy in the historiography of European integration. Before turning to Milward, however, it is important to recognize the contributions of contemporary historians, political scientists, and other analysts who provided a more complete understanding of the European Communities during the 1950s, 1960s and 1970s than did the federalists, and whose work has stood the test of time.

Analysts and observers

From the beginning, the process of European integration attracted economists, political scientists, legal scholars, and others eager to analyze one of the most innovative and interesting developments in the postwar period. The pages of *International Organization, Foreign Affairs,* and later the *Journal of Common Market Studies* (founded in 1963), are full of articles exploring the theoretical implications, practical significance, institutional design, political dynamics and policy processes of the European Communities. Clearly, the launch of the ECSC and the EEC marked not only the institutionalization of economic integration but also the birth of an academic industry loosely described as European Community studies.

The early years of the ECSC and the EEC, in particular, spawned a vast academic literature of highly variable quality, mostly in English and German. Some of these publications were federalist tracts, but many others were serious enquiries into the political, economic and legal characteristics of the new Community. The three most significant studies of the ECSC in English, in terms of their immediate impact and enduring relevance, are Ernst Haas, *The Uniting of Europe* (1958), William Diebold, *The Schuman Plan: A Study in Economic Cooperation* (1959), and Hans A. Schmidt, *The Path to European Union: From the Marshall Plan to the Common Market* (1962). It was no coincidence that all three authors were American-based (although not necessarily American-born). After all, the 1950s and 1960s were decades of lavish funding for social science in the United States in comparison with the situation in other countries and with the situation in the United States in later decades.[4]

For the purposes of this chapter, the most noteworthy point about the work of Haas, Diebold, Schmidt and others is that it was based on close observation of developments in Luxembourg in the 1950s, and therefore provided readers as well as future historians with a rich vein of information on and insights into the construction of the ECSC and the birth of the EEC. Haas is by far the best-known early scholar of the European Communities. As a young political scientist at the end of World War II, he wanted to know how the state and the state system could change, and how communities beyond the state might come into being. Intrigued by the integrative potential of international organizations, for obvious professional and personal reasons (his family had fled Nazi Germany when he was a child) the situation in postwar Europe attracted his attention. The ECSC was a wonderful laboratory. Haas spent a year in Luxembourg (1955–6) observing it in action.

The Uniting of Europe, his ensuing *magnum opus,* extrapolated from the experience of the ECSC the conditions under which sovereignty-sharing and transnational community-building could take place. The book is best known for developing the idea of spill-over (the notion that integration in one functional area would almost certainly lead to integration in others), which Haas posited not on the basis of economic determinism but on likely changes in the attitudes and behaviour of governments, parties and, especially, labour and business interest groups. His key conclusion was that 'group pressure will spill-over into the federal sphere and thereby add to the integrative impulse' (Haas 1958: xiii).

The Uniting of Europe became the foundation of a rich and varied literature on the European Communities. Reaction to it in the 1960s was mixed, however. When the pace of integration slowed later in the decade, critics panned Haas and his disciples for painting a false dawn, for forecasting an ever-upward trajectory for ever-closer union. Yet *The Uniting of Europe* had not put forth the inevitability of European union. More discerning eyewitnesses, including Haas himself, appreciated the potential pitfalls of European integration and saw *The Uniting of Europe* as a tentative step forward rather than the definitive last word on integration theory.

Although celebrated for its theoretical contribution, *The Uniting of Europe* is a much neglected contemporary chronicle of the making of Europe's first supranational entity. It contained extremely useful accounts of the day-to-day difficulties of organizing the common market in coal and steel. It also showed the mixed motives of those engaged in constructing the ECSC. Leon Lindberg, Haas's student, continued the practice of theoretical testing and empirical analysis with *The Politics of European Economic Integration* (1963), which contained valuable information on the development of the common agricultural policy and other initiatives of the European Communities.

Miriam Camps was another American analyst of the emerging European Economic Community. Her work was more broadly based and better known than Haas's in the 1960s and shed considerable light on the day-to-day dynamics of European integration. Camps was a US State Department official from 1939 to 1954, working mostly on European economic issues. She resigned from government service to marry William Camps, Master of Pembroke College, Cambridge, and spent the next twelve years as an independent analyst of the European Community, before rejoining the State Department. During that time she wrote prolifically on the two most compelling questions confronting the EEC: Britain's relationship with it and the Empty Chair Crisis of 1965–6.

First, Camps wrote a series of monographs on the launch of the EEC, the British proposal for a wider free trade area, and the formation of the European Free Trade Association (Camps 1957, 1958, 1959*a*, 1959*b*). These provided considerable insight into Britain's effort to thwart the EEC by subsuming it into a free trade area (excluding agriculture) encompassing most Western European states and, when that failed, to establish the rival European Free Trade Association. Second, Camps wrote a book on Britain's application for EEC membership and de Gaulle's veto of it (Camps 1964). Writing from the perspective of a contemporary historian, Camps based her research on extensive interviews (she knew most of the protagonists personally), speeches and published papers, and newspaper accounts. Despite her preference for British membership in the EEC, Camps was dispassionate in her analysis and objective in her assessment of Britain's reasons for applying and de Gaulle's reasons for vetoing. Nor did she subscribe entirely to the view that strategic considerations drove de Gaulle's decision. Just as Britain sought membership primarily for economic but also for strategic reasons, so too did de Gaulle veto Britain's application primarily for strategic but also for economic reasons.

Camps published another, more speculative book in 1965 on the development of the EEC, but is perhaps best remembered for her book the following year on the Empty Chair Crisis (Camps 1965, 1966). Like subsequent scholars of that seminal event in the EEC's history, Camps wondered why Commission President Walter Hallstein and Vice-President Sicco Mansholt had played into de Gaulle's hands by linking financial and institutional reforms in a way that the French president was bound to reject, a question to which we still do not have a satisfactory answer. More sympathetic to the French position than most contemporary or later observers, Camps explained that de Gaulle's reaction was based on economic, institutional and strategic considerations. Whereas most of the book consisted of an in-depth analysis of the crisis, Camps ended with conjecture about the EEC's likely development. Considering how gloomy the prospects for European integration seemed at the time, her conclusion was optimistic and mostly correct:

> It seems probable that the process that has been going on fitfully but steadily since the war will continue and that the states now joined in the European Community plus, at a minimum, the United Kingdom, Denmark, Norway, and Ireland will progressively integrate their economies and tend increasingly to conduct their external affairs in concert. (Camps 1966: 246)

Uwe Kitzinger was a contemporary historian of the EEC in the mould of Miriam Camps. A flamboyant Oxford-based academic entrepreneur (he founded and for a long time owned the *Journal of Common Market Studies*), Kitzinger wrote mostly about Britain's long march towards EEC membership in a series of books spanning the 1960s and 1970s. His best-known work, co-authored with David Butler, examined Britain's renegotiation of accession terms and subsequent referendum on continued EEC membership (Butler and Kitzinger 1976). It contained a wealth of information on the negotiations and referendum debate, and informed analysis of the outcome.

F. Roy Willis, an American academic, also wrote extensively about the EEC in the 1960s and 1970s. His best-known book, *France, Germany and the New Europe* (1965), examined the postwar *rapprochement* between the two countries, culminating in the Elysée Treaty of January 1963. Apart from its analysis of one of the most striking developments in international relations in the twentieth century, Willis's book was a source of invaluable information on French occupation policy in Germany, the Schuman Declaration, the negotiations that resulted in the ECSC, the EDC, and the EEC, and the emergence of the Elysée Treaty out of the wreckage of the French Fouchet Plan. Willis's work was particularly refreshing because of its emphasis on both the economics of the Franco–German relationship and the importance of people-to-people contacts in promoting reconciliation between both countries. In contrast to Camps, for instance, who focused exclusively on the role of national governments in the process of European integration, Willis argued that 'the basis of *rapprochement* between France and Germany was to be the mutual understanding of individuals, not of governments' (Willis 1965: 53).

Willis's other major contribution to EC studies, an edited book published in 1975, is less significant for the historiography of European integration (Willis 1975). It is noteworthy largely because three of the contributors to it (Hendrik Brugmans, Walter Lipgens and John Pindar) were avowed federalists whose chapters inevitably promoted a deterministic view of European integration, despite the difficult political and economic circumstances in Europe at the time of the book's publication. Nevertheless another contributor to the book, Françoise de la Serre, wrote one of the most perceptive analyzes ever of the Empty Chair Crisis.

Throughout the 1960s, 1970s, and early 1980s a host of doctoral dissertations appeared on the subject of European integration. Indeed, some of the leading scholars of the European Community at that time, such as Lindberg and Willis, had based their early publications on the subject on their doctoral dissertations. Like the scholarly monographs then available on the EC, the dissertations varied in usefulness and impact. Two stand out. One, by Loukas Tsoukalis, was a study of monetary policy cooperation among EC member states following the currency crises of the late 1960s and early 1970s. The other, by Haig Simonian (Tsoukalis's student), was a study of Franco–German relations (what Simonian called the privileged partnership) first under French President Georges Pompidou and German Chancellor Willy Brandt, then under their successors Valéry Giscard d'Estaing and Helmut Schmidt. The two dissertation were soon published and became widely read source books on key aspects of contemporary European integration (Tsoukalis 1977; Simonian 1985).

All of the astute observers of European integration cited in this section sympathized with the subject of their research and writing, but none was a propagandist for the European Community. All were aware of the dominant federalist narrative, but none was comfortable with it. Indeed, by delving into the minutiae of the process of integration—to the extent that their access to sources then allowed them to do so—they contributed to a growing dissatisfaction with the federalist explanation of the origin and development of the European Communities. The work of Haas, Camps, Willis, and others clearly demonstrated that the Communities owed their existence and progress to a range of competing ideas, interests and political pressures. There was nothing inexorable about the demise of the nation state or the rise of a federal Europe. De Gaulle's antics in the 1960s seemed less of an aberration than an exaggerated assertion of national interests in a process dominated by nation states.

In a sympathetic review of one of Miriam Camps's books, Eric Roll, a leading economist and senior British civil servant, remarked that there were those who saw the federalist interpretation of European integration 'as a piece of mystification to obscure sordid national interests or even more sordid personal ambitions' (Roll 1965: 134). Clearly, as Roll's comment indicates, there was widespread dissatisfaction with the standard federalist narrative of European integration. Especially as state documents pertaining to the early postwar years became available, the time was ripe for a radical reassessment of the origins and development of the European Communities. Alan Milward led the charge.

The Milwardian onslaught

Milward already had a formidable reputation as an economic historian of World War II when he turned his attention to postwar European reconstruction. He was curious to know why reconstruction had been so successful after World War II compared to the aftermath of World War I. Presumably, Europe's success after 1945 had a lot to do with the role of the United States. Indeed, the prevailing view in the popular and academic literature was that the United States had saved Western Europe from the economic crisis of 1947 by implementing the Marshall Plan. Milward soon questioned the nature and seriousness of the 1947 crisis and, as a result, the importance of the Marshall Plan. Contrary to the prevailing belief, Milward asserted that Europe's economic recovery had begun in 1945 and was well underway by 1947 when Europe faced a shortfall of dollars with which to continue to buy capital and consumer goods from the United States: 'It was the success and vigour of the European recovery, not its incipient failure [that] exacerbated this payments problem' (Milward 1984: 465). Far from rescuing Western Europe, the Marshall Plan had merely helped Western Europe to overcome a balance of payments problem (although this was hardly an inconsiderable achievement).

The Reconstruction of Western Europe (1984) had an immediate impact on the historiography of the Marshall Plan, a subject of heated discussion in academic circles for over a decade before the book was published. Left-wing historians had already questioned the motives for the Marshall Plan, dismissing it as an instrument of US cold war policy and a means of furthering US domestic and international interests, but nobody had ever doubted the plan's economic impact on Western Europe. That Milward did so in such a trenchant fashion sent shockwaves through the large community of scholars of postwar US and European history. Many of the reviews of Milward's book focused on his criticism of the Marshall Plan, which, most concluded, was excessive. Indeed, the publication soon afterwards of Michael Hogan's massive study of the Marshall Plan, and later of two studies of postwar US foreign economic policy, restored the balance in favour of the plan's economic impact (Hogan 1987; Killick 1997; Lundestad 1998).

If the Marshall Plan had not saved postwar Western Europe, Milward wondered what had. He concluded that the real saviours were the ECSC and the European Payments Union (EPU). The first facilitated a diplomatic settlement between France and Germany, without which a stable Western European order could not have come about; the second facilitated international trade, without which Western Europe could not have prospered. Federalists were already singing the praises of the ECSC, whereas the EPU had escaped widespread academic and popular attention.[5] Milward agreed with the federalists only on the import of the ECSC. Delving into its provenance, he dismissed the federalist view of 'human idealism fortunately triumphing at specific moments over the narrow, anachronistic realism of national governments', arguing instead that 'the historical evidence gives considerable support' to the idea that the ECSC was created 'as an arm of the nation states to do things which could not otherwise be achieved' (Milward 1984: 492, 494).

Milward demonstrated that the Marshall Plan had failed to promote the unity of Western Europe to which its architects aspired. Rhetorically at least, the plan was extremely ambitious. By laying the foundation for a customs union, it sought eventually to sweep away the nation state as the basis of the European political system, replacing it with a federal United States of Europe (Milward 1984: 467). However, the ensuing Organization for European Economic Cooperation (OEEC) failed to become a vehicle for European federalism because of French concerns about Germany's economic resurgence and British concerns about loss of sovereignty. Instead of going along with American plans and embracing postwar Germany, France attempted at the time to reconstruct economically at Germany's expense. One of the sweet ironies of this situation, in Milward's view, was that the architect of French national recovery was none other than Jean Monnet, whose plan for economic modernization (the

Monnet Plan) aimed to exploit German resources (notably high-grade coking coal) in order to produce steel in up-to-date French mills and meet market demands that Germany could no longer satisfy.

Origins and significance of the ECSC

Monnet eventually modified his approach to Germany not because of altruism or high idealism but because of unrelenting American diplomatic pressure to come to terms with Germany's political and economic rehabilitation. There was no question for France of accepting a US-induced customs union in which French industry simply could not compete. By early 1948, French officials were groping for a less ambitious but nonetheless far-reaching strategy that would reconcile French economic modernization (notably in the coal and steel sectors) with German economic recovery. This was the genesis of the Schuman Plan, the substance of which emerged gradually over a two-year period and 'did not, as all commentators on it have so far suggested, emerge as a *deus ex machina* from [Monnet's] Planning Commissariat in Spring 1950' (Milward 1984: 164).

Milward's overall conclusion was that Western Europe's post-World War II reconstruction was successful and enduring because of the political settlement put in place through the negotiation of the ECSC, a settlement that was based on the resolution of seemingly low-level economic but nonetheless highly contentious political issues between states. 'In place of a comprehensive political peace settlement there developed in the reconstruction period [after 1945] an institutionalized pattern of economic interdependence in Western Europe which was a better basis for Western Europe's economic and political existence than the comprehensive regulation of major political issues which was attempted after 1918' (Milward 1984: 463). By contrast with the failed Versailles Treaty of 1919, 'from the Schuman Plan negotiations emerged an altogether more pragmatic process of integration which resolved the central political problem of Western Europe and became the pattern for the European Economic Community' (Milward 1984: 475). Milward's book was therefore as much a work of political and diplomatic as of economic history.

Milward took particular pleasure in debunking the federalist narrative of European integration and dismissed the political significance of the 'extraordinary wave of enthusiasm for European federation' in the immediate postwar years, claiming that 'it was no more than a faintly disquieting and soon stilled disturbance for the ship of state, their officer governments and their crews of civil servants' (Milward 1984: 55). The idea that European integration was the result of idealism or the weakness of the nation state 'is flatly contradicted by this book. Here the interpretation is that the very limited degree of integration that was achieved came about through the pursuit of the narrow self-interest of what were still powerful nation states' (Milward 1984: 492). Nor was there anything inexorable or inevitable about European integration:

> The historical evidence is that [the ECSC] came into existence to cope with certain historically specific and well-defined economic and political problems and, those problems once solved, there could be no further momentum from the national interest towards any further stage of economic and political integration. . . . . The process of integration is neither a thread woven into the fabric of Europe's political destiny nor one woven into the destiny of all highly developed capitalist nation states. (Milward 1984: 493)

Milward directed much of his ire at Monnet, 'an assiduous self-publicist and a re-markable collector of disciples' (Milward 1984: 129, n.7), and to a lesser extent (in the footnotes) at Mayne, one of Monnet's main disciples and a leading federalist propa-gandist.[6] He was more tolerant of Schuman, not least because the French foreign minister had had the political courage to front the coal and steel proposal and, in do-ing so, had nearly lost his seat in the French parliament (advocating Franco–German *rapprochement* was not politically rewarding in France at the time). 'There is no inten-tion in this book to deny a certain welcome leaven of idealism to these men [Adenauer, Schuman, Spaak, Monnet]', Milward wrote, 'but the policies from which a limited measure of economic integration did emerge were, so the evidence clearly indicates, created by national bureaucracies out of the internal expression of national political interest, not by the major statesmen who implemented them' (Milward 1984: 492).

Impact and follow-on

The publication of *Reconstruction* had a huge impact on the historiography of European integration. Milward's stellar academic credentials, together with the ex-tent of the archival research on which the book was based, lent considerable credib-ility to his conclusions. Backed up by solid research, Milward's assertions about the state-centric nature of European integration seemed compelling, if somewhat over-stated. The main drawback of the book was that it was so badly written: only the most dedicated students of European integration would have the stamina to trudge through it.

Milward used the occasion of the publication of the paperback edition to take a swipe at those federalist who claimed that the book was 'a denial of the role of ideal-ism and an exaggeration of the role of national materialism in the making of post-war Europe', once again claiming that the historical evidence showed that the prevailing (federalist) understanding of European integration was 'an inadequate foundation of belief and theory on which to build or explain the new European order' (Milward, 1986: xix). In the original edition, Milward had been so dismissive of the federalists as to argue that his own interpretation of the history of European integration was blindingly obvious: 'I do not think many serious historians have doubted that this [interpretation] is just what would appear when … the history of these events was written in a neutral way rather than in the full flush of ardent discipleship. Indeed, a large majority of historians, having read what there is to read on the history of the origins of the European Economic Community, have probably dismissed it as myth, and it is no great thing to show to be wrong what few historians ever believed to be right' (Milward 1984: 493).

The study of postwar economic reconstruction brought Milward to the study of European integration, which was squarely the subject of his next big book. As he wrote in the preface to the paperback edition of *Reconstruction*, research on European integration in the two years since publication of the hardback edition (in 1984) had convinced him that 'there was indeed an imperative towards wholly new forms of interdependence and to the transfer of national "sovereignty" to non-national institutions, which the nation-state had to follow to make itself once more an accepted and strong unit of organization'. It could be possible, therefore, to formulate an 'historically-convincing intellectual foundation for the process of

European "integration", although it would be equally disappointing to federalists and their associates' (Milward, 1986: xix) This was a tantalizing hint of what was to come in *The European Rescue of the Nation State* (1992).

In the meantime, Milward admitted that one of the weaknesses of *Reconstruction* was that it was 'written from above not below' (Milward, 1986: xvii). Milward used the analogy of a house: his book was the roof and other studies would have to provide the walls (Milward 1984: 464). It was essential to try to fill in the details of political and economic activity within the various Western European countries and the day-to-day development of European integration using not only government files but also other materials, such as industry, labour and private papers. To that end, Milward launched a research project at the EUI on 'The Origins of the European Community', which produced many detailed studies of developments and negotiations leading to the ECSC and the EEC. Milward was grateful to the EUI for supporting research that 'must have appeared at first to be coming to wholly unwanted conclusions. To how many national governments could a similar tribute be paid?' (Milward 1986: xix). Milward liked to bite the hand that fed; the more he bit, the more it fed.[7]

A first, tentative attempt to build a supporting wall for the Milwardian edifice appeared in 1982 (even before the publication of *Reconstruction*) in the form of an edited work by Hanns Jürger Küsters on the origins of the EEC (Küsters 1982). Other walls were put in place later in the 1980s and early 1990s. These included edited works by Raymond Poidevin (1986), Klaus Schwabe (1988a), Enrico Serra (1989), and Richard Griffiths (1990).[8] In general, they painted a realistic, state-centric picture of the origins and development of European integration (Milward himself and many of his colleagues contributed to these volumes).

One of the most important books on the history of European integration could perhaps be described as an annex to Milward's edifice. That was John Gillingham's *Coal, Steel and the Rebirth of Europe* (1991), a brilliant analysis of the background and negotiations leading to the ECSC. Like Milward, Gillingham asserted the centrality of the ECSC to the stability and security, and therefore also the prosperity, of Western Europe after World War II. Like Milward as well, Gillingham emphasized the primacy of national interests. His chapter on the negotiation of the ECSC, aptly entitled 'From Summit to Swamp', followed the course of the intergovernmental conference from the rhetorical heights of the Schuman Declaration to the unseemly give-and-take of the bargaining that followed. Unlike Milward, however, Gillingham gave due credit to the role of Jean Monnet (Gillingham's hero) and the United States, in whose interests Monnet operated. Indeed, one of Monnet's unique attributes was an ability to mediate between France and the United States and reconcile the interests of both in promoting the Schuman Plan. Far from seeing the ECSC as a defeat for the United States, as Milward had portrayed it (compared to the federal goals of the Marshall Plan), Gillingham saw the ECSC as a triumph for American diplomacy. Unlike Milward as well, Gillingham was an excellent writer.

Another important feature of Gillingham's book was that it drew heavily on industry as well as government archives and placed the ECSC squarely in the history of nearly fifty years of interaction between French and German producers (almost half the book covered the period from the end of World War I to the end of World War II). The final chapter, entitled 'The Success of Failure', contrasted the economic inadequacy of the ECSC with its political success.[9] Whereas the ECSC was unable to prevent reconcentration in the German steel industry and failed to bring about a fully functioning common market, it provided a practical peace settlement for postwar Europe, inculcated cooperative practices among participating groups and governments, and laid an institutional foundation for the EEC.

Rescuing the nation state

One of the most arresting features of Milward's next *magnum opus* was its title, *The European Rescue of the Nation State* (1992; paperback edn., 2000). Milward was struck by an apparent paradox: at the same time that nation states were becoming more powerful in the postwar period, having recovered (in most cases) from the devastation of the war itself, they were surrendering sovereignty to a supranational entity which, its proponents claimed, was the antithesis of the nation state. How could nation states be strengthening and weakening at the same time? Milward concluded that 'there is no ... antithesis [between the nation state and the supranational EC] and that the evolution of the Community since 1945 has been an integral part of the reassertion of the nation state as an organizational concept' (Milward 2000: 2–3). Indeed, the two were inextricably linked: 'to supercede the nation state would be to destroy the Community. To put a finite limit to the process of integration would be to weaken the nation state, to limit its scope and to curb its power' (Milward 2000: 2–3).

Milward's central thesis was that national governments went beyond traditional international interdependence and surrendered sovereignty in key policy areas in order to ensure their own survival and enhance their own authority. Far from undermining the nation state, as federalists believed that it would, European integration was an essential means of strengthening the nation state under the circumstances in which Europe found itself in the mid-twentieth century. 'The development of the European Community, the process of European integration, was, so runs the argument of this book, a part of [the] postwar rescue of the European nation state, because the new political consensus on which this rescue was built required the process of integration, the surrender of limited areas of national sovereignty to the supranational' (Milward 2000: 4).

Milward rooted the story of the rescue of the nation state firmly in economic and social developments, although the need to accommodate West Germany in a secure postwar system obviously provided the overarching framework. Milward presented three lengthy case studies: employment and welfare (how Belgium responded to the Schuman Plan); foreign trade and economic growth (the origins of the European Economic Community); and the maintenance of agricultural incomes (the origin of the common agricultural policy). The book also included a number of essays on various aspects of European integration, including the infamous chapter on 'The Lives and Teachings of the European Saints', and a final chapter on Britain's relationship with the EEC (by the time that the second edition appeared in 2000, Milward was writing the official history of Britain's response to European integration and eventual applications for membership in the EEC).

A lengthy quotation from the case study on Belgium's response to the Schuman Plan encapsulates Milward's point about the primacy of national interests in the process of European integration and the advantage for national governments of surrendering sovereignty in specific fields:

> In all [the debate on the Schuman Plan] no trace of idealism about the wider advantages to mankind of European integration can be discovered. It was taken for granted that peace between France and Germany was essential for Belgium's security, and that this was the strongest reason for accession to the treaty. After that acceptance it was vital to ensure that Belgium's other national interests were not trampled into the ground in the rush of the French, Germans and Americans to find a common framework for the future. What emerged as a definition of Belgium's national interest was then strikingly clear. ... [It included] support from the [ECSC] for the new basis of the state in welfare, higher employment and a measure of government influence and management in key industrial sectors. ... [Moreover] supranationality brought a new advantage. A genuine restructuring of the coal industry might be easier if the immense political problems which were bound to arise ... could be shared with supranational management, or blamed on it. The Treaty of Paris can be understood ... as the moment when Belgium formally entered the mixed economy and so ratified the changes which had taken place in its government and society since 1944. ... [As a result] the Belgian state did not emerge weaker in the face of a liege authority but stronger in the face of an unruly subject. (Milward 2000: 82–3)

It was unsurprising for readers familiar with Milward's earlier work to see that *European Rescue* contained a broadside against the federalists and the neo-functionalists, whose work Milward disparaged for being ahistorical and for ignoring the importance and durability of the nation state. It also contained a stinging rebuke of Lipgens's methodology and motives. 'As an historical method', Milward wrote of the way that Lipgens had collected federalist statements made by European politicians during and immediately after the war, 'this resembled beachcombing and the sheer volume of the findings was presumably supposed to prove that it could only have been washed up by high historical tide' (Milward 2000: 16). Apart from its flawed methodology, 'Lipgens's massive study had been, after all, only the chronicle of fringe political groups' (Milward 2000: 17).

Nor was it surprising to readers of *Reconstruction* that Milward reserved his most biting criticism in *European Rescue* for the founding fathers and their disciples. Writing in the wake of the Single European Act and during the single market programme, Milward seemed especially irritated by the renewed homage being paid to Monnet and Spaak. 'The Lives and Teachings of the European Saints' showed once again that Adenauer, de Gasperi and Schuman sought above all to promote their countries' interests and found an ideal way of doing so through the process of European integration. Devoutly religious and appreciating the vague popular appeal of European unity, Schuman revelled in his new-found status as a European saint. Although also devoutly religious, Adenauer was more down to earth and forthright in his pursuit of West German sovereignty, a goal that he could only achieve, paradoxically, by sharing sovereignty with Germany's erstwhile enemies in Western Europe.

At least Milward appreciated Adenauer's, de Gasperi's and Schuman's democratic credentials. Spaak was also an elected politician, but that cut little ice with Milward, who seemed to despise Spaak because the long-time Belgian foreign minister genuinely believed in European federalism. Milward held Monnet in equally low esteem not only because Monnet, a consummate politician, operated outside the political arena, but also because he was such a self-promoter. Milward marvelled at Monnet's ability to attract devoted adherents, who cultivated an image of the Great Man at variance with the reality of Monnet's naked pursuit of French national interests.

Subsequent scholarship

The European Rescue of the Nation State cemented Milward's reputation as the foremost historian of European integration and established his explanation of the origins and development of the EC as the new orthodoxy. Rearguard actions to reassert federalism or at least to provide a more balanced perspective, notably by Sidjanski and Burgess, who first returned fire after Milward's *Reconstruction* appeared in 1984, were largely unavailing (Burgess 1986, 1989, 1995, 2000; Sidjanski 2000). *The Frontier of National Sovereignty*, a short book by Milward and Co. published in 1993, was essentially an addendum to *European Rescue* (Milward, et al. 1993). Like *European Rescue*, it contained a number of case studies to demonstrate the primacy of national interests in the process of European integration and the mutual dependence of the nation state and the supranation (the case studies were country-specific, focusing on the interests and preferences of Italy, France, Denmark, Britain and the United States at various times in the postwar period).

Like *European Rescue* only more so, *The Frontier of National Sovereignty* sought to debunk neo-functionalism, which Milward regarded as a malign and insidious quasi-theory of European integration, and replace it with a theory based on historical evidence. Milward's alternative hypothesis, that nation states chose to surrender sovereignty in a supranational entity when it suited them to go beyond traditional interdependence, had both descriptive and predictive value: it described the process of integration to date and provided a framework for envisaging when nation states might agree to surrender sovereignty in new policy areas (although the range of interests in an enlarging EC and an inability to foresee the future obviously limited the predictive value of any theory of European integration). Not surprisingly, Milward and Co. concluded that their approach to understanding the EC convincingly explained the acceleration of integration in the late 1980s, culminating in the Maastricht Treaty.

Andrew Moravcsik's *Choice for Europe*

The work of Andrew Moravcsik, which began to appear at that time, reinforced the new orthodoxy. Moravcsik took an unabashedly state-centric view of European integration, beginning with a study of the negotiations that had resulted in the Single European Act (Moravcsik 1991). Moravcsik refined Milward's approach by focusing exclusively on the commercial interests of the big member states. In his view, commercial interests alone determined the preferences of the big member states and lowest common denominator intergovernmental bargaining accounted for the contents of the SEA. Like Milward, Moravcsik wanted to develop a theory of European integration that was based on historical evidence. The case study of the SEA formed the basis for Moravcsik's trademark 'liberal intergovernmentalism', an approach to understanding key constitutive moments (mostly treaty-making and reform) in the history of the EU.

The Choice for Europe, Moravcsik's monumental study of European integration 'from Messina to Maastricht' (1955–92) developed the theory of liberal intergovernmentalism on the basis of five case studies (Moravcsik 1998). In addition to the SEA, these were: negotiating the Rome Treaty; consolidating the common market (including de Gaulle's exclusion of Britain, withdrawal from Community decision-making, and conclusion of the Luxembourg Compromise); launching and consolidating the European Monetary System; and negotiating the Maastricht Treaty. Moravcsik not only insisted on the importance of historical research for understanding and theorizing about the EU, but also trumpeted his mastery of primary sources.

Moravcsik's brilliance was dazzling but his audacity was exasperating. He became a one-man industry for promoting liberal intergovernmentalism. Many political scientists thought that his emphasis on history in general, and primary sources in particular, was overstated; many historians thought that his determination to develop an overarching theory of big decision-making in the EU distorted his interpretation of the historical evidence. In 2000 the *Journal of Cold War Studies* published a two-part article by Moravcsik elaborating upon his chapter on de Gaulle in *The Choice for Europe*, essentially using the same sources and methodology (Moravcsik 2000a, 2000b). A number of scholars responded to Moravcsik's articles in a subsequent issue of the journal, and Moravcsik responded to them in turn (Moravcsik 2000c). One wonders why the editor devoted so much space to the glorification of Moravcsik.

'Grain and Grandeur' was the title of the chapter on de Gaulle in *The Choice for Europe* and was prominent in the title of the two-part article in the *Journal of Cold War Studies*. The thesis of both the chapter and the article was that, whether in his dealings with Germany, Britain, the Commission, or anything else having to do with the EC, de Gaulle was motivated almost exclusively by commercial rather than by geopolitical considerations, contrary to what de Gaulle himself had claimed and what most scholars had assumed. 'This essay seeks to overturn the conventional wisdom', Moravcsik wrote at the beginning of his 100-page-long exegesis in the *Journal of Cold War Studies*, '[by showing that] the primary French objective [in relation to the EC] was to secure preferential commercial advantages for French industry and agriculture. ... De Gaulle's foreign policy was designed to appease powerful industrial and agricultural groups' (Moravcsik 2000a: 5).

In 2004 the *Journal of Cold War Studies* returned to the subject of Moravcsik's scholarship on de Gaulle, this time with an article by a group of political scientists casting serious doubt on Moravcsik's accuracy and methodology, specifically his use of primary sources. Holding Moravcsik to his own insistence 'on precision in such matters' (Moravcsik 2000c), the avenging political scientists discovered that 'not all of Moravcsik's quotations and references [in the de Gaulle chapter in *The Choice for Europe*] were correct' (Lieshout et al. 2004: 90). In what looked like a parody of a political science paper, with its excessive use of abbreviations (for example, *The Choice for Europe* became 'TCfE' and hard primary sources became 'HP'), Lieshout, Segers, and van der Vleuten included two appendices: one listed the sources used by Moravcsik and an assessment of their quality; the other presented a detailed, note-by-note discussion of Moravcsik's handling of those sources. The authors were especially critical of Moravcsik's excessive dependence on the diaries of Alain Peyrefitte, an ardent Gaullist who became the president's press spokesman in 1962 (Peyrefitte 1994, P 1997). Pending access to de Gaulle's own papers, Moravcsik claimed that Peyrefitte's diaries were the next best thing.

Lieshout, Segers and van der Vleuten claimed not only that Moravcsik's use of sources was incorrect but also that the sources themselves were 'softer' than Moravcsik declared them to be. Accordingly, they went on to question the validity of Moravcsik's revisionist claims. Regardless of its possible impact on Moravcsik's scholarly reputation, the entire exercise accentuated the huge impact of Moravcsik's work. Nothing could take from Moravcsik's accomplishments. He had integrated history and political science in the study of the EU in a far more comprehensive way than Milward had been able to do, cast key developments in the history of the EU in a new light, and raised the visibility and status of EU studies. Like de Gaulle in the history of the EC, Moravcsik would forever be a giant in the study of the EU.

John Gillingham's *European Integration*

Whereas Moravcsik developed a new theory grounded in historical research, John Gillingham embarked on an equally ambitious undertaking: a history of European integration (the book was simply entitled *European Integration*) from the Schuman Plan in 1950 to the Nice Treaty in 2000 (Gillingham 2003). Gillingham's credentials as a leading historian of European integration were already well established. Aware of the importance of archival sources and their general unavailability for the period after the early 1970s, he nonetheless felt compelled and confident to continue his narrative into the early 2000s. The story that he told was not simply of national interests and supranational solutions, however, but of an epic struggle 'between two principles of social, political, and economic organization: the state and the market ... the tension between these two poles is responsible for the zigs and zags characteristic of the integration process' (Gillingham 2003: xii). A strong proponent of economic liberalism, Gillingham argued:

> on the basis of economic logic and historical example that, in the absence of a demos—a sense of European nationhood—only one integrative approach can work: 'negative integration,' which takes place either through markets or institutions created to make markets operate properly .... Although other prerequisites may be necessary for the success of this 'negative' approach, its alternative—'positive integration,' the organization of Europe by means of bureaucracy and regulation in order to compensate for market failure—has never succeeded and cannot do so under current circumstances. (Gillingham 2003: xiii)

Gillingham starkly portrayed the process of European integration as a struggle between good and evil, between market forces and statism. During the first stage of European integration, in the immediate postwar period, statism was on the ascendant. Monnet, the hero of Gillingham's book on the ECSC, became something of an anti-hero in *European Integration*, although Gillingham again acknowledged Monnet's invaluable contribution to the post-World War II settlement. The difficulty with Monnet this time was his passion for planning and disinterest in democratic institutions, two problems that he bequeathed to the European Community and later the European Union. The epic battle between markets and statism took place, in Gillingham's opinion, in the 1980s; the main protagonists were British Prime Minister Margaret Thatcher and Commission President Jacques Delors. Thatcher was Gillingham's hero in *European Integration*, Delors the baddie, a characterization that turned the usual description of European integration in the 1980s on its head.

Arguably, Gillingham's ideological zeal undermined the credibility and value of *European Integration*, which appealed strongly to eurosceptics. Gillingham's description of the EU's loss of direction and lack of democratic accountability in the 1990s gave an academic gloss to eurosceptical caricatures of the Brussels bureaucracy. In fact, Gillingham remained profoundly appreciative of the benefits of European integration, regretting only its direction (or lack of direction) since the halcyon days of the single market programme. The negative outcome of the referenda on the EU constitution in France and the Netherlands in spring 2005 is fully consistent with Gillingham's conclusions in *European Integration* and is not necessarily a cause for alarm. Rather, it is a signal to EU leaders (in Brussels and the national capitals) that the EU needs to return to first principles: the continuation and consolidation of unspectacular but essential negative integration.

Other contributions

Other major contributions to the historiography of European integration in recent years range from detailed studies of national involvement to in-depth analyses of particular events and developments. The creeping forward in time of the availability of national archives means that important turning points, such as the EC's first enlargement, are now subject to thorough scrutiny. Meanwhile, the burgeoning of postgraduate studies throughout Europe (and elsewhere) and the increasing political salience of European integration account for a growing number of young historians turning their attention to the EU. Important contributions to the published literature include Wendy Asbeek Brusse's study of trade liberalization as a driver of European integration in the 1950s (Asbeek Brusse 1997*b*); Fernando Guirao's assessment of Spain's unique and usually neglected position in postwar Europe (Guirao 1998); William Hitchcock's examination of the strength of French diplomacy despite the weakness of the Fourth Republic (Hitchcock 1998); Michael Gehler's exploration of Austria's road to EU membership (Gehler 2002); and Piers Ludlow's comprehensive look at the Gaullist challenge to European integration in the 1960s, which balances Moravcsik's revisionist claims against the traditional view of de Gaulle's motives (Ludlow 2006).

Craig Parsons, another younger scholar, made a highly original contribution to the historiography of European integration with the publication of *A Certain Idea of Europe* (2003), in which he argues (as he does in Chapter 5 of this book) that France was instrumental in establishing the ECSC and the EEC only because domestic political circumstances made it possible for pro-European politicians to form coalition governments around other issues and then to advance their integrationist agendas. By contrast, edited books by established scholars, such as the British historian Ann Deighton and the German historian Wilfred Loth, continue to provide more detailed information about the construction of the European Community (Deighton 1995; Loth 2001).

The history of Britain's uneasy relationship with the European Community remains a fertile field of scholarship; it has even given rise to a book on the historiography of Britain and European integration (Daddow 2004). Given its highly emotional and politically-charged nature, it is hardly surprising that the question of Britain's EU membership has attracted considerable academic attention. The title of Edmund Dell's book, *The Schuman Plan and the British Abdication of Leadership of Europe*, suggests that the historiography of Britain's initial response to and later involvement in European integration mirrors the divisive national discourse on the subject (Dell 1995). Dell, a former government minister and a trained historian who undertook considerable research into Britain's reaction to the Schuman Declaration, is scathing in his condemnation of Britain's dismissal of the historic announcement and failure to participate in the ensuing ECSC. Wolfram Kaiser agrees that Britain lost its leading position in Europe in the postwar period and argues that its first application (in 1961) served a variety of domestic and international purposes, notably (and seemingly paradoxically) to strengthen the Anglo–American special relationship, regardless of the outcome of the accession negotiations (Kaiser 1999).

Concerned about the quality of the public and academic debate on Britain's involvement in the EC, Milward weighed in with a chapter on 'Britain and Western Europe' in the first edition of *European Rescue*, which he revised considerably in the second edition (Milward 1992, 2000). He also wrote an official history of Britain's relationship with the EC from the Schuman Plan to the failure of Britain's first application for membership, in which he argued that British policy throughout was consistent with a national strategy that sought to ease the country's transition from a Great Power to a middle-ranking European power but that proved difficult to implement for a variety of economic and political reasons (Milward 2002). As in his earlier work on the history of European integration, Milward attempted to analyze the motives and actions of the protagonists on the basis of specific interests rather than their own (and others') rhetorical justifications. Despite its massive size and impressive scholarship, however, *The Rise and Fall of a National Strategy* (2002) did not have an impact on the historiography of Britain's relationship with the EC commensurate with the impact of his earlier works on the historiography of European integration.

By contrast, John W. Young provided one of the best (and most readable) overviews of Britain's response to European integration from the end of World War II to the launch of the single currency (Young 2000). At the other end of the spectrum, some excellent 'micro histories' have filled in the details of particular episodes throughout that time. These include James Ellison's examination of British efforts to scuttle the negotiations for the Rome Treaty by promoting an alternative and geographically more inclusive free trade area (Ellison 2000); Piers Ludlow's in-depth analysis of Britain's first, ill-fated application for EC membership (Ludlow 1997); and Oliver Daddow's equally illuminating analysis of Britain's second application (Daddow 2003).

Conclusion

In *European Integration*, Gillingham remarked that 'historical writing about the subject [of this book] is in its infancy' (Gillingham 2003: xi). Although it is certainly true that much remains to be done, the historiography of European integration has nonetheless developed rapidly since the mid-1980s. Apart from the pioneering work of Milward and the follow-on work of his students and his students' students, numerous studies have appeared on almost every aspect of European integration, using not only national and EU archives but also the private papers of individual protagonists, key economic actors and various interests groups. As a result, a much fuller picture has emerged of the origins and evolution of the European Community. A number of general texts on EU history have attempted to bring the fruits of this specialized scholarship to a wider student audience, if not yet to a general readership (Bitsch 1996; Dinan 2004; Gerbet 1999; Loth 1996; Stirk 1996; Thody 1997). As in other areas of EU scholarship, the gap between the specialists' knowledge and the publics' awareness nevertheless remains formidable. Whereas that is true of most academic endeavours, the consequences of the 'knowledge gap' for the EU, being such a highly contested form of governance, are particularly regrettable.

Notes

1 Charlemagne's contemporary champions overlook the brutality of his campaign against the Saxons and the fact that he was a source of inspiration for Hitler, who named an SS division after Charlemagne (Becher 2003: 148). The Charlemagne Prize (Karlspreis) is the leading award given by the city of Aachen, site of Charlemagne's court, to advocates and architects of European integration. Recipients include Coudenhove-Kalergi, Jean Monnet and Valéry Giscard d'Estaing, Bill Clinton, and (improbably) the euro.

2 One reviewer describer Mowat's *Creating the European Community* a 'a work of devotion to the unity of Europe, and especially the idea of Christendom' (Ferrell 1974: 1545). Mowat gave a moving account of his academic calling and faith in the idea of European unity in his autobiography, *An Oxford Family Remembers* (2002).

3 The Liaison Committee organizes conferences and publishes a journal (*The Journal of European Integration History*) twice a year. A number of its conferences led to major publications on the history of European integration, including Schwabe (1988a) and Serra (1989).

4 In a swipe at the early neo-functionalists, Alan Milward claimed that the US government and US foundations funded scholarship on the European Communities in the 1950s and 1960s in order to propagate the idea of European integration as a bulwark against communism. By implication, Haas and other recipients of US funding were, either wittingly or unwittingly, agents of US policy (Milward et al. 1993: 4).

5 The EPU was the subject of an excellent, although officially commissioned, study that appeared five years after the publication of *Reconstruction* (Kaplan and Schleiminger 1989).

6 Despite his lack of a stellar federalist lineage, Monnet endeared himself to federalists not only by his achievements but also by assiduous self-promotion and an uncanny ability to cultivate followers. Mayne, who worked in the press office of the European Coal and Steel Community and later for the Action Committee for a United States of Europe, was one of Monnet's greatest admirers. Monnet is the hero of Mayne's numerous books on European integration. Monnet wrote the introduction to Mayne's *The Community of Europe* (1962) and Mayne translated Monnet's *Memoirs* (1978) into English.

7 Milward wrote several years later that, in the mid-1980s, 'the center of social life [at the EUI] was a stuffy windowless attic whose two attractions were cheap alcohol and conversation. While outside the pitilessly cheerful Italian sunlight cut into profile the shadowless edges of the buildings, inside the force of some incipient idea kept us long in that dark corner. A simple progressivist discourse about European integration was in those days surprisingly often heard in the Institute; we [Milward and Co.] were developing another speech . . . . No one listened to us, but we were handsomely funded for the work we did and we gave one direction and purpose to the Department of History which offered others a way of explaining why it was there' (Milward et al. 1993: ix, x).

8 Poidevin also wrote a sympathetic biography of Robert Schuman which nonetheless showed that the foremost European saint, as Milward called him, had feet of clay (Poidevin 1986).

9 A subsequent effort by Dirk Spierenburg and Raymond Poidevin to establish the economic success of the ECSC was largely unavailing (Spierenburg and Poidevin 1994).

Further reading

There are numerous histories of European integration but few historiographical studies of it. Kaiser (2006 forthcoming) examines both the historiography of European integration and the relationship between historiography and social science research on the EU. Milward (1984, 2000) and Gillingham (2003) demonstrate the nature and extent of historical enquiry into the process of European integration. On the historiography of British accession to the European Community, see Daddow (2004) and Milward (2002). On the historiography of de Gaulle's impact on the European Community, see Moravcsik (2000*a*, 2000*b*).

Daddow, O. (2004), *Britain and Europe since 1945: Historiographical Perspectives on Integration* (Manchester: Manchester University Press).

Gillingham, J. (2003), *European Integration, 1950–2003: Superstate or New Market Economy?* (Cambridge: Cambridge University Press).

Kaiser, W. (2006 forthcoming), 'From State to Society? A Historiography of European Integration', in Cini and Bourne (eds.), *Palgrave Advances in European Union Studies* (Basingstoke: Palgrave Macmillan).

Milward, A. (1984), *The Reconstruction of Western Europe, 1945–1951* (London: Methuen).

Milward, A. (2000), *The European Rescue of the Nation State*, 2nd edn. (London: Routledge).

Milward, A. (2002), *The Rise and Fall of a National Strategy 1945–1963: The UK and the European Community*, Vol. 1 (London: Frank Cass).

Moravcsik, A. (2000a), 'De Gaulle Between Grain and Grandeur: The Political Economy of French EC Policy, 1958–1970 (Part 1)', *Journal of Cold War Studies*, 2/2: 3–43.

Moravcsik, A. (2000b), 'De Gaulle Between Grain and Grandeur: The Political Economy of French EC Policy, 1958–1970 (Part 2)', *Journal of Cold War Studies*, 2/3: 4–68.

Appendix: Chronology of European Integration, 1945–2005

1945

February	The Yalta conference takes place
May	World War II ends in Europe
July–August	The Potsdam conference takes place

1946

September	British Prime Minister Winston Churchill calls for a 'United States of Europe'

1947

March	US President Harry S. Truman issues an anti-communist manifesto (The Truman Doctrine)
	Britain and France sign a defensive alliance (the Dunkirk Treaty)
May	The UN Economic Commission for Europe is established
June	US Secretary of State George C. Marshall announces a plan to assist European reconstruction (the Marshall Plan)
July	The Committee for European Economic Cooperation is established
October	The General Agreement on Tariffs and Trade (GATT) is launched
December	The International Committee of the Movements for European Unity is established

1948

January	The Benelux customs union is launched
February	The Communist Party consolidates power by staging a coup in Czechoslovakia
March	France, Britain, and the Benelux countries sign a defensive alliance (the Brussels Treaty)
April	The US Congress enacts the Marshall Plan (formally called the European Recovery Programme)
	The Organization for European Economic Cooperation (OEED) is established
May	The Congress of Europe takes place in The Hague
June	The Berlin blockade begins

1949

April	The North Atlantic Treaty is signed in Washington, DC
	The International Ruhr Authority is established

May	The Federal Republic of Germany (West Germany) is established The Council of Europe is launched The Berlin blockade ends

1950

May	French Foreign Minister Robert Schuman issues the 'Schuman Declaration'
June	Negotiations begin to establish the European Coal and Steel Community (ECSC) The Korean war begins
October	French Prime Minister René Pleven calls for a European Defence Community (EDC)
November	The European Convention for the Protection of Human Rights and Fundamental Freedoms is signed

1951

February	Negotiations begin to establish the EDC
April	The Paris Treaty establishing the ECSC is signed

1952

May	The Paris Treaty establishing the EDC is signed
August	The ECSC is launched in Luxembourg
September	The ECSC Assembly holds its first session in Strasbourg

1953

March	An *ad hoc* assembly adopts a draft treaty to establish the European Political Community

1954

August	The French National Assembly rejects the EDC treaty
October	Agreement is reached in Paris to expand the Brussels Treaty into the Western European Union

1955

May	Germany joins the North Atlantic Treaty Organization (Nato)
June	The Messina conference on reviving European integration takes place The Spaak Committee meets for the first time
October	A referendum is held on the future of the disputed Saar territory Jean Monnet launches the Action Committee for a United States of Europe, an international pressure group

1956

April	The Spaak Committee recommends establishing an atomic energy community and a customs union

May	Foreign ministers approve the Spaak Committee's recommendations at the Venice Conference
June	Negotiations begin to establish the European Economic Community (EEC) and the European Atomic Energy Community (Euratom)
October–November	The Suez crisis erupts
October	The Soviet Union puts down an uprising in Hungary

1957

| January | Based on the outcome of the October 1955 referendum, the Saar rejoins Germany |
| March | Treaties establishing the EEC and Euratom are signed in Rome |

1958

January	The EEC and Euratom are launched
	The Commission takes office under the presidency of Walter Hallstein
March	The assembly of the new communities (later called the European Parliament) holds its first plenary session
May	The French Fourth Republic collapses in political turmoil
July	A conference on establishing the common agricultural policy (CAP) takes place in Stresa
September	French voters endorse the Fifth Republic in a referendum
December	Charles de Gaulle is elected president of the new Fifth Republic

1959

| January | The first stage of transition to a common market begins |
| September | The Stockholm Convention establishes the European Free Trade Association (EFTA) |

1960

| December | The Organization for Economic Cooperation and Development (OECD) is established |

1961

July	The EEC signs an association agreement with Greece
August	Britain applies to join the EEC (together with Denmark, Ireland, and Norway)
November	France launches the Fouchet Plan for a European political community

1962

| January | The second stage of transition to a common market begins |
| April | The Fouchet Plan collapses amid acrimony among the EEC member states |

July	US President John F. Kennedy outlines a 'grand design' for transatlantic relations

1963

January	De Gaulle vetoes Britain's EEC membership application
	De Gaulle and German Chancellor Konrad Adenauer sign the Elysée Treaty of Franco–German friendship
July	The Yaoundé Convention between the EEC and seventeen African states and Madagascar is signed
September	The EEC signs an association agreement with Turkey

1965

March	Hallstein introduces controversial budget proposals
April	The Merger Treaty, fusing the executives of the EEC, ECSC, and Euratom, is signed
July	The Empty Chair Crisis begins

1966

January	The third and final stage of transition to a common market begins
	The Empty Chair Crisis ends with the Luxembourg Compromise on decision - making in the Council of Ministers

1967

May	Britain applies a second time to join the EEC (together with Denmark, Ireland, and Norway)
July	The Merger Treaty comes into force
	A new Commission takes office under the presidency of Jean Rey
November	De Gaulle vetoes Britain's application for EEC membership a second time

1968

May	Students and workers riot in Paris
July	The customs union is completed eighteen months ahead of schedule

1969

April	De Gaulle resigns as president of France
July	Britain, Denmark, Ireland, and Norway reactivate their membership applications
December	At a summit in The Hague, EU leaders decide to revive the EEC through a programme for 'completion, deepening, enlargement'

1970

January	A new Commission takes office under the presidency of Franco Malfatti

April	Member states reach agreement to finance the EEC through its 'own resources'
June	Accession negotiations with Britain, Denmark, Ireland, and Norway resume
October	Luxembourg Prime Minister Pierre Werner presents a plan for economic and monetary union (EMU)
	Foreign ministers adopt a plan drawn up by Belgian diplomat Etienne Davignon for foreign policy cooperation (European Political Cooperation)
November	Foreign ministers hold their first meeting under the auspices of European Political Cooperation

1971

January	The second Yaoundé Convention and Arusha agreement comes into force
August	The United States announces the suspension of dollar convertibility, formally ending the Bretton Woods system

1972

January	Accession treaties are signed in Brussels with Britain, Denmark, Ireland, and Norway
March	The monetary 'snake' is launched
	Commission Vice-President Sicco Mansholt becomes the interim Commission president
September	Norwegians reject EEC membership in a referendum
October	At a summit in Paris, EEC leaders agree 'to transform the whole complex of … relations [between their countries] into a European Union' by the end of the decade

1973

January	Britain, Denmark, and Ireland join the EEC
	A new Commission takes office under the presidency of François - Xavier Ortoli
July	The Conference on Security and Cooperation in Europe (CSCE) opens in Helsinki
October	Arab oil producers quadruple the price of oil and embargo the port of Rotterdam
December	EEC leaders discuss the oil crisis at a summit in Copenhagen

1974

April	A new British government renegotiates the terms of the country's EEC membership
September	EEC leaders decide to form the European Council

1975

February	The Lomé Convention between the EEC and forty-six developing countries is signed

March	The European Council meets for the first time and concludes the renegotiation of Britain's membership terms
	The European Regional Development Fund is established
June	British voters endorse continued EEC membership in the country's first ever national referendum
	Greece applies to join the EEC
July	EEC leaders agree to establish the Court of Auditors and strengthen the budgetary powers of the European Parliament
August	Thirty-five participating states conclude the CSCE
December	Belgian Prime Minister Leo Tindemans issues a report on European Union (the Tindemans Report)

1976

July	The EEC opens accession negotiations with Greece

1977

January	A new Commission takes office under the presidency of Roy Jenkins
March	Portugal applies to join the EEC
July	Spain applies to join the EEC

1978

July	The European Council agrees to establish the European Monetary System (EMS)
October	The EEC opens accession negotiations with Portugal
December	Member states decide to launch the EMS in January 1978; eight decide to participate in system's exchange-rate mechanism (ERM)

1979

February	The EEC opens accession negotiations with Spain
March	Launch of the EMS
May	The accession treaty with Greece is signed in Athens
June	The first direct elections to the European Parliament are held
September	Dirk Spierenburg presents a report on Commission reform
October	The Second Lomé Convention is signed
November	The 'Three Wise Men' present a report on EEC reform
	The British budgetary question begins to dominate EU politics

1981

January	Greece joins the EEC
	A new Commission takes office under the presidency of Gaston Thorn

November   The Genscher–Colombo initiative is launched

1982

February   Greenlanders decide in a referendum to leave the EEC

1983

June   EEC leaders issue the Stuttgart Declaration

1984

February   The European Parliament adopts the Draft Treaty Establishing the European Union

June   The second direct elections to the European Parliament are held

          EEC leaders decide at a summit in Fontainebleau to resolve the British budgetary question

December   The Third Lomé Convention is signed

1985

January   A new Commission takes office under the presidency of Jacques Delors

March   A committee under the chairmanship of Irish Senator James Dooge recommends holding an intergovernmental conference on treaty reform

June   Accession treaties are signed with Portugal and Spain

          The Commission publishes its White Paper on the single market

          EEC leaders decide to hold an intergovernmental conference

September   The intergovernmental conference begins

December   The intergovernmental conference ends with agreement on the Single European Act (SEA)

1986

January   Portugal and Spain join the EEC

February   Foreign ministers sign the SEA

1987

April   Turkey applies to join the EEC

July   The SEA comes into effect

1988

January   French Prime Minister Edouard Balladur issues a memorandum on EMU

February   German Foreign Minister Hans-Dietrich Genscher endorses the idea of EMU

          EC leaders agree on the Delors I budget package

June	EC leaders decide to establish a committee under Commission President Delors to consider the steps necessary to achieve EMU

1989

June	The Delors report on EMU is released
	The third direct elections to the European Parliament are held
July	Austria applies to join the EC
November	The Berlin Wall is breached, symbolizing the end of the cold war
December	EC leaders decide to hold an intergovernmental conference on EMU and adopt a Charter of Fundamental Social Rights for Workers

1990

May	A charter establishing the European Bank for Reconstruction and Development is signed
June	France, Germany, and the Benelux countries sign the Schengen Agreement
	EC leaders decide to hold an intergovernmental conference on political union concurrently with the intergovernmental conference on EMU, beginning in December 1990
July	Stage I of EMU begins
	Cyprus applies to join the EC
	Malta applies to join the EC
October	Germany is reunited
	Britain joins the exchange rate mechanism of the EMS
November	The US–EC Transatlantic Declaration is signed
December	Two intergovernmental conferences begin in Rome (one on monetary union, the other on political union)

1991

June	War breaks out in Yugoslavia
July	Sweden applies to join the EC
December	The intergovernmental conference ends at a summit in Maastricht
	The Soviet Union collapses

1992

January	The EC recognizes the independence of Croatia and Slovenia
February	Foreign ministers sign the Treaty on European Union in Maastricht
March	Finland applies to join the European Union (EU)

May	EC and EFTA countries sign an agreement to establish the European Economic Area (EEA)
	EC leaders reach an agreement on CAP reform
	Switzerland applies to join the EC
June	Danish voters reject the Maastricht Treaty in a referendum
September	Britain suspends participation in the exchange rate mechanism of the EMS
	The currency crisis deepens
	French voters narrowly approve the Maastricht Treaty in a referendum
November	Norway again applies to join the EC
December	Swiss voters reject EEA membership in a referendum, implicitly rejecting EC membership
	EC leaders agree on opt-outs for Denmark from the Maastricht Treaty and on the Delors II budget package
	The single market programme comes to an end

1993

February	The EC opens accession negotiations with Austria, Finland, and Sweden
April	The EC opens accession negotiations with Norway
May	Danish voters approve the Maastricht Treaty in a second referendum
June	At Copenhagen summit, EC leaders agree on accession criteria
August	The currency crisis ends
November	The Maastricht Treaty comes into effect; as a result, the EU comes into being
December	The Commission publishes a White Paper on growth, competitiveness, and employment

1994

January	Stage II of EMU begins
March	A dispute over the institutional implications of enlargement ends with the Ioannina Compromise
	Hungary applies to join the EU
April	Poland applies to join the EU
June	The fourth direct elections to the European Parliament are held
	Accession treaties with Austria, Finland, Sweden, and Norway are signed
January	Stage II of EMU begins
	The European Monetary Institute is established
November	Norwegians again reject EU membership in a referendum
December	The European Energy Charter is signed

1995

January	Austria, Finland and Sweden join the EU
	A new Commission takes office under the presidency of Jacques Santer
June	The Reflection Group holds its first meeting to prepare a new intergovernmental conference on treaty reform
	Europe agreements with Estonia, Latvia and Lithuania are signed
	Romania applies to join the EU
October	Latvia applies to join the EU
November	Estonia applies to join the EU
	The EU and twelve Mediterranean countries sign the Barcelona Declaration
December	The United States and EU sign the New Transatlantic Agenda
	The Reflection Group issues its report on the forthcoming intergovernmental conference
	Lithuania applies to join the EU
	The Dayton peace plan for former Yugoslavia is signed in Paris
	Bulgaria applies to join the EU

1996

January	The Czech Republic applies to join the EU
March	An intergovernmental conference on treaty reform begins in Turin
June	Slovenia applies to join the EU
December	EU leaders agree on the Stability and Growth Pact

1997

June	EU leaders conclude the intergovernmental conference and agree on the Amsterdam Treaty
October	The Amsterdam Treaty is signed
November	The European Council holds special jobs summit in Luxembourg

1998

March	Inaugural session of European Conference (London)
	The EU opens accession negotiations with Poland, Hungary, the Czech Republic, Estonia, Slovenia and Cyprus
May	At special summit, EU leaders agree that eleven member states will participate in the final stage of EMU (all except Britain, Denmark, Greece, and Sweden) and choose the first president of the European Central Bank (ECB)
June	The ECB is launched in Frankfurt

1999

January	Stage III of EMU (a single monetary policy and irrevocably fixed exchange rates among participating currencies) begins
March	The Santer Commission resigns
	EU leaders agree on the *Agenda 2000* budget package
May	The Amsterdam Treaty comes into force
June	The fifth direct elections to the European Parliament are held
July	Manuel Marín becomes interim Commission president
September	A new Commission takes office under the presidency of Romano Prodi
October	EU leaders agree to strengthen cooperation on Justice and Home Affairs
December	EU leaders recognize Turkey as a candidate for EU membership

2000

February	The EU opens accession negotiations with Latvia, Lithuania, Slovakia, Bulgaria, Romania, and Malta
	An intergovernmental conference on treaty reform begins
March	EU leaders launch a strategy for economic modernization (the Lisbon Strategy)
September	Danish voters decide in a referendum not to adopt the euro
December	The intergovernmental conference ends with agreement on the Nice Treaty
	EU leaders proclaim the Charter of Fundamental Rights

2001

January	Greece adopts the euro
June	In a very low turnout, Irish voters reject the Nice Treaty in a referendum

2002

January	Euro notes and coins are introduced
February	the Convention on Future of Europe begins in Brussels
August	The ECSC comes to an end
October	In a larger turnout, Irish voters accept the Nice Treaty in a second referendum

2003

February	The Nice Treaty comes into effect
April	Accession treaties with Cyprus, the Czech Republic, Estonia, Hungary, Latvia, Lithuania, Malta, Poland, Slovenia, and Slovakia are signed in Athens

June	The Convention on the Future of Europe ends with agreement on a Draft Constitutional Treaty
October	The EU launches an intergovernmental conference to finalize the Constitutional Treaty

2004

May	Cyprus, the Czech Republic, Estonia, Hungary, Latvia, Lithuania, Malta, Poland, Slovenia, and Slovakia join the EU
June	EU leaders reach agreement on the Constitutional Treaty
	The sixth direct elections to the European Parliament are held
October	EU leaders sign the Constitutional Treaty in a ceremony in Rome
November	A new Commission takes office under the presidency of José Manuel Barroso

2005

May	French voters reject the Constitutional Treaty in a referendum
June	Dutch voters reject the Constitutional Treaty in a referendum
	EU leaders decide to put the Constitutional Treaty on hold

References

Abelshauser, W. (1994), ' "Integration à la carte": the Primacy of Politics and the Economic Integration of Western Europe in the 1950s', in Martin (ed.), *The Construction of Europe: Essays in Honour of Emile Noël* (Dordrecht: Kluwer), 1–18.

Acheson, D. (1969), *Present at the Creation* (New York: W.W. Norton).

Adamsen, H. (1981), *Investitionshilfe für die Ruhr: Wiederaufbau, Verbände und Soziale Marktwirtschaft 1948–1949* (Wuppertal: Peter Hammer Verlag).

Adler, M. (1969–70), 'Specialization in the European Coal and Steel Community', *Journal of Common Market Studies*, 8: 175–91.

Aldcroft, D. H. (2001), *The European Economy 1914–2000*, 4th edn. (New York: Routledge).

Allen, D. (1997), 'EPC/CFSP, the Soviet Union, and the Former Soviet Republics: Do the Twelve have a Coherent Policy?', in Regelsberger et al. (eds.), *Foreign Policy of the European Union: From EPC to CFSP and Beyond* (Boulder, CO: Lynne Rienner), 219–35.

Allen, D. (1996), 'Cohesion and the Structural Funds', in Wallace and Wallace (eds.), *Policy Making in the European Union*, 3rd edn. (Oxford: Oxford University Press), 243–66.

Alphand, H. (1977), *L'étonnement d'être* (Paris: Fayard).

Alter, K. J. (1996), 'The European Court's Political Power', *West European Politics*, 19: 458–87.

Andrews, S. (1973), *Agriculture and the Common Market* (Ames: Iowa State University Press).

Aron, R., and Lerner, D. (eds.) (1957), *France Defeats EDC* (New York: Praeger).

Asbeek Brusse, W. (1997a), 'Liberalising Intra-European Trade', in Griffiths (ed.), *Explorations in OEEC History* (Paris: OECD), 123–37.

Asbeek Brusse, W. (1997b), *Tariffs, Trade and European Integration, 1947–1957: From Study Group to Common Market* (New York: St. Martin's Press).

Ashworth, W. (1974), 'Industrialization and the Economic Integration of Nineteenth Century Europe', *European Studies Review*, 4: 291–314.

Audland, C. (1993), 'The Heath Negotiations', unpublished paper presented at the Chatham House conference, Previous Enlargement Negotiations, 29 March.

Auswärtiges Amt (1978), Akten zur deutschen Auswärtigen Politik 1918–1945, Series B, 12 (Göttingen: Vandenhoeck and Ruprecht).

Averyt, W. (1977), *Agropolitics in the European Community: Interest Groups and the Common Agricultural Policy* (New York: Praeger Publishers).

Baker, D., and Seawright, D. (1998), *Britain for and against Europe: British Politics and the Question of European Integration* (Oxford: Oxford University Press).

Balassa, C. (1978), *Organized Industry in France and the European Common Market: Interest Group Attitudes and Behavior*, Unpublished dissertation, Johns Hopkins University, Baltimore, MD.

Ball, G. W. (1973), *The Past Has Another Pattern* (New York: W.W. Norton & Company).

Barbero, A. (2004), *Charlemagne: Father of a Continent* (Berkeley: University of California Press).

Barbezat, D. (1997) 'The Marshall Plan and the Origin of the OEEC', in Griffiths (ed.), *Explorations in OEEC History* (Paris: OECD), 33–44.

Baun, M. (1996), *An Imperfect Union: The Maastricht Treaty and the New Politics of the European Union* (Boulder, CO: Westview Press).

Baun, M. (2000), *A Wider Europe* (Boulder, CO: Rowman & Littlefield).

Becher, M. (2003), *Charlemagne* (New Haven, CT: Yale University Press).

Becker, F. (2001), *Bilder von Krieg und Nation. Die Einigungskriege in der bürgerlichen Öffentlichkeit Deutschland 1864–1913* (Munich: Oldenbourg).

Bell, P. M. H. (1997), *France and Britain 1940–1994: The Long Separation* (London: Longman).

Berghahn, V. R. (1986), *The Americanization of West German Industry 1945–1973* (New York: Berg).

Bethlen, I. (1932), 'The Danube States and the Tardieu Plan', *Political Science Quarterly*, 47: 352–62.

Bidault, G. (1965), *Resistance: The Political Biography of Georges Bidault* (London: Weidenfeld & Nicolson).

Bitsch, M.-T. (1996), *Histoire de la construction européenne de 1945 à nos jours* (Paris: Editions Complexe).

Bjøl, E. (1966), *La France devant l'Europe* (Copenhagen: Munksgaard).

Blasius, R. A. (1984), *Dokumente zur Deutschlandpolitik*, Series 1: 1 (Frankfurt: Alfred Metzner).

Bloes, R. (1970), *Le 'Plan Fouchet' et le problème de l'Europe politique* (Bruges: Collège d'Europe).

Boskin, M. J. (1987), *Reagan and the Economy: The Successes, Failures, and Unfinished Agenda* (San Francisco: ICS Press).

Bossuat, G. (1992), *La France, l'aide américaine et la construction européenne, 1944–1954* (Paris: Comité pour l'Histoire Économique et Financière de la France).

Bossuat, G. (1993), 'Armaments et relations franco-allemands (1945–1963)', in Centre des Hautes Études de l'Armement, *Histoire de l'armement en France de 1914 à 1962* (Paris: ADDIM).

Bossuat, G. (1995), 'Les hauts fonctionnaires français et le processus d'unité en Europe occidentale d'Alger à Rome, 1943–1958', *Journal of European Integration History*, 1/1: 87–109.

Bowie, R. (1989), 'Réflexions sur Jean Monnet', in Fondation Jean Monnet pour l'Europe, *Témoignages à la mémoire de Jean Monnet* (Lausanne: Fondation Jean Monnet pour l'Europe), 81–8.

Boyce, R. (1994), 'Was there a "British" Alternative to the Briand Plan?', in Catterall and Morris (eds.), *Britain and the Threat to Stability in Europe, 1918–45* (Leicester: Leicester University Press).

Breuning, K. (1969), *Die Vision des Reiches* (Munich: Max Hueber).

Brinkley, D. (1991) (ed.), *Jean Monnet and the European Integration Movement* (New York: St. Martin's Press).

Brugmans, H. (1966), *L'ideé europeénne, 1918–1965*, 2nd eds. (Bruges: De Tempel).

Brunet, J. (1993), 'Le MRP et la construction européenne, 1955–1957', in Berstein, Mayeur, and Milza (eds.), *Le MRP et la construction européenne* (Paris: Complexe).

Bullen, R. (1988), 'The British Government and the Schuman Plan, May 1950–March 1951', in Schwabe (ed.), *Die Anfänge des Schuman-Plans 1950–1951* (Brussels: Bruylant), 199–210.

Burgess, M. (1986) (ed.), *Federalism and Federation in Western Europe* (London: Croom Helm).

Burgess, M. (1989), *Federalism and European Union: Political Ideas, Influences, and Strategies in the European Community, 1972–1987* (London: Routledge).

Burgess, M. (1995), *The British Tradition of Federalism* (London: Leicester University Press).

Burgess, M. (2000), *Federalism and the European Union: The Building of Europe, 1950–2000* (London: Routledge).

Burley, A.-M., and Mattli, W. (1993), 'Europe before the Court: A Political Theory of Legal Integration', *International Organization*, 47: 41–76.

Butler, D., and Kitzinger, U. (1976) *The 1975 Referendum* (New York: St. Martin's Press).

Byrnes, M. (2000) 'Unfinished Business: The United States and Franco's Spain, 1944–47', *Diplomacy & Statecraft*, 11/1: 129–62.

Cairncross, A. (1986), *The Prices of War: British Policy on German Reparations, 1941–1949* (Oxford: Blackwell).

Cairncross, A. (1992), *The British Economy since 1945: Economic Policy and Performance* (Oxford: Blackwell).

Callot, E. (1986) *L'action et l'oeuvre politique du Mouvement républicain populaire* (Paris: Champion-Slatkine).

Cameron, D. (1992), 'The 1992 Initiative: Causes and Consequences', in Sbragia (ed.), *Euro-politics: Institutions and Policy Making in the New European Community* (Washington, DC: Brookings Institution), 23–74.

Camps, M. (1957), *The European Common Market and Free Trade Area*, Policy Memorandum No. 15 (Princeton, NJ: Center of International Studies, Princeton University).

Camps, M. (1958), *The First Year of the European Economic Community*, Policy Memorandum No. 17 (Princeton, NJ: Center of International Studies, Princeton University).

Camps, M. (1959a), *The Free Trade Area Negotiations*, Policy Memorandum No. 18 (Princeton, NJ: Center of International Studies, Princeton University).

Camps, M. (1959b), *The European Free Trade Association: A Preliminary Appraisal*, Political and Economic Planning, Occasional Papers, No. 4 (London: Political and Economic Planning).

Camps, M. (1964), *Britain and the European Community* (Princeton, NJ: Princeton University Press).

Camps, M. (1965), *What Kind of Europe? The Community since De Gaulle's Veto* (Oxford: Oxford University Press).

Camps, M. (1966), *European Unification in the Sixties: From the Veto to the Crisis* (New York: McGraw-Hill).

Carson, M. (2003), 'From Commodity to Public Health Concern: The Transformation of Food Policy in the European Union', Paper delivered at European Union Studies Association Conference, Nashville, 27–29 March 2003.

Charvet, J.-P. (2001), 'European Farming and World Markets', in Buller and Hoggart (eds.), *Agricultural Transformation*, Food and Environment: *Perspectives on European Rural Policy and Planning*, Vol. 1 (Aldershot: Ashgate), 9–28.

Cienciala, A. M. (1968), *Poland and the Western Powers 1938–1939* (London: Routledge & Kegan Paul).

Cini, M. (1996), *The European Commission: Leadership, Organization and Culture in the EU Administration* (Manchester: Manchester University Press).

Clout, H. (1984), *A Rural Policy for the EEC?* (London and New York: Methuen).

Comité Intergouvernemental créé par la conférence de Messine. Rapport des chefs de délegation aux ministres des Affairs etrangères (Spaak Report). Brussels, 21 April 1956.

Committee for the Study of Economic and Monetary Union (1989), *Report on Economic and Monetary Union in the European Community* (Luxembourg: Office for Official Publications of the European Communities).

Communauté Européennes (1969), *Le Plan Mansholt* (Brussels: Communauté Européennes).

Contogeorgis, G. (1978), 'The Greek View of the Community and Greece's Approach to Membership', in Wallace and Herreman (eds.), *A Community of Twelve? The Impact of Further Enlargement on the European Communities* (Bruges: De Tempel), 16–34.

Cophornic, G. (1994), 'SFIO et UEO: La recherche d'une unite', in Bossuat and Girault (eds.), *Europe Brisée, Europe Retrouvée* (Paris: Sorbonne), 263–88.

Council for European Union (2001), Economic and Finance Ministers, Brussels, 12 February 2001.

Coundehove-Kalergi, R. (1922), 'Paneuropa', *Neue Freie Presse*, 16 November.

Criddle, B. (1969), *Socialists and European Integration* (London: Routledge).

Curzon, V. (1979), *The Essentials of Economic Integration: Lessons from EFTA* (London: Macmillan).

Daddow, O. (2003) (ed.), *Harold Wilson and European Integration: Britain's Second Application to Join the EEC* (London: Frank Cass).

Daddow, O. (2004), *Britain and Europe since 1945: Historiographical Perspectives on Integration* (Manchester: Manchester University Press).

D'Appollonia, A. C. (2002), 'European Nationalism and European Union', in Pagden (ed.), *The Idea of Europe: From Antiquity to the European Union* (Cambridge: Cambridge University Press), 191–208.

De Gaulle, C. (1954), *Mémoires de guerre*, Vol. 1, *L'Appel, 1940–1942* (Paris: Plon).

De Gaulle, C. (1963), Press conference, 14 January, www.ena.lu/mce.cfm.

De Gaulle, C. (1967), Press conference, 17 May, www.ena.lu/mce.cfm.

De Gaulle, C. (1970), *Mémoires d'espoir* (Paris: Plon).

De Gaulle, C. (1970–1), *Discours et messages*, 5 vols. (Paris: Plon).

De Gaulle, C. (1985), *Lettres, notes et carnets*, Vol. 8, (Paris: Plon).

Deighton, A. (ed.) (1995), *Building Postwar Europe: National Decision-Makers and European Institutions, 1948–1963* (Basingstoke: Macmillan).

De la Gorce, P. M. (1979), *Apogée et Mort de la Quatrième République* (Paris: Grasset).

Dell, E. (1995), *The Schuman Plan and the British Abdication of Leadership in Europe* (Oxford: Clarendon Press).

Délorme, H., and Tavernier, Y. (1969), *Les paysans français et l'Europe* (Paris: Armand Colin).

Delwit, P. (1995), *Les partis socialistes et l'intégration européenne: France, Grande Bretagne, Belgique* (Brussels: Université de Bruxelles).

De Rougemont, D. (1961), *Vingt-huit siècles d'Europe* (Paris: Payot).

De Schoutheete de Tervarent, P. (1997), 'The Creation of the Common Foreign and Security Policy', in Regelsberger et al. (eds.), *Foreign Policy of the European Union: From EPC to CFSP and Beyond* (Boulder, CO: Lynne Rienner), 41–66.

Dickhaus, M. (1995) 'The Functioning of the European Payments Union', in Olesen (ed.), *Interdependence versus Integration: Denmark, Scandinavia and Western Europe 1945–1960* (Odense: Odense University Press), 82–95.

Dickhaus, M. (1997) 'It is only the provisional that lasts', in Griffiths (ed.), *Explorations in OEEC History* (Paris: OECD), 183–200.

Diebold, W. (1959), *The Schuman Plan: A Study in Economic Cooperation, 1950–1959* (New York: Praeger).

Diebold, W. (1988), 'A personal note', in Schwabe (ed.), *Die Anfärge des Schuman-Plans 1950–1951* (Brussels: Bruylant), 23–31.

Diebold, W. (1997) 'From the ITO to the GATT—and Back?', in Kirshner (ed.), *The Bretton Woods–GATT System: Retrospect and Prospect after Fifty Years* (New York: M.E. Sharpe), 152–80.

Dinan, D. (2004), *Europe Recast: A History of European Union* (London: Palgrave).

Document de Travail (1950), Jean Monnet Archives, Lausanne AMG 3/3/9, available at http://www.eu-history.leidenuniv.nl/ (section Historical Documents).

Duchêne, F. (1994), *Jean Monnet: First Statesman of Interdependence* (New York: W.W. Norton).

Dumke, R. H. (1991), 'Tariffs and Market Structures', in Lee (ed.), *Germany Industry and German Industrialization* (London: Routledge), 48–73.

Dunthorn, D. J. (2000), 'The Prieto–Gil Robles Meeting of October 1947: Britain and the Failure of the Spanish anti-Franco Coalition, 1945–50', *European History Quarterly*, 30/1: 49–75.

Dyson, K. (1994), *Elusive Union: The Process of Economic and Monetary Union in Europe* (London: Longman).

Dyson, K., and Featherstone, K. (1999), *The Road to Maastricht: Negotiating Economic and Monetary Union* (Oxford: Oxford University Press).

Dziemanowski, M. K. (1969), *Joseph Pilsudski: A European Federalist 1918–22* (Stanford, CA: Hoover Institution Press).

EC Bulletin (1972), 'The Enlarged Community: Outcome of the Negotiations with the Applicant States', *Bulletin of the European Economic Community*, January 1972, Supplement 1/1972. www.ena.lu/mce.cfm.

EC Bulletin (1985), 'Political Agreement on the Accession of Spain and Portugal (29 March 1985), *Bulletin of the European Economic Community*, March 1985. www.ena.lu/mce.cfm.

EC Bulletin (1994), 'Declaration by the Member States and Declaration by the Four Applicant Countries', *Bulletin of the European Communities*, March 1994.

Ehrmann, H. (1954), 'The French Trade Associations and the Ratification of the Schuman Plan', *World Politics*, 7/2: 453–81.

Ehrmann, H. (1957), *Organized Business in France* (Princeton, NJ: Princeton University Press).

Eichengreen, B. (1995), 'The European Payments Union', in Eichengreen, *Europe's Postwar Recovery* (Cambridge: Cambridge University Press), 169–98.

Eichengreen, B., and Wyplosz, C. (1993), 'The Unstable EMS', *Brookings Papers on Economic Activity*, 1: 51–144.

Eisenberg, C. (1996), *Drawing the Line: The American Decision to Divide Germany, 1944–1949* (Cambridge: Cambridge University Press).

Elgey, G. (1993), *Histoire de la Quatrième République*, 4 vols., 2nd edn. (Paris: Fayard).

Ellison, J. (2000), *Threatening Europe: Britain and the Creation of the European Community, 1955–1958* (Basingstoke: Macmillan).

Erdmann, K. D. (1982–90) (ed.), *Akten der Reichskanzlei: Weimarer Republik. Kabinette Brüning I und II*, Vol. 1 (Boppard am Rhein: Boldt).

Esposito, C. (1994), *America's Feeble Weapon: Funding the Marshall Plan in France and Italy, 1948–1950* (Westport, CT: Greenwood Press).

Eulenburg, F. (1926), 'Gegen die Idee einer europäischen Zollunion', in Heiman (ed.), *Europäische Zollunion* (Berlin: Reimar Hobbing).

European Commission (1977), *Twenty-Five Years of the Common Market in Coal: 1952–1977* (Brussels: Agriculture Information Service for the Directorate-General for Agriculture).

European Commission (1980a), 'Milk: Problem Child of European Agriculture', in *Green Europe* (Newsletter of the Common Agricultural Policy), No. 166 (Brussels: Agriculture Information Service of the Directorate-General for Agriculture).

European Commission (1980b), 'European Agriculture 1979', in *Green Europe* (Newsletter of the Common Agricultural Policy), No. 168 (Brussels: Agriculture Information Service of the Directorate-General for Agriculture).

European Commission (1984), 'Milk: The Quota System', in *Green Europe* (Newsletter of the Common Agricultural Policy), No. 203 (Brussels: Agriculture Information Service of the Directorate-General for Agriculture).

European Commission (1987), 'Twenty Years of European Agriculture', in *Green Europe* (Newsletter of the Common Agricultural Policy), No. 217 (Brussels: Agriculture Information Service of the Directorate-General for Agriculture).

European Commission (1991), *The Development and Future of the Common Agricultural Policy*. Document drawn up on the basis of COM(91)100 and COM(91)258. *Bulletin of the European Communities*, Supplement 91/5 (Luxembourg: Office for Official Publications of the European Communities).

European Commission (1994), *Rapport sur les résultats des négociations d'adhésion de l'Autriche, de la Suède, de la Finlande, et de la Norvège à l'Union européenne établi sous la responsabilité de la présidence du Conseil en coopération avec les services de la Commission* (Brussels: General Secretariat of the Council).

European Commission (1997), 'Agenda 2000: For a Stronger and Wider Union', *Bulletin of the European Union*, Supplement 5/97 (Luxembourg: Office for Official Publications of the European Communities).

European Commission (1998), *Report on Economic and Monetary Union*, IP/98/273, Brussels, 25 March 1998.

European Commission (2000), 'Euro Attitudes–Euro Zone', *Eurobarometer*, Brussels, May 2000.

European Commission (2002), 'Euro Attitudes–Euro Zone', *Eurobarometer*, Brussels, October 2002.

European Council (1988), European Council in Hanover, June 1988, Conclusions of the Presidency, SN 2683/88.

European Council (1990), European Council in Rome, October 1990, Conclusions of the Presidency, SN 304/90.

European Council (1993), European Council in Copenhagen, June 1993, Conclusions of the Presidency, SN 180/1/93, Part 7.

European Parliament (1989), 'Activities: Conclusions of the Presidency, European Council, Strasbourg, 8 and 9 December 1989', SN 441/2/89.

Fauri, F. (1997), 'Free but Protected? Italy and the Liberalisation of Foreign Trade in the 1950s', in Griffiths (ed.), *Explorations in OEEC History* (Paris: OECD), 139–48.

Fauvet, J. (1959), *La Quatrième République* (Paris: Fayard).

Fearne, A. (1991), 'The History and Development of the CAP 1945–1985', in Ritson and Harvey (eds.), *The Common Agricultural Policy and the World Economy: Essays in Honour of John Ashton* (Wallingford: CAB International), 6–33.

Fearon, J. (1991), 'Counterfactuals and Hypothesis Testing in Political Science', *World Politics*, 43: 169–95.

Fennell, R. (1997), *The Common Agricultural Policy: Continuity and Change* (Oxford and New York: Oxford University Press).

Ferrell, R. H. (1974), Review of Mowat, *Creating the European Community* (1973) in *American Historical Review*, 79/5: 1545.

Fischer, W. (1961), 'Der Deutsche Zollverein, die Europäische Wirtschaftsgemeinschaft und die Freihandelszone', *Europa Archiv*, 5: 105–14.

Fischler, F. (2003), 'Quality in Agriculture', speech delivered at the Informal Meeting of the EU Ministers for Agriculture, Corfu, 13 May 2003, available at http://europa.eu.int/rapid/pressReleasesAction.do?reference=SPEECH/03/238&format=HTML& aped=0&language=EN&guiLanguage=en

Först, W. (1979), 'Die Politik der Demontage', in Först, *Entscheidungen im Westen* (Cologne: Grote Verlag).

France, Foreign Ministry (1993), *Documents Diplomatiques Français, 1958*, Vol. 2 (Paris: Imprimerie Nationale).

France, Foreign Ministry (1995), *Documents Diplomatiques Français, 1960*, Vol. 1 (Paris: Imprimerie Nationale).

Freisberg, E. (1965), *Die Grüne Hürde Europas: Deutsche Agrarpolitik und EWG* (Cologne: Westdeutscher Verlag).

Freymond, J. (1974), *Le IIIe Reich at la réorganisation économique de l'Europe 1940–1942* (Leiden: Sijthoff).

FRUS (1993), *Foreign Relations of the United States, 1958–1960*, 7/58 (Washington, DC: Government Printing Office).

Gardner, R. N. (1997), 'The Bretton Woods–GATT System after Fifty Years: A Balance Sheet of Success and Failure', in Kirshner (ed.), *The Bretton Woods–GATT System: Retrospect and Prospect after Fifty Years* (New York: M.E. Sharpe), 181–209.

Garton Ash, T. (1993), *In Europe's Name* (New York: Random House).

Gati, C. (1990), *The Bloc that Failed: Soviet–East European Relations in Transition* (Bloomington: Indiana University Press).

Gehler, M. (2002), *Der lange Weg nach Europa: Österreich vom Ende der Monarchie bis zur EU*, Bd. 1, *Darstellung* (Innsbruck: Studien Verlag).

George, S. (1998), *An Awkward Partner: Britain in the European Community*, 3rd edn. (Oxford: Oxford University Press).

Gerbet, P. (1956), 'La genèse du Plan Schuman', *Revue Française de Science Politique*, 6/3: 525–53.

Gerbet, P. (1962), *La genèse du plan Schuman: des origines à la déclaration du 9 mai 1950* (Lausanne: Centre de recherches européennes).

Gerbet, P. (1994), *La construction de l'Europe* (Paris: Imprimerie Nationale).

Gerbet, P. (1999), *La construction de l'Europe*, 2nd edn. (Paris: Imprimerie Nationale).

Gernert, A. (1998), 'Nation-Buildung versus *Nationalbewegung*: Italien 1850–1914', in Timmermann (ed.), *Entwicklung der Nationalbewegungen in Europa 1850–1914* (Berlin: Duncker & Humblot).

Giauque, J. G. (2002), *Grand Designs and Visions of Unity: The Atlantic Powers and the Reorganization of Western Europe, 1955–1963* (Chapel Hill: University of North Carolina Press).

Giersch, H., Paqui, K., and Schmieding, H. (1994), *The Fading Miracle: Four Decades of Market Economy in Germany* (Cambridge: Cambridge University Press).

Gillingham, J. (1985), *Industry and Politics in the Third Reich: Ruhr Coal, Hitler and Europe* (London: Methuen).

Gillingham, J. (1987), 'Die franzoesische Ruhrpolitik und die Urspruenge des Schuman-Plans', *Vierteljahrshefte für Zeitgeschichte*, 35: 1–24.

Gillingham, J. (1991), *Coal, Steel, and the Rebirth of Europe, 1945–1955* (Cambridge: Cambridge University Press).

Gillingham, J. (1997), 'The Marshall Plan and the Origins of Neo-Liberal Europe', in Labohm (ed.), *Netherlands Journal of International Affairs* (special edition), October: 25–30.

Gillingham, J. (1998), 'Jean Monnet et le 'Victory Program' americain', in Bossuat and Wilkens (eds.), *Jean Monnet et les Chemins de la Paix* (Paris: Publications de la Sorbonne), 236–52.

Gillingham, J. (2000), 'Jean Monnet and the New Europe', in Schuker (ed.), *Deutschland und Frankreich vom Konflikt zur Aussöhnung* (Munich: Oldenbourg Verlag).

Gillingham, J. (2002), 'Background to Marshall Plan Technical Assistance: Productivity in American Ideology', in Barjot (ed.), *Catching up with America: Productivity Missions and the*

Diffusion of American Technological Culture after the Second World War (Paris: Presse de l'Université de Paris-Sorbonne).

Gillingham, J. (2003), *European Integration, 1950-2003: Superstate or New Market Economy?* (Cambridge: Cambridge University Press).

Godley, W. (1979), 'The United Kingdom and the Community Budget', in Griffiths (ed.), *The Economic Development of the EEC* (Cheltenham: Edward Elgar), 427-41.

Goldbach, M. L. (1991), *Dokumente zur Deutschlandpolitik*, Series 1: 4 (Frankfurt am Main: Alfred Metzner).

Goldschmidt, B. (1980), *Le complexe atomique: histoire politique de l'énergie nucléaire* (Paris: Fayard).

Görtemaker, M. (1994), *Unifying Germany, 1989-90* (New York: St. Martin's Press). 155.

Grant, C. (1994), *Delors: Inside the House that Jacques Built* (London: Nicholas Brealey).

Grant, W. (1997), *The Common Agricultural Policy* (Basingstoke: Macmillan).

Griffiths, R. T. (1988), 'The Schuman Plan Negotiations: The Economic Clauses', in Schwabe (ed.), *Die Anfänge des Schuman-Plans 1950-1951* (Brussels: Bruylant), 35-71.

Griffiths, R. T. (1990) (ed.), *The Netherlands and the Integration of Europe 1945-1957* (Amsterdam: NEHA).

Griffiths, R. T. (1994), 'Europe's First Constitution: The European Political Community, 1952-1954', in Martin (ed.), *The Construction of Europe: Essays in Honour of Emile Noël* (Dordrecht: Kluwer), 19-39.

Griffiths, R. T. (1995a), 'The National and International Ramifications of Post-war Reconstruction', in Olesen (ed.), *Interdependence versus Integration: Denmark, Scandinavia and Western Europe 1945-1960* (Odense: Odense University Press), 24-39.

Griffiths, R. T. (1995b), 'The European Integration Experience', in Middlemas (ed.), *Orchestrating Europe: The Informal Politics of the European Union 1973-95* (London: Fontana Press), 1-70.

Griffiths, R. T. (1997) (ed.), *Explorations in OEEC History* (Paris: OECD).

Griffiths, R. T. (2000), *Europe's First Constitution: The European Political Community, 1952-1954* (London: Federal Trust).

Griffiths, R. T. (2002), 'Waarom Kunnen wij het GLB niet hervormen?', in Asbeek Brusse (ed.), *De Toekomst van het Europese Gemeenschappelijk Landbouwbeleid* (Utrecht: Lemma), 49-62.

Griffiths, R. T., and Ward, S. (1996), 'The End of a Thousand Years of History: The Origins of Britain's Decision to Join the European Community, 1955-61', in Griffiths and Ward (eds.), *Courting the Common Market: The First Attempt to Enlarge the European Community* (London: Lothian Foundation Press), 1-37.

Gros, D., and Thygesen, N. (1998), *European Monetary Integration from the European Monetary System to Economic and Monetary Union*, 2nd edn. (Harlow: Addison-Wesley Longman).

Guirao, F. (1996), 'The United States, Franco and the Integration of Europe', in Heiler and Gillingham (eds.), *The United States and the Integration of Europe: Legacies of the Postwar Era* (New York: St. Martin's Press), 79-101.

Guirao, F. (1998), *Spain and the Reconstruction of Western Europe, 1945-57: Challenge and Response* (London: Macmillan).

Haas, E. (1958), *The Uniting of Europe: Economic and Social Forces 1950-1957* (Stanford, CA: Stanford University Press).

Hanrieder, W. (1989), *Germany, America, Europe* (New Haven, CT: Yale University Press).

Hanson, P. (1989), 'Trends and Policies in East-West Economic Relations: A View from the West', in Bertsch and Saunders (eds.), *East-West Economic Relations in the 1990s* (London: The Macmillan Press), 55-66.

Hantos, E. (1925), *Die Handelspolitik in Mitteleuropa* (Jena: Gustav Fischer).

Hay, D. (1957), *Europe: The Emergence of an Idea* (Edinburgh: Edinburgh University Press).

Hayek, F. (1948), 'The Economic Conditions of Interstate Federalism', in Hayek, *Individualism and Economic Order* (Chicago: University of Chicago), 255–72.

Heater, D. (1992), *The Idea of European Unity* (Leicester: Leicester University Press).

Heisenberg, D. (1999), *The Mark of the Bundesbank: Germany's Role in European Monetary Cooperation* (Boulder, CO: Lynne Rienner).

Heisenberg, D. (2003), 'Cutting the Bank Down to Size: Efficient and Legitimate Decision-making in the European Central Bank after Enlargement', *Journal of Common Market Studies*, 41/3, September: 397–420.

Henderson, W. O. (1939), *The Zollverein* (Cambridge: Cambridge University Press).

Hendriks, G. (1991), *Germany and European Integration: The Common Agricultural Policy–an Area of Conflict* (Oxford: Berg).

Herriot, E. (1930), *The United States of Europe* (London: Harrop).

Heusdens, J. J., and de Horn, R. (1980), 'Crisis Policy in the European Steel Industry in the Light of the ECSC Treaty', *Common Market Law Review*, 17/1: 31–74.

Hill, B. (2000), *Farm Incomes, Wealth and Agricultural Policy*, 3rd edn. (Aldershot: Ashgate).

Hill, B. E. (1984), *The Common Agricultural Policy: Past, Present and Future* (London and New York: Methuen).

Hill, C. (1997), 'The Actors Involved: National Perspectives', in Regelsberger et al. (eds.), *Foreign Policy of the European Union: From EPC to CFSP and Beyond* (Boulder, CO: Lynne Rienner), 85–97.

Hillary, P. (1993), 'Ireland's Accession Negotiations and European Community Entry', unpublished paper presented at the Chatham House conference, Previous Enlargement Negotiations, 29 March.

Hirschman, A. O. (1970), *Exit, Voice and Loyalty: Responses to Decline in Firms, Organizations and States* (Cambridge, MA: Harvard University Press).

Hitchcock, W. (1998), *France Restored: Cold War Diplomacy and the Quest for Leadership in Europe, 1944–1954* (Chapel Hill: University of North Carolina Press).

Hix, S. (1999), *The Political System of the European Union* (London: Macmillan).

Hobsbawm, E. (1990), *Nations and Nationalism since 1780* (Cambridge: Cambridge University Press).

Hoffmann, S. (1966), 'Obstinate or Obsolete? The Fate of the Nation-State and the Case of Western Europe', *Daedelus*, 95/3: 862–915.

Hoffmeyer, B. (1982), 'The EEC's Common Agricultural Policy and the ACP States', Centre for Development Research, CDR Research Report No. 2, Copenhagen.

Hogan, M. (1987), *The Marshall Plan: America, Britain, and the Reconstruction of Europe, 1947–1952* (Cambridge: Cambridge University Press).

Hogan, M. (1998), *A Cross of Iron: Harry S. Truman and the Origins of the National Security State, 1945–1954* (Cambridge: Cambridge University Press).

Holmes, P., and Kempton, J. (1999), 'The EU in the Global Economy', in Dyker (ed.), *The European Economy* (New York: Addison-Wesley Longman).

Ioakiminidis, P. C. (1993), 'Widening versus Deepening the European Community: The Lessons from the Past with Reference to the Greek Case', unpublished paper presented at the Chatham House conference, Previous Enlargement Negotiations, 29 March.

Irving, R. E. M. (1973), *Christian Democracy in France* (London: George Allen & Unwin).

Jacobsen, H.-D. (1990), 'West Germany's Economic Relations with the East: Political Goals and Economic Possibilities', in Baldwin and Milner (eds.), *East–West Trade and the Atlantic Alliance* (New York: St. Martin's Press), 99–117.

Jarausch, K. (1994), *The Rush to German Unity* (Oxford: Oxford University Press), 23.

Jenkins, R. (1989), *European Diary 1977–1981* (London: Collins).

Jones, E., Frieden, J., and Torres, F. (1998), *EMU and the Smaller Countries: Joining Europe's Monetary Club* (New York: St. Martin's Press).

Jouve, E. (1967a), *Le Général de Gaulle et la Construction de l'Europe (1940–1966)*, Vol. 1 (Paris: Librairie générale de droit et de jurisprudence).

Jouve, E. (1967b), *Le Général de Gaulle et la Construction de l'Europe (1940–1966)*, Vol. 2 (Paris: Librairie générale de droit et de jurisprudence).

Kaiser, W. (1999), *Using Europe, Abusing the Europeans: Britain and European Integration, 1945–1963*, 2nd edn. (Basingstoke: Macmillan).

Kaplan, J., and Schleiminger, G. (1989), *The European Payments Union: Financial Diplomacy in the 1950s* (Oxford: Clarendon Press).

Kaplan, L. A. (1988), *The United States and NATO: The Enduring Alliance* (New York: Pergamon Press).

Keeler, J. (1996), 'Agricultural Power in the European Community: Explaining the Fate of CAP and GATT Negotiations', *Comparative Politics*, 28/2: 127–49.

Kersten, A. (1988), 'A Welcome Surprise? The Netherlands and the Schuman Plan Negotiations', in Schwabe (ed.), *Die Anfänge des Schuman-Plans 1950–1951* (Brussels: Bruylant), 284–304.

Keynes, J. M. (1940), *How to Pay for the War: A Radical Plan for the Chancellor of the Exchequer* (London: Macmillan).

Kiesewetter, H. (1987), 'Economic Preconditions for Germany's Nation-Building in the Nineteenth Century', in Schulze (ed.), *Nation-Building in Central Europe* (Leamington Spa: Berg), 81–105.

Killick, J. (1997), *The United States and European Reconstruction, 1945–1960* (Edinburgh: Edinburgh University Press).

Kirshner, O. (1997) (ed.), *The Bretton Woods–GATT System: Retrospect and Prospect after Fifty Years* (New York: M.E. Sharpe).

Kitzinger, U. (1973), *Diplomacy and Persuasion: How Britain Joined the Common Market* (London: Thames and Hudson).

Klein, F. (1998), 'Between Compiègne and Versailles: The Germans on the Way from a Misunderstood Defeat to an Unwanted Peace', in Boemke, Feldman, and Glaser (eds.), *The Treaty of Versailles* (Cambridge, Cambridge University Press), 130–50.

Knudsen, A.-C. (2001a), 'Creating the Common Agricultural Policy: The Story of Cereals Prices', in Loth (ed.), *Crises and Compromises: The European Project 1963–1969* (Baden-Baden: Nomos Verlag), 131–54.

Knudsen, A.-C. (2001b), *Defining the Policies of the Common Agricultural Policy: A Historical Study* (Florence: European University Institute).

Koester, U., and Bale, M. (1984), *The Common Agricultural Policy of the European Community: A Blessing of a Curse for Developing Countries?*, World Bank Staff Working Papers, No. 630 (Washington, DC: The International Bank for Reconstruction and Development).

Koskenniemi, M. (2002), *The Gentle Civilizer of Nations: The Rise and Fall of International Law 1870–1960* (Cambridge: Cambridge University Press).

Krajcovic, M. (1999), 'Internationale und aussenpolitische Zusammenhänge der slowakischen Nationalbewegung 1914–1945', in Timmermann (ed.), *Nationalismus und Nationalbewegung in Europa 1919–1945* (Berlin: Duncker & Humblot), 83–98.

Kramer, A. (1990), *The West German Economy* (Oxford: Berg).

Kramer, H. (1993), 'The European Community's Response to the New Eastern Europe', *Journal of Common Market Studies*, 31/2: 213–44.

Küsters, H. J. (1982) (ed.), *Die Gründung der europäischen Wirtschaftsgemeinschaft* (Baden-Baden: Nomos Verlag).

Küsters, H. J. (1986), *Les fondements de la Communauté économique européenne* (Brussels: European Communities).

Küsters, H. J. (1988), 'Die Verhandlungen über das institutionelle System zur Gründung der Europäischen Gemeinschaft für Kohle und Stahl', in Schwabe (ed.), *Die Anfänge des Schuman-Plans 1950–1951* (Brussels: Bruylant), 73–102.

Küsters, H. J. (1995), 'West Germany's Foreign Policy in Western Europe, 1949–58: The Art of the Possible', in Wurms (ed.), *Western Europe and Germany: The Beginnings of European Integration, 1945–1960* (Oxford: Berg), 55–86.

Lacouture, J. (1998), *Mitterrand: Une histoire de Français* (Paris: Editions du Seuil).

Laffan, B. (1997), *The Finances of the European Union* (Basingstoke: Macmillan).

Lagerfeld, S. (1990), 'Europhoria', *Wilson Quarterly*, 14: 57–67.

Langewiesche, D. (2000), *Nation, Nationalismus, Nationalstaat in Deutschland und Europa* (Munich: Beck).

Lapie, P. (1971), *De Léon Blum à De Gaulle* (Paris: Fayard).

Large, D. C. (1996), *Germans to the Front: West German Rearmament in the Adenauer Era* (Chapel Hill: University of North Carolina Press).

Laurent, P.-H. (1990), 'Reality not Rhetoric: Belgian–Dutch Diplomacy in Wartime London, 1940–44', in Smith and Stirk (eds.), *Making the New Europe* (London: Pinter), 168–86.

Lee, S. (1995), 'German Decision-Making Elites and European Integration: German 'Europapolitik' during the Years of the EEC and Free Trade Area Negotiations', in Deighton (ed.), *Building Postwar Europe: National Decision-Makers and European Institutions, 1948–1963* (Basingstoke: Macmillan), 38–54.

Lee, S. (2001), *Victory in Europe: Britain and Germany since 1945* (London: Longman).

Lefebvre, D. (1992), *Guy Mollet, le mal aimé* (Paris: Plon).

Leffler, M. P. (1992), *A Preponderance of Power: National Security, the Truman Administration and the Cold War* (Stanford, CA: Stanford University Press).

Lieshout, R. H., Segers, M. L. L., and van der Vleuten, A. M. (2004), 'De Gaulle, Moravcsik, and the Choice for Europe: Soft Sources, Weak Evidence', *Journal of Cold War Studies*, 6/4 (Fall): 89–139.

Light, M., Loewenhardt, J., and White, S. (2000), 'Russia and the Dual Expansion of Europe', ESRC 'One Europe or Several?' Policy Paper 02/2000: 1.

Lindberg, L. N. (1963), *The Politics of European Economic Integration* (Stanford, CA: Stanford University Press).

Lindberg, L. N., and Scheingold, S. (1970), *Europe's Would-Be Polity* (Englewood Cliffs, NJ: Prentice-Hall).

Lingard, J., and Hubbard, L. (1991), 'The CAP and Its Effects on Developing Countries', in Ritson and Harvey (eds.), *The Common Agricultural Policy and the World Economy: Essays in Honour of John Ashton* (Wallingford: CAB International), 241–57.

Lipgens, W. (ed.) (1985), *Documents on the History of European Integration*, Vol. 1 (Baden-Baden: Nomos Verlag).

Lipgens, W. (ed.) (1986), *Documents on the History of European Integration*, Vol. 2 (Baden-Baden: Nomos Verlag).

Lipgens, W., and Loth, W. (1988) (eds.), *Documents on the History of European Integration*, Vol. 3 (Berlin: De Gruytes).

Lister, L. (1960), *Europe's Coal and Steel Community* (New York: Twentieth Century Fund).

Lister, M. (1988), *The European Community and the Developing World: The Role of the Lomé Convention* (Aldershot: Avebury).

Loedel, P. (1999), *Deutsche Mark Politics: Germany in the European Monetary System* (Boulder, CO: Lynne Rienner).

Loth, W. (1996), *Der Weg nach Europa: Geschichte der europäischen Integration 1939–1957*, 3rd edn. (Göttingen: Vandenhoeck & Ruprecht).

Loth, W. (2001) (ed.), *Crises and Compromises: The European Project 1963–1969* (Baden-Baden: Nomos Verlag).

Ludlow, N. P. (1997), *Dealing with Britain: The Six and the First UK Membership Application* (Cambridge: Cambridge University Press).

Ludlow, N. P. (2006), *The European Community and the Crises of the 1960s: Negotiating the Gaullist Challenge* (London: Routledge).

Ludlow, P. (1982), *The Making of the European Monetary System: A Case Study of the Politics of the European Community* (London: Butterworth).

Ludlow, P. (2003), 'An Opportunity or a Threat? The European Commission and the Hague Council of December 1969,' *Journal of European Integration History*, 9/2: 11–25.

Lundestad, G. (1998), *'Empire' by Integration: The United States and European Integration, 1945–1997* (Oxford: Oxford University Press).

Lynch, F. (1993), 'Restoring France: The Road to Integration', in Milward et al., *The Frontier of National Sovereignty: History and Theory, 1945–1992* (London: Routledge), 58–87.

Lynch, F. (1997), *France and the International Economy: From Vichy to the Treaties of Rome* (New York: Routledge).

Mack Smith, D. (1996), 'Documentary Falsification and Italian Biography', in Blanning and Carradino (eds.), *History and Biography* (Cambridge: Cambridge University Press).

Mahant, E. (1969), 'French and German Attitudes to the Negotiations about the European Economic Community, 1955–1957', Unpublished dissertation, London University.

Marjolin, R. (1986), *Le travail d'une vie: mémoires, 1911–1986* (Paris: R. Laffont).

Marjolin, R. (1989), *Architect of European Unity: Memoirs, 1911–1986* (London: Weidenfeld & Nicolson).

Markovits, A., and Gorski, P. (1993), *The German Left: Red, Green, and Beyond* (Oxford: Oxford University Press).

Marks, S. (1985), Review of Milward *The Reconstruction of Western Europe, 1945–1951* (1984), *The American Historical Review*, 90/2: 408.

Marquina Barrio, A. (1986), *España en la politica de Seguridad Occidental* (Madrid: Ediciones Ejercito).

Marsh, D. (1992), *The Bundesbank: The Bank that Rules Europe* (London: Heinemann).

Marsh, P. (1978), 'The Development of Relations between the EEC and the CMEA', in Shlaim and Yannopoulos (eds.), *The EEC and Eastern Europe* (Cambridge: Cambridge University Press), 25–69.

Marsh, P. (1999), *Bargaining on Europe: Britain and the First Common Market, 1860–1893* (New Haven, CT: Yale University Press).

Martin, J. S. (1950), *All Honorable Men* (Boston: Alyson Publications).

Massigli, R. (1978), *Une comédie des erreurs* (Paris: Plon).

Mastny, V. (1996), *The Cold War and Soviet Insecurity: The Stalin Years* (Oxford: Oxford University Press).

Mayer, H. (1977), 'Early at the Beach and Claiming Territory? The Evolution of German Ideas on a New European Order', *International Affairs*, 73: 721–37.

Mayne, R. (1962), *The Community of Europe: Past, Present and Future* (New York: W.W. Norton).

McElligott, A. (1994), 'Reforging *Mitteleuropa* in the Crucible of War', in Stirk (ed.), *Mitteleuropa: History and Prospects* (Edinburgh: Edinburgh University Press), 129–59.

McNamara, K. (1988), *The Currency of Ideas* (Ithaca, NY: Cornell University Press).

Meade, J. E., Liesner, H. H., and Wells, S. J. (1962), *Case Studies in European Economic Integration* (Oxford: Oxford University Press).

Mee, C. (1975), *Meeting at Potsdam* (New York: Penguin Books).

Michalski, A. (1995), A Reluctant Partner: The Pattern of Denmark's Involvement in the European Community, unpublished Ph D thesis, London School of Economics.

Michalski, A., and Wallace, H. (1992), *The European Community: The Challenge of Enlargement* (London: Royal Institute for International Affairs).

Michelmann, H. J., Rude, J., Stabler, J., and Stoney, G. (eds.) (2001), *Globalization and Agricultural Trade Policy* (Boulder, CO: Lynne Rienner).

Milward, A. (1984), *The Reconstruction of Western Europe, 1945–1951* (London: Methuen; paperback edn., 1986).

Milward, A. (1988), 'The Belgian Coal and Steel Industries and the Schuman Plan', in Schwabe (ed.), *Die Anfänge des Schuman-Plans 1950–1951* (Brussels: Bruylant), 437–54.

Milward, A. (1992), *The European Rescue of the Nation State* (London: Routledge; paperback edn., 2000).

Milward, A. (2000), *The European Rescue of the Nation State*, 2nd ed. (London: Routledge).

Milward, A. (2002), *The Rise and Fall of a National Strategy 1945–1963: The UK and the European Community*, Vol. 1 (London: Frank Cass).

Milward, A., and Brennan, G. (1996), *Britain's Place in the World: A Historical Enquiry into Import Controls 1945–60* (London: Routledge).

Milward, A., Lynch, F., Romero, F., Ranieri, R., and Sørensen, V. (1993), *The Frontier of National Sovereignty: History and Theory, 1945–1992* (London: Routledge).

Mitchell, B. R. (1992), *International Historical Statistics, Europe 1750–1988* (New York: Stockton Press).

Monnet, J. (1943), Note de Réflexion. Address to the National Liberation Committee, 5 August 1943, Algiérs. Available at http://www.eu-history.leidenuniv.nl/ (section historical documents).

Monnet, J. (1976), *Mémoires* (Paris: Feyard).

Monnet, J. (1978), *Memoirs* (New York: Doubleday).

Moravcsik, A. (1991), 'Negotiating the Single European Act: National Interests and Conventional Statecraft in the European Community', *International Organization*, 45/1: 651–88.

Moravcsik, A. (1998), *The Choice for Europe: Social Purpose and State Power from Messina to Maastricht* (Ithaca, NY: Cornell University Press).

Moravcsik, A. (2000a), 'De Gaulle between Grain and Grandeur: The Political Economy of French EC Policy, 1958–1970 (Part 1)', *Journal of Cold War Studies*, 2/2: 3–43.

Moravcsik, A. (2000b), 'De Gaulle between Grain and Grandeur: The Political Economy of French EC Policy, 1958–1970 (Part 2)', *Journal of Cold War Studies*, 2/3: 4–68.

Moravcsik, A. (2000c), 'Beyond Grain and Grandeur: An Answer to Critics and an Agenda for Future Research', *Journal of Cold War Studies*, 2/3: 117–42.

Mowat, R. C. (1973), *Creating the European Community* (New York: Barnes and Noble).

Mowat, R. C. (2002), *An Oxford Family Remembers* (Oxford: New Cherwell Press).

Nation, R. C. (1992), *Black Earth, Red Star: A History of Soviet Security Policy, 1917–1991* (Ithaca, NY: Cornell University Press).

Naumann, F. (1915), *Mitteleuropa* (Berlin: Reimer).

Neitzel, S. (2000), *Weltmacht oder Untergang: Die Weltreichslehre im Zeitalter des Imperialismus* (Paderborn: Schöningh).

Nello, S. S. (1991), *The New Europe: Changing Economic Relations between East and West* (Brighton: Harvester/Wheatsheaf).

Neville-Rolfe, E. (1984), *The Politics of Agriculture in the European Community* (London: European Centre for Policy Studies).

Neyer, J. (2000) 'The Regulation of Risks and the Power of the People: Lessons from the BSE Crisis', *European Integration Online Papers (EioP)*, 4/6. http://eiop.or.at/eiop/pdf/2000-006.pdf

Noël, G. (1988), *Du pool vert à la politique agricole commune: Les Tentatives de Communauté agricole européenne entre 1945 et 1955* (Paris: Economica).

Nugent, N. (1992), 'The Deepening and Widening of the European Community: Recent Evolution, Maastricht, and Beyond', *Journal of Common Market Studies*, 30: 311–28.

Nuttall, S. (1997), 'Two Decades of EPC Performance', in Regelsberger et al. (eds.), *Foreign Policy of the European Union: From EPC to CFSP and Beyond* (Boulder, CO: Lynne Rienner), 67–84.

OECD (1964), *Low Incomes in Agriculture: Problems and Policies* (Paris: Organization for Economic Cooperation and Development).

OECD (1965), *Agriculture and Economic Growth* (Paris: Organization for Economic Cooperation and Development).

OECD (2001), *Multifunctionality: Towards an Analytical Framework* (Paris: Organization for Economic Cooperation and Development).

OECD (2003a), *Farm Household Incomes in OECD Countries* (Paris: Organization for Economic Cooperation and Development).

OECD (2003b), *Agricultural Policies in OECD Countries: A Positive Reform Agenda* (Paris: Organization for Economic Cooperation and Development).

O'Neill, F. (1981), *The French Radical Party and European Integration* (London: Gower).

Oppenheimer, P. (1974), 'Monetary Union: A Survey of the Main Issues', *The Economist*, 122: 23–48.

Padoa-Schioppa, T. (1987), *Efficiency, Stability and Equity: A Strategy for the Evolution of the Economic System of the European Community* (Oxford: Oxford University Press).

Padoa-Schioppa, T. (1994), *The Road to Monetary Union in Europe: The Emperor, the Kings, and the Genies* (Oxford: Oxford University Press).

Pagden, A. (1995), *Lords of all the World: Ideologies of Empire in Spain, Britain and France c.1500–c.1800* (New Haven, CT: Yale University Press).

Parsons, C. (2003), *A Certain Idea of Europe* (Ithaca, NY: Cornell University Press).

Patterson, L. A. (1997), 'Agricultural Policy Reform in the European Community: A Three-Level Game Analysis', *International Organization*, 51/1: 135–65.

Pearce, J. (1981), *The Common Agricultural Policy: Prospects for Change* (London: Routledge & Kegan Paul)

Pearson, R. (1983), *National Minorities in Eastern Europe 1848–1945* (Basingstoke: Macmillan).

Pegg, C. H. (1983), *Evolution of the European Idea 1914–1932* (Chapel Hill: University of North Carolina Press).

Pelkmans, J. M. (1997), *European Integration: Methods and Economic Analysis* (Harlow: Longman).

Peterson, M. (1979), *International Interest Organizations and the Transmutation of Postwar Society* (Stockholm: Almqvist & Wiksell International).

Peyrefitte, A. (1994), *C'était de Gaulle*, Vol. 1 (Paris: Fayard).

Peyrefitte, A. (1997), *C'était de Gaulle*, Vol. 2 (Paris: Fayard).

Peyrefitte, A. (2000), *C'était de Gaulle*, Vol. 3 (Paris: Fayard).

Phlips, L. (1983), *The Economics of Price Discrimination* (Cambridge: Cambridge University Press).

Pinder, D. (1983), *Regional Economic Development and Policy: Theory and Practice in the European Community* (London: Allen & Unwin).

Pitman, P. (1998), 'France's European Choices', unpublished dissertation, Columbia University, New York.

Poidevin, R. (1984), 'René Mayer et la politique extérieure de la France, 1943–1953', *Revue d'histoire de la deuxième guerre mondiale et des conflits contemporains*, 34/134: 73–97.

Poidevin, R. (1986) (ed.), *Histoire des débuts de la construction européenne (mars 1948–mai 1950)* (Brussels: Bruylant).

Poidevin, R. (1988), 'Le rôle personnel de Robert Schuman dans les négociations CECA (juin 1950–avril 1951)', in Schwabe (ed.), *Die Anfänge des Schuman-Plans 1950–1951* (Brussels: Bruylant), 105–16.

Pomian, J. (1972), *Joseph Retinger: Memoir of an Eminence Grise* (Brighton: Sussex University Press).

Pompidou, G. (1969), Statement given by George Pompidou to the ORTF, The Hague, 2 December 1969, www.ena.lu/mce.cfm.

Pond, E. (1993), *Beyond the Wall: Germany's Road to Unification* (Washington, DC: The Brookings Institution).

Prate, A. (1995), *La France en Europe* (Paris: Economica).

Price, H. B. (1955), *The Marshall Plan and its Meaning* (Ithaca, NY: Cornell University Press).

Ranieri, R. (1988), 'The Italian Steel Industry and the Schuman Plan Negotiations', in Schwabe (ed.), *Die Anfänge des Schuman-Plans 1950–1951* (Brussels: Bruylant), 345–56.

Rayner, A. J., Ingersent, K. A., and Hine, R. C. (1993), 'Agriculture in the Uruguay Round: An Assessment', *The Economic Journal*, 103: 1513–27.

Reisman, S. (1997), 'The Birth of a World Trading System: ITO and GATT', in Kirshner (ed.), *The Bretton Woods–GATT System: Retrospect and Prospect after Fifty Years* (New York: M.E. Sharpe), 82–6.

Renouvin, P. (1949), *L'idée de fédération européene dans le pensée politique du XIXe siècle* (Oxford: Clarendon Press).

Reynolds, D. (1997), 'The European Response: Primacy of Politics', *Foreign Affairs*, May/June, 76/3: 171–84.

Rieger, E. (2000), 'The Common Agricultural Policy: Politics Against Markets', in Wallace and Wallace (eds.), *Policy Making in the European Union*, 4th edn. (Oxford: Oxford University Press), 179–210.

Rioux, J. (1984), *La Quatrième République* (Paris: Seuil).

Roll, E. (1965), Review of Camps, *Britain and the European Community* (1964), *The Economic Journal*, March: 132–4.

Röpke, W. (1942), *International Economic Disintegration* (London: William Hodge).

Röpke, W. (1946), *The Solution of the German Problem* (New York: G. P. Putnam's Sons).

Ross, G. (1995), *Jacques Delors and European Integration* (Cambridge: Polity Press).

Royo, S. (2004), 'Portugal and Spain in the European Union after 17 Years: Iberian Lessons for Post-Community Europe', paper presented at the conference 'Europe and the World: Integration, Interdependence, Exceptionalism?', 12–14 March, Chicago.

Rueff, J. (1959), 'Zur Wirtschaftsreform in Frankreich: Bericht zur Finanzlage... 30. September 1958', *ORDO*, 11: 3–67.

Ruge, S., and Schumann, S. (1972), 'Die Reaktion des deutschen Imperialismus auf Briands Paneuropaplan 1930', *Zeitschrift für Geschichtswissenschaft*, 20: 40–70.

Ruggie, J. G. (1998), 'What Makes the World Hang Together? Neo-Utilitarianism and the Social Constructivist Challenge', *International Organization*, 52/4: 855–85.

Ryan, H. B. (1987), *The Vision of Anglo-America* (Cambridge: Cambridge University Press).

Sandholtz, W. (1993), 'Choosing Union: Monetary Politics and Maastricht', *International Organization*, 47: 1–39.

Sandholtz, W., and Stone Sweet, A. (eds.) (1998), *European Integration and Supranational Governance* (New York: Oxford University Press).

Sandholtz, W., and Zysman, J. (1989), '1992: Recasting the European Bargain', *World Politics*, 42/1: 95–128.

Scheinman, L. (1965), *Atomic Energy Policy in France under the Fourth Republic* (Princeton, NJ: Princeton University Press).

Schenk, C. (1994), *Britain and the Sterling Area: From Devaluation to Convertibility in the 1950s* (London: Routledge).

Schmidt, H. A. (1962), *The Path to European Union: From the Marshall Plan to the Common Market* (Baton Rouge: Louisiana State University Press).

Schmitt, C. (1940), *Positionen und Begriffe im Kampf mit Weimar-Genf-Versailles 1923–1939* (Hamburg: Hanseatische Verlagsanstalt).

Schmoller, G. (1916), 'Die Handels- und Zollannäherung Mitteleuropa', *Jahrbuch für die Gesetzgebung, Verwaltung und Volkswirtschaft in dem Deutschen Reich*, 40: 529–50.

Schuman, R. (1963), *Pour l'Europe* (Paris: Nagel).

Schwabe, K. (1988a) (ed.), *Die Anfänge des Schuman-Plans 1950–1951* (Brussels: Bruylant).

Schwabe, K. (1988b) (ed.), *Beitrage des Kolloquiums in Achen. May 1986* (Baden-Baden: Nomos Verlag).

Schwabe, K. (2001), 'The Cold War and European Integration, 1947–63', *Diplomacy and Statecraft*, 12/4: 18–34.

Schwartz, T. (1985), From Occupation to Alliance: John J. McCloy and the Allied High Commission in the Federal Republic of Germany, unpublished dissertation, Harvard University, Cambridge, MA.

Schwarz, H.-P. (1979), 'Adenauer und Europa', *Vierteljahrshefte fuer Zeitgeschichte*, 27: 471–523.

Schwarz, H.-P. (1980), *Vom Reich zur Bundesrepublik: Deutschland Im Wiederstreit der aussenpolitischen Konzeptionen in den Jahren der Besatzungsherrschaft 1945–1949* (Stuttgart: Neuwied).

Schwarz, H.-P. (1986), *Adenauer: Der Aufstieg 1876–1952* (Stuttgart: Deutsche Verlags-Anstalt).

Schwarz, H.-P. (1995), *Konrad Adenauer: A German Politician and Statesman in a Period of War, Revolution and Reconstruction*. Vol. 1: From the German Empire to the Federal Republic 1876–1952 (Providence, RI: Berghahn Books).

Searle, J. (1995), *The Construction of Social Reality* (New York: Free Press).

Seeley, J. R. (1871), 'United States of Europe', *Macmillan's Magazine*, 23: 436–48.

Seeley, J. R. (1897), *The Expansion of England* (London: Macmillan).

Self, P., and Storing H. (1962), *The State and the Farmer* (London: George Allen & Unwin).

Serra, E. (1989) (ed.), *Il Rilancio dell'Europa e i Trattati di Roma* (Brussels: Bruylant).

Sheingate, A. (2001), *The Rise of the Agricultural Welfare State: Institutions and Interest Group Power in the United States, France, and Japan* (Princeton, NJ: Princeton University Press).

Sidjanski, D. (2000), *The Federal Future of Europe: From the European Community to the European Union* (Ann Arbor: University of Michigan Press).

Siebert, F. (1973), *Aristide Briand 1862–1932* (Zurich: Eugen Rentsch).

Simonian, H. (1985), *The Privileged Partnership: Franco–German Relations in the European Community: 1969–1984* (Oxford: Clarendon Press).

Sobell, V. (1990), *The CMEA in Crisis: Toward a New European Order?* (New York: Praeger).

Sohl, H.-G. (1983), *Notizen* (Bochum-Wattenscheid: Hans-Günther Sohl).

Soutou, G. (1991), 'Georges Bidault et la construction européenne, 1944–1954', *Revue d'histoire diplomatique*, 105: 3–4.

Soutou, G. (1996), *L'alliance incertaine: les rapports politico-stratégiques franco–allemands, 1954–1996* (Paris: Fayard).

Soutou, G. (2001), 'France and the Cold War, 1944–63', *Diplomacy and Statecraft*, 12/4: 35–52.

Spierenburg, D., and Poidevin, R. (1994), *The History of the High Authority of the European Coal and Steel Community: Supranationality in Operation* (London: Weidenfeld and Nicolson).

Spinelli, A., and Rossi, E. (1988), *The Ventotene Manifesto* (London: Federal Trust).

Stambrook, F. G. (1963–4), 'A British Proposal for the Danubian States: The Customs Union Project of 1932', *Slavonic and East European Review*, 42: 64–88.

Stirk, P. M. R. (1996), *A History of European Integration since 1914* (London: Pinter).

Stirk, P. M. R. (1999), 'Carl Schmitt's Völkerrechtliche Grossraumordnung', *History of Political Thought*, 20/2: 357–74.

Stirk, P. M. R., and Weigall, D. (1999) (eds.), *The Origins and Development of European Integration* (London: Pinter).

Story, J. (1988), 'The Launching of the EMS: An Analysis of Change in Foreign Economic Policy', *Political Studies*, 36: 390–420.

Strikwerda, C. (1993), 'The Troubled Origins of European Economic Integration: International Iron and Steel and Labor Migration in the Era of World War I', *American Historical Review*, 98: 1106–29.

Swinbank, A. (1978), *The British Interest and the Green Pound* (Reading: Center for Agricultural Strategy, University of Reading).

Swann, D. (1988), *The Economics of the Common Market*, 6th edn. (Harmondsworth: Penguin Books).

Szokolóczy-Syllaba, J. (1965), *Les organisations professionnelles françaises et le marché commun* (Paris: Armand Colin).

Tangermann, S. (1998), 'An Ex-Post Review of the 1992 MacSharry Reform', in Ingersent, Rayner, and Hine (eds.), *The Reform of the Common Agricultural Policy* (London: Macmillan), 12–53.

Thatcher, M. (1993), *The Downing Street Years* (London: HarperCollins).

Thiemeyer, G. (1999), *Vom 'Pool Vert' zur Europäischen Wirtschaftsgemeinschaft: Europäische Integration, Kalter Krieg und die Anfänge der Gemeinsamen Europäischen Agrarpolitik 1950–1957* (Munich: Oldenbourg).

Thody, P. (1997), *An Historical Introduction to the European Union* (London: Routledge).

Timmermann, H. (1990), 'The Soviet Union and Western Europe: Conceptual Change and Political Reorientation', in Harle and Iivonen (eds.), *Gorbachev and Europe* (New York: St. Martin's Press), 103–29.

Trachtenberg, M. (1999), *A Constructed Peace: The Making of the European Settlement 1945–1963* (Princeton, NJ: Princeton University Press).

Tracy, M. (1989), *Government and Agriculture in Western Europe*, 3rd edn. (New York: New York University Press).

Triepel, H. (1899), *Völkerrecht und Landesrecht* (Leipzig: C.L. Hirschfeld).

Tsoukalis, L. (1977), *The Politics and Economics of European Monetary Integration* (London: Allen and Unwin).

Ungerer, H. (1997), *A Concise History of European Monetary Integration: From EPU to EMU* (Westport, CT: Quorum Books).

Vanke, J. (2001a), 'De Gaulle's Atomic Defense Policy in 1963', *Journal of Cold War History*, 1/2: 119–26.

Vanke, J. (2001b), 'An Impossible Union: Dutch Objections to the Fouchet Plan, 1959–1962', *Journal of Cold War History*, 2/1: 95–112.

Van Schendelen, M. P. C. M. (1996), ' "The Council Decides": Does the Council Decide?', *Journal of Common Market Studies*, 34/4: 531–48.

Ventresca, R. (2004), *From Fascism to Democracy: Culture and Politics in the Italian Election of 1948* (Toronto: University of Toronto Press).

Vernon, R. (1997) 'The U.S. Government at Bretton Woods and After', in Kirshner (ed.), *The Bretten Woods–GATT System: Retrospect and Prospect after Fifty Years* (New York: M.E. Sharpe), 52–69.

Voth, H. J. (2001), 'The Prussian *Zollverein* and the Bid for Economic Superiority', in Dwyer (ed.), *Modern Prussian History 1830–1947* (Harlow: Pearson), 168–88.

Voyenne, B. (1954), *Petite histoire de l'ideé europeéne*, 2nd edn. (Paris: Campagne Européenne de la Jennesse).

Wallander, C. (2003), 'Western Policy and the Demise of the Soviet Union', *Journal of Cold War Studies*, 5: 137–77.

Warner, G. (1999), 'Jugoslawischer Nationalismus zwischen den Weltkriegen', in Timmermann (ed.), *Nationalismus und Nationalbewegung in Europa 1919–1945* (Berlin: Duncker & Humblot), 282–300.

Watt, D. C. (1990), Review of Lipgens (ed.), *Documents on the History of European Integration*, Vol. 1 (1985) in *International Affairs*, 66/2: 392–3.

Weiler, J. H. H. (1981), 'The Community System: The Dual Character of Supranationalism', *The Yearbook of European Law*, 1: 267–306.

Weiler, J. H. H. (1990–1), 'The Transformation of Europe', *Yale Law Journal*, 100: 2403–83.

Wexler, I. (1983), *The Marshall Plan Revisited: The European Recovery Program in Economic Perspective* (Westport, CT: Greenwood Press).

White Paper (1970), *The United Kingdom and the European Communities* (London: HMSO).

White Paper (1975), *Membership of the European Community: Report on Renegotiation* (London: HMSO).

Williamson, J. (1975), 'The Implications of European Monetary Integration for Peripheral Areas', in Needleman (ed.), *Economic Sovereignty and Regional Policy* (Dublin: Gill & Macmillan).

Willis, F. Roy (1965), *France, Germany, and the New Europe, 1945–1963* (Stanford, CA: Stanford University Press).

Willis, F. Roy (1968), *France, Germany, and the New Europe, 1945–1967*, 2nd edn. (Stanford, CA: Stanford University Press).

Willis, F. Roy (1975) (ed.), *European Integration* (New York: New Viewpoints).

Winand, P. (1993), *Eisenhower, Kennedy, and the United States of Europe* (New York: St. Martin's Press).

Winkler, H. A. (2002a), *Der lange Weg nach Westen*, Vol. 2 (Munich: Beck).

Winkler, H. A. (2002b), *The Long Shadow of the Reich: Weighing Up German History* (London: German Historical Institute).

Wirsing, G. (1932), *Zwischeneuropa und die deutsche Zukunft* (Jena: Diederich).

Woodward, E. L., and Butler, R. (1946), *Documents on British Foreign Policy, 1919–1939*, Series 2: 1 (London: HMSO).

Wünsche, H. (1989), 'Wirtschaftliche Interessen und Prioritäten: Die Europavorstellungen von Ludwig Erhard', in Hrbek and Schwarz (eds.), *40 Jahre Römische Verträge: der deutsche Beitrag: Kokumentation der Konferenz anlässlich des 90. Geburtstages von Hans von der Groeben* (Baden-Baden: Nomos Verlag), 50–64.

Young, A. R. and Wallace, H. (2000), 'The Single Market: A New Approach to Policy', in Wallace and Wallace (eds.), *Policy Making in the European Union*, 4th edn. (Oxford: Oxford University Press), 85–114.

Young, J. W. (2000), *Britain and European Unity 1945–1999* (Basingstoke: Macmillan).

Zelikow, P., and Rice, C. (1995), *Germany Unified and Europe Transformed: A Study in Statecraft* (Cambridge, MA: Harvard University Press).

Zubok, V., and Pleshakov, C. (1996), *Inside the Kremlin's Cold War: From Stalin to Khrushchev* (Cambridge, MA: Harvard University Press).

Index